Fourteen Ounces of Prevention:
A Casebook for Practitioners

14 OUNCES OF PREVENTION

A Casebook for Practitioners

Edited by:

**Richard H. Price,
Emory L. Cowen,
Raymond P. Lorion, and
Julia Ramos-McKay**

AMERICAN
PSYCHOLOGICAL
ASSOCIATION

Library of Congress Cataloging-in-Publication Data

Fourteen ounces of prevention.

    1. Mental illness—Prevention. I. Price, Richard H.
RA790.f66   1988   616.89′05   88-14471
ISBN 1-55798-036-5 (pbk.) (acid-free paper)

Copies may be ordered from
Order Department
P.O. Box 2710
Hyattsville, MD 20784

In the United Kingdom and Europe, copies may be ordered from
American Psychological Association
3 Henrietta Street
Covent Garden
London WC2E 8LU
England

Published by the
American Psychological Association
750 First Street, NE
Washington, DC 20002

Reprinted November 1995

Printed in the United States of America

Contents

Acknowledgments

This casebook was conceived and initiated by the American Psychological Association's (APA) Board of Professional Affairs Task Force on Promotion, Prevention and Intervention Alternatives in Psychology. The Task Force began its work in September, 1983. Members of that Task Force and the editors of this casebook include Richard H. Price (chair), Emory L. Cowen, Raymond P. Lorion, and Julia Ramos-McKay. At earlier points in time, Steven Goldston (1983–1984), Tom Hollon (1983), and Joel Goldstein (1985) also served on the Task Force.

Special thanks from the Task Force go to Bev Hitchins who served as APA Staff Liaison to the Task Force. Throughout the nearly 5 years of the Task Force's existence, Bev showed enormous managerial skills, patience, persistence, and loyalty to the goals of the Task Force. Unquestionably, the Task Force would not have been nearly so productive nor would it have achieved its goals so fully without her efforts. In addition, sincere thanks go to Barbara Strane of The University of Michigan who aided materially in making institutional arrangements and organizing the efforts of the Task Force.

The editors gratefully acknowledge the Board of Professional Affairs for seeing the need to address the issue of prevention more fully and more formally than had been done by any national organization and for supporting this initiative by creating the Task Force. Subsequently, through the collaboration with the National Council of Community Mental Health Centers (NCCMHC), the APA was able to broaden its support for its project. Special thanks go to NCCMHC members Tom Wolff and Carolyn Swift and NCCMHC staff members Frank Bailey, Bruce Emery, and Laurie Poul for their assistance and collaboration in helping the APA secure the necessary funding to publish this book. With their collaboration, the NCCMHC and APA were granted funds by the PEW Charitable Trusts in October, 1986. The APA especially appreciates the attention and encouragement that PEW officer Roseann Siegel gave to this project from its inception.

The prevention programs described in this casebook were first presented at the National Conference on Prevention sponsored by the APA, the NCCMHC, and the PEW Memorial Trust. That conference was held in Bethesda, Maryland, in May, 1987, and included not only representatives of each of the prevention programs described in this volume but also a large number of policymakers and legislators concerned with the goal of prevention. Our thanks to all of them for their contributions.

Many thanks also go to the authors of each prevention program. Their creativity and concern for the development of scientifically sound prevention models has provided a major contribution to the field of prevention. We hope these program models will also offer concrete options to individual practitioners who see the need to institute a prevention program in their own community.

Contributors

Angela M. Adan, MA Department of Psychology, University of Illinois

David G. Altman, PhD Health Promotion Resource Center, School of Medicine, Stanford University

Bernard L. Bloom, PhD Department of Psychology, University of Colorado

Gilbert J. Botvin, PhD Laboratory of Health Behavior Research, The New York Hospital, Cornell Medical Center

Donna M. Bryant, PhD Frank Porter Graham Child Development Center, University of North Carolina, Chapel Hill

Frances A. Campbell, PhD Frank Porter Graham Child Development Center, University of North Carolina, Chapel Hill

Emory L. Cowen, PhD Center for Community Study, University of Rochester

William S. Davidson II, PhD Department of Psychology, Michigan State University

Robert D. Felner, PhD Department of Psychology, University of Illinois

William F. Hodges, PhD Department of Psychology, University of Colorado

Dale L. Johnson, PhD Department of Psychology, University of Houston-UP

Raymond P. Lorion, PhD Department of Psychology, University of Maryland

Nathan Maccoby, PhD School of Medicine, Stanford University

David L. Olds, PhD Department of Pediatrics, University of Rochester Medical Center

Donald E. Pierson, EdD Center for Field Service and Studies, College of Education, University of Lowell

Richard H. Price, PhD Department of Psychology and Institute for Social Research, The University of Michigan

Craig T. Ramey, PhD Frank Porter Graham Child Development Center, University of North Carolina, Chapel Hill

Julia Ramos-McKay, PhD Behavioral Science Unit, Hartford Police Department, Manchester, CN

Robin Redner, PhD Department of Psychology, Michigan State University

Mary Jane Rotheram-Borus, PhD Division of Child Psychiatry, Columbia University

Lawrence J. Schweinhart, PhD High/Scope Educational Research Foundation, Ypsilanti, MI

Myrna B. Shure, PhD Division of Psychology, Department of Mental Health Science, Hahnemann University

Phyllis R. Silverman, PhD Institute of Health Professions, Massachusetts General Hospital

Joseph J. Sparling, PhD Frank Porter Graham Child Development Center, University of North Carolina, Chapel Hill

George Spivack, PhD Hahnemann University Prevention Intervention Research Center, Hahnemann University

Ciporah S. Tadmor, PhD Obstetrics Department, RAMBAM Medical Center and the Samuel Neaman Institute for Advanced Studies in Science and Technology at Technion, Haifa

Stephanie Tortu, PhD Laboratory of Health Behavior Research, The New York Hospital, Cornell Medical Center

Barbara H. Wasik, PhD Frank Porter Graham Child Development Center, University of North Carolina, Chapel Hill

David P. Weikart, PhD High/Scope Educational Research Foundation, Ypsilanti, MI

Richard H. Price, Emory L. Cowen, Raymond P. Lorion, and Julia Ramos-McKay

Introduction

This book is dedicated to the idea that good psychological science is a critical ingredient in programmatic efforts to prevent human suffering, maladaptation, and illness. With this book, we intend to provide psychologists, and indeed citizens at large, with examples of successful prevention programs that can be adopted in local communities and be made part of the practice of psychologists nationwide.

In 1984, the National Institute of Mental Health (NIMH) reported that 43 million people in the United States, 19% of the nation's population, were suffering from some form of psychological disorder or distress. There will never be enough mental health professionals to provide help for such widespread distress. For that reason, prevention advocates have argued that we must mount large-scale preventive efforts, as public health pioneers did in dealing with diseases such as polio, smallpox, and measles.

Although a growing number of psychologists agree that a wide range of psychological and health problems are preventable, the logic of prevention must be turned into concrete reality. To do that, we must identify model programs that work. Identifying effective programs has two aspects. First, research evidence for claims of program effectiveness must be examined carefully. Many preventive measures that look as if they should work actually may not. Second, once identified, model programs can serve as examples to be repeated in other settings such as schools, communities, or work organizations. This idea led the American Psychological Association's (APA) Task Force on Prevention, Promotion, and Intervention Alternatives in Psychology to launch a major effort to search for effective model prevention programs.[1] This book represents the end product of the Task Force's efforts.

In this introduction, we describe the activities of the Task Force in searching for model prevention programs in the context of a larger history of resurgent interest in prevention and the criteria the Task Force used to select model programs. Brief previews of the programs described in the volume are also included here.

The Task Force: Mandate and History

In winter 1978, the APA's Policy and Planning Board appointed an ad hoc Task Force chaired by Edward S. Bordin to consider the emerging roles and activities for psychologists which, in the light of changing times and problem definitions, might help to balance the practices of current delivery systems. The Task Force held two meetings in early 1979, solicited the views of experts, and established a set of criteria to be used in evaluating alternative models. The Task Force's first and strongest recommendation was that APA establish a Continuing Committee on Promotion, Prevention, and Alternative Interventions in Psychology. The Task Force also proposed eight specific activities for the new committee to undertake.

Based on those recommendations, the APA's Board of Directors appointed a Task Force on Promotion, Prevention, and Intervention Alternatives in 1981 to report through the Committee on Professional Practice of the Board of Professional Affairs. The Board of Directors instructed the

---

[1]The Task Force included psychologists Emory L. Cowen, Raymond P. Lorion, Richard H. Price, and Julia Ramos-McKay, as well as Beverly Hitchins of the American Psychological Association.

new task force to focus specifically on psychological approaches to the promotion of health and prevention of the range of physical and mental health problems such as those associated with coping skills, stress reduction, and acquisition of healthy behaviors and life-styles.

The mission statement of the new task force included specific recommendations that (a) the delivery settings and agencies of programs be studied, and proposals be made for developing and evaluating new approaches in settings with diverse characteristics; (b) legislation and other initiatives affecting these new approaches be monitored and assessed at the federal, state, and local levels; and (c) liaison be maintained with other professional and scientific organizations interested in prevention and promotion.

Although the Task Force had its first meeting in November, 1981, personnel changes limited its early operation and planning efforts. By September, 1982, however, the four-member Task Force was reconstituted. The first agenda item was to identify those elements in its broad, complex charge that could be realistically addressed within the constraints of limited resources. An early decision was made to focus on what was seen as the Task Force's single most central charge, that is to identify and support the development of newly evolving and needed approaches in psychology including the promotion of health, the prevention of disorder, and emergent intervention alternatives that maximize growth and minimize dysfunction.

The key words *identify* and *support* implied two distinct but important processes: (1) to identify innovative, well-documented "model" programs, exemplifying the categories of promotion, prevention, and emergent intervention alternatives; and (2) to spearhead the preparation of a volume describing these models in practitioner-oriented ways. The longer-term benefit that the Task Force hoped would accrue from these steps was to facilitate more widespread field applications of demonstrably effective preventive programs as alternatives to traditional, after-the-fact repair services.

The Emergence of Prevention as a National Priority

APA's appointment of the original Task Force on emerging roles in 1978 took place shortly after the submittal of the Final Report of the 1978 U.S. President's Commission on Mental Health. Among that report's distinguishing features were its strong emphases on the concept of prevention, including the recommendation that NIMH be designated as a lead agency in furthering prevention; and the need for effective new service-delivery models for the unserved and underserved. Those conclusions put into bold relief a set of views that had been slowly gaining momentum over a long time period which were in response to perceived insufficiencies in the existing mental health and other service delivery systems.

The growing clarity of these problems and the heavy human and social costs of health and mental health problems for vulnerable populations stimulated consideration of conceptual alternatives. If even the best and most sophisticated attempts to cure psychological or physical illness can account for only a minor fraction of the prevalence of illness, might it not be easier, farther reaching, more humane, and more effective to seek prevention strategies from the start? That very real question stimulated a search for viable alternatives.

Prevention is one such option and is a sweeping alternative, which challenges pivotal assumptions of the health and mental health systems, not simply their practices. Rather than trying to undo established pathology, the goal of prevention orientation is to develop initiatives to forestall problems in people at risk and to build strengths and competencies to advance their well-being.

Primary prevention efforts cluster around two broad strategies: (1) system-directed approaches such as social policy development and modification of social environments designed to reduce sources of stress and to enhance life opportunities; and (2) person-centered strategies such as educational programs to impart adaptive skills and competencies as well as preventive interventions for risk groups such as divorcing parents and children of divorce. These two strategies have produced programs that reflect a healthy diversity. A core quality that links prevention efforts and sets them apart from past practice is their intentional targeting to well people. In that regard, these prevention efforts reflect the popular wisdom that an ounce of prevention is worth a pound of cure.

There have been important signposts of the growth, vitality, and promise of the prevention movement beyond the President's Commission Report. Although these developments have been energetic and well motivated, they have also been somewhat uncritical. The question, Which of many preferred prevention contributions are enduring rather than ephemeral?, guided the Task

Force's interpretation of its mandate and subsequent activities. From its inception, the overarching goal of the Task Force was to identify a diverse range of documented, effective prevention programs—the best our field can offer at this time—and to build bridges around those programs to span the sometimes wide gulf between theory and research on the one side and application and dissemination on the other. How might the potential benefits of these special prevention programs best be harnessed to affect not just the lives of the few people who were part of them, but the large unidentified masses who stand to benefit from exemplary model programs? To Task Force members, an answer to this question was a way of bringing the goal of prevention closer to fruition.

The Need for a Practitioner Focus

In the past, most mental health practitioners who saw themselves as working "in the trenches" tended to ignore prevention because they viewed it, in part, as a luxury for those with surplus time and money. Because of the pressure to meet the great need for psychological services, many providers, who otherwise might have worked in prevention programs, attached a low priority to prevention programs and research within their own work settings. In their experience, the number of people needing services continued to grow while resources for providing such services diminished. Moreover, prevention programs being developed by researchers did not necessarily address the needs of service providers. More recently, however, progress in the field of prevention research and a clamor by providers for usable prevention programs has led to the development of programs that can be applied in a variety of settings.

The recent expansion of work sites in which psychologists practice, including industrial settings, employee assistance programs, law enforcement agencies, and sports programs, requires providers of psychological services to be knowledgeable about appropriate ameliorative interventions and appropriate prevention techniques. For example, a police psychologist may develop programs to prevent or minimize stress and negative reactions in police officers, in addition to treating officers who are experiencing symptoms of psychological distress. A sports team that employs a psychologist may be interested not only in treatment for team members but also in ways to prevent such problems as substance abuse and

physical injuries. Prevention research and programming can no longer be seen as a luxury to be carried out by others; employers of psychological-service providers have begun to see prevention programming as a critical skill.

The recent proliferation of prevention programs is a response to real and urgent needs. Programs to provide specific interventions for children who are at risk for particular problems, programs to teach children interpersonal skills, and programs to teach children to say "No" to drugs and to recognize and react to "good touches" and "bad touches" are now available. Many of these programs appear to be designed for easy use and require little training on the part of the practitioner. The busy practitioner, pressed for time because of service provision needs, takes these programs at face value and assumes that they have been developed through the appropriate research.

Unfortunately, all "prevention" programs are not *real* prevention programs. Practitioners must know how to evaluate each program. To do so, they must consider not only its appropriateness and ease of application but also the quality of the research upon which a program stands, how well specified its target groups are, the actual nature of the intervention, and whether expected outcomes have been demonstrated. For those reasons, the Task Force concluded that it could best contribute to the field by conducting a search for model preventive programs with well-documented program features and solid, supporting program-outcome findings.

The Task Force's Search for Model Programs

Before beginning our search for model programs, the Task Force identified several benchmarks to be used in its search. First, we hoped to find programs relevant to all stages of the life span. Prevention is important not only for children but for adults and the elderly as well. In addition, we hoped to find programs that could be delivered in many different community settings including hospitals, schools, service agencies, and the workplace. Finally, we hoped that the exemplary prevention programs identified would be aimed at a wide range of different health, mental health, and criminal justice outcomes.

The Task Force contacted over 900 experts throughout the country who we believed were knowledgeable about prevention programs. In response to our inquiries, we received nearly 300 replies describing a wide range of prevention efforts. The Task Force then set about examining these programs and searching for evidence of effectiveness. In the end, we identified 14 programs that we believe can serve as models. There are surely many effective programs that we were unable to identify as our search was certainly not exhaustive. What follows is a brief sketch of the search itself, the criteria we developed, the procedures we used to evaluate candidates for model programs, and some information about the kinds of program submissions we received.

Criteria for the Selection of Model Programs

Task Force members discussed at length the diverse ways in which the concept of a model program could be realized. The prime concern was how to determine whether an intervention worked. At one extreme, we could rely entirely upon the availability of rigorous empirical data to decide this question. From this perspective, a model would represent an intervention strategy with irrefutable scientific evidence of its capacity to reduce the incidence of identifiable disorders.

At the other extreme, one might rely upon community acceptance. From this perspective, a model would represent an intervention strategy that appeared useful and adoptable across multiple settings. Evidence that the strategy worked would be reflected in the positive responses of those who provided and received the intervention. Less emphasis would be placed upon the outcomes of formal evaluations on the assumption that those charged with the allocation of scarce community resources would have examined program outcomes according to local norms.

Members of the Task Force concluded that the selection of model interventions should be based on quantitative outcomes. However, we felt that consideration must also be given to the diversity of targets, desired outcomes, and setting conditions for which preventive interventions are designed. To reflect that diversity, a three-dimensional matrix was created within which to locate identified interventions.

The first dimension related to the life stage of intervention recipients. Prevention strategies can be focused at all points across the life span from the prenatal period to old age. Thus, a life-span continuum was created which included the following major developmental periods: prenatal through preschool (0 to 4 years); elementary school (5 to 12 years); adolescence (13 to 21 years); adulthood (22 to 65 years); and retirement (65

and beyond). We also considered program outcome. Initially, this dimension focused on distinguishing among mental-health, substance-abuse, physical-health, criminal-justice and educational outcomes. We classified each program in terms of its specific preventive goals. We focused on the setting in which the program activities occurred. We considered (among others) educational, occupational, medical, social service, and home settings as well as a combination of these settings.

Within this three-dimensional framework, we classified interventions which successfully completed the initial program screening. Of the approximately 300 program descriptions received in response to more than 900 practitioner surveys distributed, 52 were considered sufficiently promising to warrant detailed examination of program materials and evaluation findings. Eventually, 14 of those 52 were selected as exemplary programs.

In screening, we considered program descriptions in terms of multiple criteria. Conceptually, these criteria addressed four aspects of the interventions: (a) the problem addressed, (b) the program's targeted goals, (c) the procedures followed in reaching those goals, and (d) the evidence documenting the successful attainment of program goals. Specifically, members of the Task Force examined program descriptions and sought information about the characteristics of the intervention. We used the following selection criteria for model prevention programs.

• Clear description of the emotional or behavioral condition to be prevented and the group at risk

• Description of the skills necessary to conduct the intervention

• Statement of a rationale for the intervention

• Description of the actual intervention

• Rationale for the timing of the delivery, duration, and chronology of intervention activities

• Specification of the program steps taken to recruit intervention recipients

• Specification of the observable and measurable program objectives

• Description of the evaluation, follow-up data, and program monitoring

• Description of how the program relates to other groups, organizations, and agencies in the community

• Recognition and resolution of ethical issues

• Transferability of the intervention to other settings

• Roles of psychologists and other professional and nonprofessional caregiver resources

As noted earlier, 52 of the approximately 300 program descriptions submitted provided sufficient information on issues to warrant further examination. Each of the 300 submissions was reviewed by two Task Force members and rated along a 5-point continuum in terms of overall promise for more detailed scrutiny, importance of the problem, and probable quality of the evaluation. Interrater agreements were examined for each program description. In cases of marked disagreement, a third or fourth rater was used.

The developers of these 52 programs submitted detailed program materials, manuals, research reports, and other indicators of effectiveness. Task Force members examined the informative and scientific quality of these materials and selected 14 model programs. Although these 14 programs varied in their reported evaluation findings, each had specifically documented the achievement of intended outcomes. Moreover, each was judged to be exportable, that is, a program that had a defined, replicable set of procedures that could be adopted by practitioners. Finally, in selecting the final set of programs, the Task Force attempted to provide at least reasonable coverage of the three-dimensional matrix of the life span, service settings, and prevention outcomes.

Characteristics of Programs Submitted

Examination of the initial pool of submitted programs provides useful insight into the profile of preventive interventions at the time of the Task Force's survey (1983–1984). In general, these preventive interventions were targeted predominantly to children and adolescents. Less than 20% of the programs submitted focused on adults or the elderly. Demographically, recipients of preventive interventions tended to be disproportionately poor, minority-group members, and otherwise disenfranchised groups. Programs were provided for the most part within schools and social service agencies, and most prevention service providers were nonprofessional community caregivers, educators, and members of program recipients' families.

Some readers may be surprised by the fact that relatively few programs survived the initial screening. One reason for that is that only one third of the programs systematically evaluated their efforts, and a significant number of these lacked program manuals or other means of documenting their efforts. Because these programs had only vaguely defined procedures, they had little chance to be replicated successfully in other settings. With such high attrition, it is misleading to use the total number of submissions as a framework for assessing the efficacy of existing prevention programs. A more accurate indicator of the state of the field might be the 52 programs that we examined in detail. Of these, nearly 25% lacked follow-up information considered essential by Task Force members to document the enduring achievement of preventive goals. A number of others appeared to have methodologically flawed evaluations that cast a shadow on program outcome findings or insufficient documentation to permit program replication. Although the final group of 14 programs are not flawless, they may provide a reasonable estimate of the profile of currently mature preventive intervention strategies.

Many of the programs not selected represented interesting, potentially promising ideas which had not yet evolved into fully developed preventive interventions. For some, too little time had passed to assess the preventive strategy's impact on the desired outcome. Others simply lacked systematic program evaluations. In some of those cases, the strategy's value as a preventive intervention was accepted without question by its adherents, that is, the need to evaluate the program was not perceived.

The range and substance of the submittals persuaded the Task Force members to believe that effective prevention programs will increase significantly over the coming years as necessary outcome data are obtained using longitudinal evaluations. We view the results of the original survey optimistically and look forward to continued healthy growth in the development of viable preventive interventions.

Overview of the Model Programs

This volume is divided into three sections describing programs focused on infancy and early childhood, school-age children and adolescents, and prevention programs for youth and adults. The targets of these programs are diverse. They include preschool minority children, poor teenage mothers, school-age children in health classes, young people who have just entered the juvenile justice system, grade school children experiencing a transition to high school, newly separated couples, mothers about to undergo caesarean birth, bereaved widows, and members of entire communities at risk of cardiovascular disease.

Authors were asked to follow a uniform structure in their presentations and to aim their presentation at practitioners interested in replicating these programs in their home communities. We proposed a uniform structure in which all authors begin with a brief discussion of the program's issues, problems, and goals; describe how the program actually works; discuss briefly the research evidence for program effectiveness; highlight the program's limitations as well as positive aspects; and offer practical suggestions for starting a new program.

What follows, we feel, are descriptions of prevention programs that are the product of considerable ingenuity focused on the goal of prevention. Although there is a need for many more such model programs, as well as for their adoption in the work of practicing psychologists, the present volume is, nevertheless, an exciting beginning.

SECTION I

Early Childhood Programs

Section I provides readers with descriptions of five approaches to the prevention of emotional, behavioral, and cognitive disorders in preschool and primary grade children. The intervention models described here represent the diverse routes by which optimizing development may be approached concretely. The primary recipient of such interventions may be the child, the parent, or both. Involvement may begin in utero or in the final preschool years. The programs may last for months or years. Whatever the case, it is apparent from the evidence described in the following pages that technologies now exist to achieve and maintain significant developmental gains in high-risk children.

In chapter 1 "Prenatal/Early Infancy Project," Olds focuses his efforts on infants born to low-income adolescent mothers. To prevent a wide range of maternal and child health problems associated with poverty, Olds involves participants, starting in the second trimester of pregnancy, in a nurse home-visitation program designed to improve the mother's understanding of, and capacity to respond to, infant needs. By initiating the intervention early and continuing it through the child's second year, Olds demonstrates that distinct, albeit interrelated, outcomes such as maternal nutrition, caregiving skills, and occupational success affect such infant health indicators as reduced rates of prematurity, child abuse and neglect, and behavioral problems.

Participants in Pierson's "Brookline Early Education Program" (chapter 2) are also involved during pregnancy. In this case, however, the program continues until the child enters kindergarten. In the intervening years, a range of intervention strategies is made available to educate and support parents in responding to their children's educational needs. In addition, the program monitors the health status of the children and provides an organized prekindergarten experience for participants. These intervention components produce positive educational and behavioral effects lasting at least through second grade. Moreover, the inclusion of a cost-effectiveness analysis makes evident the importance of matching the intensity of program effort to the educational and economic resources of recipients.

Ramey, Bryant, Campbell, Sparling, and Wasik's, "Carolina Early Intervention Program," described in chapter 3, seeks to prevent intellectual underdevelopment in high-risk children by combining a highly structured developmental daycare center with parent support. Children enter this program at 6 weeks of age and continue their involvement until they enter kindergarten. Each element of this intervention represents a carefully researched component of an overarching theoretical framework in which an expanding array of ecological influences is appreciated and affected. Evaluation data obtained to date show that this intervention both reduces the occurrence of cognitive delay in poor, minority children and achieves a broad range of academically relevant developmental gains.

The "Houston Parent–Child Development Program," described by Johnson in chapter 4, focuses on the child between the ages of 1 and 3. During this period, parents (the involvement of the father is considered central to the program's success) participate in a structured 550-hour experience designed to educate them about child rearing and to support their growth as effective parents. Given the primarily Mexican-American population served, special attention is paid to ensuring the program's cultural sensitivity. Evaluations conducted at two later points during the child's primary grade involvement provide strong evidence of the intervention's positive academic and behavioral effects.

Finally, Schweinhart and Weikart provide an overview of the "High Scope/Perry Preschool Program" in chapter 5. This intervention involves low-income children between 3 and 4 years of age in a developmentally appropriate prekindergarten curriculum. Similar to other programs in this section, the child's involvement is supported by a focused approach to parental education and support. Unique to this program is its extended evaluation. By monitoring the status of program and nonprogram children over a 19-year period, the investigators provide highly encouraging evidence of the long-term benefits of targeted early childhood interventions. Positive consequences of program participation are reported in diverse domains, including academic success, intellectual development, the avoidance of antisocial behaviors, and employment. Cost-benefit analysis shows that the program is a sound economic investment that returns up to 600% on taxpayers' investment.

Although these five programs are unique in many ways, they share at their core a common ecological understanding of behavior, which is reflected in efforts to enhance child development by strengthening parents and relevant systems as well as individual children. They also share cultural sensitivity and attention to the details that operationalize the interventions. All of the programs have been effective with high-risk populations whose access to educational, economic, health, and other salient resources is seriously limited. Finally, each supports the premise that rigorous evaluative research is an invaluable program developmental tool.

David L. Olds

1

The Prenatal/ Early Infancy Project

The Prenatal/Early Infancy Project consisted of a program of nurse home visitation designed to prevent a wide range of maternal and child health problems associated with poverty. The program was established to improve women's prenatal health habits, infant caregiving skills, social support, use of community services, and educational and occupational achievements and to help women reduce unwanted additional pregnancies and their reliance on welfare. These changes in maternal behavior and experience were expected to lead to a reduction in child health disorders including prematurity and low birth weight, growth and nutritional problems, accidents, ingestions, acute infectious illnesses, cognitive delays, behavioral problems, and child abuse and neglect.

Our research team at the Prenatal/Early Infancy Project viewed these maternal and child afflictions as expressions of a dysfunctional caregiving system. By caregiving system, we meant not only parents and families, but the larger communities in which they lived including the social and material resources available to parents to help them care for their children, as well as those forces that work against their providing optimal care such as employment, poverty, single parenthood, and racial and class discrimination. Viewing these problems from this broad perspective had important implications for the way the program was designed.

Background

In recent decades, our society has experienced high rates of young-adolescent and single-parent families. Becoming a parent too early and without adequate social support leads to dropping out of school, interference with employment, and welfare dependence (Card & Wise, 1978; Furstenberg, 1980). Moreover, teenaged and unwed women produce a disproportionate number of low-birth-weight and preterm babies (Naeye, 1981; Garn & Petzold, 1983). Tragically, the adverse sequelae of preterm delivery and low birth weight are most likely to emerge when children are born into impoverished homes, where parents have few personal and social resources (Sameroff & Chandler, 1975).

Even if children are born full term and with adequate birth weight, they are at considerably greater risk for disorders in health and socio-emotional and cognitive functioning if they are born to unmarried teenagers living in impoverished circumstances (Phipps-Yonas, 1980). Moreover, if teenagers give birth to a second child soon after the birth of a first, their second child is at

This research was supported by grants from the Ford Foundation (Grant No. 875-0559) and a Faculty Scholars Award from the W.T. Grant Foundation to the author (Grant No. 861080-86). I wish to thank Karen Hughes for preparation of the manuscript; Joannie Pinhas for her comments on the manuscript; Al Baldwin for introducing me to naive psychology and for his review of the manuscript; and Elizabeth Chilson, Diane Farr, Georgianna McGrady, Jacqueline Roberts, and Lyn Scazafabo for their work with the families enrolled in the program.

increased risk for pregnancy complications, later health problems, and death, compared with first children born to other mothers of the same age (McCormick, Shapiro, & Starfield, 1984). Studies of social class differences in low birth weight (Miller and Merritt, 1979) and later child health and development (Miller, Court, Walton, & Knox, 1960; Elardo, Bradley, & Caldwell, 1975) suggest that a major explanation for these social class differences can be traced to maternal prenatal health behaviors and subsequent infant caregiving. Commonalities in the origins of the problems addressed by this program are highlighted when they are viewed from an ecological perspective (Bronfenbrenner, 1979). The ecological model refers to the interdependence among social systems operating at the level of the marital and parent–child dyad, the family system as a whole, the interrelations among these systems, and larger socioeconomic influences operating at the level of the community.

One implication of the ecological model is that the health habits and caregiving behaviors of disadvantaged parents need to be understood in terms of the circumstances with which they have to contend. Stress can often interfere with caregiving (Belle, 1982) and maternal prenatal health behaviors (Newton & Hunt, 1984) by contributing to higher rates of maternal depression (Fergusson, Hons, Horwood, Shannon, 1984). Moreover, it is suggested increasingly that stress in and of itself can affect health directly, by suppressing the functioning of the immune system (Locke, 1982).

Although the evidence regarding social support as a moderator of stress is more difficult to interpret, it is commonly observed that individuals who are isolated from supportive social networks have higher rates of mortality and morbidity (Berkman & Syme, 1979), and isolated parents are at much greater risk for smoking cigarettes during pregnancy (McCormick et al., 1986), heavy prenatal alcohol consumption (Stephens, 1985), and caregiving dysfunction (Garbarino & Crouter, 1978).

Some people have argued that the best way to improve the caregiving system is through national policies aimed at creating jobs and reducing unemployment, the subsidy of housing for a larger portion of the population, and income maintenance arrangements. Although we at the Prenatal/Early Infancy Project would support such approaches, these kinds of solutions are not politically feasible at this time and are long-range solutions of unknown consequences for maternal and child health.

Notwithstanding the influence of larger social and economic influences, we decided to test a more focused prevention strategy that is within the purview of health professionals, that is potentially more easily implemented on a wide scale, and that has increasing scientific documentation concerning its effectiveness. Although the program we devised emphasized regular medical care, we started from the assumption that many health and psychosocial dysfunctions are attributable to environmental conditions that are beyond the reach of traditional office or clinic practice. Our approach to this issue was to have the home-visiting nurses in our program try to minimize the stressful situations that characterize living under oppressive social and economic conditions.

Our strategy relied on nurse home visitation during an important phase in the life cycle of high-risk families—pregnancy and the first 2 years of the baby's life. By improving the conditions for pregnancy, birth, and early child rearing, it was expected that the environmental adversity leading to a number of later health problems would be reduced, saving the individual untold suffering and saving society an exorbitant part of its health-care costs. The content of the Elmira home-visiting program was designed to meet the needs of parents for information, emotional support, and the relief of life stress, in an attempt to address simultaneously those factors that undermine parents' own personal achievements, their health habits, and the care of their children.

We believed that it was important to test the effectiveness of the program in a randomized trial. Other intervention studies directed toward improving the outcomes of pregnancy and early child rearing had often been difficult to interpret because of problems with the design of the research or program. Many programs, for example, provided a variety of services that might be of help to socially disadvantaged families, but their evaluations were carried out with control groups that were not randomly assigned. Consequently, the treatment and control groups often were not equivalent at the beginning of the study. In other cases, more rigorously designed studies were carried out on interventions focused on single variables such as reducing prenatal smoking (Sexton & Hebel, 1984), supplementing prenatal nutrition (Rush, Stein, & Insoln, 1980), or encouraging parents to childproof their homes (Dershewitz & Williamson, 1977). These kinds of focused interventions do not address the full range of stressful family and community circumstances that often interfere with optimal maternal health habits and caregiving. In designing the present study, we tried to learn from the experience of these earlier investigators.

Our work was carried out during a period of decline in community-health nursing services. Even though nurse home visiting recently has been given considerable attention as a means of promoting child health (Kempe, 1976; Wynn & Wynn, 1979), its funding has been cut drastically in our large cities, where the need for this type of intervention is greatest (Chavigny & Korske, 1983). The reticence of state and local legislatures to fund nurse home-visiting services is due, in part, to the absence of good empirical evidence that home visitation services are indeed effective (Combs-Orme, Reis, & Ward, 1985).

The Setting

The program was carried out in a small, semi-rural county of approximately 100,000 residents in the Appalachian region of New York State. At the time the study was initiated, the community was well served from the standpoint of both health and human services. Prenatal care was available through nine private obstetricians and a free antepartum clinic sponsored by the health department. Pediatric care was provided by two sophisticated pediatric practices (with a total of 11 pediatricians) and eight physicians in family practice. A variety of social services was available for children and families. In spite of an abundance of health and human services, the community has consistently exhibited the highest rates of reported and confirmed cases of child abuse and neglect in the State (New York State Department of Social Services, 1973–82). Moreover, in 1980 the community was rated the worst standard metropolitan statistical area in the United States in terms of its economic conditions (Boyer & Savageau, 1981).

The Sample

Because we were interested in preventing a wide range of maternal and child health problems, we used general criteria (risk factors) for the identification of the families most likely to benefit from the service. At the time that we designed the study, the literature suggested that being a teenager, being unmarried, and being poor increased the likelihood of poor health and developmental outcomes on the part of the child and arrested

personal development on the part of the mother (Birch & Gussow, 1970; Card & Wise, 1978).

Because the literature was not clear on which of these factors was most important in predicting poor outcomes, we recruited women with any one of these three risk characteristics. We limited the program to women having first children. We reasoned that women having first children would be more receptive to the nurses' offers of help, that the skills and resources that they developed in coping with their first pregnancies and children would be carried over to subsequent children, and that it would be easier for women to return to school and work if they had only one child to manage. Thus, by targeting first-time parents,[1] we expected to increase the long-term impact of the program and its cost-effectiveness. Because we also were interested in creating a program that was not stigmatized as being exclusively for the poor or for parents at risk for child abuse or neglect, we welcomed the enrollment of anyone bearing a first child, regardless of their risk status. In so doing, we think that we increased the willingness of women to participate. Morever, by creating sample heterogeneity through the enrollment of these nonrisk women, we also were better able to determine the extent to which the effects of the program were greater for families at higher risk.

Consequently, we actively recruited women who were at less than 25 weeks of gestation if they had no previous live births and had any *one* of the following characteristics: (a) young age (< 19 years), (b) single-parent status, or (c) low socioeconomic status (SES). Anyone bearing a first child, however, was welcome to register. Some women were registered after the 25th week of gestation because of problems with dating the pregnancy, but all women were enrolled prior to the 30th week. They were recruited through the health department antepartum clinic, the offices of private obstetricians, Planned Parenthood, the public schools, and a variety of other health and human service agencies. Approximately 10% of the target population was not invited to participate, because they registered for prenatal care after the 25th week of gestation. An additional 10% of the target population (poor, unmarried, or teenaged women bearing first children) were dismissed because they were not referred from the offices of private obstetricians. Five hundred

---

[1]Throughout this chapter, we refer to parents (rather than mothers) because about 40% of the women were married at registration and a significant number of the unmarried women were living with the father of the baby. To the extent possible, the program focused on fathers as well as mothers.

women were interviewed between April 1978 and September 1980, and 400 enrolled. There were no differences in age, marital status, or education between those 400 women who participated and the 100 who declined. Ninety-four percent of the non-Whites (mostly Blacks) enrolled, as opposed to 80% of the Whites (P = .02). At registration, 47% of the participating women were under 19 years of age, 62% were unmarried, and 61% came from families in Hollingshead's social class CS IV and V (semiskilled and unskilled laborers) (Hollingshead, 1976). Eight-five percent of the women met at least one of the age, marital status, or SES criteria, and 23% had all three risk characteristics.

This statistical profile of the sample does not fully describe its risk status. From the nurses' reports, we learned that a substantial number of the families lived under oppressive circumstances such as households with open sewers, caving-in roofs, bedrooms located in a dirt basement, and no running water or cooking facilities. Violence, alcoholism, and drug abuse were common. One young woman was mysteriously beaten unconscious during pregnancy and had no recollection of the incident. Another was jailed for holding up a local establishment with a knife and had to be visited by her nurse in the county jail. Many women reported having been abused as young children.

The Home Visitation Program

Theoretical Foundations

The program embraced a variety of psychological theories, including cognitive development (Piaget, 1952), attachment (Bowlby, 1969), and social learning (Bandura & Walters, 1963). It was influenced most, however, by the ecological framework articulated by Bronfenbrenner (1979) and the concepts of naive psychology (Baldwin, 1967).

The ecological framework played a role in systematizing environmental influences on parental health habits, qualities of infant caregiving, and the child's health and development. The ecological perspective recognizes the importance of parental caregiving while, by virtue of its attention to the situational determinants of parental behaviors, avoids blaming parents for caregiving dysfunction. One policy implication of this is that to be successful, programs must be able to influence in significant ways the enduring environment in which the family is functioning.

Many of the assumptions of the program plan also were built on the framework of naive psychology or a commonsense orientation to parental behavior (Baldwin, 1967). Parents were conceived of as being influenced by culturally defined norms for appropriate behavior during pregnancy and early child rearing. Most of those norms (especially those that led to aspirations for the child's well-being and success in life) are shared by all members of the society, although there can be numerous variations on how to best achieve those aspirations. The nurses (who were all parents themselves) operated on the assumption that the new parents were committed to the well-being of their child and that family members would behave, for the most part, in accordance with what most parents would define as appropriate behavior during pregnancy and the early child-rearing years. A failure to follow through with that commitment was assumed to reflect a lack of knowledge regarding what children need, interference from other life pressures, or mental illness. Because the program was grounded in commonsense concepts, the content of the program was congruent with family members' ways of thinking about what constitutes the optimal conditions for pregnancy, birth, and early care of the child. Naive psychology also provides a basis for interpreting the behavior of others and empathizing with their experiences, both of which were crucial for the nurses' effective work with families.

At the same time, we reviewed the scientific literature regarding influences on the well-being of the mother and child and incorporated our findings into a systematic parent education program. At times, "commonsense" notions came into conflict with the empirical literature. Many new parents, for example, believed that picking up a crying newborn would spoil it and lead to more crying later, a view refuted by careful longitudinal research (Ainsworth, 1973). Because of the importance of parental responsiveness for the development of a secure attachment, the nurses held to their position that it was wise to pick up a crying newborn, which did not make sense to some new parents. When the evidence was less conclusive, the nurses were less insistent. For example, at the time our program was carried out, it was standard pediatric advice to delay the introduction of solids until the child was about 2 months of age, and then only to introduce new foods one at a time. Many parents, however, introduced their babies to cereal at a much earlier time (often to promote sleeping through the night), because this had been a standard practice in their families for several generations. Because the evidence on the value of delaying the introduction of solids was equivocal, the nurses did not push as hard on this topic. In general, when conflicts arose between the commonsense or culturally defined norms for caregiving and professional advice, the nurses accepted the culturally defined behaviors unless there was clear evidence that those behaviors posed an imminent threat to the mother or child.

Although each of these theoretical perspectives by itself was an inadequate basis for organizing the intervention, in combination they helped create a more coherent approach to the complexities encountered by the nurses as they attempted to optimize families' adjustment to parenthood.

Building the Nurse–Parent Relationship: The Importance of Timing

In working with parents, we believed that it was essential to build the program on a foundation of respect for them, an appreciation for differences in their life-styles, and their strengths. Because we wanted to avoid giving parents the message that they were incompetent or incapable of caring for their children, it was important to begin in the program during pregnancy. Offering help once the baby was born might have been interpreted as an indication that we thought parents had made mistakes or were incapable of caring for their children. Morever, because some of our objectives (such as the prevention of low birth weight and prematurity) had to be accomplished by the time of the child's birth, assistance had to begin during pregnancy at the latest. In general, we reasoned that women would be more likely to accept support when they were going through the profound biological, psychological, and social changes produced by pregnancy.

Program Content

During their home visits, the nurses carried out three major activities: (a) parent education about influences on fetal and infant development; (b) the involvement of family members and friends in the pregnancy, birth, early care of the child, and support of the mother; and (c) the linkage of family members with other formal health and human services. In the following sections, each of

these activities is analyzed in terms of how it enables parents to create a healthy environment for their baby's development.

Parent Education

In the home-based education program, the nurses provided parents with information on fetal and infant development in order to improve parental health habits and behaviors that theoretically affect the child's well-being. The nurses also encouraged parents to complete their own educations, to obtain vocational training, and to make decisions for themselves about finding employment and bearing additional children.

Prenatal education. It is important to note that the nurse's activities during pregnancy varied considerably among families. The material covered depended, in large part, on the mother's stage of pregnancy (Rubin, 1975). During the first trimester and part of the second, time was set aside for the mother to verbalize her feelings and reactions to the pregnancy, as well as to determine the feelings and support of significant others. During the second trimester, often coinciding with the recognition of fetal movement, the mother began to orient to the fetus as a living being. At this time, she became more eager to learn about fetal growth and development, as well as about how her health and behavior could affect the growth and development of her baby. As the mother began to anticipate labor and delivery during the third trimester, she became more concerned with preparation for labor, delivery, and early infant care (Rubin, 1975). Although the program was structured, it was designed to capture the interest of women as they progressed through the developmental stages of pregnancy and to address an issue when it presented the greatest opportunity for change.

The home visitation schedule during pregnancy called for the initial visit to be made within 7 days after enrollment. The nurses visited families once every other week throughout pregnancy with visits of 60 to 90 minutes duration. The women's primary support person was invited to attend every visit, but he or she was especially encouraged to attend special visits that addressed (a) nutrition and health habits; (b) fetal development and the physiology of pregnancy; (c) preparation for labor, delivery, and newborn care; and (d) the women's plans for returning to school, work, and methods of family planning. The nurse tried to schedule these visits when the primary support person could be present.

During pregnancy, the nurses concentrated on achieving the following educational objectives:

1. *Help women improve their diet and monitor their weight gain.* The nurses carried out systematic evaluations of the women's diet using 24-hour diet recalls at least every other visit and monitored their weight gain by plotting it on a standard weight-gain chart. The nurses reviewed daily nutritional requirements and suggested a diet plan that coincided with the women's food preferences and their life-styles. The nurses addressed specific problems, such as nausea and vomiting, over- and undereating, pica, and inadequate finances, and offered practical tips about how to shop resourcefully. The nurses reinforced the physician's recommendations for vitamins, iron supplements, and special diets, and this helped women plan ways of improving their intake to ensure more complete antepartum nutrition.

2. *Help women eliminate the use of cigarettes, alcohol, and drugs.* The nurses assessed the women's use of cigarettes, alcohol, and drugs and devised plans to reduce their use. Early in the sequence of visits, the nurses explained in detail how these substances affect fetal development and the mother's health. Individualized plans were developed for reducing their intake using behavioral analysis techniques. The nurses encouraged a reduction in smoking, for example, by helping women identify the contexts in which they usually smoked, by substituting nutritious snacks in the place of cigarette smoking, by gradually reducing the nicotine levels in the brand of cigarettes they smoked (nicotine fading), and by encouraging women to follow the advice offered in smoking cessation pamphlets and to attend smoking clinics.

3. *Teach parents to identify the signs of pregnancy complication.* The nurses discussed in detail the common signs of pregnancy complication and preterm delivery, including conditions associated with hypertensive disorders of pregnancy (such as blurred vision, dizziness, edema), genitourinary tract infection (e.g., vaginal discharge and burning sensation with urination), and the symptoms of preterm or complicated labor. The nurses helped women distinguish false labor (Braxton–Hicks contractions) from real contractions and urged the women to call the physician's office or clinic at the first sign of any complication.

4. *Encourage regular rest, appropriate exercise, and good personal hygiene related to obstetrical health.* The nurses taught the women the importance of regular rest (including resting several times per day and lying on the left side to promote uterine blood flow), the maintenance of exercise consistent with prepregnant levels, sexual activity that reflected knowledge about the potential health risks to mother and fetus (avoiding a partner with venereal disease, avoiding sexual activity if intercourse was uncomfortable or if there were sign of premature labor), and basic hygienic practices that reduce the chances of genitourinary tract infections.

5. *Prepare parents for labor and delivery.* All women were encouraged to attend the local childbirth education classes offered by the local hospitals. If the mother was unable or unwilling to attend, the nurse covered the topics of labor and delivery and demonstrated the breathing and relaxation exercises during the home visits. The nurses arranged a tour of the labor and delivery rooms for those women who did not attend the formal classes. (One of the most common reasons that women did not attend was that they had no one to accompany them as a support person.) As indicated above, all women were taught to identify the complications of pregnancy and labor and to notify the physician or emergency room, depending on the type of problem identified. The labor and delivery routines followed by the local hospitals were discussed with both mother and her support person.

6. *Prepare parents for the early care of the newborn.* The nurses encouraged optimal care of the newborn by helping parents prepare for the child. The nurses taught the parents about newborn competencies and the value of early and extended contact between parents and the newborn (Klaus & Kennell, 1976). Parents were encouraged to spend the first hour after delivery getting to know their new family member and to request rooming-in. The advantages and disadvantages of rooming-in were discussed so that the parents would be able to make the choice without feeling coerced and so that they would continue to feel that their birthing experience was under their control. Similarly, parents were encouraged to choose a feeding method (after considering the advantages and disadvantages of breast versus bottle feeding); to obtain baby clothes, equipment, and a place for the baby to sleep upon returning home from the hospital; and to choose a source of pediatric care. One of the most critical features of the program involved the nurses dis-

cussing variations in newborn crying patterns and temperament with parents (Thomas, Chess, & Birch, 1963). The nurses emphasized the tremendous variability in the extent to which newborns cry, and they stressed that infants who cried a lot were not intending to make life difficult for parents and that their crying was not an indication that the parents were incompetent.

7. *Encourage appropriate use of the health care system.* The nurses urged the women to attend all prenatal appointments, to make a list of their concerns and questions before the visit (so that they could make best use of their time with the physician), to comply with the physician's recommendations, to call the physician whenever any sign of pregnancy complication arose, and to discuss the results of their prenatal visits with the nurses themselves.

8. *Encourage mothers to make plans regarding subsequent pregnancies, returning to school, and finding employment.* A central aspect of the nurses' educational program was to encourage parents to clarify their plans for completing their education, returning to work, and bearing additional children. The nurses emphasized that the decision to return to school or seek employment after delivery should be made after parents fully considered what was in their own and their babies' best interest. Toward the end of pregnancy and throughout the first 2 years postpartum, the nurses helped them make concrete plans for child care and advised them in methods of finding jobs and interviewing. The advantages of different methods of birth control were discussed and birth control devices presented. The discussions of family planning were carried out in the context of the women's desires for their continued education, work, and achievement of what they considered to be their optimal family size. The nurses tailored the specific content of their home visits to the individual needs of each family. For example, the nurses helped all interested women find employment but gave special consideration to those who were poor and lacked other sources of income; they discussed family planning with all families but gave extra attention to those who

wanted to avoid additional pregnancies. The nurses refrained from imposing family planning methods on couples who had already decided that they wanted to have large families with their children spaced closely together.

Infancy education. The infancy curriculum focused on five developmental periods, each of which was described in terms of the adaptive tasks of the mother and development of the infant. As during pregnancy, the curriculum was organized so that the nurses were able to cover issues of common concern to all new parents, while responding to the individual needs of each family. Because support persons often were unable to attend all home visits, the nurses made special efforts to encourage their attendance at selected visits. The frequency of visits during each of the five developmental periods and the visits support persons were especially encouraged to attend are specified in Table 1–1.

In general, each visit (which lasted from 60 to 90 min) started with an inquiry about how the mother was doing. The focus of the visit then shifted to the baby. As with the prenatal curriculum, the nurse decided how much material to cover and in what order. The specific educational objectives for the infancy period were as follows:

1. *Improve parents' understanding of the infant's temperament.* The nurses continued to help parents understand their infant's temperament after delivery. The nurses encouraged the parents, for example, to administer some of the items of the Brazelton Newborn Examination (Brazelton, 1973), so the parents might increase their confidence in handling their newborn and become sensitized to their child's individual way of responding to the world. With this information, parents could organize their infant's environment to minimize distress and optimize development. A passive infant, for example, may need extra stimulation, because it does not engage others as readily. By contrast, an irritable child who responds poorly to change may need to be protected from hordes of well-wishing relatives and friends. In general, the concepts of temperament and individual personality, beginning in the ear-

Table 1–1. Visits of Support Persons

Child's age	Stage	Frequency of visits	Support person attendance
0–6 weeks	Integration and adaptation	Weekly	2 days and 10 days
6 weeks–4 months	Consolidation	Every 2 weeks	4 months
4 months–14 months	Attachment	Every 3 weeks	8 months
14 months–20 months	Mobility	Every month	17 months
20 months–24 months	Autonomy/socialization	Every 6 weeks	20 months and 24 months

liest days after delivery, formed a consistent theme throughout the 2 years after delivery. The nurses spent a considerable portion of their time during the child's first 6 months helping parents understand how to interpret cries. For those whose babies cried excessively (a surprisingly small proportion, on the basis of nurses' reports), the nurse taught methods of coping with a colicky infant, with techniques such as holding, rocking, swaddling, carrying, talking, and singing to the baby.

2. *Promote the infant's socioemotional and cognitive development.* The nurses encouraged parents and other family members to engage in sensitive, growth-promoting care of the infant, including interpreting and responding to the infant's cues (e.g., crying, changes in activity level, grimacing, smiling, refusing to feed); communicating with the child by holding, talking, singing, naming objects, and reading; playing interactive games (such as patty-cake, peek-a-boo, hide and seek); making play things that were appropriate for the child's stage of development; turning routine care such as feeding and diaper changing into opportunities for communication and play; and organizing the child's daily routine to create variety. As the child grew older and more mobile, the nurses discussed the child's need to explore and later to develop a sense of autonomy. The nurse suggested methods of controlling undesirable behavior (e.g., negativism, temper tantrums, getting into everything, resistance to toilet training) with techniques such as removing and distracting the child, which do not involve physical punishment and yelling. Much time was spent helping parents understand their children's need for responsive caregivers whom they could learn to trust to respond to their needs.

The nurses carried out these activities after they assessed the child and family and decided which particular aspect of the child's development and the parents' caregiving deserved the greatest attention. They achieved these objectives by modeling appropriate caregiving, discussing the child's developmental course, and providing parents with a library of materials on these topics written for individuals with varying reading levels. They tried to introduce topics when parents seemed to be most interested or concerned with them. Sometimes, however, the nurses introduced issues because the parents seemed unaware of the problem, such as the excessive punishment of infants and a failure to respond to crying because of a fear of spoiling the child.

3. *Promote the physical health of the child.* The nurses assessed the extent to which parents knew how to provide routine care of the child including appropriate feeding, dressing, and bathing; managing common problems such as rashes, spitting up, and constipation; and preventing accidents and ingestions. Where needed, the nurses taught basic caregiving skills. They discussed the use of infant car seats and safety belts; the use of safety locks on kitchen cabinet doors; the prevention of falls from beds, tables, and couches and of burns from hot liquids (such as tea, coffee, baths); and the avoidance of cribs with small slats and thin plastic sheets on sleeping surfaces. The nurses also spent considerable time on the child's age-specific nutritional needs, how to know when the child had eaten enough, and how to hold the child during feeding in ways that would promote parent–child communication. The nurses taught parents about immunizations, well-baby care, and how to take the child's temperature and recognize signs of illness (such as a consistent refusal to eat, change in activity level, lethargy or irritability). The nurses encouraged the parents to call a physician or emergency room if the child appeared ill, to be prepared to provide the child's temperature and describe other signs of illness, and to assist the physician in deciding whether an office or emergency-room visit was warranted.

Enhancing Informal Support

The nurses sought to enhance the informal support available to women during pregnancy, birth, and the first 2 years after delivery. Early in the sequence of visits, the nurses asked the women to identify family members and friends whom they felt close to and could count on to help them. On the basis of this assessment, the nurses identified the mother's primary and secondary support person and urged each woman to invite these persons to participate in the home visits. In the visits, the nurses encouraged the women's family and friends to help the women with household responsibilities, to accompany them to the hospital at the time of delivery, to be present for the birth, to aid in the subsequent care of the child, and to reinforce the advice of the nurses in their absence. The nurses encouraged them to be sensitive to the women's needs and to help them follow appropriate health behaviors—without nagging and finding fault. The women's husbands or boyfriends and their own mothers were especially called on to participate in the home visits. These individuals were assumed to play decisive roles in determining the extent to which the women would improve their health habits, finish their educations, find work, secure appropriate child care, and address the needs of the child. In order to facilitate the involvement of friends and family members in the home visits, the nurses visited some women on weekends and evenings, when the women's family members and friends could participate.

In identifying individuals who might serve as supports for the mother, the nurses assessed the extent to which each individual of significance in the mother's life supported the mother and the goals of the program; the nurse tried to assess the likelihood that the program would create or intensify hostilities among members of the support network or between the mother and the support person. It was not uncommon for the women to be involved, for example, with men who were engaged in illegal activities or who were abusive to them. In some of the cases, the nurses were able to serve as a support to the women as they broke away from these destructive relationships. In others, the women seemed to be committed to maintaining contact, at almost any cost.

Linkage with Formal Services

The nurses also connected families with formal health and human services, in order to reduce family stresses that the family was unable to handle alone. Parents were urged to keep prenatal and well-child care appointments and to call the physician's office when a health problem arose, so that the office staff might help them make decisions as to whether sick or emergency-room visits were necessary. The nurses sent regular reports of their observations regarding medical, social, and emotional conditions to both the obstetricians and pediatricians who provided the mothers' and babies' care. Each physician received at least two written reports; where needed, case conferences and phone contacts were used to communicate more completely or more rapidly. In this way, the physicians and office nurses could provide more informed and sensitive care in the office, and by communicating regularly with the mothers' and babies' primary health care providers, the nurses could clarify and reinforce physicians' recommendations in the home. When necessary, parents were referred to other services such as Planned Parenthood, mental health counseling, legal aid, and the nutritional supplementation program for women, infants, and children (WIC). Thus, to the extent possible, the resources of the formal health and human service system were summoned to meet the needs of the families visited by the nurse.

Results

We tested the effects of the program by comparing those families who had been randomly assigned to receive the nurse with families who had been randomly assigned to service conditions that did not involve home visiting (free transportation for regular prenatal and well-child care and sensory and developmental screening for the child at 1 and 2 years of age).[2] Even though the program ended at the child's second birthday, we followed the children and families until the children were 4 years of age to determine the long-range impact of the program. Details of the research design can be found in our empirical reports (Olds, Henderson, Chamberlain, & Tatelbaum, 1986; Olds, Henderson, Tatelbaum, & Chamberlin, 1986).

During pregnancy, we found that, compared to women who had been assigned to receive the transportation and screening services, women who had received the nurse made better use of the formal services that were available to them. They experienced greater informal social support, improved their diets more, and reduced the number of cigarettes smoked.

The positive effects of the program on birth weight and length of gestation were concentrated on the very young teenagers, for whom we observed a 395 gram improvement in birth weight, and smokers, for whom we observed a 75% reduction in preterm delivery (Olds, Henderson, Tatelbaum, & Chamberlin, 1986).

After delivery, we compared women who had received the postnatal nurse home visitation program with those assigned to receive either the screening or the transportation and the screening. One of the most important issues that we examined after delivery was the impact of the program on the rates of verified cases of child abuse and neglect. For the group of women with all three of the risk characteristics used for sample recruitment (the poor, unmarried teenagers), we found a 75% reduction in the incidence of verified cases of child abuse and neglect—a reduction from 19 to 4%. This picture of maltreatment

---

[2]Forty-six non-Whites were removed from the analyses reported here because the sample of non-Whites was too small to cross-classify race with other variables of importance in the statistical analyses. Results for these non-White cases are presented elsewhere (Olds, Henderson, Birmingham, Chamberlin, & Tatelbaum, 1983).

prevention was painted by a number of other sources of data:

1. There was a trend for the nurse-visited, poor, unmarried teenagers themselves to tell us that their children were easier to care for.

2. Our interviewers observed less punishment and restriction and a greater number of growth-promoting playthings in the homes of nurse-visited, poor, unmarried teenagers.

3. Our medical record abstractors found that the nurse-visited, poor, unmarried teenagers took their children to the emergency room fewer times during the first year of life for upper respiratory infections than did the poor, unmarried teenagers in the comparison group.

4. During the second year of the child's life, nurse-visited women took their children to the emergency room 56% fewer times for accidents and ingestions than did women who had been assigned to the comparison group.

When we further examined the impact of the program on maltreatment and emergency-room visits, we found that as women's sense of control over their lives declined, the incidence of both maltreatment and emergency-room visits increased among women who had been assigned to the comparison services. However, among those women who had been assigned a nurse to visit them after delivery, the incidence of maltreatment and emergency-room visits remained relatively low—even among women who had little sense of control over their lives when they registered in the program (Olds, Henderson, Chamberlain, & Tatelbaum, 1986).

In examining the impact of the program on the women's own life-course development, we found that between birth and the child's fourth birthday, nurse-visited, poor, unmarried women worked 82% longer than their counterparts in the comparison group. During the first 2 years postpartum, only the nurse-visited, poor, unmarried, older women worked longer than their counterparts in the comparison group; but during the 2-year period after the program ended at the child's second birthday, the poor, unmarried teenagers began to work more than their counterparts in the comparison group as well.

Data derived from interviews with mothers at the 10th and 22nd months of the infants' life help explain the increased employment observed for the nurse-visited, poor, unmarried teenagers during the 24- to 48-month period. In these interviews, the nurse-visited, poor, unmarried teens reported greater concern about eventually finding employment than the poor, unmarried teens in the comparison group. In other words, the nurse-visited, poor, unmarried teenagers wanted to work more but were unable to do so, probably because of their young age. (At 10 months postpartum, the average teenage mother had just turned 18 years of age). Once they became older (and more employable), they indeed worked more than their counterparts in the comparison group.

During the 46-month period following delivery, nurse-visited women had 22% fewer subsequent pregnancies than did women in the comparison group, an effect that was concentrated among poor, unmarried women for whom there was a 42% reduction.

Positive Aspects, Negative Side Effects, and Limitations of the Program

Positive Aspects

Our results indicate that home visitation is a useful vehicle for the delivery of prevention services. It provides a means of reaching out to parents who distrust formal service providers or who lack self confidence—those least likely to show up for office-based services. If properly carried out, home visitation can eventually increase parents' confidence, so they can express themselves more comfortably and feel less threatened about using other formal services.

Without a major home visitation component, a significant portion of the families who most need the service will not receive it. Clearly, home visitation cannot overcome the lack of participation by all insecure, distrustful parents—who can simply refuse to answer the door or can conveniently not be at home. A persistent, caring nurse, however, can be remarkably successful in engaging a significant portion of those who are unreachable through other means.

Another advantage of the program was that the nurses were able to acquire a more complete understanding of those factors in the home and family that interfered with parents' efforts to cope with the pregnancy and early care of the child. By assessing the home environment, the nurses could provide more sensitive, informed services themselves and could help other service providers do the same. Because the parents in our program did not always articulate their needs clearly, it helped to have sensitive home-visiting nurses get to know them so that appropriate services could be provided.

By approaching pregnancy and early child rearing from an ecological framework, the nurses in our program were able to achieve considerable leverage in improving pregnancy outcomes (Olds, Henderson, Tatelbaum & Chamberlin, 1986), maternal life-course development (Olds et al., 1983), as well as qualities of maternal caregiving (Olds, Henderson, Chamberlain, & Tatelbaum, 1986). Improvements in these various areas of maternal and child functioning had a synergistic effect on one another. By calling attention to the adverse effects of maternal smoking and inadequate weight gain on fetal development, for example, the nurses helped women change those prenatal health behaviors that lead to intrauterine growth retardation and begin to appreciate how their behavior affected their children's well-being later in life. Morever, because growth-retarded babies have more aversive cries, some investigators have argued that they are at increased risk for child abuse (Lester & Zeskind, 1978). Consequently, the prevention of low birth weight in itself may reduce the incidence of subsequent maltreatment. In a similar way, by involving other family members in the pregnancy, birth, and early care of the child, the nurses increased the social resources for mother and baby, which is important by itself. The enhancement of social support may be important for the prevention of child neglect as well, in view of its association with social isolation (Seagull, 1987).

In an analogous way, by linking parents with other health and human services, the nurses helped reduce many of the stresses that lead to maternal depression (Fergusson et al., 1984), poor prenatal health habits (Stephens, 1985), and interference with caregiving (Belle, 1982). By helping young women find ways to continue their education, find jobs, and plan future pregnancies, the nurses helped them increase their financial resources and reduce the stresses associated with caring for several young children. These aspects of the program undoubtedly also contributed to its success in reducing child abuse and neglect and improving other aspects of maternal caregiving.

Negative Side Effects

Although the program has shown promising results in a variety of areas of maternal and child functioning, it is important to acknowledge that our efforts to help families may not have always brought about their intended effect—our supposedly supportive interventions may sometimes have produced harm. In designing the program, we attempted to anticipate the kinds of problems that might be created by the program in order to avoid or minimize them. With so much pressure on parents to uphold high standards in caring for their children, for example, feelings of anxiety and guilt were almost inevitable, unless specific precautions were taken. Under a great deal of stress, a mother may unwillingly react harshly to her child. By discussing such problems before they arose, the nurses helped parents rehearse problem-solving methods and minimized guilt by pointing out that many parents react similarly when faced with the same problems. Similarly, because 50 to 80% of the women who smoke at the start of pregnancy find it impossible to give it up, even with the assistance of a smoking cessation program (Windsor, 1986), we urged the nurses to avoid making women who were unsuccessful feel guilty.

Some parents simply felt overwhelmed by the volume of information imparted in the program. To counteract this, the nurses promoted change in small ways and outlined clear, specific, sequential, and attainable goals. The nurses also looked for signs of overload such as blank or puzzled expressions, wandering attention, or lack of verbal response. When this occurred, the nurse made sure that what they were saying addressed the needs and interests of the family. If the women were still unable to concentrate, the nurses shortened the length of the visit.

This kind of intervention can also lead to the nurses' interference with parents' own way of doing things. Examples include interference with the timing of feeding solids and spoiling young babies by picking them up when they cry, as noted earlier. The nurses addressed issues like these by (a) advising parents during pregnancy that health professionals and parents sometimes have different views and (b) encouraging parents to make their own decision after carefully considering which method they wished to follow. The nurses avoided challenging the family practice unless it posed an imminent threat to the mother or child.

The nurses' efforts to establish rapport and impart useful information increased the possibility that parents would become dependent on them. To prevent this, the nurses encouraged parents to assume the initiative in solving problems that confronted them. Achieving independence, however, sometimes required allowing dependence in times of unusual stress. The first few weeks after delivery, for example, are often difficult for new mothers, so the nurses routinely visited more frequently during this time.

One of the more serious unintended effects involved the nurses' interfering with family dynamics and thereby exacerbating family conflict. The nurses tried to avoid these problems by listening respectfully to everyone's opinions and by urging them to listen carefully to each other. When serious family conflict emerged, the nurses referred the family for professional counseling. In general, it was our judgment that promoting the involvement of other family members diminished the potential conflict that home visiting might have created if the home visitor were to have focused her attention exclusively on the mother.

The primary risk in linking families with health and human services was in increasing the family's dependence on formal services. This problem was minimized by helping parents continue their education, find employment, and turn to friends and relatives for other assistance.

Limitations

Even though the program was more effective than we originally expected, it was not without limitations. The rate of child abuse and neglect, for example, although substantially reduced in the nurse-visited condition, was still 4 to 5%—a rate too high by any standard, especially for such young children. We tried to analyze why the nurses were unable to prevent the more intractable cases of maltreatment, but our data did not provide any explanations. (We see corresponding limitations in program impact on other outcomes, such as preterm delivery and low birth weight.) Because there is no empirical pattern to the failure of the program to prevent certain cases of maltreatment and other problems, it is useful to examine the limitations of the program on purely theoretical grounds.

Although the present program was designed to address those underlying emotions and cognitions that play an important role in caregiving, it may be that long histories of abuse or neglect in women's childhoods, in certain cases, continue to undermine their ability to form relationships and their quality of caregiving (Main & Goldwyn, 1984; Ricks, 1985), even in the presence of a 2½-year comprehensively designed program.

Although the nurses in the present program tried to moderate the effects of poverty on family life by linking parents with needed services in the community, ultimately there are structural constraints limiting what is possible with this kind of intervention. Communities with high rates of unemployment, drug abuse, and other conditions antithetical to productive living exert powerful, insidious forces that work against the influence of the nurse. In light of this, it is not unreasonable for the nurses to fail in their prevention efforts in certain cases.

Other structural, community-wide factors need to be considered as well. Even though the nurses tried to imbue parents with an appreciation for the importance of nonviolent child-rearing methods, their efforts were counteracted by the cultural acceptance of physical punishment as a method of discipline. When questioned about their disciplinary practices during the research interviews, many parents apologized for not spanking their children *more* frequently.

In spite of its limitations, however, the present program does provide a basis for considerable hope that the incidence of a number of serious maternal and child health problems can indeed be reduced with home visitation services. Before these findings are used as a basis for a major public-policy initiative, it is important that they be replicated with different nurses and with families living in different circumstances.

Because our study was carried out in a semi-rural, essentially White community, we cannot say how effective it might be in a poor urban area with a primarily Black population. We suspect that it would be as effective there, in part because of promising results for the small Black sample in our original study (Olds et al., 1983), but we have no good evidence on this point.

Even if the questions of generalizability were resolved, significant questions would remain about whether such services are indeed cost-effective and how they should be funded. Preliminary cost-benefit analyses suggest that a major portion of the cost for home visitation can be offset by avoided foster-care placements, hospitalizations, emergency-room visits, and child-protective-service worker time incurred during the same period that the home-visiting is provided. Short-range projections (through the child's sixth year of life) of cost savings to the government resulting from the nurse-visited, unmarried women returning to the work force and reducing the number of subsequent children show even greater cost savings (Olds, Lombardi, & Henderson, 1986). Given the association between early maltreatment and subsequent psychosocial dysfunctions such as juvenile delinquency (Gargarino & Plantz, 1986) and violent behavior (Lewis, Shanok, & Balla, 1979), the long-range financial savings to the community may be substantially greater.

Even if our final cost-benefit analysis confirms these preliminary results, questions will remain about which government agency should fund this kind of service. The intervention itself is most likely to be carried out through departments of public health, yet the cost savings and human benefits are likely to be seen in a number of other government agencies such as social services, mental health, and education. Because of this, we recommend that the program costs be shared by a number of government agencies in proportion to the cost savings that are anticipated in each of their budgets.

Practical Suggestions for Starting a New Program

The present program and research required the active involvement of virtually every health and human service available to women and children in the community. Any attempt to replicate the program will require comparable community development. To elicit the cooperation of these service agencies, we developed a proposal to carry out the study and presented it to representatives of the local pediatric and obstetric groups; the county health department; the two local hospitals; the department of mental health, mental retardation, and alcoholism services; family services; Planned Parenthood; and the public schools. Representatives of these groups raised concerns about (a) the credentials and background of the nurses who would be selected as home visitors; (b) the possible interference with patient-care activities in the health department, physicians' offices, and hospitals; and (c) the possible duplication of services and consequent reduction in need for their own programs that served poor women and children. We considered each of their concerns and resolved them as we refined the program plan. The representatives also raised problems with the research, which we have discussed elsewhere (Olds, 1988). As the study proceeded, we informed them of the findings of the study. They in turn played a central role in seeing to it that the program was continued by the county health department after the original experimental phase of the study was completed.

One of the issues raised by the local steering committee concerned the qualifications of the nurses who were involved in the home visitation. In retrospect, this is one of the most important issues to consider in planning this kind of home visitation program. We decided that it was important to hire nurses who were parents themselves and who displayed considerable life experience and wisdom in addition to their formal training. Although it is possible to educate helping professionals in methods of forming effective therapeutic relationships, we believed that it was even more important to find individuals who had demonstrated a wealth of personal experience that would help them relate effectively with the families and make sound judgments in the field.

If the selection of nurses is so important to the success of the program, how is the current nursing shortage likely to affect the viability of the program? It has been our experience that this kind of position is extremely attractive to many nurses, in part because of the work hours, the autonomy that it provides in the job definition, and the opportunities created for the nurses to follow through with their desire to serve others. Consequently, the position is likely to be very competitive with other attractive nursing positions. Moreover, it has been our experience that nurses with both the professional and the personal attributes that would make them good home visitors can be found in virtually every community in the country.

Conclusions

We have taken the position that the development of programs and policies for socially disadvantaged families should be based to a greater extent on rigorously conducted research, but we recognize that the problems faced by poor women, children, and their families during this stage in the life cycle are so pressing that program and policy planners cannot wait for the definitive study to direct their work. Indeed, given the complexities of these problems and the variety of community contexts in which a single program might be established, we will never be able to prescribe a single program plan for prenatal and infancy home visitation. Nevertheless, we hope that the results of our study will give program planners and policy makers a sense of direction as they try to promote the health of socially disadvantaged pregnant women and their children.

References

Ainsworth, M. (1973). The development of infant–mother attachment. In B. Caldwell & H. Ricciuti

(Eds.), *Review of child development research* (Vol. 3, pp. 1–94). Chicago: University of Chicago Press.

Baldwin, A. L. (1967). *Theories of child development.* New York: John Wiley and Sons, 1967.

Bandura, A., & Walters, R. H. (1963). *Social learning and personality development.* New York: Holt, Rinehart, and Winston.

Belle, D. (Ed.). (1982). *Lives in stress: Women and depression.* Beverly Hills, CA: Sage Publishing.

Berkman, L., & Syme, L., (1979). Social networks, host resistance, and mortality: A nine-year follow-up study of Alameda County residents. *American Journal of Epidemiology, 109,* 186–204.

Birch, H., & Gussow, H. (1970). *Disadvantaged children: Health, nutrition, and school failure.* New York: Harcourt, Brace and World.

Bowlby, J. (1969). *Attachment and loss: Vol. 1: Attachment.* New York: Basic Books.

Boyer, R., & Savageau, D. (1981). *Places rated almanac.* New York: Rand McNally, 1981.

Brazelton, T. B. (1973). *Neonatal behavioral assessment scale.* London: Heineman.

Bronfenbrenner, U. (1979). *The ecology of human development: Experiments by nature and design.* Cambridge, MA: Harvard University Press..

Card, J. J., & Wise, L. L. (1978). Teenage mothers and teenage fathers: The impact of early childbearing on the parents' personal and professional lives. *Family Planning Perspectives, 10,* 199–205.

Chavigny, K., & Korske, M. (1983). Public health nursing in crisis. *Nursing Outlook, 31,* 312–316.

Combs-Orme, T., Reis, J., & Ward, L. D. (1985). Effectiveness of home visits by public health nurses in maternal and child health: An empirical review. *Public Health Reports, 100,* 490–499.

Dershewitz, R. A., & Williamson, J. W. (1977). Prevention of childhood household injuries: A controlled clinical trial. *American Journal of Public Health, 67,* 1148–1153.

Elardo, R., Bradley, R., & Caldwell, B. (1975). The relation of infants' home environment to mental test performance from six to thirty-six months: A longitudinal analysis. *Child Development, 46,* 71–76.

Fergusson, D., Hons, L., Horwood, L., & Shannon, F: (1984). Relationship of family life events, maternal depression, and child-rearing problems. *Pediatrics, 73,* 773–776.

Furstenberg, F. F. (1980). *Unplanned parenthood: The social consequences of teenage childbearing.* New York: The Free Press.

Garbarino, J., & Crouter, N. (1978). Defining the community context for child maltreatment. *Child Development, 49,* 604–616.

Garbarino, J., & Plantz, M. C. (1986). Child abuse and juvenile delinquency: What are the links? In J. Garbarino, C. Schellenbach, J. Sebes, & Associates (Eds.), *Troubled youth, troubled families.* New York: Aldine.

Garn, S. M., & Petzold, A. S. (1983). Characteristics of the mother and child in teenage pregnancy. *American Journal of Diseases of Children, 137,* 365–368.

Hollingshead, A. (1976). *Four factor index of social status.* Unpublished manuscript, Yale University.

Kempe, C. (1976). Approaches to preventing child abuse: The health visitor concept. *American Journal of Diseases of Children, 130,* 941–947.

Klaus, M., & Kennell, J. (1976). *Maternal–infant bonding.* St. Louis: C. V. Mosby.

Lester, B. M., & Zeskind, P. S. (1978). Brazelton scale and physical size correlates of neonatal cry features. *Infant Behavior and Development, 1,* 393–402.

Lewis, D. O., Shanok, S. S., & Balla, D. A. (1979). Perinatal difficulties, head and face trauma, and child abuse in the medical histories of seriously delinquent children. *American Journal of Psychiatry, 136,* 419–423.

Locke, S. E. (1982). Stress, adaptation, and immunity: studies in humans. *General Hospital Psychiatry, 4,* 49–58.

Main, M., & Goldwyn, R. (1984). Predicting rejection of her infant from mother's representation of her own experience: Implications for the abused–abusing intergenerational cycle. *Child Abuse and Neglect, 8,* 203–217.

McCormick, M. C., Brooks-Gunn, J., Shorter, T., Holmes, J. H., Wallace, C. Y., & Heagarty, M. C. (1986). *Environmental stress, social supports, health behaviors, and mental illness as risk factors for low birthweight in low-income women.* Unpublished manuscript, University of Pennsylvania, Philadelphia.

McCormick, M. C., Shapiro, S., & Starfield, B. (1984). High-risk young mothers: Infant mortality and morbidity in four areas in the United States, 1973–1978. *American Journal of Public Health, 74,* 18–23.

Miller, F., Court, S., Walton, W., & Knox, E. (1960). *Growing up in New Castle Upon Tyne.* London: Oxford University Press.

Miller, H., & Merritt, A. (1979). *Fetal growth in humans.* Chicago: Year Book Publishers.

Naeye, R. (1981). Teenaged and pre-teenaged pregnancies: Consequences of the fetal-maternal competition for nutrients. *Pediatrics, 67,* 146–150.

New York State Department of Social Services. (1973–1982). *Annual report of Child Protective Services in New York State.* Albany: New York State Department of Social Services.

Newton, R. W., & Hunt, L. P. (1984). Psychosocial stress in pregnancy and its relation to low birth weight. *British Medical Journal, 288,* 1191–1194.

Olds, D. (1988). Common design and methodological problems encountered in evaluating family support services: Illustrations from the Prenatal/Early Infancy Project. in H. Weiss & F. Jacobs (Eds.), *Evaluating Family Programs.* Chicago: Aldine Press.

Olds, D., Henderson, C. Birmingham, M., Chamberlin, R., & Tatelbaum, R. (1983). *Final report to Maternal and Child Health and Crippled Children's Services Research Grants Program, Bureau of Community Health Services, HSA, PHS, DHHS* (Grant No. MCJ-36040307).

Olds, D., Henderson, C., Chamberlin, R., & Tatelbaum, R. (1986). Preventing child abuse and neglect: A randomized trial of nurse home visitation. *Pediatrics, 78,* 65–78.

Olds, D., Henderson, C., Tatelbaum, R., & Chamberlin, R. (1986). Improving the delivery of prenatal care and outcomes of pregnancy: A randomized trial of nurse home visitation. *Pediatrics, 77,* 16–28.

Olds, D., Lombardi, J., & Henderson, C. (1986). *Final report to the William T. Grant Foundation* (Grant No. 840723-80) New York: William T. Grant Foundation.

Phipps-Yonas, S. (1980). *Teenage pregnancy and motherhood: A review of the literature. American Journal of Orthopsychiatry, 50,* 403–431.

Piaget, J. (1952). *The origins of intelligence in children.* New York: International Universities Press.

Ricks, M. H. (1985). The social transmission of parental behavior: Attachment across generations. In I. Bretherton & E. Waters (Eds.), *Growing points of attachment theory and research.* Monographs of the Society for Research in Child Development, 50, 211–227.

Rubin, R. (1975). Maternal tasks of pregnancy. *Maternal-Child Nursing Journal, 4,* 143–153.

Rush, D., Stein, Z., & Insoln, M. (1980). A randomized controlled trial of prenatal supplementation in New York City. *Pediatrics, 65,* 683–697.

Sameroff, A., & Chandler, M. J. (1975). Reproductive risk and the continuum of caretaking casualty. In F. D. Horowitz (Ed.), *Review of child development research (Vol. 4, pp. 187–245).* Chicago: University of Chicago Press.

Seagull, E. A. W. (1987). Social support and child maltreatment: A review of the evidence. *Child Abuse and Neglect, 11,* 41–52.

Sexton, M. S., & Hebel, J. R. (1984). A clinical trial of change in maternal smoking and its effects on birthweight. *Journal of the American Medical Association, 251,* 911–915.

Stephens, C. J. (1985). Perception of pregnancy and social support as predictors of alcohol consumption during pregnancy. *Alcoholism: Clinical Experience and Research, 9,* 344–348.

Thomas, A., Chess, S., & Birch, M. (1963). *Behavioral individuality in early childhood.* New York: New York University Press.

Windsor, R. A. (1986). *Behavioral impact and cost analyses of smoking cessation methods for pregnant women: The Birmingham trial* (Smoking Behavior and Policy, Discussion Paper Series). Cambridge, MA, Harvard University.

Wynn, M., & Wynn, A. (1979). Some developments in child health care in Europe. *Hospital Medicine, 15,* 65–70.

Donald E. Pierson

2

The Brookline
Early Education Project

In schools across this country and around the world, educators continually hear disconcerting evidence of children's unfulfilled potential and failure in school. While the catastrophic manifestations of these concerns—school dropouts, juvenile delinquency, illiteracy, adolescent pregnancy, and drug and alcohol abuse—require intensive and expensive intervention, many observers contend that the precursors of school success and failure can be influenced by relatively inexpensive provision of parent and early childhood education programs.

Issues and Goals

In the early 1970s in Brookline, Massachusetts, Superintendent of Schools Robert I. Sperber heard reports from school personnel that as many as one third of the primary grade students had learning or adjustment difficulties that might require remedial attention. Concerned about the implications for costs of special education and prompted by a desire to prevent rather than remediate children's difficulties in school, Sperber initiated the Brookline Early Education Project (BEEP).

With funding from two private foundations (Carnegie Corporation of New York and The Robert Wood Johnson Foundation), BEEP drew from the resources and collaborative planning of medical, psychological, social service, and research authorities. Parents, school personnel, and community representatives were also actively engaged in identifying the issues and thrust of the program. The following eight issues arose in the planning process and shaped the programs and research design.

1. *Importance of the early years.* It seemed obvious that children would benefit in many ways if parents, educators, health care givers, indeed the entire community, could become better informed about the nature of learning and child development in the first 5 years of life. This is not to deny the importance of education in later years, but rather to acknowledge a need for sound information about child development among parents and their support networks.

2. *Lead role of the school.* Although it was assumed that any number of agencies in a community could take the lead in administering early education, part of the significance of this model is to demonstrate the viability of the public schools carrying out that lead role.

3. *Primacy of the parents' role.* By offering parent education, the aim is to acknowledge, inform, and support parents in their efforts while avoiding approaches that might deny, usurp, or undermine their role.

4. *Relationship of health and development to learning.* In promoting education for young children, we realized that learning, health status, and development are inextricably related. Therefore, there must be close collaboration between educators and primary health care givers.

5. *Open enrollment with active recruitment.* All of the federally funded programs and several state-based initiatives in early education have been restricted to low-income families. Although it is appropriate to target services to those most in need, this targeting also encourages the stigma of a deficit orientation. By opening the program to all, we tried to reinforce the expectation that everyone could benefit. At the same time, we accepted the challenge to make sure that families who would not seek such an opportunity would hear about it and feel comfortable in joining.

6. *Continuity from birth to kindergarten.* Many experts argue the critical importance of working with parents and children at one age versus another. In BEEP, we wanted to make certain that we started early enough and continued long enough to ensure that gains were maintained throughout the preschool years.

7. *Team teaching model.* We realized that we all had much to learn about delivering parent and early childhood education, and we were determined to avoid the isolation that is characteristic of teachers in many elementary schools. Staff schedules, therefore, incorporated weekly time for planning, information sharing, and supervision.

8. *Cost-effectiveness design.* To gain some insight into how much one needs to invest in order to make the program worthwhile, we incorporated three cost levels into our parent education model: minimum, moderate, and maximum intensity of services.

Guided by the planning around these issues, BEEP has conducted research and demonstration programs for more than a decade. The ultimate goal is to determine the benefits of a comprehensive, school-based parent and early childhood education program for children's functioning in school.

Program Description

Family Enrollment

When the pilot project began in the spring of 1973, we attempted to identify and recruit all families who were expecting the birth of a child in the coming months. All families residing in Brookline were eligible to enroll in BEEP if they had a child born during the enrollment period. In addition, to gain more population diversity than would be possible in Brookline alone and to further Brookline's involvement in the urban–suburban desegregation programs, minority families in adjoining areas of Boston were also invited to enroll.

Recruitment strategies were designed to enroll families who would not have the confidence or network of contacts to participate in an innovative education program. Kindergarten teachers, principals, counselors, social workers, public health nurses, obstetricians, hospitals, maternity shops, and recreation programs cooperated in displaying brochures and referring families. The most successful recruiters, however, were participating families who brought their friends.

We invited prospective participants to come to our early education center to learn about what the program could offer. The center was conveniently located, first above an obstetrician's office, then in a former college dormitory, and, ultimately, as space became available, in rooms in several elementary schools. Families inevitably decided to enroll once they learned of the attractive lending library of toys and books, the indoor and outdoor play areas, the informal meeting rooms, and the friendly atmosphere at the Center.

When enrollment for the pilot program closed in the fall of 1974, 285 families had enrolled. These families reflected the diversity sought in the recruiting campaign. For instance, about 50% of the parents had a college education; 44% were expecting their first child; 39% were minorities; 18% did not speak English; and the ages of the mothers ranged from 14 to 41 years.

It is important for readers to understand that sample sizes varied over time and across analyses. Sample attrition occurred at an annual rate of approximately 10% because of family mobility. Consequently, approximately half of the original sample of BEEP participants resided in the Brookline and Boston area at the time of the kindergarten assessment. Because the demographic profile of those remaining did not differ from that of the original sample, we concluded that our findings were not systematically biased because of attrition. At the time of the kindergarten assessment, a total of 132 BEEP participants were available for evaluation. Additional funds received from the sponsoring foundations at the time of the second grade assessment allowed us to locate and assess an additional 37 BEEP participants residing outside of the immediate geographic area. Because of this, a total of 169 BEEP participants were assessed in the second grade.

Parent Education and Support

Committed to the idea that the family is the most important educational force for the young child, members of BEEP worked to inform and support parents by providing valid information, nurturant resources, and a sense of community. The staff who worked most closely with parents were called "teachers" to encourage identification with, and it was hoped, to influence the roles of elementary teachers. The teaching staff reflected the range of cultural and ethnic backgrounds of the families; all had backgrounds in child development and were parents themselves.

A curriculum guide (Yurchak, 1975) was developed to structure the teacher's role. Discussions with parents focused on recognizing the child's strengths, needs, and emerging developmental characteristics. Weekly team meetings, occasional peer and videotaped observations, and regularly scheduled case review sessions with the program supervisor were vital to the efforts for program quality.

The amount of parent education offered to each family was controlled by random assignment of families to one of three levels of program intensity. We explained this structure to all families prior to their enrollment; participants understood that they were required to accept the random cost-level assignment if they enrolled. To our knowledge, no one declined to participate because of their assignment, although many expressed disappointment because of an assignment discrepant with their desires.

The most expensive level of parent education (projected to cost $1,200 per child per year) involved frequent home visits, center-based meetings, and limited child care. Each of these components was scheduled once every 3 or 4 weeks. The second or moderate level of program intensity ($800) involved the same offerings less frequently, once every 6 weeks. The least expensive cost level ($400) involved no outreach through home visits, meetings, or child care. Thus, parents assigned to this level had to take the initiative to use the BEEP Center on a drop-in basis, to make telephone inquiries to staff when questions arose, to borrow from the lending library, and to take advantage of ideas mentioned in the newsletter.

As the children grew to 3 years of age, the more expensive home visits were supplanted by school-based parent education components of parent–teacher conferences and guided classroom observations. Discussions at this age focused increasingly on the child's school behavior.

The total number of contacts between parents and staff was substantial at each program level. For instance, the mean number of contacts over the 5 years was 167, 114, and 87 for the respective program levels. Within each level, there was wide variation in patterns of participation, reflecting both the program's responsiveness to individual family needs and the initiative of participants.

Diagnostic Monitoring

Periodic health and developmental exams were administered at the Center for the purpose of ensuring that no child would progress through the preschool years with an undetected health or developmental condition that might hamper abilities to function successfully in school. Required for all children enrolled in BEEP, the exams were held at the following intervals after program entry: 2 weeks, 3 months, 6 months, 14 months, 24 months, 30 months, 42 months, and entry to kindergarten.

Each exam consisted of physical, neurologic, and developmental assessments conducted by a multidisciplinary team of psychologists, nurses, and pediatricians available through a collaboration with Children's Hospital Medical Center of Boston. Parents were expected to observe each exam, and the results were shared with them verbally and in writing. When concerns were identified that required medical or social service attention, referrals were made to primary care physicians and community agencies.

Early Childhood Programs

For the children's first 2 years, there was no separate formal education component for the children. Children came to the Center with their parents and enjoyed the variety of materials and activities available there. Beginning at age 2, weekly playgroups were held for all children, organized by small groups of six to eight children. Each session followed a predictable routine that was geared to providing developmental tasks to the children.

At ages 3 and 4 years, a daily morning prekindergarten program was offered to all children. Classes typically consisted of 15 to 20 children and three adults. Several classes were bilingual. Curriculum emphasis, influenced by the High/Scope Program (Hohmann, Banet & Weikart, 1979; also see chapter 5 of this book), was on structuring the space, materials, and human resources to afford each child an opportunity to develop a sense of effectiveness in the mastery and social skills necessary for success in school. Individual goals for each child were mutually determined, within a framework provided, by teachers and parents.

The prekindergarten program was the only phase of BEEP in which parents were asked to share the program expense. A sliding scale fee was established that ranged from $25 to $800 per child annually on the basis of each family's expressed ability to pay. Extended day care was available each afternoon in the same setting for an additional fee paid to a parent-organized cooperative which provided this service.

Outcomes

The BEEP interventions concluded when participating children entered kindergarten. Meanwhile, the children's progress in school was evaluated in the fall and spring of the kindergarten year and again in the spring of the second grade year. A summary of the results follows (for more detailed reports, see Pierson et al., 1983; Pierson, Walker & Tivnan, 1984; Bronson, Pierson & Tivnan, 1984).

Note that as originally designed, BEEP did not include a randomly assigned no-treatment control sample. Hence, its evaluations were conducted within a quasi-experimental design in which demographically similar comparisons samples were assembled for each of the major assessment points. Specifically, for the kindergarten analysis, the status of BEEP participants was compared with that of 362 demographically comparable children who were enrolled in the Brookline kindergartens during the prior 2 years. Similar to BEEP children, the members of the comparison group included only those children whose parents agreed to have them tested.

For the second grade assessment, a different comparison group was formed. In this case, comparison children were obtained from the classrooms in which BEEP children were enrolled. These comparisons were selected randomly from among available children matched for age and gender with their BEEP counterparts. Sample sizes for this analysis were 169 for each group.

Language Proficiency

Nineteen of the BEEP families who enrolled their child at birth and completed the entire program did not originally speak English in their homes. When these children (13 Hispanic and 6 Chinese) entered kindergarten, all were evaluated as ready to be integrated into the regular kindergarten classrooms. This accomplishment of bilingual proficiency was consistent with the parents' early program goals. This BEEP outcome also enabled the schools to avoid the costly provision of transitional bilingual program support in kindergarten and the elementary grades for these children.

Kindergarten Classroom Observations

Independent observers who were trained to observe and record a variety of social, mastery, and use-of-time variables found significant advantages for the BEEP participants over comparison children in both fall and spring of the kindergarten year. The behaviors that were categorized as "social" and "use of time" showed the greatest effects.

Kindergarten Teacher Reports

Ratings by teachers of the children's progress revealed few overall differences, with advantages recorded for BEEP participants only in the fall on a reading readiness scale. Analyses for possible effects of children's background characteristics did reveal significant interactions, with advantages for participants over comparison children in those subgroups traditionally associated with having difficulties in school, such as families with less educated parents.

Second Grade Classroom Observations

Observations were collected on six occasions in the spring of second grade, and again independent observers found significant overall advantages for the BEEP children versus comparison children. The percentage of children falling below the designated competence level was reduced by one half, from 28.4% in the comparison group to 14.2% in the BEEP sample. At this age, when schools are beginning to emphasize academic subjects more than socialization, the greatest advantages for the BEEP participants were on the mastery, rather than the social or use-of-time items.

Second Grade Reading

Classroom teachers also reported their assessments of children's skills in the spring of second grade. Here the area of reading showed advantages for the BEEP participants that were analogous to the classroom observations. We regarded a report of "able to decode words and comprehend stories in a 2-2 basal reader" as evidence of competence. The percentage of the 169 children in each group that fell below this competence expectancy was reduced from 32.5% for the comparison group to 19.3% for BEEP participants.

Cost-Effectiveness Analyses

Findings with important policy implications resulted from analyzing the second grade data by both intensity of parent education program and parent education background. For children whose parents were highly educated (i.e., mother a college graduate), 19.5% of the comparison group had reading difficulty. The percentages of children with difficulty were reduced for the three successive levels of program intensity: to 12.5% for the minimum, 9.7% for the moderate, and 3.0% for the maximum. Thus, although children whose parents were highly educated had relatively little difficulty with reading, the BEEP programs still had an impact in further reducing this incidence. For children whose parents were not highly educated (i.e., mother was not a college graduate), 50.0% of the comparison group had reading difficulty in second grade. Moreover, unless the BEEP parent education program was at least moderate in intensity, this high incidence of difficulty was not reduced. The three BEEP program levels resulted in the following percentages of children with reading difficulty: minimum, 52.2%; moderate, 31.6%; and maximum, 28.6%.

In other words, when working with families who had a limited educational background and when the parent education component consisted of outreach through regularly scheduled home visits, meetings, and guided classroom observations, the proportion of children with reading difficulty in second grade was reduced from about one half to less than a third. No benefit in reading outcomes could be discerned for these children when the parents were left to take advantage of the parent education opportunity on their own initiative.

Parent Involvement

The crux of BEEP's programs was the encouragement of parents to become informed advocates for their children's education and health. In order to ascertain evidence of impact on parents, second grade teachers were asked to keep a record of all contacts with parents during a 6-week period in the spring. BEEP parents initiated more than twice as many contacts as comparison group parents (132 vs. 54) for purposes categorized as "discussion of child's progress." This difference was evident across levels of parent education. Other categories of communication, not pertaining to the child's progress, showed no differences between the BEEP and comparison groups.

Limits and Opportunities

The BEEP has demonstrated that a comprehensive, school-based early education program can result in substantial benefits for a cross section of families. The results should lead to recognition of certain limitations while pointing the way to many opportunities.

Limits

First, it is important to recognize that this program aimed to be both supportive of parents and directed toward the goal of reducing school failure. Program strategies and the measures for their evaluation were both oriented toward identifying the fundamentals of competent functioning in school. It would be unreasonable to expect other programs with a different focus to have similar effects.

Second, the magnitude of the intervention's impact suggests that it is possible to reduce by about one half the number of children who experience reading difficulty in second grade. While this is substantial and certainly worthy of policy action, we must be cautious not to present early education as a promise for the eradication of all learning difficulties.

Third, children whose parents had limited educational backgrounds and resources seemed to benefit from the program only when the intervention included a concerted outreach to the family. It is unrealistic to expect these families to take the initiative and benefit from educational opportunities that are remote from their daily priorities of survival.

Fourth, the comprehensive BEEP model incorporated collaborations for health monitoring and referral and social work counseling and referral, as well as carefully supervised educational services. As partial replications of the intervention are considered, it will be necessary to account for the range of service needs that families have while targeting limited resources in the most strategic manner possible.

Fifth, given the magnitude of the challenge, it seems clear that state, federal, and private foundation support will be needed to assist impoverished areas in implementing high-quality early education programs.

Finally, perhaps the greatest strength of early education programs is also their limitation. That is, parents uniformly praise the merits of such programs and testify about how helpful the information and support have been to them in understanding and appreciating their infants and preschool children. But children are young for only a relatively brief period of their lives, and family needs and pressures continue beyond the preschool years. Thus, the period of parental advocacy for infants and young children may be rather ephemeral unless supplemented by strategies for their continuation in later years. Each community must recognize that the more visible stresses and devastating outcomes of adolescence and young adulthood are part of a cycle connected to the quality of life in general and to the well-being of young children in particular. A broad base of citizens, and not just the parents of young children, should be mobilized to improve educational opportunities for people of all ages beginning at birth and continuing through adolescence.

Opportunities

The experiences in Brookline confirm that with careful planning and adequate resources, early education in the schools can serve as a community-based prevention program. Moreover, the benefits of the BEEP early education model are evident across the socioeconomic spectrum and are crucially important for low-income families and useful for middle-income families. The challenge for local policy makers is to determine how the BEEP pilot programs can best be adapted and delivered to meet the needs of the local community.

In Brookline, the School Committee has evaluated the BEEP results and decided that local investments in early education will pay lasting dividends for the schools and community. The following components for parent and early childhood education have been incorporated into the local school budget:

• Primary specialist to supervise prekindergarten and kindergarten programs

• Three transition-to-kindergarten classes for 4- and 5-year-old children with a curriculum based on the BEEP parent involvement model

• Daily bilingual prekindergarten class for 3- and 4-year-old children

• Weekly bilingual playgroup for 2-year-old children and their parents

• Afternoon home visits in selected school districts by specially trained kindergarten teachers for families with infants

• Home visits and referral services by specially trained bilingual staff for limited-English-speaking families with infants

• Drop-in center with lending library for families with young children

• Seminars and discussion groups administered by adult education for parents

• Health and developmental exams administered by the public health department for preschool children.

In communities where the schools are not able or ready to take the leadership role in establishing early education opportunities, other agencies can meet the need. The possibilities are numerous: public health departments, private pediatric clinics, hospitals, Head Start centers, public libraries, mental health or other community agencies, alliances of private child care providers, university-based laboratory schools, or community psychology programs. Indeed, the most important consideration is not which agency takes the lead, but rather that some agency respond to this opportunity in a manner that effectively mobilizes and coordinates all of the community's relevant resources, including the schools, on behalf of families and young children.

Practical Suggestions

The next generation of early education programs needs to strike a balance between capitalizing on the creative energy of developing unique ideas and incorporating the essential insights and practices known to work in previous models. The lessons from BEEP include eight considerations.

1. *Set clear goals.* With a clear statement of goals, the program has a basis for unified focus and effective programs. Without such a statement, the program is likely to waver around individual priorities and understandings. In BEEP, the prevention of school failure was the overriding goal.

2. *Offer open enrollment with recruitment.* To avoid the stigma of a deficit orientation for at-risk families, the program should be available to all residents within a given geographic boundary. At the same time, it is critical to reach out to families who lack a tradition of educational involvement.

3. *Include a health component.* All families want, most of all, to have a healthy baby. Within the context of discussions about the baby's health, the interrelationship of educational agenda for parents and children can be introduced.

4. *Plan for cost-effectiveness.* Keeping in mind the second grade results that showed that children from families whose mother had a limited educational background benefited from BEEP only with consistent outreach to involve parents, it is important to match the program offerings with familial characteristics. For instance, the expensive resources of home visits should ordinarily be reserved for families who lack the confidence or means to come to the center or school for a conference.

5. *Select and train staff carefully.* Regardless of prior planning, once the program becomes operative it takes on the personality of the staff. The selection of staff who can empathize with parents is therefore crucial. Inclusion of a variety of race, gender, and ethnic models among the professional staff is essential for establishing a range of competent models with whom the parents and children can identify. Ongoing staff training, skillful supervision, and cooperative teamwork characterize successful programs.

6. *Respect family needs and values.* Individuals working at the intersection of education and mental health must continually keep in mind the aim of strengthening families. It is an important responsibility, and sometimes a difficult dilemma, to distinguish between harmless aberrant behavior that can be overlooked and potentially harmful deviations that require intervention. Frequent case conferences are necessary for staff to gain

confidence in their ability to make this distinction. After all, they must on the one hand enable families to become more self-sufficient and on the other hand take a strong stance to assist children when parents or caretakers are negligent.

7. *Use appropriate evaluation measures.* The extension of early education opportunities can be advanced if programs accept a reasonable degree of accountability. It is no longer necessary to prove whether early education can work. What is needed, particularly to gain more local support, is to document that specified goals have been attained. The measures must be consistent with the goals and program operations.

8. *Develop ties with elementary schools.* The benefits realized by parents and children during the preschool years can be reinforced and extended if the elementary school staff have an integral role in the program. This approach not only lends perspective to the early education endeavor, but generates strategies for improving the elementary schools.

Conclusion

As the conclusion of BEEP's foundation-sponsored research study approached, the Brookline Superintendent of Schools appointed an Early Education Advisory Committee to review the findings and experiences of BEEP and to develop recommendations for the School Committee. The following statement was developed by Brookline's Early Education Advisory Committee and adopted by vote of the Brookline School Committee on April 6, 1981. This statement serves as a premise for Brookline's continuing commitment to early education; it is offered here as a starting point for other communities interested in early education:

Statement of Philosophy for Parent and Early Childhood Education

Schools that recognize the value of extending their efforts to the family and the earliest years of the child's life can enhance the learning of the children and the well-being of the community. This conviction is based on the work of the Brookline Early Education Project and on a substantial body of related research on child development.

Clearly, certain conditions in the first five years of life influence healthy development and success in school. Preventive health care which monitors all areas of the child's development helps reduce the need for later costly remediation. Consistent opportunities for children to listen to and speak with nurturing adults, especially during the first three years of life, facilitate optimal language and cognitive development. Opportunities orchestrated for the child to practice and master a range of skills—problem solving, perceptual, motor, and social—encourage motivation for self-directed learning and enable children both to esteem themselves and to respect the rights and dignity of others.

Parents are better able to assume responsibility for their child's success in school if they feel confident of their abilities to contribute to their child's learning and to the school and community. Information pertaining to child development plus support for the child rearing role from other adults increase parents' willingness to participate actively.

Especially in these stringent economic times, if some of the school's investments to prepare children for success in school and for responsible adulthood are oriented toward the earliest years and toward building a strong constituency of parents, cost-effective benefits will be realized. Further, if the capabilities of other public and private agencies, such as health agencies, libraries, day care and nursery schools, colleges and universities, private employers and state agencies, are fully and systematically enlisted by the schools, the resources available to enhance children's learning will be increased despite imminent reductions in tax-based expenditures for public education.

A high quality of education for young children, involving partnership relations between schools and parents as well as full utilization of community resources, is the best insurance policy available to a community that is concerned with realizing a high quality of life for all of its citizens.

References

Bronson, M. B., Pierson, D. E., & Tivnan, T. (1984). The effects of early education on children's competence in elementary school. *Evaluation Review, 8,* 615–629.

Hohmann, M., Banet, B., & Weikart, D. (1979). *Young children in action: A manual for preschool education.* Ypsilanti, MI: High Scope Press.

Pierson, D. E., Bronson, M. B., Dromey, E., Swartz, J. P., Tivnan, T., & Walker, D. K. (1983). The impact of early education as measured by classroom observations and teacher ratings of children in kindergarten. *Evaluation Review, 7,* 191–216.

Pierson, D. E., Walker, D. K., & Tivnan, T. (1984). A school-based program from infancy to kindergarten for children and their parents. *Personnel and Guidance Journal, 62*(8), 448–455.

Yurchak, M. J. H. (1975). *Infant-toddler curriculum of the Brookline Early Education Project.* Brookline, MA: Brookline Early Education Project.

Craig T. Ramey, Donna M. Bryant, Frances A. Campbell, Joseph J. Sparling, and
Barbara H. Wasik

CHAPTER

3

Early Intervention for High-Risk Children: The Carolina Early Intervention Program

Every American ought to have the right to be treated as he would wish to be treated, as one would wish his children to be treated. This is not the case.—John F. Kennedy

In the United States today, one in five children are growing up in poverty. For Black children, the poverty rate is almost 50% (U.S. Census Bureau, 1986). Poor children are at increased risk for academic underachievement, dropping out of school, juvenile delinquency, teenage pregnancy, eventual underemployment, and high birth rates. Such conditions are not conducive to our country's well-being. A democracy requires a citizenry capable of informed and constructive participation. Undereducated and unemployed adults are unlikely to meet these requirements.

To ignore or consciously dismiss the plight of the poor from the nation's conscience is to risk possibly catastrophic consequences. The creation of a permanent and growing underclass is an economic drain and a moral dilemma. Avoidance or ignorance of the problems of the poor can be especially vicious because the poor are too easily identified and subject to stereotype—all too frequently they are members of racial and ethnic minorities. Our society must make concerted, extensive, and sincere efforts to alter the plight of the poor and their children. From the understanding that many patterns of behavior are learned, it follows that education will be a key process in behavioral and social change.

This chapter is about the forces that are changing our conceptions of education and about how one research program in North Carolina has been pursuing new educational practices to assist the intellectual development of children from poor and undereducated families.

Toward the Prevention of Intellectual Underdevelopment

It is widely believed that experience is related to intellectual development in humans. For this reason, many parents go to great efforts to select their children's teachers and classmates with care. This implied belief in environmental causality is relatively new, historically. In philosophy, it was first articulated by John Locke in 1690, but as a scientific concept it is much more recent. In his influential review of then available scientific evidence, J. McVicker Hunt in 1961 challenged

The research described in this chapter has been supported by grants from the National Institute of Child Health and Human Development; the U.S. Department of Education; the Administration for Children, Youth, and Families; the Spencer Foundation; the Carnegie Foundation; the Department of Human Resources of the State of North Carolina; and the Department of Social Services of Orange County, North Carolina. We wish to thank Marie Butts, Jean Godwin, Jodi Freeze, and Tarlouh Wiggins for preparing the manuscript and Laura Caldwell, Mary Helms, and Kaye Fendt for data analyses.

the prevailing view of intelligence as fixed or immutable and development as predetermined.

Hunt concluded his classic work, *Intelligence and Experience* (1961), with the following observations:

> It is no longer unreasonable to consider that it might be feasible to discover ways to govern the encounters that children have with their environments, especially during the early years of their development, to achieve a substantially faster rate of intellectual development and substantially higher adult level of intellectual capacity. (p. 363)

This perspective on intellectual malleability might have remained an academic issue had John Kennedy not been elected President in 1960. Kennedy's platform, galvanized in part by his primary win in West Virginia—a southern state then known for its widespread poverty—emphasized social and racial equality. This emphasis derived, in part, from social science findings concerning the devastating associations among racism, poverty, and social and psychological dysfunction.

Kennedy's social activism in general led to Lyndon Johnson's Great Society programs and more specifically led to the launching in 1965 of Project Head Start, the embodiment of early educational concern for disadvantaged and minority children. Edward Zigler, the first director of the Office of Child Development, the federal agency responsible for implementing Head Start, recently noted,

> Originally, the program was designed only as a 6- or 8-week preschool during the summer preceding the child's entry into kindergarten, but many had faith that this minimal effort would solve all the problems of children from urban and rural slums. (Zigler & Freedman, 1987, p. 87)

Such hopes were dashed by the report from the Westinghouse Learning Corporation (1969), which concluded that no permanent IQ effects could be attributed to participation in Head Start. This and other evidence led Arthur Jensen (1969) to conclude, "compensatory education has been tried and it apparently has failed" (p. 2). One reaction to the Westinghouse and Jensen conclusions was to create more intensive early education programs that began earlier in childhood, were more comprehensive in services, and lasted longer. At the Frank Porter Graham Child Development Center, work on one such program was begun in 1971; it continues today and is the subject of this chapter.

Between 1972 and 1980, six cohorts of high-risk children were recruited during the last trimester of their mother's pregnancy and randomly assigned to a treatment or control group. Randomization should ensure, with the limits of sampling theory, initial equivalence of groups, thus allowing future group differences to be plausibly attributed to the intervention program. For the first four cohorts (known as the Abecedarian Project), the children were randomly assigned either to a group that received a systematic educational day care beginning by 3 months of age or to a control group that received no systematic educational program. The same selection criteria were used for the fifth and sixth cohorts (known as Project CARE), but the children were randomly assigned to one of three conditions: (a) a systematic center-based educational program beginning before 3 months of age, (b) a home-based intervention program beginning before 3 months of age, or (c) a control group that received no systematic educational program. In this chapter, our focus is not on the home-based intervention condition, but on comparing findings on the children who attended the Frank Porter Graham Child Development Center with those on their control counterparts. This is the sample that we refer to as the Carolina Early Intervention Program (CEIP). Seventy children were enrolled in the intervention program and 76 in the control group. Throughout this project, retention has been high. After 54 months, 87% of intervention children and 89% of controls were actively enrolled in the program.

Table 3–1 contains a summary of entry characteristics of the children's families. In general, the mothers tended to be young, Black, poor, single, and with less than a high school education. Thus, their children were considered at high risk for delayed intellectual development and poor readiness for public school success.

In the remainder of this chapter, we shall describe the theoretical rationale for our prevention

Table 3–1. Entry Characteristics for Carolina Early Intervention Program Mothers

Characteristic	Control (N = 76)		Intervention (N = 70)	
	M	SD	M	SD
Wechsler Adult Intelligence Scale–Full Scale IQ	85.2	10.1	85.7	12.1
Age	20.8	5.5	20.1	4.2
Last grade completed	10.4	1.8	10.7	1.7
Percent married	21.1	—	18.6	—
Percent Black	95	—	94	—

efforts, link that theoretical rationale to our intervention practices, briefly present some intellectual performance results, and conclude with a discussion of issues concerning the generality of our findings. We shall present some recommendations for future programs.

A Conceptual Model for Early Intervention

Because many factors affect the growth and development of young children, we have developed a model to make more explicit the factors that were considered with respect to creating our early intervention program. We have used this model as an aid in understanding the development of children and the environmental interventions that have been designed to enhance their development during the so-called preschool years. This model is an extension of a transactional model of infant education developed by Ramey, Trohanis,

and Hostler (1982) and is consistent with a biosocial systems theory approach to development as presented by Ramey, MacPhee, and Yeates (1982) and Ramey, Bryant, Sparling, and Wasik (1984). An abbreviated version of our full model is presented schematically in Figure 3–1.

Within this model, we are concerned with four levels of influence: (a) the biological and social histories of the child and caregivers, (b) the current status of individual family members (e.g., child and caregiver), (c) the transactions that occur among individuals within the family and between individuals and forces outside the family, and (d) the future status of family members and their relationships.

Development of young children and their families is assumed to be a process characterized by reciprocal influence and mutual regulation and the product of multiple causes operating at various levels of influence within our model. Therefore, to understand development, with respect to intervention, it is necessary to describe how fac-

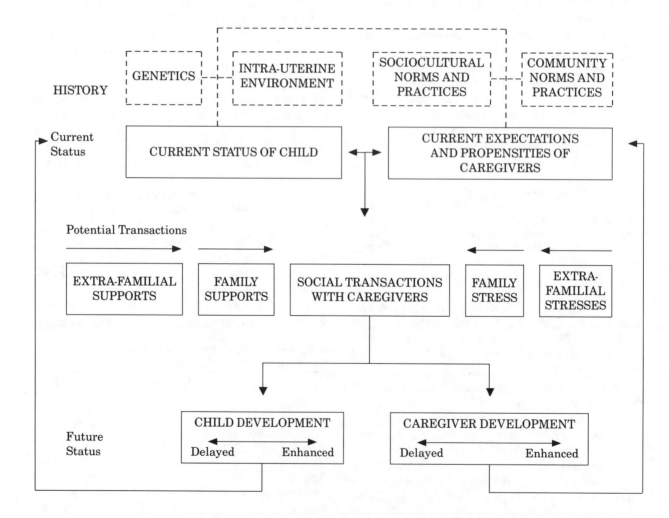

Figure 3–1. Biosocial systems model for differential development during early childhood.

tors relate to one another within the historical present and to describe how alterations in various elements of the system may influence future performance of individuals.

In Figure 3–1, a historical level of influence has been included for conceptual completeness. This historical level consists of four components, two of which have a direct impact on the child's status at birth: genetic influences and the quality of the intrauterine environment. The other two factors (community norms and practices and sociocultural norms and practices) probably act directly on the child's caregivers but only indirectly on the child because of the young child's limited ability to represent these complex forces symbolically. These factors and their interrelationships are represented within dashed boxes in our model to indicate that these cannot be manipulated for the purposes of family-oriented educational interventions.

Systems-Level Assumptions

Two general key assumptions pertinent to early education undergird our general model. These assumptions include

1. A family system is an adaptation to the broader biosocial network of which it is a part. Individual families adapt to their life circumstances as best they know how.

2. For the young child who lacks a sophisticated cognitive symbol system, proximal events (in time and space) are of greater developmental importance than are distal events. As the infant's symbolic capability increases, however, distal events become functional codeterminants of the child's actions.

Assumptions About the Child

Six dimensions of the child's development are particularly important, in part because they are characteristics likely to be responded to by caregivers. These child characteristics include (a) physical characteristics, (b) health status, (c) temperament, (d) cognitive level, (e) psychomotor coordination, and (f) social skills. These six child dimensions assume developmental importance particularly in relation to current expectations and propensities of the child's primary caregivers.

Assumptions About the Caregiver's Expectations and Propensities

The caregiver's expectations and propensities can be divided into two categories: personality characteristics and parenting style. By personality characteristics, we mean expectations and propensities of the caregivers as adults that limit or enhance their abilities to function as optimal caregivers. Included in the personality category are emotional health, locus of control, self-esteem, problem-solving abilities, and psychological coping and adaptation skills. In the category of parenting style, we are especially concerned with the parents' propensity to act in developmentally encouraging ways.

Assumptions About Caregiver–Child Transactions

We assume that variations among caregivers and children act to codetermine specific behavioral interchanges at a transactional level. By transactional, we mean an interchange between two or more individuals that leaves each individual altered. The transactions of greatest educational importance are assumed to be the young child's social interactions with adult caregivers. There are at least seven dimensions along which social interactions vary that have been consistently related to the developmental advancement of children. These include affection, involvement, responsiveness, nonpunitiveness, variety, organization, and age appropriateness. Thus, the behavioral interchanges between the developing child and the more sophisticated adult caregivers are construed to directly affect both the future status of the child and the future expectations and propensities of caregivers.

Assumptions About Family Supports and Stresses

Within our model, family support is divided into social, material, and information resources. Family stress is hypothesized to relate to (a) the degree of the family's organization, (b) the extent to which a positive social climate is present, (c) the quality of the family's interactions with people outside the household, and (d) the stability of the family's composition through time. Extrafamilial stresses are assumed to have a direct bearing on family stress and, as a consequence, an indirect, but potentially powerful, effect on the social interactions that occur between young children and adults. These indirect effects occur primarily, we think, by affecting the opportunity and propensity for interacting positively with the developing child on the seven dimensions described. Three extrafamilial stresses that are particularly noteworthy include the degree to which the family is stigmatized, the degree to which the family is systematically and negatively discriminated against, and the extent to which the family is not valued according to either community norms and practices or sociocultural norms and practices.

To deal effectively with familial and extrafamilial stresses, therapeutic and, more recently, preventive interventions have been developed with the goal of providing extrafamilial supports to enhance the family's capacity for functioning; in effect, to counter stress by providing additional family resources or supports. These supports can be divided into four major classes: health, mental health, education, and economic programs.

Components of the Carolina Early Intervention Program

Consistent with our conceptual model, the CEIP is construed as a multidisciplinary extrafamilial support system designed to prevent intellectual underdevelopment in high-risk children. The program is composed of both intervention modalities and intervention content areas. The modalities of intervention are developmental day care that begins between 6 and 12 weeks of age, a toy lending library, a home visiting program, and parent group meetings. The program content is composed of a specific child-oriented curriculum, a parent problem-solving curriculum, and an informal network of family support resources.

We conceptualize the modality components of the intervention to enhance the child's intellectual functioning in the following ways:

• Developmental day care will directly enhance the child's development by providing systematic and daily exposure to professional caregivers who by inclination and education are affectionate, involved, responsive, and nonpunitive. These caregivers provide a set of experiences that are healthful, organized, varied, and developmentally appropriate through a planned environment and curriculum.

• The toy lending library will increase both material and informational supports to the family and will also facilitate positive social interactions with family caregivers.

• The home-visiting program will provide informational and social resources that will enhance developmentally encouraging expectations and propensities of mothers and, perhaps, other family members.

• The parent group program will increase the social resources available to families by linking parents who are facing similar issues with each other and with informed and resourceful persons from the community.

In sum, we conceive the CEIP as a multifaceted and intensive effort to affect positively the immediate and intermediate causal factors that are hypothesized to play prime roles in the intellectual development of children.

In the next few sections, we describe the structural and operational features of our intervention components.

Educational Modalities

Developmental day care. It is our experience that developmental day care should include a safe, healthful, and comfortable environment. It must also have certain characteristics that guarantee that the child will not be deprived of the educational and social experiences that are a part of good traditional parent–child care. One characteristic necessary for a positive day care experience is a good adult to child ratio. In our program, the ratios range from 1:3 for infants to 1:6 or 7 for 4-year-olds.

Group size is a major consideration in providing a program of educational care for children in the early years. Factors such as funding, licensing, and availability of space all affect group size decisions, but within these restrictions groups that seem to provide the best opportunities for learning are small groups of three to seven or eight children. This grouping shows our bias toward an arrangement whereby an adult is responsible for and responsive to a group of children, as opposed to the style in which an adult is assigned to an activity or learning area.

We feel that certain premises are basic to the recruitment and training of the teaching staff. Of first importance is the need to select teachers whose ethnic and cultural values are perceived as supportive by the families. We also give much attention and time to organized in-service staff training because the teaching staff is considered a primary factor in the quality of the program. The training program is designed to be directly applicable to teachers' daily activities and to the improvement of their professional skills. This frequently involves presentations of information about child development. Opportunities for the staff to communicate their needs for such information are therefore built into the training program.

A prime concern of any program designed to foster child development is to do everything possible to create an intact, healthy, and well-nourished child. Adequate nutrition is essential for sound physical development and a major factor in intellectual and behavioral growth as well. The act of eating together can also be used to help the child establish natural and warm human relationships. Our day-care program provides good food that meets nutritional standards. Teachers try to educate children about the importance of good nutrition through enjoyable activities such as eating meals together in a slow-paced and conversational setting. Breakfast and lunch are provided at the center as well as an afternoon snack. Each classroom has a dining area large enough to allow the children and teachers to sit at the table together. Children are allowed ample time to eat, and the adult helps provide interesting table conversation to make mealtime a pleasant experience.

Assuming that children benefit from interacting with both male and female adults, we encourage the presence of men in our day care and have always had at least one male teacher, assistant teacher, and driver.

An outdoor playground is an ideal place to challenge motor development and stimulate social interactions. The quality of the equipment is vital. Our outdoor playground equipment is chosen on the basis of its usefulness for children across developmental age ranges, adaptability for fostering a variety of skills, safety, and sturdiness. The outdoor equipment includes swings, slides, jungle gyms, sandboxes, and a paved track for wheeled toys. Adult supervision is as careful outdoors as it is indoors.

Field trips are a regular part of our educational program to broaden the knowledge base of young children. The public bus system stops in front of the center so it can be used as transportation (and a bus ride is a field trip in and of itself) as well as using the center's vans. Field trips are often planned in conjunction with the educational activities that a teacher has been using with the class. Individual classes make some field trips alone, such as to the library or grocery store, or team up with one or two other classes to make trips to the zoo, the science museum, or the farm.

Parents are encouraged to transport their child to and from the day-care center. However, this is very difficult for some families because of their lack of means of transportation or their irregular work hours. To ensure that children from such families attend the center as regularly as possible, we provide transportation for those children who need it. Our center owns two 12-seat vans, and a transportation supervisor schedules and supervises travel to and from the center. The driver and another adult are on each trip.

Toy lending library. A toy library is an old concept that has taken on new meaning in our day-care program, where it has a subtle influence on various aspects of the curriculum and the program goals. Selection of materials becomes an extension of curriculum planning, providing opportunities for choosing toys that allow home play to extend the skills that the child practices in day care. The library stocks many toys that come with guidebooks. Toys that do not have guidebooks are provided with cards containing suggestions for parent and child activities with the toy. The process of choosing an appropriate toy each time, which is the parents' responsibility, is subtle training in a child's developmental needs and abilities.

Home visiting. Home visiting has been an integral part of the CEIP. In the Abecedarian Project, home visitors mainly filled a social work role, meeting regularly with parents to help fill basic needs. In Project CARE, teachers made home visits following a more specific agenda. The goal of home visiting is for the teacher or home visitor to interact with parents in the home setting, to provide information about child development and community resources, to provide emotional support to parents, and to help parents learn ways to facilitate their child's cognitive and social development. Through home visiting, teachers learn about routines experienced by the child at home, and the family learns about routines experienced by the child in the child development center. Each teacher makes visits to the families of the children in his or her classroom.

During home visits, the teacher introduces to the families the educational activities that are currently being used in the classroom. They encourage parents to use or to modify the activities in a way that will encourage their child's learning. They also describe the problem-solving approach that we advocate for handling day-to-day child-rearing concerns. Occasionally, home visitors help families learn about or locate needed community resources.

Parent groups. Parent groups serve two major functions in the CEIP. The first is parent support. They make it possible for parents to share information and concerns on child rearing. Being part of such a group allows the parents to see that they are not alone in many of their concerns. Groups can provide contacts with parents that can help to build networks and social supports that will last beyond the life of the education program and can be a concurrent source of support during the life of the program.

The second major function that parent groups serve is to provide information or access to resources in the community that may not be available otherwise. For example, it is often possible to ask a person from the community to talk with parents in groups about topics of interest to them or to describe programs that might benefit family members.

Program Content

Child curriculum. From the beginning, it has been our opinion that a well-specified child curriculum is needed in the day-care and home visit intervention modalities. Many creative contributions to the education of young children are made by teachers and visitors, but it is not enough to leave these professionals on their own without the resources of a specific curriculum. Without an adopted curriculum, the variation in the program provided by different teachers will be too wide to represent a consistent education across years and across classrooms.

Our infant and child curricula (Sparling & Lewis, 1981, 1984, 1985) have had certain characteristics in common. All have been (a) divided into gamelike episodes, (b) applied in cycles, and (c) integrated into all aspects of the child's day.

The succinct learning activities, called *Learningames,* cover a full spectrum of developmental skill areas. The areas, organized into four broad themes are presented in Table 3–2. The skill areas are further divided into skill goals, each related to one of the hundreds of specific learning activities that make up our overall curriculum.

A second characteristic of our curricula is that they are applied in cycles. Two-week time periods constitute our basic curriculum interval. During this interval, the teacher and parent complete a

Table 3–2. Themes and Skill Areas in the Carolina Early Intervention Program Educational Curriculum

Broad themes	Specific skill area
Cognitive and fine motor	1. Awareness of object permanence 2. Awareness of positions in space 3. Puzzle skills 4. Sorting skills 5. Matching skills 6. Awareness of cause and effect 7. Sensory awareness
Social and self	8. Awareness of self-image 9. Skills in sharing with an adult 10. Skills in interacting with other children 11. Skills in imitating gestures 12. Self-help skills 13. Awareness of needs and feelings
Motor	14. Rhythm skills 15. Balance skills 16. Skills in throwing, pushing, and pulling
Language	17. Dialogue skills 18. Skills in using books 19. Skills in talking about picture–object pairs 20. Skills in talking about concept pictures 21. Skills in talking about action pictures 22. Skills in talking about object pictures 23. Skills in talking about relationship pictures

cycle that includes observation, implementation, and assessment.

The third characteristic of our curricula is the natural integration of learning in everyday activities. The care routines of diapering, feeding, dressing, and special one-to-one times, when facilitated throughout the day by the well-trained staff, become the vehicles for making the learning activities into many rich and varied experiences for each child. We believe that it is important not to shunt the learning activities off into a discrete curriculum time during the day.

The adult is encouraged to help the child to generalize the learning activities through seven principles. These general principles are described as adult skills. If these are commonly present in the adult's behavior, variations on the learning activities are likely to occur to the adult throughout the caregiving day. The skills (or principles) are as follows:

1. To *prepare* the materials and ideas necessary for child-learning activities.

2. To *attend* to the child's behaviors that reveal his or her learning status.

3. To *model*, through adult behavior, appropriate language and problem solving.

4. To *support*, with smiles and praise, steps the child takes toward mastery.

5. To *prompt* the child's most appropriate behavior, making it likely to happen.

6. To *rescue* the child by revising a task that is too difficult.

7. To *build* by adding challenging elements to a task the child has previously completed.

In aggregate, these skills describe the adult's behavior as she or he effectively becomes a partner with young children. As noted earlier, it is the assumption of our education model that the adult–child transaction is of particular developmental importance. Education in the early years of life is primarily an adult-mediated process. The behaviors and insights the adult brings to the adult–child transaction can facilitate or impede the young child's learning. Even though the child does indeed learn from independent exploration of the environment, the interactions that are mediated or insightfully structured by the adult are the ones in which large steps of developmental progress are more likely to be made. Therefore, in our curricula, less is said about the prepared environment and more attention is paid to elements of interaction such as language.

The language with which an adult surrounds and explains an activity is perhaps the most powerful tool of mediated learning. Within the domain of language, we have rated pragmatics as a more important intervention avenue than either semantics or syntax (McGinness & Ramey, 1981). Adults in our program pay special attention to the functions (pragmatics) to which they put language. For example, they attempt to increase the proportion of informational talk and reduce the proportion of directive talk as they interact with children.

In summary, the child curriculum as it functions in our intervention model might be described as cyclic, gamelike, integral to home and day care, covering 23 child development areas under four broad categories, promoting seven generalizable adult skills, and biased toward adult–child transactions involving informational language.

The parent problem-solving curriculum. The parent problem-solving program is designed to help parents learn a strategy or plan for effective resolution of everyday problems that arise as a function of child rearing. The problem-solving strategy is one that can also be used to help parents deal with other decisions and stresses in their lives. Home visitors are trained to help parents learn a specific problem-solving approach through in-service training sessions, role playing, and written materials (Wasik, 1984). To help the parent learn problem-solving strategies, the program has two parts. The first introduces the parents to the usefulness of using a systematic strategy to help them solve problems, teaches them the seven steps in our problem-solving model, and illustrates the problem-solving program with a number of typical parenting problems. In the second phase, the parent selects problems of child rearing and uses the newly learned problem-solving strategy to accomplish their objectives. The home visitor is taught to help the parent learn to do each of the following:

1. Identify problems,

2. Identify what the parent wants to happen in a given situation,

3. Identify several alternative solutions,

4. Consider the consequences for each solution,

5. Select the best solution at that time,

6. Carry out the solution, and

7. Evaluate whether the solution worked.

After the parents acquire a basic familiarity with this problem-solving approach, the home visitor prompts, encourages, and models good problem-solving strategies with respect to everyday problem situations.

An important part of our problem-solving program is that it is integrated with *Learningames* and with positive, nonpunitive child management techniques.

Although the emphasis in these content areas has been on the adult in the role of parent, it is important to mention that one reason the problem-solving component has been included in the overall program is because it is seen as a set of skills that makes it easier for the parents to deal with all of their day-by-day interactions. If, as a result of these skills, parents have fewer problems in nonparental situations, there may be a reduction in the incidence of poor emotional health and poor self-esteem and the possible creation of a more internal locus of control. These factors are hypothesized to have impact on the adults' overall functioning and, in turn, the adults' ability to interact effectively and positively with the child.

Program Evaluation

The CEIP is a research program as well as an intervention program. The main research questions focus on the efficacy of early intervention to prevent developmental problems among high-risk children. Because we did not attempt to evaluate the independent contributions of each aspect of the CEIP, we are not able to attribute any specific outcome(s) to specific program components. The CEIP is a test of the intervention package. However, all aspects identified within the model presented earlier have an associated research component. Over the years, more than 40 investigators and many research associates and assistants have been involved in conducting research within this program.[1] Our research continues today as we examine forces that affect the lives of these children and their families as the children progress through school. The results presented in this chapter focus on development during the so-called preschool years.

The central question around which CEIP activities have been organized concerns the efficacy of the intervention program to promote intellectual performance and to prevent intellectual delays and deficits. We believe, therefore, that assessment of intellectual functioning is a good way to determine the average level of child risk expressed in the control sample and to assess the preventive impact of the intervention treatment. Intellectual functioning is currently best assessed using standardized IQ tests, the definitive criteria of the *Diagnostic and Statistical Manual of Mental Disorders (Third Edition. Revised) (DSM-III-R)* for clinical level intellectual retardation.

In the CEIP, standardized developmental tests have been administered at 6-month intervals. The specific tests were chosen primarily on the basis of the psychometric adequacy of the instruments available for a given age level.

Three aspects of the efficacy of early intervention are particularly germane to our research. The first concerns the course of intellectual development in relation to population norms for intervention and control children. The second question concerns the power of this particular early intervention program to counteract risk factors for delayed development. The third issue is to determine whether this early intervention program is more effective in reducing risks for intellectual delays in some domains than it is in others. We shall present data on each of these three issues in turn.

Developmental Course

Figure 3–2 contains a plot of the mean Bayley Mental Development Index (MDI; Bayley, 1969) scores at 6, 12, and 18 months and the Stanford-Binet IQ scores at 24, 36, and 48 months for the 69 control children on whom we have data at all assessment occasions and the 63 intervention group children with complete data.

Several features about Figure 3–2 are noteworthy. First, group differences favoring the inter-

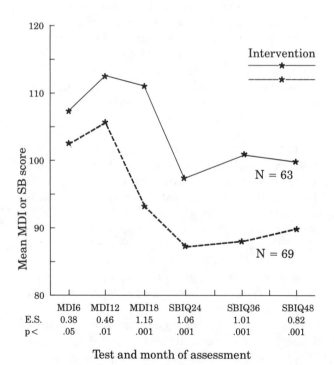

Figure 3–2. Mean Bayley Mental Development (MDI) Index and Stanford-Binet IQ (SB) scores for preschool and control and intervention children in the Carolina Early Intervention Program.

[1]More than 200 articles and books have been published, concentrated in the fields of child development, pediatrics, education, and public policy. A bibliography is available upon request.

vention children were obtained at each of these six measurement occasions. The effect size at 6 months was .38 standard deviations and at 4 years was .82 standard deviations. However, it should be noted that the divergence between the two groups appears to have stabilized by 24 months and was maintained until age 4. Thus, it appears that this intense and comprehensive early intervention had a measurable impact within the first year of life, an impact that was sustained over the preschool period.

It is also noteworthy that the control group children evidenced their decline from national average during the first 2 years of development and then stabilized in performance during the latter part of the preschool years. Averaging across the assessments at 2, 3, and 4 years, the difference between the intervention and control group was 12 IQ points, with intervention children scoring at national average. We interpret these data to be consistent with the hypothesis that early intervention can prevent intellectual delay in high-risk children.

Although these data are straightforward with respect to the efficacy issue, they raise, but do not answer, other important questions. For example, it is not clear what specific etiological factors cause the developmental curve obtained for the control group. As Landesman and Butterfield (1983) have pointed out, the developmental course of mild retardation is likely to be determined by biological and social factors and to vary in prevalence across different cultures, countries, and time periods. This brings us to the question of the clinical relevance of these group data.

Clinical Implications

What is the clinical significance of these data? Figure 3–3 shows the percentage of children in the control and intervention conditions with IQ scores at or below 84. A score of 84 or lower in the *DSM-III-R* classification system would result in a diagnosis of borderline intellectual functioning or mental retardation. We have restricted our concerns to the postinfancy period from 2 to 4 years with performance on the Stanford-Binet (Terman & Merrill, 1972) as the criterion variable. As Figure 3–3 indicates, there are significant differences between groups at each of these three occasions. Averaging across the three assessments, we find that the mean percentage of control group children who score 84 or below is 39.6% and for the intervention group children,

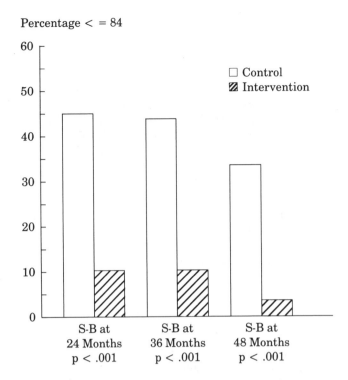

Percentage < = 84

Figure 3–3. Percentages of preschool control and intervention children with IQ scores lower than 84 in the Carolina Early Intervention Program.
S-B = Stanford-Binet Intelligence scale.

8.3%. If the performance of the control group indicates risk during this developmental period, then the early intervention program has reduced the risk for borderline or lower intellectual functioning by a total of 79%.

Although the numbers become quite small when we restrict ourselves to those children who would be classified as mildly retarded (i.e., IQ 50–70) during this developmental period, in the control group one child at 24 months and six children at both 36 and 48 months would be diagnosed as mildly retarded. At none of the three assessment occasions did any of the intervention children score 70 or below. Thus, from a clinical perspective it appears that this form of intervention can significantly reduce the incidence of diagnosable dysfunction during the middle-to-late preschool period.

Developmental Risk and Response to Intervention

Both the Bayley MDI and the Stanford–Binet result in a single score for intellectual functioning. The McCarthy Scales of Children's Abilities (Terman & Merrill, 1972) provide information about specific areas of development: memory, motor, perceptual–performance, quantitative, and verbal. This information can help us answer two important questions about development: (a) Are high-risk children at increased risk for delay in some areas of development more than others? and (b) Does our intervention affect certain areas of development more than others? Table 3–3 presents 42-month and 54-month McCarthy results for the overall score (GCI) and for the five subscales. The pattern of scores in these areas shows that the control children scored uniformly lower than did intervention children in each of them except for the motor scale score at 42 months. Overall, the intervention group's performance was at national average. These results indicate that this sample of children is at risk for delayed development in many areas and that our intervention helps children improve their functioning in several areas, not just one or two.

Table 3–3. Scores on the McCarthy Scales of Children's Abilities From Carolina Early Intervention Program Repeated Measures Preschool Samples

	Control (N = 69)		Intervention (N = 63)		Effect size[a]
	M	SD	M	SD	M
3½-year-olds test results					
General Cognitive Index	94.4	12.7	103.2	10.4	0.69
Memory Scale	50.1	7.1	52.6	5.9	0.35
Motor Scale	49.1	7.9	51.3	8.0	0.28
Perceptual–Performance Scale	44.6	8.8	48.9	7.5	0.49
Quantitative Scale	45.9	9.1	51.5	7.2	0.62
Verbal Scale	48.3	7.3	52.8	6.3	0.62
4½-year-olds test results					
General Cognitive Index	92.7	13.4	101.4	10.1	0.65
Memory Scale	48.5	7.9	52.3	6.4	0.48
Motor Scale	46.7	8.5	50.1	7.2	0.40
Perceptual–Performance Scale	43.6	8.3	48.4	7.8	0.58
Quantitative Scale	43.2	8.4	47.6	6.8	0.52
Verbal Scale	48.8	9.1	54.4	7.1	0.62

Note. For 3½-year-olds, control *n* = 69 and intervention *n* = 63. For 4½-year-olds control *n* = 68 and intervention *n* = 61.
[a]Effect size is determined by subtracting the mean performance of the control group from that of the intervention group and dividing the difference by the standard deviation of the control group.

The Issue of Generality

The generalizability of our findings is of importance for both scientific and practical reasons. Scientifically, the issue is primarily one of the reproducibility of our findings. In that context, there is simply no substitute for replication. Replication under identical conditions is, however, practically impossible. Too many factors vary historically and geographically to achieve an exact copy of the circumstances of our project. The best that one can hope for is that similar findings are obtained under similar circumstances. The extent to which circumstances are similar is at present a judgment call.

In this vein, let us note some contextual features of the community in which this research is being conducted. Chapel Hill, North Carolina, is an affluent, liberal, university town of approximately 50,000 people. In the year that the program began, there were 67 identifiable public and private agencies that explicitly provided services for poor families. These included such traditional supports as the Department of Social Services, various church groups, and housing programs for the homeless. In addition, the town contains a large university teaching hospital that provides much of the medical care that the poor receive. By virtue of this sample's being in a somewhat small town with a university teaching hospital, their health care has been at a very high level. Thus, all families in our program—both intervention and control—probably received more services than are available in more typical towns and cities. Although we cannot prove this, we suspect, consistent with our conceptual model, that this high level of community resources and services tended to elevate the performance of control group children over what would have been obtained in more representative settings with fewer services readily available. Thus, it is our view that the group IQ difference of approximately one standard deviation represents a conservative estimate of what might be obtained with a similar intervention in less resourceful settings.

Another scientific issue of generalizability concerns the question of who benefits from participation in such intervention programs. In recent articles (Ramey, Yeates, & MacPhee, 1984; Ramey, Yeates, & Short, 1984), we have presented evidence that children benefited from the program independently of their mother's assessed intelligence, age, education, or type of family. Thus, it is our hypothesis that comprehensive, broad-based programs such as ours are likely to be beneficial to a wide range of high-risk children.

We are currently exploring this hypothesis with other scientists, educators, and practitioners from across the nation in the Infant Health and Development Program—a randomized intervention trail, in eight U.S. cities, based on a modified CEIP protocol. That program involves 985 low-birth-weight infants and their families. Results from that program are expected to be available in 1989.

Conclusions

Our main conclusion is that CEIP data are consistent with the hypothesis that systematic and comprehensive early intervention can be an effective method for preventing developmental delay in high-risk children during the preschool years. Our data suggest that the 15-point IQ difference typically reported between Blacks and Whites in the United States (Jensen, 1969) can be effectively eliminated during the preschool years and that high-risk, socially disadvantaged children can perform at least at national average on standardized tests of intelligence if they and their families are provided additional educational and family support services.

To be sure, these results were achieved by an apparently expensive intervention in a rather small-scale experiment. Therefore, it will be particularly important to examine the results from the Infant Health and Development Program to determine the likelihood of broad generalization of our findings. That work is in progress. As for the expense, it is clear that the psychological costs of poverty are intergenerational and devastating. Poverty and its associated mental retardation, school failure, teen pregnancy, and crime threaten our cities and ultimately our economy and democracy. For these reasons we must ask ourselves this question: How much is it worth to us as a nation to assist the development of disadvantaged children?

References

Bayley, N. (1969). *Bayley skills of infant development.* New York: Psychological Corp.

Hunt, J. (1961). *Intelligence and experience.* New York: The Ronald Press Company.

Jensen, A. R. (1969). How much can we boast IQ and scholastic achievement? *Harvard Educational Review, 39,* 1–123.

Landesman, S., & Butterfield, E. (1983). Mental retardation: Developmental issues in cognitive and social adaptation. In M. Lewis (Ed.), *Origins of intelligence* (pp. 479–519). New York: Plenum Press.

McGinness, G., & Ramey, C. T. (1981). Developing sociolinguistic competence in children. *Canadian Journal of Early Childhood Education, 1,* 22–43.

Ramey, C. T., Bryant, D. M., Sparling, J. J., & Wasik, B. H. (1984). A biosocial systems perspective on environmental interventions for low birth weight infants. *Clinical Obstetrics and Gynecology, 27,* 672–692.

Ramey, C. T., MacPhee, D., & Yeates, K. O. (1982). Preventing developmental retardation: A general systems model. In L. A. Bond & J. M. Joffe (Eds.), *Facilitating infant and early childhood development* (pp. 343–401). Hanover, NH: University Press of New England.

Ramey, C. T., Trohanis, P. L., & Hostler, S. L. (1982). Introduction. In C. T. Ramey & P. L. Trohanis (Eds.), *Finding and educating high-risk and handicapped infants* (pp. 1–19). Baltimore: University Park Press.

Ramey, C. T., Yeates, K. O., & MacPhee, D. (1984). Risk for retarded development among disadvantaged families: A systems theory approach to preventive intervention. *Advances in special education, 4,* 249–272.

Ramey, C. T., Yeates, K. O., & Short, E. J. (1984). The plasticity of intellectual development: Insights from preventive intervention. *Child Development, 55,* 1913–1925.

Sparling, J., & Lewis, I. (1981). *Learning games for the first three years: A program for parent/center partnership.* New York: Walker.

Sparling, J., & Lewis, I. (1984). *Learning games for threes and fours: A guide to adult and child play.* New York: Walker.

Sparling, J., & Lewis, I. (1985). *Partners for learning.* Winston–Salem, NC: Kaplan Press.

Terman, L. M., & Merrill, M. Q. (1972). *Stanford-Binet intelligence scale: 1972 norms.* Boston: Houghton-Mifflin.

Wasik, B. H. (1984). *Coping with parenting through effective problem solving: A handbook for professionals.* Unpublished manuscript. Frank Porter Graham Child Development Center, University of North Carolina at Chapel Hill.

Westinghouse Learning Corporation. (1969). *The impact of Head Start: An evaluation of Head Start on children's cognitive and affective development.* Athens, OH: Ohio University.

Zigler, E., & Freedman, J. (1987). Early experience, malleability, and Head Start. In J. J. Gallagher & C. T. Ramey (Eds.), *The malleability of children* (pp.85–95). Baltimore: Paul H. Brooks.

Dale L. Johnson

CHAPTER

4

Primary Prevention of Behavior Problems in Young Children: The Houston Parent–Child Development Center

When young children are aggressive with other children; are inattentive, overactive, fearful; and do not mind their parents, they are labeled as children with behavior problems, conduct disorders, or emotional problems. In many cases, such problems begin very early and constitute a source of difficulty for parents, teachers, peers, and not least in importance, for the children themselves.

Estimates of the percentage of children in school who have behavior problems range from 20% to 30% (Dohrenwend et al., 1980; Glidewell & Swallow, 1969; Rubin & Balow, 1978). Thus, large numbers of children could presumably benefit from psychological treatment. Even if treatment resources were available, many children are not referred to them (Shepherd, Oppenheim, & Mitchell, 1966), and there is pessimism about the effectiveness of interventions with conduct disorders or behavior problems (Rutter & Garmezy, 1983). Children who have been engaged repeatedly in aggressive, antisocial behaviors by the age of 10 tend to be rejected by peers and teachers and are a source of serious concern for parents. Furthermore, untreated, or unchanged, these disorders tend to persist and may continue to be problematic in adolescence and adulthood for many children (Loeber, 1982; Olweus, 1979; Robins, 1978). Obviously, the early prevention of these disorders, before a vicious circle of antiso-

cial behavior and social rejection develops, would be highly desirable.

The Houston Parent–Child Development Center (H-PCDC) described here represents an attempt to develop methods for the primary prevention of behavior problems in young Mexican-American children. The H-PCDC is an example of true primary prevention in that the children, who were 1 year old at the program's inception, were not selected because they were already identified as having behavior problems. They were normal infants who were selected for the project because their families were impoverished. The risk factors, therefore, were poverty and minority status.

Actually, little is known about whether this group of children is more or less likely to develop behavior problems than other children. There have been five reported surveys of Mexican-American children that permit comparison with majority group children (Flores de Apodaca, Lowenthal, Linden, & Lowenthal, 1983; O'Donnell, Stein, Machabanski, & Cress, 1982; Touliatos & Lindholm, 1976, 1980; Tuddenham, Brooks, & Milkovich, 1974). Taken together, they allow one conclusion: There is no compelling reason to believe that Mexican-American children in low-income families differ from majority-group children in the development of behavior problems. It must be added, however, that the question remains essentially unanswered because none of the surveys used appropriate epidemiological sampling procedures. Despite this serious caveat, it seems reasonable to assume that this group of children is at least no less likely to develop behavior problems than other groups of children.

The primary prevention of disorders depends largely on an understanding of the etiologies of the disorders to be effected. However, when the H-PCDC began in late 1969, there was much theory but little empirical evidence to indicate how behavior problems developed, and therefore there was little to guide the program development process. As it happens, our conceptions of the kinds of parent–child relationships that would promote the development of competence in children seem to have been supported by recent research.

Most efforts to prevent the development of behavior problems in children have been either parent focused (e.g., Glidewell, Gildea, & Kaufman, 1973; Hereford, 1963) or child focused (e.g., Spivack & Shure, 1974). These programs have demonstrated short- but not long-term prevention effects. They were based on assumptions about the origins of behavior problems—the parent models on assumptions that parental behaviors cause child behavior problems, and the child models on the idea that cause is to be found in the child's competencies.

Another way of viewing this situation, which underlies the H-PCDC approach (Johnson, 1975), is that behavior problems arise out of children's interactions with the significant persons in their environment. This is essentially a transactional perspective on the development of behavior problems (Sameroff & Chandler, 1975). In this perspective, the child interacts with others, including parents, and in each interaction each person adapts to or is changed by the interaction. Neither person in a dyadic relationship exclusively causes any particular developmental outcome; the outcome is a product of their interactional history.

Evidence supportive of this point of view has been provided by Patterson (1986) and Olweus (1980). Both researchers found that if the child was temperamentally difficult, parents tended to use increasingly coercive and ineffective child-rearing methods. These were countered, in turn, by the child's resistive behaviors. Thus, the quality of social interaction is dependent on the developmental and constitutional characteristics of all of the people involved in the situation at all times. For example, a parent interacting with a neurologically impaired child can be expected to behave quite differently from a parent interacting with a neurologically normal child of the same age.

The Houston Parent–Child Development Center

The H-PCDC was a product of the war on poverty of the Johnson administration. It began as a Parent–Child Center (PCC) when such programs were supported as branches of the Head Start family of early childhood activities. Subsequently, PCCs became PCDCs, that is, research and development centers designed to create state-of-the-art compensatory early childhood education programs. The charge to PCDC developers was to design programs that would optimize the school performance of low-income children. Such programs were to begin within the first 3 years of the child's life and closely involve parents in order to provide long-range continuity of training. In addition, families had to meet poverty guidelines and were to be provided with a wide array of services, for example, access to health clinics. Three of the original PCCs, in Birmingham, New Orleans, and Houston, met criteria set for PCDC program development. Although similar in many ways, these three PCDCs differed in program length, ethnic groups involved, educational methods, and, to a lesser extent, evaluation procedures. A detailed description of the PCDCs is provided by Andrews et al. (1982).

The development of the H-PCDC rested on the belief that parent–child education programs can be optimally effective only if they are designed to meet the specific parenting needs of the participating families. The assumption that a standard program could be developed and then applied to families with such diverse life-styles as reservation Navajos, Blacks in the Bronx, or Mexican Americans in Texas was rejected as absurd. Therefore, an essential feature of the H-PCDC is that it was designed specifically for a certain group of families. Replication would always demand that the particular needs of other groups be assessed and a program, perhaps containing many elements of the H-PCDC program, be designed. For Mexican-American families in Houston, a program that had its first year in the home, that included fathers, and that conducted much of its verbal interactions in Spanish was appropriate. With another ethnic group and in another setting, other program elements would have to be devised to respond to the needs of that group.

This cultural sensitivity to the needs of a certain group of families is at the heart of the H-PCDC endeavor. In a sense, it is the process rather than the product that has priority.

The major goal of the H-PCDC is to help families to optimize the competence of their children. Planning a program to achieve this for low-income Mexican-American families in Houston involved a number of steps. First, the Development Center staff conducted surveys with families in Houston barrios asking them to tell us what they wanted for their children. We conducted these door-to-door surveys as open-ended discussions and supplemented them with day-long observations of parent–child interaction in selected households. Next, we brought these ideas from the survey and observation sources to groups of representative families for discussion. We also met with groups of professionals, including Mexican-American professionals, to hear their opinions about the needs of low-income Mexican-American families. Finally, when the program was underway, we revised and enhanced the goals on an ongoing basis with input from the H-PCDC Parents Advisory Council. Program staff, all of whom were bilingual and most of whom were Mexican Americans from the neighborhoods being served, also provided continual feedback about goals. Finally, program goals and procedures were developed in consideration of information from the behavioral science literature, especially that having to do with pedagogical practice, parent–child interactions, and the development of child competence.

The Two-Stage Program

The planning and review process resulted in the design of a two-stage program beginning when the child was 1 year of age and ending at age 3. A total of approximately 550 hours of family involvement in the program was required over the 2-year period.

We had been informed early from many sources that it was unlikely that Mexican-American women would leave home with their infants to participate in what amounted to a public program, that is, a social activity that included people who were not the mother's immediate relatives. In response, we began the H-PCDC with a year of home visits. During that period, we scheduled 25 visits of 1½ hours each. The in-home educators who made the visits were women from the barrios who were trained to carry out the lessons with mothers in the home. The most important guideline for the H-PCDC staff was that they worked as resource persons, bringing information to the mothers that they could use about child development and child training. With this information, the mothers taught their own children as they wished.

The general focus of the in-home sessions was on the mother's understanding of her infant's developmental progress and on the impact that she has on that development. Discussion topics included language development, how infants learn from toys and games, cognitive development, and physical growth and change. In-home educators were trained in listening skills to provide first-level counseling for mothers who were isolated so often from traditional social support systems.

The first-year program also included several family workshop sessions held on weekends to maximize participation by fathers, siblings, and other family members. These sessions were organized around such human relations training topics as decision making and communication in the family. We included this program element because most of the families had fathers present and we knew the fathers were very much involved in the welfare of their children. Weekend sessions in a picniclike context fit in well with cultural customs for family events and provided a way to bring entire families in contact with the programs. These sessions were also used to keep the fathers informed about the purposes and procedures of the program. Mothers also participated in English-language classes conducted by H-PCDC staff during this year.

Activities conducted for those enrolled in the second program year took place at the project Center four mornings per week. This Center-based format was used to take advantage of opportunities for learning provided by group interactions. The 2-year-olds participated in a nursery school while their mothers attended classes on such home management topics as arranging the home for safety, budgeting, sewing, and forming consumer cooperatives. The mothers also participated in sessions that were child directed, such as learning to use the Palmer concept training curriculum (training the child to use appropriately such concepts as "over," "behind," and "above"), dealing with problem behaviors (e.g., temper tantrum and separation anxiety), and toy making. Microteaching techniques using videotapes of mothers interacting with their children were used to help mothers refine their teaching skills. In addition, mothers and fathers, who participated in evening sessions scheduled each month, were invited to suggest program elements that they thought would be useful. The suggestions that came forth and were implemented were drivers' education for mothers, sex education for mothers, automobile repair, and family planning information for fathers (the last two were suggested by fathers).

Components of the H-PCDC's 2-year program were designed to enhance the generalization of learning by (a) making sure that practice was guided by knowledge of principles and (b) providing occasions to apply learnings in a variety of settings.

Teachers in the first year were paraprofessionals; in the second year, both professionals and paraprofessionals were involved. All sessions were conducted in a bilingual format with Spanish used most commonly because all of the mothers were fluent in that language and only about one third were fluent in English. Mexican cultural materials were used whenever possible to encourage pride in ethnic origin and to promote positive self-esteem in the participants. Delivery of services was given careful consideration. For example, transportation was provided to the mothers for trips to the Center and for community health clinic visits. In both years, community workers, including a nurse, attended to social and medical needs and provided training in how to make effective use of such services.

The theoretical orientation of the H-PCDC was eclectic, with ideas of cognitive development guided by Piagetian concepts and those of child management guided by social learning theory.

In summary, the following constitute critical elements of the Houston program.

1. Participation is for 2 years, beginning when the child is 12 months of age.

2. The program has a sequential pattern as it moves from home in the first year to the Center in the second.

3. The model is designed to include the entire family.

4. The major program focus is on the mother–child interaction in the family setting.

5. Bilingual communication is encouraged.

6. Learning takes place in groups of mixed sizes and in varied settings.

7. A variety of educational methods is used.

8. Child-rearing resources are made available to families.

9. Staff include bilingual professionals and paraprofessionals.

10. Supportive services are provided to help families cope with acute financial, medical, and other problems.

11. The program is culturally sensitive.

Program Effectiveness

Research Design

The program evaluation design included the random assignment of families to program and control groups, the use of relatively large numbers of participants, the annual assessment of the child beginning at age 1, and the use of multimethod measurement. All assessments were carried out with bilingual versions of the measures by bilingual data collectors.

Participants. Door-to-door surveys were conducted to locate families for the project. Families were eligible if they had a 1-year-old child who was not neurologically impaired or chronically ill, if they met poverty guidelines, and if the mother was not employed in ways that would interfere with participation. The project was then explained to eligible families by a community worker, who told them that there were two programs, the Child Development Project and the Parent–Child Development Center, and these were described in detail. They were told that families would be assigned to one group or the other by chance, and they were asked if they would participate no matter to which group they were assigned. If they agreed they were enrolled. A table of random numbers was used to make group assignments.

Participants entered in annual groups, or cohorts, of about 100 families each year. Research data were collected for eight cohorts between 1970 and 1977. Demographic characteristics of the families varied some from year to year, but thorough analyses of intake characteristics showed no consistent differences between program and control groups. Significant group differences were found on a few background characteristics for some cohorts, but all of these differences were nonsignificant when cohorts were combined. Analyses carried out at various end-of-program and follow-up periods showed no signs of group differences; that is, there was no evidence to suggest that randomization had resulted in biased groups or that differential attrition had occurred in the follow-up samples.

Participant characteristics described in detail by Johnson, Breckenridge, and McGowen (1984) were typical of all cohorts. Boys and girls were equally represented. Nearly 90% of the families had the father present. Family incomes averaged $6,000 per year. On average, families included three children, and parents had 7 years of education. About 40% of the parents were born in Mexico, and parents divided themselves into three approximately even groups in preferring to speak Spanish, English, or both languages.

End-of-Program Results

The results at the end of the program have been reported in Andrews et al. (1982) and do not need to be repeated in detail here. In summary, on videotaped mother–child interaction measures, significant group differences were found indicating that program mothers were more affectionate, used more praise, used less criticism, were less rigidly controlling, and were more encouraging of their child's verbalizations. In an observation of the mother and child at home, program mothers were found to provide a more educationally stimulating environment. Program mothers also held more modern, less traditional attitudes about families. These general results have been replicated across successive cohorts.

For the children, small but significant differences were found on the Stanford–Binet Intelligence Scale. Differences on the Concept Familiarity Index, a criterion measure for the Palmer Concept Training curriculum, were significant for only one cohort.

First follow-up. The first attempt to determine whether involvement with the program reduced the likelihood that behavior problems would emerge was carried out when children were from 4 to 7 years of age through an interview with 128 of the mothers (Johnson & Breckenridge, 1982). The researchers designed the interview to elicit either positive or negative descriptions of the child's behaviors over a wide range of situations. A Multivariate Analysis of Variance (MANOVA) of the coded responses showed main effects for group and sex as well as a Group × Sex interaction. Boys in the control group were more destructive, more overactive, more negative attention seeking, and less emotionally sensitive than children in the other three groups.

Second follow-up. The second follow-up was carried out in schools when children were in Grades 2 through 5, that is, 5 to 8 years after program completion (Johnson & Walker, 1987). Teachers completed the Acting Out, Moody, Learning Behavior Rating Scale (AML), an 11-item measure of acting-out behaviors, moody, withdrawn behaviors, and learning problems (Cowen, et al., 1973) for 132 children. The Classroom Behavior Inventory (CBI; Schaefer & Edgerton, 1976) was also completed. Significant group differences were found for acting-out behaviors, with control children more restless, impulsive, obstinate, and disruptive, and more often involved in fights. Boys showed more acting-out problems than girls. Differences approached significance ($p < .065$) on moody, withdrawn behaviors. No differences appeared on the single learning problems item. Similar results were obtained on the CBI Hostile–Considerateness scale: Control children were more hostile and less considerate. The other significant finding was that boys in the control group were more dependent than boys in the program. Four times as many children in the control group as children in the program were referred for special services, but because the total number of children referred was low, differences were not significant.

To assess the clinical significance of the results, a cutoff point for the AML was developed from literature sources and scores of PCDC children referred for treatment. The score level selected was one that would suggest probable cause for referral. Using this cutoff point, a significant group difference was found. It could be inferred that if treatment resources had been available, and they were not, a significantly larger number of children in the control group would have been referred. Thus, the primary prevention effects appear to be both statistically and clinically significant.

This follow-up also found that children in the program did significantly better on the school-administered Iowa Tests of Basic Skills composite score ($p < .02$) than children in the control group (Johnson & Walker, 1985). This result taken with those for the prevention of behavior problems suggests that the overall program goal of fostering competence in children was attained.

Why the Program Works

With a program as extensive and complex as the H-PCDC and having such general goals, it may not be possible to define specifically how it has had primary prevention effects on the emergence of behavior problems. However, by comparing the H-PCDC with other primary prevention efforts and by examining the network of effects obtained by the H-PCDC, it may be possible to develop hypotheses about the sources of effects.

The central question is not why the H-PCDC achieved primary prevention effects documented at the time of the first follow-up. Other primary prevention efforts have had comparable results. Rather, the question is why H-PCDC effects have continued 5 to 8 years after program completion, a unique finding. Several factors may explain these results. First, it must be noted that in terms of sheer length, the PCDC is somewhat unusual among parent–child programs. The 550 hours required is roughly equivalent to three semesters of college class time. It is not only the length of time, but the intensity of the experience for the parents that we believe contributes to the impact of the program. Parents, fathers as well as mothers, become highly involved with the program, organize graduation ceremonies, form alumni groups, and have fought for funds to keep the program in operation in virtually each of the past 17 years. Program features such as its cultural sensitivity, provision of access to resources, and service delivery methods contribute to this level of parental enthusiasm for the program. Perhaps most important is that in all aspects the program promotes the parents' sense of efficacy and autonomy.

Other program features have also been found effective in other prevention efforts. The H-PCDC forms the basis of a social support system that was certainly active while families were in the program and in some instances persisted several years later.

Parent training in child management skills may also be an important feature in the long-term effectiveness of the program. A third follow-up has just revealed that mothers in the program are significantly less likely than mothers in the control group to believe that physical punishment is more important than using psychological methods of discipline. This result was obtained when children were in early adolescence and suggests that knowledge during the program has become a part of the belief structure of many of the mothers. Whether it provides a guide to action was not determined. But if mothers in the program do believe that physical punishment is not necessary for discipline, it may also mean that they have not been caught up in the cycle of coercive parent–child relationships described by Patterson (1986) and Olweus (1980).

The emphases on parent–child education and on the parent and child's participating jointly in the program when the child was very young may have central significance for explaining long-term effects. Breckenridge (1980) used videotapes of mother–child interaction at child age 2 to predict behavior problems identified in the first follow-up. He found that maternal high criticism, low warmth, low use of praise, and rigid control were associated with follow-up measures of high destructiveness, negative attention seeking, and restlessness in children. These same maternal behaviors also differentiated groups at the end of the program. The H-PCDC program has had a similar impact on the kinds of maternal behaviors that promote positive behaviors in young children.

This is not to suggest that a simple linear relation exists between maternal behaviors and child outcomes. It is obviously easier to be affectionate toward a loving child and to praise a child who has accomplished certain tasks. Rather, it is assumed that the child contributes to the mother's behavior and that Breckenridge was measuring a product of the mother–child interaction. It appears that the program has affected the early mother–child interaction by enhancing attachment formation. In turn, it is assumed that this early relationship decreases the possibility that coercive or rejecting interactions would develop. Support for this hypothesis is now available. Lewis, Feiring, McGuffog, and Jaskir (1984) reported that insecure attachment at age 1 is associated with behavior problems at age 6. Erickson, Sroufe, and Egeland (1985) have reported similar findings. The affection, use of praise, lack of criticism, and flexible control displayed by the mothers on the H-PCDC videotapes are the kinds of behaviors that have been found to promote secure attachment in infants (Bretherton & Waters, 1985). Secure children, including H-PCDC graduates, seem to get along more harmoniously with adults and children. They are able to follow suggestions, cooperate, and act constructively. The H-PCDC finding that program boys were more independent than control boys suggests that these results occur without loss of autonomy.

It is hypothesized that the H-PCDC's effectiveness is based on (in probable order of importance) (a) development of an early and positive pattern of mother–child interaction; (b) knowledge of positive disciplinary skills by mothers, maternal sensitivity to child's emotional state, and developmental stage; (c) increased sense of parental efficacy; and (d) mother's knowledge of resources.

These hypotheses about program effects are to be tested in later research.

Limitations of the Program

The H-PCDC, like all other early childhood programs, although extensive in its involvement with families, is far from comprehensive. Furthermore, current knowledge about family development would probably have led the planners of the H-PCDC to do some things differently today than were done in 1970, some of which are fairly serious.

It was clear as we recruited families for the project that those who were in most need of help often chose not to participate. For example, parents involved with drugs or prostitution, who typically had high-risk infants, did not make themselves available to the project. In addition, adolescent mothers rarely participated. Perhaps this reflects the fact that they were sheltered by their own parents, but we do not know for certain why they did not accept invitations to take part. Thus, although the service delivery system of the program was exceptionally effective, it did not reach all parents in need of assistance.

Most programs fail to provide services over a long period of time and thus are not available to parents when new child-rearing problems or family stresses arise. For example, there is little in the parents' experience with the child during the first 3 years that prepares them for coping with the problems of parenting an adolescent. The third follow-up has found both bafflement by many parents about adolescence and a lack of resources for dealing with these problems. Because the rate of marital dissolution has been fairly high (about 25% in 10 years) in our sample, many women are left alone with minimal financial resources to rear adolescent children. The mandate for the PCDC designs did not permit the kind of long-term continuity of services that real life seems to require. Perhaps future programs can consider these issues.

Another possible program limitation is that the emphasis on the parent–child dyad may have distracted somewhat from an emphasis on the development of the parents. The original plan for the H-PCDC called for vocational development training for the fathers, but limited funds eliminated that aspect of the program. An effective design might include the same emphasis for mothers. An example of a program in which a major component involves the development of the mother's educational and vocational skills is titled Avance.

Located in San Antonio, it is designed largely for young and undereducated mothers (Rodriguez, 1983).

The range of behavior problems that can be affected by the H-PCDC has not been investigated. Certainly, it cannot be supposed that such severe child disorders as infantile autism and certain types of attention deficit disorder would be expected to be affected by the program. For example, one child in the program group appeared quite normal as he and his mother began the program. At age 3, he was untestable. A referral for a neurological examination revealed that he had a serious, progressive neurological condition. His parents worked hard to provide him with emotional support and cognitive stimulation, but the limits set by his neurological disorder were great. The scope of preventive action needs to be explored, but clearly there are limits to what can be expected of parent–child education programs.

Program Dissemination

The original PCDC plan, formulated by Mary Robinson while she was with the Office of Economic Opportunity, was to take some of the existing PCCs and convert them to research and development centers. These became the three PCDCs in Birmingham, New Orleans, and Houston. According to the plan, if these proved effective when evaluated at the end of the program, each would be replicated in three new sites, and these in turn would be evaluated by an external evaluation group. If they were effective, then the models would be ready for widespread dissemination with federal, state, and foundation monies.

The three original models were judged to be effective; Bank Street College was awarded the replication management contract, and Educational Testing Service undertook the evaluation. Instead of three replication sites for each model only one site for each model was actually implemented. These were in Detroit, Indianapolis, and San Antonio. The replications were well underway when severe budget problems brought the project to a halt. At present, the three original sites exist as PCCs with no research involvement. All follow-up work is entirely separate from the ongoing programs and has been funded by the Hogg Foundation and the Spencer Foundation.

The dissemination plan, although not fully implemented, revealed what is needed to replicate programs of this type and that knowledge is available. In developing the H-PCDC model for replication, curriculum materials and training manuals were prepared. The current H-PCDC could function as a training site, if provided supplementary assistance. Furthermore, there is no reason why elements of the H-PCDC could not be used in creating new, but similar, programs. As explained above, the simple use of program modules is not sufficient. It is essential that there be a careful analysis of local needs using information from many sources.

In searching for effective primary prevention methods, it is not enough to consider only the H-PCDC model. Participants of other programs having similar features should be followed and assessed for behavior problems. The viability of this approach is suggested by the fact that one project, somewhat similar to the H-PCDC, the Perry Point Preschool Program (Schweinhart & Weikart, 1983; also see Chapter 5 in this book) obtained near-significant results for behavior problems several years after program completion. On the other hand, many existing parent education or early childhood programs could very likely be improved by the addition of H-PCDC elements.

Conclusions

It now appears to be possible to prevent the emergence of behavior problems in children. *Prevention* is perhaps too strong a word; more accurately, it appears to be possible to *reduce* the rate of the emergence of behavior problems in children. This reduction in rate is nevertheless of great importance because it means that for substantial numbers of families interactions will be characterized by harmony rather than by conflict. Much more needs to be learned about this form of primary prevention, and research efforts should be directed toward identifying the essential features of programs like H-PCDC for the prevention of behavior problems. It seems unlikely that such programs need to be so extensive. This is a major issue in that the major obstacle to wider application of the procedures described here is cost. There is a reluctance in the United States at this time to allocate funds for the support and development of families, and low-cost programs would be more attractive than those that are more expensive. Perhaps most important, however, is the development of a national consensus that family integrity is important and deserving of support as a national priority. When that occurs, the primary prevention of behavior problems in children will become a social reality available to many instead of a potentiality available to only a few.

References

Andrews, S. R., Blumenthal, J. B., Johnson, D. L., Kahn, A. J., Ferguson, C. J., Lasater, T. M., Malone, P. E. & Wallace, D. B. (1982). The skills of mothering: A study of Parent Child Development Centers. *Monographs of the Society for Research in Child Development, 47* (6, Serial No. 198).

Breckenridge, J. N. (1980). *Predicting child behavior problems from early mother–child interaction.* Unpublished masters thesis, University of Houston.

Bretherton, I., & Waters, E. (Eds.). (1985). Growing points of attachment theory and research. *Monographs of the Society for Research in Child Development, 50* (1 & 2, Serial No. 209).

Cowen, E., Dorr, D., Clarfield, S., Kreling, B., McWilliams, S. A., Pokracki, R., Pratt, D. M., Terrell, D., & Wilson, A. (1973). The AML: A quick-screening device for early identification of school maladjustment. *American Journal of Community Psychology, 1,* 12–35.

Dohrenwend, B. P., Dohrenwend, B. S., Gould, M., Link, B., Neugebauer, R., & Wunsch-Hitzig, R. (1980). *Mental illness in the United States: Epidemiological estimates.* New York: Praeger.

Erickson, H. F., Sroufe, L. A., & Egeland, B. (1985). The relationship between quality of attachment and behavior problems in preschool in a high-risk sample. In I. Bretherton & E. Waters (Eds.), Growing points of attachment theory and research (pp. 147–166). *Monograph of the Society of Child Development, 50* (1 & 2, Serial No. 209).

Flores de Apodaca, R., Lowenthal, B., Linden, N., & Lowenthal, A. S. (1983). Quick socio-emotional screening of Mexican-American and other ethnic Head Start children. *Hispanic Journal of Behavioral Sciences, 5,* 81–92.

Glidewell, J. C., Gildea, M. C. L., & Kaufman, M. K. (1973). The preventive and therapeutic effects of two school mental health programs. *American Journal of Community Psychology, 1,* 295–329.

Glidewell, J. C., & Swallow, C. S. (1969). *The prevalence of maladjustment in elementary schools* (Report prepared for the Joint Commission on Mental Illness and Health of Children). Chicago: University of Chicago.

Hereford, C. F. (1963). *Changing parental attitudes through group discussion.* Austin, TX: University of Texas Press.

Johnson, D. L. (1975). The development of a program for parent–child education among Mexican-Americans in Texas. In B. Z. Friedlander, G. M. Sterritt, & G. E. Kirk (Eds.), *Exceptional Infant* (Vol. 3, pp. 374–398). New York: Brunner/Mazel.

Johnson, D. L., Breckenridge, J. N. (1982). The Houston Parent–Child Development Center and the primary prevention of behavior problems in young children. *American Journal of Community Psychology, 10,* 305–316.

Johnson, D. L., Breckenridge, J. N., & McGowen, R. J. (1984). Home environment and early cognitive development in Mexican-American children. In A. W. Gottfried (Ed.), *Home environment and early mental development* (pp. 151–195). New York: Academic Press.

Johnson, D. L., & Walker, T. (1985, April). *A follow-up evaluation of the Houston Parent–Child Development*

Center: School performance. Paper presented at the meeting of the American Educational Research Association, Chicago.

Johnson, D. L., & Walker, T. (1987). The primary prevention of behavior problems in Mexican-American children. *American Journal of Community Psychology, 15,* 375–385.

Lewis, M., Feiring, C., McGuffog, C., & Jaskir, J. (1984). Predicting psychopathology from early social relations. *Child Development, 55,* 123–136.

Loeber, R. (1982). The stability of antisocial and delinquent child behavior: A review. *Child Development, 5,* 1431–1446.

O'Donnell, J. P., Stein, J. N., Machabanski, H., & Cress, J. N. (1982). Dimensions of behavior problems in Anglo-American and Mexican-American preschool children: A comparative study. *Journal of Consulting and Clinical Psychology, 50,* 643–651.

Olweus, D. (1979). Stability of aggressive reaction patterns in males: A review. *Psychological Bulletin, 86,* 852–875.

Olweus, D. (1980). Familial and temperamental determinants of aggressive behavior in adolescent boys: A causal analysis. *Developmental Psychology, 16,* 644–660.

Patterson, G. R. (1986). Performance models for antisocial boys. *American Psychologist, 41,* 432–444.

Robins, L. N. (1978). Sturdy childhood predictors of adult antisocial behaviour: Replications from longitudinal studies. *Psychological Medicine, 8,* 611–622.

Rodriguez, G. G. (1983). *Final report: Project CAN Prevent.* San Antonio: Avance.

Rubin, R. A., & Balow, B. (1978). *Prevalence of teacher-identified behavior problems: A longitudinal study. Exceptional Children, 45,* 102–111.

Rutter, M., & Garmezy, N. (1983). Developmental psychology and psychopathology in children. In P. H. Mussen (Ed.), *Handbook of child psychology* (Vol. 4, pp. 775–911). New York: Wiley.

Sameroff, A. J., & Chandler, M. J. (1975). Reproductive risk and the continuum of caretaking casuality. In F. Horowitz (Ed.), *Review of child development research* (Vol. 4, pp. 187–244). Chicago: University of Chicago Press.

Schaefer, E. S., & Edgerton, M. (1976). *Classroom Behavior Inventory.* Unpublished manuscript.

Schweinhart, L. J., & Weikart, D. (1983). The effects of the Perry Preschool Program on youths through age 15—a summary. In Consortium for Longitudinal Studies (Eds.), *As the twig is bent: Lasting effects of preschool programs* (pp. 71–101). Hillsdale, NJ: Erlbaum.

Shepherd, M., Oppenheim, A. N., & Mitchell, S. (1966). Childhood behavior disorders and the child guidance clinic. *Journal of Child Psychology and Psychiatry, 7,* 39–52.

Spivack, G., & Shure, M. B. (1974). *Social adjustment of young children: A cognitive approach to solving real-life problems.* San Francisco: Jossey-Bass.

Touliatos, J., & Lindholm, B. W. (1976). Behavior problems of Anglo and Mexican-American children. *Journal of Abnormal Child Psychology, 4,* 299–304.

Touliatos, J., & Lindholm, B. W. (1980). Psychopathology of Anglo and Chicano children. *Journal of Clinical Child Psychology, 9,* 55–56.

Tuddenham, R. D., Brooks, J., & Milkovich, L. (1974). Mothers' reports of behavior of ten-year olds: Relationships with sex, ethnicity, and mother's education. *Developmental Psychology, 10,* 959–995.

Lawrence J. Schweinhart and David B. Weikart

CHAPTER

5

The High/Scope Perry Preschool Program

In the two decades since it completed its operation, the High/Scope Perry Preschool Program has come of age in several ways. In 1962 through 1967, the program served 3- and 4-year-olds; in 1988, the longitudinal study is continuing with 28-year-olds. The early evidence of program effectiveness has been overshadowed by evidence of long-term effectiveness 14 years after children completed the program. The program's pragmatic rationale—a desire to help children at risk of school failure to do better in school—has been elaborated into a path-analytic causal model based on the interactionist approach to human development. The High/Scope curriculum, developed in the Perry Program, is now used by thousands of early childhood teachers. The research evidence generated by this local effort in Ypsilanti, Michigan, has come to influence public policy throughout the United States and around the world.

Put simply, the Perry Preschool Program was successful because it brought the right experiences to the right children at the right time in their lives. The children served were at special risk of school failure because their parents lacked education and income and lived in a stressful environment. Without intervention, these children would have started school with significantly less of the knowledge, skills, and positive dispositions needed for school success. The Perry Preschool Program enabled the children to develop these qualities—not enough to overcome failure totally, but enough to make an important and lasting difference in their lives.

Rationale for the Perry Preschool Program

Influencing the Success Stream

We believe that early childhood education can help children who live in poverty because it can positively alter the causal chain that leads from childhood poverty to school failure to subsequent adult poverty and related social problems. This cycle of poverty is not inevitable for every person in the United States, but it does characterize some lives. Two out of five children from the poorest fifth of families remain in the poorest fifth as young adults; 7 out of 10 remain in the poorest two fifths (Hill & Ponza, 1983).

Poor children are more likely to fail in school. The National Assessment of Educational Progress in 1982 found that in cities, advantaged students averaged 22 percentage points higher on mathematics tests than disadvantaged students (Education Commission of the States, 1983). The 1982 high school dropout rate was 17% for the poorest quartile of youngsters, more than three times as great as the 5% rate for the richest quartile (National Center for Education Statistics, 1983).

Students who fail in school are likely to become adults who live in poverty. The poverty rate for high school dropouts in 1986 was 19%, while it was only 10% for high school graduates and 4% for those who attended college (U.S. Bureau of the Census, 1987a). Although some have argued that this relation is due not to what is actually learned in the extra years of school but to the traits of people who go to school longer (Jencks et al., 1979) or the social response to longer schooling (Collins, 1979), the empirical connection itself is not in dispute.

Poverty and school failure are associated with juvenile delinquency and crime (Loeber & Dishion, 1983). Whereas school success causes students to have strong social bonds to the school and the community, school failure alienates students from these institutions, permitting them to engage in delinquency (Elliott, Ageton, & Canter, 1979).

Teen pregnancy and poverty go hand in hand. In one study of 24-year-old women, the poverty rates were 54% for teenage mothers (age 17 or younger), but only 33% for older mothers and 15% for women still childless. Currently, nearly three fourths of the families headed by mothers aged 15 to 24 live in poverty (U.S. Bureau of the Census, 1987a).

The Role of Early Childhood in Human Development

The transactional understanding of human development views behavior as the result of the continuous interplay of a person's maturation and experiences in settings. Persons and settings achieve stable patterns of relationship even as they shape and reshape each other. People grow in the traditional settings of childhood family, schooling, workplace, and adulthood family. Each setting is a context for the formation of habits of interaction between the individual and other persons. Any "intervention" is an attempt to influence the habitual interactions that characterize traditional institutional settings.

Early childhood is an opportune time for intervention because of its position in the child's physical, social, and mental development. Physically, preschool-aged children have matured to the point that they have achieved both fine and gross motor coordination and are able to move about freely and easily. Socially, children are able to move away from familiar adults and social contexts into new settings. The fear of strangers is now not as common as it was earlier, and youngsters welcome relations with new peers and adults. Mentally, children have developed the abilities to speak and listen and can use objects for their own purposes. Piaget sees the preschool-aged child as in the preoperational stage and moving to the concrete operational stage, learning from real objects and developing the ability to learn from

symbols (Piaget & Inhelder, 1969). When the child is fully concrete operational at age 6 or 7, schools begin instruction in the symbol-based skills of reading, writing, and arithmetic.

Introductions to new settings are crucial times for human development because they entail the creation of new habits of interaction between the new person and other persons and objects in the setting. The person's initial behavior in the setting is the key element in the creation of these new habits. Thus, the best times in life for interventions are the months or years just before individuals enter new settings. The intervention should focus on changing the individual's initial behavior in the setting so that it promotes the formation of desirable patterns of interaction in the new setting. If expected behaviors in the new setting were based only on superficial appearances, desirable behavioral change could be limited to changes in superficial behavior. But when expected behavior in the setting is rooted in underlying skills and dispositions, the desirable behavioral change must likewise be rooted in these skills and dispositions. Thus, an early childhood program in the year or two prior to school entry should focus on developing the child's skills and dispositions that underlie adaptive functioning in the school setting.

The skills to be developed in early childhood are not the abstract skills of reading, writing, and arithmetic. Nor are they merely the recognition of numbers and letters, the presumed building blocks of these skills. Rather, they are the thinking skills appropriate to early childhood—putting things in groups and in series and solving problems in space and time and in social situations. They are the dispositions of intellectual curiosity, persistence in completing activities, and an open friendliness toward adults and other children (Katz, 1985).

What Made the Perry Preschool Program Work?

An explanation of why the Perry Preschool Program worked must include an examination of the history of the program within the context of the rest of the early childhood program research tradition of the past few decades. We shall pay specific attention to the work of the other members of the Consortium for Longitudinal Studies (1983; Lazar, Darlington, Murray, Royce, & Snipper, 1982), the High/Scope Preschool Curriculum Comparison study (Schweinhart, Weikart, & Larner, 1986; Weikart, Epstein, Schweinhart, &

Bond, 1978), and the National Day Care study (Ruopp, Travers, Glantz, & Coelen, 1979).

History of the Perry Preschool Program

The Perry Preschool study (Berrueta-Clement, Schweinhart, Barnett, Epstein, & Weikart, 1984; Schweinhart & Weikart, 1980; Weikart, Bond, & McNeil, 1978; Weikart, Deloria, Lawser, & Weigerink, 1970) demonstrated the potential benefits of high-quality early childhood development programs for poor children. In the study, 3- and 4-year-olds from families of low socioeconomic status (SES) were randomly assigned either to a group that attended the Perry Preschool Program or to a group that did not. Pairs of children matched on initial IQ were randomly split between the groups, then reassigned if necessary to equate the groups' sex ratio and average SES; siblings were assigned to the same group. The resultant groups of children, 58 in the preschool group and 65 in the control group, were not statistically different from each other (at $p < .10$) on any background characteristic except maternal employment during the child's preschool years, and this variable was not significantly correlated with the reported outcomes (Berrueta-Clement et al., 1984). This design permits subsequent group differences to be considered effects of the preschool program.

The Perry Preschool Program used the High/Scope curriculum (Hohmann, Banet, & Weikart, 1979; Weikart & Schweinhart, 1987), an educational approach based largely on Piaget's interactional theory of child development. Most children attended the program for 2 years at ages 3 and 4. The classroom program was in session five mornings a week for 7 months of the year, with home visits by a teacher to each parent once a week. Because it was a new, experimental program, classroom groups had about 25 children and 4 teachers, for a teacher–child ratio between 1:5 and 1:6.

Early Childhood Program Quality

High quality is the common characteristic that the Perry Preschool Program shares with other successful early childhood programs for children living in poverty. High-quality early childhood programs can be operated anywhere if conditions of quality are maintained—in public schools, in Head Start programs, in community agencies, or in private homes. At the same time, low-quality programs can be operated in any of these places— programs that cost people money even as they fail to deliver on the potential that they promise to young children. So what exactly is quality?

Experimentally designed research on early childhood programs helps answer this question, but does not fully resolve it. Most of this research has compared children who attended a program with those who did not. This design can tell us how successful programs are but requires us to make educated inferences about which of their elements are responsible for this success. To date, several studies of curriculum and components of quality have been conducted. Yet, in the final analysis, recommendations for program quality must rely not only on scientific studies but also on the varied program experiences that we and the rest of the early childhood community have accumulated over the years (Epstein et al., 1985).

Research on the Perry Preschool Program and other early childhood programs suggests that effective early childhood programs have all of the following seven components:

1. A developmentally appropriate curriculum based on child-initiated activities;

2. Group or classroom enrollment limits of fewer than 20 3- to 5-year-olds, with at least two adults assigned to each group of children;

3. Staff trained in early childhood development;

4. Supervisory support and in-service training for the curriculum;

5. Parent involvement as partners with program staff;

6. Sensitivity to the noneducational needs of the child and family; and

7. Developmentally appropriate evaluation procedures.

These are discussed in the following sections.

The developmentally appropriate curriculum. The Perry Preschool Program used a developmentally appropriate curriculum based on child-initiated learning activities. It recognized children's intellectual, social, and physical needs and encouraged children to initiate their own learning activities within a supportive environment (Hohmann et al., 1979). This curriculum was based largely on a view of the child as an active, self-initiating learner (Piaget, 1970). In

Piaget's view, children learn by actively exploring reality with all of their senses. In a developmentally appropriate curriculum, children have many opportunities to initiate their own activities and take responsibility for completing them. The role of staff and parents is to help children make decisions, not to make all of the decisions for them. Staff do not rely on workbooks or attempt to maintain strict control. They are preparing children for academic learning but not by presenting precisely sequenced lessons of reading, writing, and arithmetic. By emphasizing children's decision-making and problem-solving capacities, they are preparing children for the real-life work demands that they will eventually face.

Today, the early childhood field recognizes the value of child-initiated activity in helping young children achieve their full potential. Significantly, the 54,000-member National Association for the Education of Young Children has issued position statements (1986a, 1986b) on developmentally appropriate practices in early childhood programs (those that serve children from birth to age 8; in particular, those that serve 4- and 5-year-olds). For example, in the recommended curriculum, the statements say, "Children select many of their own activities from among a variety of leaning areas the teacher prepares" (National Association for the Education of Young Children, 1986b, p. 23) and "Adults provide opportunities for children to choose from among a variety of activities, materials, and equipment; and time to explore through active involvement" (National Association for the Education of Young Children, 1986a, p. 10).

A year of training and practice in the High/Scope curriculum (Hohmann, et al., 1979) enables teachers to implement such a child-initiated, developmentally appropriate approach. The High/Scope curriculum centers on a plan–do–review process and a set of key experiences for young children. In the plan–do–review process, each child makes a plan with the teacher at the beginning of the class, carries it out, then makes a new plan and carries it out, and so on, finally rejoining the teacher to review what he or she did. This process enables young children to plan and carry out their own activities, supported by a facilitative teacher. The key experiences for young children are activities that teachers and children engage in together to further specific aspects of children's cognitive and social development. Such activities enable the child to develop such skills as placing objects in categories, ranking them by

size, thinking about space and time, and solving interpersonal conflicts.

Recent research supporting the importance of child-initiated activity in early childhood programs comes from the High/Scope Foundation's long-term Preschool Curriculum Comparison study. This study has examined the effects on young people through age 15 of three well-implemented programs based on different preschool curriculum models—a direct-instruction curriculum, the High/Scope curriculum, and a typical nursery school curriculum (Schweinhart et al., 1986). The direct-instruction curriculum emphasized teacher-directed instruction, while both the High/Scope and nursery school curricula emphasized child-initiated learning activity. The High/Scope curriculum was based in part on joint planning by teachers and children, whereas the nursery school curriculum was based on teachers striving to respond to the child's needs and interests.

The mean IQ of the children in the three programs, regardless of the curriculum model used, rose 27 points, from 78 to 105, during the programs' first year, and the children's IQs averaged 94 at age 10. On the basis of these data, we had concluded that well-implemented preschool programs had a positive effect, regardless of which curriculum was used.

The most recent phase of the curriculum study was conducted at age 15. We were surprised to discover that members of the High/Scope and nursery school groups each reported engaging in only about half as many delinquent acts as did members of the direct-instruction group. The High/Scope group reported an average of 5 offenses, the nursery school group reported an average of 7, and the direct-instruction group reported an average of 13 ($p < .05$, $n = 54$). Persons reporting more than 15 delinquent acts constituted only about 8% of the High/Scope and nursery school groups, compared with 44% of the direct-instruction group.

This study cannot tell us whether the direct-instruction group reported more delinquency than it would have without the program. It does tell us that the direct-instruction group reported more delinquency than did the other curriculum groups. We can only surmise that the direct-instruction preschool program may have failed to take full advantage of the opportunities that were available to positively influence the development of young children's social problem-solving skills. After all, its stated objectives were academic, whereas both of the other curricula included social objectives such as children learning to get along with other children.

In attempting to understand these findings, Kamii (1986) applied Piaget's theory of moral development and concluded that the direct-instruction curriculum prevented children from developing autonomy because the teacher was authoritarian and used rewards and punishments. By contrast, the other two curricula encouraged children's autonomy because they allowed teachers and children to discuss their points of view with one another. What is clear is that the results of this study imply that child-initiated learning programs for preschool-aged children are preferable to direct-instruction academic programs. Because this conclusion is important and this is but one study, more research is needed.

Creating a supportive context for child-initiated learning. *Enrollment limits.* Low enrollment limits are essential to maintain the small group size and low number of children per staff member that are essential to a high-quality early childhood program. According to the National Day Care study (Ruopp et al., 1979; Travers & Goodson, 1980), 3- to 5-year-olds develop best in classroom groups with enrollment limits of 16 to 20 children and two adults present—a teacher or caregiver and an assistant. The study found that children in such groups, as compared with those in larger groups, received more staff attention; engaged more frequently in reflection, verbal initiative, and cooperation; engaged less frequently in aimless wandering and noninvolvement in free play; and experienced significantly greater improvement in knowledge and skills.

The National Day Care study found that for 3- to 5-year-olds with two adults in the classroom, an enrollment limit of 20 was required for children merely to maintain a normal rate of development of knowledge and skills (Ruopp et al., 1979), and therefore this limit seems appropriate to programs for children of average or better intellectual ability and socioeconomic circumstances. By the same token, the findings suggest that an enrollment limit of 16 should be required for a Head Start or state prekindergarten program expected to enhance the development of children who live in poverty or are otherwise at risk of school failure. (Although High/Scope's successful Perry Preschool program had enrollments of up to 25 poor children, it also had four teaching staff assigned to each group; consequently its staff–child ratios were between 1:5 and 1:6.)

Staffing. Adults who provide care and education for young children need specialized training and experience in child development and early childhood education. A key finding of the National Day Care study established the value of *child-related training*—courses and practica in day care, early childhood education, child development, child psychology, and elementary education. When programs had a greater percentage of staff with child-related training, the children more frequently experienced positive social interaction with the lead caregiver; more frequently exhibited task persistence, reflectiveness in adult-directed activities, and verbal initiative during free play; showed noninvolvement less frequently; and experienced significantly greater improvement in knowledge and skills. When programs had staff with more years of day-care experience, the children exhibited less frequent aimless wandering and, during free play activities, more frequent task persistence and less frequent noninvolvement; they also experienced greater improvements in knowledge, skills, and vocabulary. It should be noted that the general educational levels per se of staff were not strongly related to such desirable outcomes (Ruopp et al., 1979; Travers & Goodson, 1980).

The care and education of young children is a teaching specialization, just as other teachers specialize in the age ranges of lower or upper elementary, middle school, or high school. Successful teaching of children at one age level—for example, sixth grade—does not qualify a teacher to work with 4- or 5-year-olds. In fact, it may even present a problem if the teacher cannot or does not shift to the nurturant, nondirective teaching style and expectations appropriate for 4- and 5-year-olds.

Supervisory support and in-service training. Administrators need to understand and actively support the goals and operation of an early childhood program and its child development curriculum. They should

• Be prepared to explain and defend the curriculum to parents, other teachers and staff, other administrators, and community leaders

• Ensure that staff, children, and the program itself are evaluated by developmentally appropriate measures and standards

• Provide the program with the equipment and resources necessary for a child development curriculum

• Hire qualified staff and encourage teamwork among the staff assigned to each classroom

• Allocate staff time for daily planning

• Allocate staff time for monthly in-service training sessions and assure that these sessions enable staff to apply in the program the child development principles that they learn

• Work with staff and parents to address child care needs that may be created for employed parents because part-day and even full-school-day school programs do not completely meet these needs.

Administrators are especially responsible for the in-service training of early childhood staff. Such training ought to take place at least monthly and should systematically address issues that arise in the day-to-day classroom application of principles of child development and child-initiated learning. In addition to its instructional value, in-service training also affords staff the opportunity to receive emotional support for their classroom efforts from other teachers and administrators. In-service training can take a variety of forms. For example, some principals or program directors have their staff participate in training opportunities provided by the district's or agency's early childhood specialist. Those who do not have such opportunities available to them can encourage early childhood staff to form study groups in which they read and discuss early childhood materials such as articles in the National Association for the Education of Young Children (NAEYC) journal, *Young Children*. In addition, administrators can support and encourage staff attendance at various early childhood conferences, where they will associate with other early childhood educators and stay current as the early childhood field develops.

Parent involvement. A high-quality early childhood program involves parents and is sensitive to their needs. Program staff should strive to form a partnership with parents, recognizing their crucial importance in a child's development. The staff can explain child development principles to parents, even as parents can help staff better understand the children and their family backgrounds. If parents want to help their 4-year-old learn how to read, the staff can show them how to read stories aloud and demonstrate positive

regard for books, the activities that best support the skills and dispositions that are appropriate for the child at this age.

Early childhood program staff should join with parents as partners in the education of young children. This partnership means that the staff should neither be too authoritarian towards parents, claiming to know what's best for the child regardless of parental perceptions, nor be too accommodating to parental pressure to place inappropriate academic expectations on young children. The early childhood program staff should be authoritative experts on principles of child development and treated as such both by parents and by the program administrator. On the other hand, staff should recognize that parents are in the position to be the all-time experts on their children's behavior and traits and family background. Parents will be with their children over the years and can profitably learn to see their children's behavior in developmental terms.

Sensitivity to the noneducational needs of children and families. In 1987, 57% of mothers of children under age 5 were in the labor force, although a decade earlier in 1977 only 40% of them were (U.S. Bureau of Labor Statistics, 1987). Most of these young children need child care arrangements for the full work day. If they are in part-day or full-school-day public school programs, they need some kind of child care arrangement for the remainder of the work day. Nearly half of this child care is provided by family members and other relatives, either in the child's home or their own. A little over one fourth is provided by nonrelatives in private homes, and nearly one fourth is provided in day care centers and nursery schools (U.S. Bureau of the Census, 1987b).

It is helpful for public school kindergarten and prekindergarten teachers to get to know the child care providers of the children in their classes, whether these providers operate day-care centers, day-care homes, or less formal arrangements. The public school might serve as a convenient site for meetings of the community's early childhood teachers and caregivers, enabling them to provide mutual support, discuss problems, and study early childhood education. The primary point of day-to-day contact between program providers and parents can be the dropping off, release, and transportation of the children, although busing may curtail such contact even as it facilitates the transitions in the child's day.

Poverty is another condition affecting children and families. Children and families living in poverty have noneducational needs that must be addressed if an education program is to make sense. Programs can provide meals to children living in poverty who otherwise may lack adequate nutrition. Teachers can assist families suffering from the stresses of poverty to access agencies to help them with their problems. Agencies that provide early childhood programs can also offer literacy training to parents who could profit from such training.

The poverty rate among children under age 6 was 22% in 1986 (U.S. Bureau of the Census, 1987a). The national Head Start program has focused primarily on children living in poverty since it began operation in 1965. Today, nearly half of the states have initiated their own early childhood programs focused on children who are poor or otherwise at risk of school failure (National Governors' Association, 1987).

Evaluation. Early childhood teachers make decisions about children, and administrators make decisions about teachers, decisions that are based on either formal or informal evaluations of teachers' and childrens' behavior and activities. Formal evaluation procedures, by making explicit the criteria by which such decisions are made, can make them more fair (Goodwin & Driscoll, 1980; Spodek, 1982). The two main objects of early childhood evaluation are (a) program quality and (b) the extent to which a program enhance children's development.

Observers assess program quality by comparing what they observe in an early childhood program to a set of standards for quality. Such program rating measures include the Early Childhood Environment Rating Scale (Harms & Clifford, 1980) and the NAEYC standards of program quality (1984). Further curriculum assessment depends on the particular curriculum model that one is assessing. Trained observers may assess the implementation of the High/Scope early childhood curriculum with High/Scope's Preschool Implementation Profile, which focuses on room arrangement, materials and equipment, the daily routine, the content of teacher–child interactions, team evaluation and planning, working with parents, inservice training, and supervision.

The goal of early childhood care and education is the enhancement of children's development of knowledge, thinking and social skills, and dispositions for learning. The assessment of children's performance on these dimensions can provide assurance that children and the program staff are accomplishing what they should be expected to accomplish. Children's performance may be assessed by tests, systematic in-program observa-

tion by trained observers, and ratings by teachers. The various types of tests for young children include tests that screen children for potential educational problems, tests that diagnose the nature of these problems, tests that measure children's school readiness, and tests of curriculum outcomes.

Any test or other assessment method that is used should meet the established criteria for validity and reliability (American Educational Research Association, American Psychological Association, & National Council on Measurement in Education, 1985). In the assessment of young children's performance, developmental validity (appropriateness to children's developmental levels) and predictive validity (prediction of children's later school success or failure) have special importance.

Tests that resemble academic achievement tests, including many readiness tests, are wholly inappropriate for young children in content, format, and the sustained attention that they require. Except for carefully defined intellectual skills, most young children are not ready for many of the skills of reading and arithmetic computation expected in elementary school. Children's progress in developing academic skills does not need to be assessed before first grade. Early childhood education can indeed make a positive contribution to children's academic achievement in the long run but should not be expected to do so in the short run. Early childhood education does not speed up children's academic achievement; rather, it builds a solid foundation for it.

High/Scope's Child Observation Record is an example of an instrument used to assess developmentally valid curriculum outcomes through the systematic in-program observation of young children's performance by trained teachers or other observers. It is based on written records of children's performance over 6 weeks using the key experiences of language, representation, classification, seriation, number, spatial and temporal relations, movement, and social/emotional development. The Child Observation Record itself contains 32 items representing these key experiences. In a field test, interrater agreements on these items averaged 75% for exact agreements and 94% for close agreements (1 point apart on the 3- to 7-point scales). We recommend that persons using this measurement system have a thorough understanding of the High/Scope curriculum. Copies of the Child Observation Record and accompanying manual are available from the High/Scope Press, Ypsilanti, MI.

Putting It All Together

Every component addressed here is important to the operation of a high-quality early childhood program. The most important component is the child development curriculum. In fact, most of the other components directly support the implementation of this kind of curriculum. But it is still possible to strive for a high-quality program when obstacles prohibit the full realization of one or more of the components. For example, a kindergarten classroom with 25 or 30 children can nevertheless maintain a developmentally appropriate curriculum based on child-initiated learning activities. This is not a reason to become complacent about large class sizes, but neither is it a legitimate excuse to stop striving for high quality.

Outcomes of the Perry Preschool Program

The Perry Preschool Program, with a sample size of 123 children and very little attrition, demonstrated effects on children's school success and later on their socioeconomic success and social responsibility as young adults. Combined with other research, the empirical case for the value of good early childhood programs for children living in poverty is substantial.

Effects on School Success

Participants scored significantly higher on various tests of intellectual ability after one year of the Perry Preschool Program and maintained a significant advantage through the end of first grade. The IQ difference between experimental and control groups diminished over time, however, and by second grade was no longer statistically significant (Weikart, Bond, & McNeil, 1978). Nevertheless, early education led the subjects to increased academic achievement, as measured by standardized tests, throughout the elementary and middle-school grades. Teacher ratings of children's social and emotional maturity after kindergarten also showed significant overall trends favoring the group that had attended preschool (Weikart, Bond, & McNeil, 1978). By age 15, youths who had attended preschool placed a higher value on schooling and had stronger commitments to school than did the no-preschool group (Schweinhart & Weikart, 1980).

Through secondary school, youths who had attended preschool, as compared with the no-pre-

school subjects, had better grades and fewer failing grades. They were less likely to be classified as mentally retarded and spent fewer years in special education (for students considered handicapped) during their years in school, but were instead assigned more frequently to remedial, compensatory education (for students considered educationally disadvantaged). At age 19, persons who had attended preschool had higher scores than those with no preschool on a measure of literacy and competence in skills of everyday life (the Adult Performance Level Survey—American College Testing Program, 1976). They also expressed more favorable attitudes toward high school than did the other group.

Effects on Socioeconomic Success and Social Responsibility

Early education led subjects to better jobs, higher earnings and job satisfaction, and less unemployment by age 19. Subjects who had attended preschool were more likely to be supporting themselves on their own or their spouse's earnings at the time they were interviewed; they also reported receiving less public assistance than the no-preschool subjects. Examination of official records showed that preschool led to reduced use of general welfare assistance. Compared with the no-preschool subjects, a higher percentage of subjects who had attended preschool reported that they regularly saved money.

Fewer of the preschool subjects had ever been arrested, and that group had a lower total number of arrests. Youths who had attended preschool were less likely to come to the attention of juvenile authorities. Those with preschool had fewer offenses as adults than did those without preschool: More of the preschool subjects had records of committing no offenses and fewer had records of five or more offenses. Preschool also led to reductions in some types of self-reported delinquent behavior. Those who had attended preschool had lower median scores on a scale measuring delinquent-event frequencies weighted by seriousness. At age 19, women in the preschool group reported fewer pregnancies and births than did the women in the no-preschool group. Figure 5–1 summarizes Perry study findings at age 19.

A General Causal Model

The Perry study combines with other research to support the following causal model of how high-

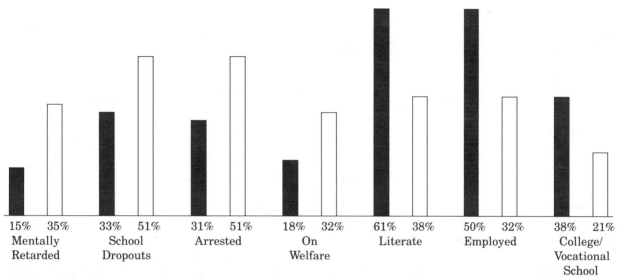

| 15% | 35% | 33% | 51% | 31% | 51% | 18% | 32% | 61% | 38% | 50% | 32% | 38% | 21% |
| Mentally
Retarded | | School
Dropouts | | Arrested | | On
Welfare | | Literate | | Employed | | College/
Vocational
School | |

Figure 5–1. High/Scope Perry Preschool study age 19 findings. All group differences are statistically significant, *p* < .05, two-tailed. Data on retarded and dropouts came from school records (*N* = 112); arrests from police records (*N* = 121); welfare from social services records (*N* = 120); literacy from a performance test (*N* = 109); employment and postsecondary enrollment from self-report (*N* = 121). The original *N* was 123.

quality early childhood programs help poor children. First, there is abundant evidence that high-quality early childhood programs do prepare poor children better for the intellectual and social demands of schooling, as measured for example by IQs and teacher ratings (McKey et al., 1985). Second, these children experience less failure as they begin school and probably assume a more favorable position in the school success flow, as measured by placement on grade versus retention in grade or placement in special education (Lazar et al., 1982; Schweinhart & Weikart, 1980). Third, the Perry study and a few others show that preschool participation, via increased school success, can lead to greater success and social responsibility in adult life (Berrueta-Clement et al., 1984).

Cost–Benefit Analysis

An economic cost–benefit analysis of the Perry Preschool Program and its long-term effects revealed that the program was an excellent investment for taxpayers, returning $6 for every dollar invested in a 1-year program and $3 for every dollar invested in a 2-year program (based on constant dollars discounted at 3% annually). In the words of the research and policy committee of the Committee for Economic Development (1985), "It would be hard to imagine that society

could find a higher yield for a dollar of investment than that found in preschool programs for its at-risk children" (p. 44).

The total benefits to taxpayers for the program (in constant 1981 dollars discounted at 3% annually), depicted in Figure 5–2, were about $28,000 per participant, about six times the size of the annual program operation cost of $5,000 per participant. For each program participant, taxpayers saved about $5,000 for special education programs, $3,000 for crime, and $16,000 for welfare assistance. Additional postsecondary education costs added about $1,000 per participant. Because of increased lifetime earnings (predicted because of more years of school completed), the average participant was expected to pay $5,000 more in taxes.

One child-year of the Perry Preschool Program cost about the same as one student-year in a special education classroom. It cost about 80% as much as one year of college education. It cost less than half as much as imprisoning a criminal for a year. The Perry Program was a novel program under development rather than a test of cost efficiency. It was relatively expensive because it maintained a teacher–child ratio of 1:5 to 1:6. The same kind of program has demonstrated equally good results when it had a teacher–child ratio of 1:8 and even 1:10. With such ratios, the program cost of approximately $5,000 per child-

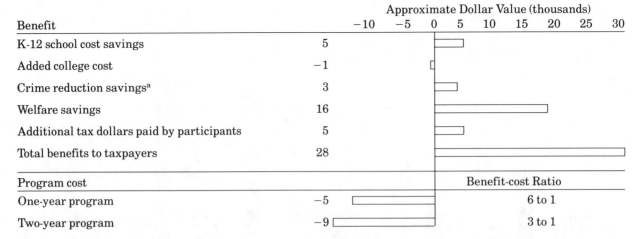

Benefit		Approximate Dollar Value (thousands)
		−10 −5 0 5 10 15 20 25 30
K-12 school cost savings	5	
Added college cost	−1	
Crime reduction savings[a]	3	
Welfare savings	16	
Additional tax dollars paid by participants	5	
Total benefits to taxpayers	28	
Program cost		**Benefit-cost Ratio**
One-year program	−5	6 to 1
Two-year program	−9	3 to 1

Figure 5–2. Perry Preschool program per-child costs and benefits to taxpayers. Table entries are constant 1981 dollars, discounted at 3% annually. Based on findings from J. R. Berrueta-Clement et al., *Changed lives: The effects of the Perry Preschool program on youths through age 19,* Monographs of the High/Scope Educational Research Foundation, 8 (Ypsilanti, MI: High/Scope Press, 1984, p. 91).
[a]Savings to citizens as taxpayers and as potential crime victims.

year could be reduced to as little as $3,000 per child-year (in 1981 dollars).

Family Socioeconomic Status and Early Childhood Education

These findings apply to children who live in poverty and are at risk of school failure. There is less evidence of preschool program effectiveness for children who are not poor or otherwise at risk of school failure. Evaluation of the Brookline Early Education Project (BEEP) in Massachusetts found that the school problems of participating middle-class children were reduced by a comprehensive 5-year intervention program, but only to a modest extent. At the end of Grade 2, 14% of BEEP's middle-class participants exhibited inappropriate classroom learning behavior, compared with 28% of the control group; 19% of participants had difficulty in reading, compared with 32% of the control group (Pierson, Walker, & Tivnan, 1984).

The Perry Preschool study and other research on early childhood education testify to the universal importance of good early childhood experience, in families and in programs. Poverty is not a permanent characteristic of a person; it is an environmental condition, just as a preschool program is an environmental condition. From this perspective, the Perry study and studies like it are not so much comparisons between a program and the lack of a program as they are comparisons between environments for young children that vary in quality. The finding is that develop-

mentally rich environments are much better for children than are developmentally poor environments. Thus, a developmentally poor early childhood program is not good for children, and a developmentally rich family environment, regardless of family income, is good for children.

The Prevalence of Early Childhood Program Quality

The quality of today's early childhood programs, then, will affect the development of the children who attend these programs—regardless of whether these children come from high-, middle-, or low-income families and regardless of whether these programs are viewed as nursery schools or as child-care programs. Similarly, the quality of young children's homes will affect their development, but this is a matter that is not directly open to public policy development.

According to the U.S. Bureau of the Census (1986), parents reported that 39% of 3- and 4-year-olds were enrolled in nursery school or other organized educational programs in 1985. On the basis of an earlier analysis (National Center for Education Statistics, 1982), we estimate that two thirds of these children were in child-care programs with organized educational activities and that one third of them were in nursery school programs. Given that the labor force participation rate for mothers of children under age 6 was 57% in 1987 (U.S. Bureau of Labor Statistics, 1987), we estimate that an additional 32% of 3- and 4-year-olds are in child-care settings that do not, in parents' judgments, provide organized educational activities. We suspect that most of these children are among the 27% of children under age 5 whose primary child-care arrangements are with family members or other relatives, rather than the 17% who receive care from nonrelatives in private homes or the 13% who receive child care in centers or schools (U.S. Bureau of the Census, 1987b). Much of the care provided by family members is surely of the highest quality; we are simply suggesting that mothers are less likely to characterize such care as including "organized educational activities."

The importance of early childhood is underscored by its position at the nexus between private, family concerns and public concerns. This position also explains the ambiguity about the prevalence of quality in the settings where young children spend their time. Society is reluctant to assess the quality of family environments for young children, yet considers it important to assess the program environments of young children. The overlap between family and program environments for 27% of children under age 5 exacerbates the dilemma.

In the absence of widespread assessments of the quality of early childhood programs in the United States, it is still important to consider the achievability of quality. The research cited here suggests that a good early childhood program can take place in any setting that has adequate resources and qualified staff—in a private nursery school, a public school, a Head Start program, a day-care center, or a day-care home. Each type of setting has its strengths and weaknesses.

Because schools, federal agencies, and private agencies and individuals can all provide good early childhood programs, we believe that they all deserve support through public policies and appropriate funding, in the foreseeable political future. This approach helps minimize the turf battles that inevitably occur when funds are exclusively assigned to one type of agency. It also recognizes the variety of existing program providers. Of course, a designated agency or department must still be selected to distribute the funds, both at the state and local levels, in a demonstrably impartial manner.

How to Start a Preschool Program

Starting a preschool program means meeting a community need that is not already addressed by other community agencies. The first step, then,

in planning a preschool program is to assess the number of children in the population to be served and the number already receiving the service. The best way to identify preschool programs is to check with the community's child-care referral agency, if there is one, or to check with the local department of social services and the phone book. The decennial U.S. census provides the best estimates of numbers of children of specified age and demographic characteristics in a designated geographic area of the country. If the unmet need is not great enough, a new preschool program should not be initiated. If the unmet need is great enough, it would be wise to communicate with agencies already providing preschool programs so that they recognize that the new program does not constitute a threat to their current level of service provision.

The next step in developing a preschool program is to identify the funding and resources available. If parental fees are a source of funding, these fees can be set in light of current fees for similar services in the community and the calculation of the program's operating budget. A high-quality program will cost more than a merely adequate one, so the need for quality must be built into the program's advertising and parent education from the beginning. If funding for the program is sought from the government, foundations, or other donors, a fund-raising effort must be planned and implemented. A key question is whether available funds are already being provided to operating programs. Generally, government agencies and foundations will require the submission of a proposal including a carefully considered plan of program operation.

Once funds are secured or a funding plan is in operation, staff can be hired. The most important background requirement to consider in hiring teaching staff is that they have training in early childhood development. Experience in early childhood programs is also important, as is the ability to get along well with children and adults. Identifying a program site is obviously an early step along with purchasing materials. Input from a trained, experienced early childhood teacher is very helpful throughout this process.

After the program begins, its quality should be maintained as previously described. Compromises may have to be made from time to time, but a program that makes too many compromises with quality over the long haul may not be worth the effort. For instance, an extraordinary teacher can operate a good early childhood program with 20 4-year-olds. But this teacher is likely to expend excessive energy to bring this about and may well look to other career options after a time. The wise preschool program provider will do what it takes to get a teaching assistant for this teacher and reduce the staff–child ratio to 1 to 10.

The Need for Advocacy

Despite the persuasive arguments for high-quality early childhood programs for children who live in poverty, nearly two thirds of such 4-year-olds in the United States still do not receive an early childhood education program regardless of level of quality (Center for Education Statistics, 1986). The federal government provides a billion dollars a year for Head Start and about a billion dollars a year for various child care programs. Half of the states now provide about a third of a billion dollars in state funding for early childhood programs for children at risk of school failure (Schweinhart, Koshel, & Bridgman, 1987). This is not enough.

Funding and the provision of programs are not enough, unless these programs are of the quality necessary to ensure long-term effects. The wise investor seeks the greatest return on investment at the lowest risk. The Perry Preschool study suggests that the public preschool investor will get the greatest return at an acceptable risk level on a high-quality program, as defined here, provided for children at risk of school failure. Of course, acceptable risk is still risk. Research decreases risks but does not provide guarantees. Research on good early childhood programs for poor children is scientifically valid and presents the prospects of high return on investment, both economically and in terms of human lives. The risk is surely worth it.

References

American College Testing Program. (1976). *User's guide: Adult APL survey.* Iowa City, IA: American College Testing Program.

American Educational Research Association, American Psychological Association, & National Council on Measurement in Education. (1985). *Standards for educational and psychological testing.* Washington, DC: American Psychological Association.

Berrueta-Clement, J. R., Schweinhart, L. J., Barnett, W. S., Epstein, A. S., & Weikart, D. P. (1984). *Changed lives: The effects of the Perry Preschool Program on youths through age 19* (Monographs of the High/Scope Educational Research Foundation, No. 8). Ypsilanti, MI: High/Scope Press.

Center for Education Statistics. (1986). Pre-school enrollment: Trends and implications. In *The condition of education.* Washington, DC: Superintendent of Documents.

Collins, R. (1979). *The credential society.* New York: Academic Press.

Committee for Economic Development, Research and Policy Committee. (1985). *Investing in our children.* Washington, DC: Author.

Consortium for Longitudinal Studies. (1983). *As the twig is bent: Lasting effects of preschool programs.* Hillsdale, NJ: Erlbaum.

Education Commission of the States. (1983). *The third national mathematics assessment: Results, trends and issues.* Denver: Author.

Elliott, D. S., Ageton, S. S., & Canter, R. J. (1979). An integrated theoretical perspective on delinquent behavior, *Journal of Research in Crime and Delinquency, 16,* 3–27.

Epstein A. S. (1985). Quality in early childhood programs: Four perspectives. In *High/Scope Early Childhood Policy Papers* (No. 3, pp. 1–9). Ypsilanti, MI: High/Scope Press. (ERIC Document ED 262 903).

Goodwin, W. L., & Driscoll, L. A. (1980). *Handbook for measurement and evaluation in early childhood education.* San Francisco: Jossey-Bass.

Harms, T., & Clifford, R. M. (1980). *Early Childhood Environment Rating Scale.* New York: Teachers College Press.

Hill, M. S., & Ponza, M. (1983). Poverty and welfare dependence across generations. *Economic Outlook USA,* 61–64. Ann Arbor, MI: Institute for Social Research.

Hohmann, M., Banet, B., & Weikart, D. P. (1979). *Young children in action: A manual for preschool educators.* Ypsilanti, MI: High/Scope Press.

Jencks, C. (1979). *Who gets ahead? The determinants of economic success in America.* New York: Basic Books.

Kamii, C. (1986). Autonomy vs. heteronomy. *Principal, 66*(1), 68–70.

Katz, L. G. (1985). Dispositions in early childhood education. *ERIC/EECE Bulletin, 18*(2), 1 & 3.

Lazar, I., Darlington, R., Murray, H., Royce, J., & Snipper, A. (1982). Lasting effects of early education, *Monographs of the Society for Research in Child Development, 47,*(2–3), 1–151.

Loeber, R., & Dishion, T. (1983). Early predictors of male delinquency: A review. *Psychological Bulletin, 94,* 68–99.

McKey, R. H., Condelli, L., Ganson, H., Barrett, B., McConkey, C., & Plantz, M. (1985). *The impact of Head Start on children, families and communities* (Final Report of the Head Start Evaluation, Synthesis, and Utilization Project). Washington, DC: CSR, Inc.

National Association for the Education of Young Children. (1984). *Accreditation criteria & procedures of the National Academy of Early Childhood Programs.* Washington, DC: Author.

National Association for the Education of Young Children. (1986a). NAEYC position statement on developmentally appropriate practice in early childhood programs serving children from birth to age 8. *Young Children, 41*(6), 4–19.

National Association for the Education of Young Children. (1986b). NAEYC position statement on developmentally appropriate practice in programs for 4- and 5-year-olds. *Young Children, 41*(6), 20–29.

National Center for Education Statistics. (1982). *Preprimary enrollment 1980.* Washington, DC: Author.

National Center for Education Statistics. (1983). *Two years in high school: The status of 1980 sophomores in 1982.* Washington, DC: Author.

National Governors' Association. (1987). *Results in education: 1987.* Washington, DC: Author.

Piaget, J. (1970). Piaget's theory. In P. H. Mussen (Ed.), *Carmichael's manual of child psychology* (3rd ed., pp. 703–732). New York: Wiley.

Piaget, J., & Inhelder, B. (1969). *The psychology of the child.* New York: Basic Books.

Pierson, D. E., Walker, D. K., & Tivnan, T. (1984). A school-based program from infancy to kindergarten for children and their parents. *The personnel and Guidance Journal, 62,* 448–455.

Ruopp, R., Travers, J., Glantz, F., & Coelen, C. (1979). *Children at the center: Summary findings and policy implications of the National Day Care study* (Vol. 1). Cambridge, MA: Abt Associates.

Schweinhart, L. J., Koshel, J. J., & Bridgman, A. (1987). Policy options for preschool programs. *Phi Delta Kappan, 68,* 524–529.

Schweinhart, L. J., & Weikart, D. P. (1980). *Young children grow up: The effects of the Perry Preschool program on youths through age 15* (Monographs of the High/Scope Educational Research Foundation, No. 7). Ypsilanti, MI: High/Scope Press.

Schweinhart, L. J., Weikart, D. P., & Larner, M. B. (1986). Consequences of three preschool curriculum models through age 15. *Early Childhood Research Quarterly, 1*(1), 15–35.

Spodek, B. (Ed.). (1982). *Handbook of research in early childhood education: Part V. Research methods in early childhood education.* New York: Free Press.

Travers, J., & Goodson, B. D. (1980). *Research results of the National Day Care study* (Final report of the National Day Care Study, Vol. 2). Cambridge, MA: Abt Associates.

U.S. Bureau of the Census. (1986). *School enrollment–Social and economic characteristics of students: October 1985 (Advance report)* (Current Population Reports, Series P-20, No. 409). Washington, DC: U.S. Government Printing Office.

U.S. Bureau of the Census. (1987a). *Money income and poverty status of families and persons in the United States: 1986 (Advance data from the March 1987 Current Population Survey)* (Current Population Reports, Series P-60, No. 157). Washington, DC: U.S Government Printing Office.

U.S. Bureau of the Census. (1987b). *Who's minding the kids? Child care arrangements: Winter 1984–85* (Series P-70, No.9). Washington, DC: U.S. Government Printing Office.

U.S. Bureau of Labor Statistics. (1987). *Over half of mothers of children one year old or under in labor force in March 1987* (News release USDL 87-345). Washington, DC: Author.

Weikart, D. P., Bond, J. T., & McNeil, J. T. (1978). *The Ypsilanti Perry Preschool Project: Preschool years and longitudinal results through fourth grade* (Monographs of the High/Scope Educational Research Foundation, No. 3). Ypsilanti, MI: High/Scope Press.

Weikart, D. P., Deloria, D, Lawser, S., & Wiegerink, R. (1970). *Longitudinal results of the Ypsilanti Perry Preschool Project* (Monographs of the High/Scope Educational Research Foundation, No. 1). Ypsilanti, MI: High/Scope Press.

Weikart, D. P., Epstein, A. S., Schweinhart, L. J., & Bond, J. T. (1978). *The Ypsilanti Preschool Curriculum Demonstration Project: Preschool years and longitudinal results* (Monographs of the High/Scope Educational Research Foundation, No. 4). Ypsilanti, MI: High/Scope Press.

Weikart, D. P., & Schweinhart, L. J. (1987). The High/Scope Cognitively Oriented Curriculum in early education. In J. L. Roopnarine & J. E. Johnson (Eds.), *Approaches to early childhood education* (pp. 253–268). Columbus, OH: Charles E. Merrill Co.

SECTION
II

Prevention Programs for Children and Youth

In this section, the authors present five exemplary primary prevention programs for children and youth. The 1978 President's Commission on Mental Health described children and youth as seriously *under*served groups. The Commission argued that "repair" services available to these groups were both limited and restricted in effectiveness. Effective alternatives seemed urgently needed.

The flexibility and adaptability of children and youth make them ideal targets for prevention programs, many of which can be set naturally in educational contexts. The view that building health and wellness from the start can forestall serious and costly problems for individuals and for society has increasing appeal recently.

The conviction that children and youth are prime targets for prevention programming turns attention naturally to the social institutions that shape their development, that is, the family and the school. Both merit serious consideration in prevention planning. The primary importance of families and the parent–child transaction, as forces that shape well-being, was illustrated in section I on preventive programs for very young children.

Schools, however, offer real advantages in logistics and accessibility for preventive programming with older children and youth. All children in modern society spend 30–35 hours a week for many years in school. There, they find key mentors and identification models. Because children come together in schools under a single roof and

administrative aegis and because education is a natural vehicle for prevention, schools offer special opportunities for preventive programming. Moreover, when prevention models are shown to be effective, schools (and their curricula) provide ideal mechanisms for constructively shaping the lives of thousands of children. Much of the excitement of the program models described in this section stems from that realization. Four of these programs are school based.

Both Shure and Spivack's and Rotheram-Borus' class-based programs, presented in chapters 6 and 7 respectively, train skills and competencies known to enhance children's adjustment. Both rest on the knowledge base that maladjusted or clinical groups lack those skills and that the presence of those skills promotes good adjustments. The well-documented Hahnemann program, described by Shure and Spivack, trains children in a family of interpersonal problem-solving skills including the abilities to generate alternative solutions and to evaluate their consequences. Young children have been shown to acquire those skills both in school- and home-training programs; as they acquire those skills, their adjustment improves. Moreover, both skill and adjustment gains have been shown to have staying power. Detailed program-training manuals are now available from preschool through the elementary range. The program is being widely implemented in schools in Philadelphia and elsewhere. The precepts of the Hahnemann program are reflected in many other prevention programs, including substance abuse prevention programs, across the full elementary and secondary range.

Rotheram-Borus' carefully evaluated program, based on a rationale and structural principles similar to the Hahnemann program, teaches a family of appropriate assertiveness skills (i.e., thoughts, feelings and behavior that help children to realize personal goals in a socially acceptable manner). The program rests on a knowledge base that children and youth who lack these skills have adjustment problems. Once again, children and youth were found to acquire the program skills and to improve on teacher-rated behavior, peer popularity measures, and school performance indices. Those gains were maintained 1 year later in new classes with new teachers. These two programs illustrate a school-based, curricular, preventive approach to promoting psychological wellness. The challenges that remain are to accelerate dissemination of such documented programs and to develop related programs based on knowledge linking other families of competencies to wellness and sound educational development in children and youth.

Botvin and Tortu's intriguing life skills training program, described in chapter 8, "Preventing Adolescent Substance Abuse Through Life Skills Training," is targeted primarily to junior high school students and provides information about the negative consequences of substance abuse and how to resist social pressures. The life skills training program helps students to increase self-esteem and learn how to deal with social anxiety. The basic 12-session program, which can be taught by teachers, older peers, or both, is part of the school's seventh grade health curriculum. Briefer booster units are available for eighth and ninth graders. Demonstrations of significant reductions in cigarette smoking, marijuana use, alcohol consumption, and social anxiety and increases in independence, psychosocial knowledge, and improved attitudes have paved the way to more extensive program implementation. Both individuals and society stand to gain from such programming.

In chapter 9, "The School Transitional Environment Project," Felner and Adan's school-based work was fueled by data showing serious attendance and dropout problems among urban high school students. It, however, models a qualitatively different approach, that is, environmental modification. Directed to the often troublesome transition from junior high to high school, the program sought both to reduce the flux and complexity of that transition and to provide significant sources of support during that critical pe-

riod. Important short-term gains were shown in participants' attendance, grades, and self-concepts. Over the full high school period, participants had fewer absences, received better grades, and had a 22% lower dropout rate than the controls. The project has been replicated in a different geographic and sociocultural context with similar findings. If the estimate is correct that the average cost to society of a high school dropout now exceeds $10,000, then a low-cost program of this type has much to offer both in fiscal (i.e., cost-benefit) and human (i.e., realization of potential) terms.

Davidson and Redner's youth diversion program illustrates the important point that specifically targeted prevention programs can be carried out effectively in settings other than schools. Set within the juvenile justice (court) system, a goal of this program is to prevent the severe and continuing problems of youthful offenders. The work of carefully selected student and community volunteers includes relationship building, youth advocacy, family management activities, and one-on-one behavioral contracting with youthful offenders, 8 hours a week for 18 weeks. Among the project's unique features are its longitudinal nature and replication in three communities. Participating offenders had 50% lower recidivism rates and fewer police contacts than outright release or court-processed controls over a 2½-year follow-up period. This project also documents significant human and cost-benefit gains from a targeted prevention program.

The prevention programs for children and youth reported in this section range in (a) specificity versus generality of targeting; (b) settings in which they were conducted; and (c) the program's basic methodology (e.g., competence enhancement, social system modification, preventive intervention following crisis or transition). However, they share the vital qualities of an underlying preventive focus and demonstrable effectiveness.

The pioneering programs reported in this section have considerable modeling and heuristic value and illustrate that preventive programs for children and youth can work very effectively and are useful. Realistically, however, even taken together, they only scratch the surface of this innovative, exciting approach. There is a natural hand-in-glove relationship among prevention programming, children and youth, and the schools. With appropriate support, those relationships should flourish as the prevention field continues to develop.

Myrna B. Shure and George Spivack

6

Interpersonal Cognitive Problem Solving

Emory Cowen (1980) suggested that primary prevention's two key features are preventing dysfunction and promoting health. With these as objectives, our approach to prevention introduces interpersonal cognitive problem solving to children. Its most important feature is that children are not taught what to think or do, but how to think so they can decide for themselves what, and what not, to do. Therefore, when we talk about thinking, we are talking about solving typical, everyday problems that come up with others. We have found that those who are able to do that are better adjusted than those who cannot think that way, or those who are restricted in their freedom to think that way.

Educators and clinicians have assumed that relieving emotional tension paves the way for one to think straight. These programs support the reverse idea—that ability to think straight paves the way for emotional relief, prevents dysfunction, and promotes health.

Goals and Issues

What problem-solving thinking skills differentiate between children who show behavior problems and those who do not? How early can we distinguish them?

Thinking Skills

Two such skills clearly distinguished children as early as age four. One, *alternative-solution think-*ing, is the ability to think of multiple ways to solve an interpersonal problem such as how one child can get to play with a toy another child will not give up. If a child asks and is refused, the child might hit the other child with the toy, not as an impulsive reaction to frustration, but because the child has decided that hitting is one way to get the toy. If so, the next question is whether the child also thought about the potential consequences of hitting and whether that might have influenced the decision to hit. The child might have foreseen that he or she could be hit back and was not concerned. If the child goes ahead and does it anyway, it could be because he or she could not think of anything else to do.

Initial research was supported by the Hahnemann NIH Institutional grant 720–20–0150 through its daughter grant mechanism. Subsequent research with 4- and 5-year-olds was supported by grant #20372, and with 10- to 12-year-olds by #s MH 27741 and MH 35989, all from National Institute of Mental Health, Washington, DC.

For our enterprise, from research to training programs, we are indebted to Milton Goldberg, then executive director of the early childhood programs, and Irvin J. Farber, director of research of the School District of Philadelphia, who gave us support from the beginning, as did the administrative staff of the Philadelphia Get Set Prekindergarten Program: Jeffrey O. Jones, followed by Bertram Snead (directors); Rosemary Mazzatenta (assistant director), and Vivian Ray (chief psychologist). Without the efforts of the many supervisors and principals, our work would have been impossible. The teachers and parents who participated in training deserve special tribute for the creative suggestions for improving the program scripts. But it was that disarming troupe of critics, ages four and five, who provoked us to constant change. It is an open question whether they or we learned more.

Behaviors

We learned that children who cannot think of more than a couple of ways to solve these kinds of problems, and who are unable or unlikely to think of consequences to acts, are often impatient (i.e., "I have to have it now"), overemotional, aggressive, unaware or unconcerned about the feelings of others, less likely to be liked by other children, or possibly overly timid, withdrawn, or shy. Our research findings with 4- and 5-year-old children in urban settings at or below the poverty level (Shure, Spivack, & Jaeger, 1971), confirmed by research findings for low- and middle-socioeconomic groups (e.g., Granville et al., 1976; Olson, Johnson, Belleau, Parks, & Barrett, 1983; Snyder & Shanks, 1982; Turner & Boulter, 1981), also apply to older children (e.g., Asarnow & Callan, 1985; McKim, Weisserg, Cowen, Gesten, & Rapkin, 1982; Richard & Dodge, 1982; Shure, 1980).

We call these skills Interpersonal Cognitive Problem Solving (ICPS). If these skills distinguish adjustment groups in relatively normal children, would enhancing them through an intervention reduce the need for impulsivity, inhibition, or other dysfunctional behaviors? Indeed, could such interventions help prevent these kinds of behaviors from occurring at all?

On the basis of our early research (Shure & Spivack, 1970), we concluded that it is the process of problem solving and not the content of solutions that contributes to behavioral adjustment in the long run. In any one instance, the problem solution an individual thinks of may play a part in what he or she does. However, the real question concerns the process the person went through in coming to that solution. Was it one of a number of possibilities? Did the person consider and weigh consequences? In this sense, we are interested in how children think in contrast to what they think. Although impulsive youngsters may focus on negative, forceful ways of getting a toy (e.g., hit or grab), inhibited children may focus on saying "please." After concluding that being stuck on one solution was more critical than the solution's content, we decided that ICPS training should concentrate on a process, not on content. Thus, ICPS, which the children called, I Can Problem Solve, was born.

Rationale for ICPS Skills as Focus of Intervention

The ICPS approach is based on the premise that people who are preoccupied with the end goal rather than how to obtain it, who cannot think through ways to solve a typical interpersonal problem, or who do not consider consequences and the possibility of alternative routes to the goal are susceptible to impulsive mistakes, frustration, aggressive behavior, or evasion of problems by withdrawal. In any case, initial needs remain unabated; if such behaviors occur repeatedly, unpleasant emotions are aroused, interpersonal relationships suffer, and varying degrees of maladaptive behaviors ensue. An implicit assumption is that the availability of ICPS thinking facilitates interpersonal adjustment and psychological health. Our programs have put this assumption to the test.

The Need for ICPS Intervention

There is increasing evidence that antisocial or aggressive behavior, rebelliousness, poor peer relations, and poor academic achievement are significant early predictors of later psychopathology (Cowen, Pederson, Babigian, Izzo, & Trost, 1973; Kohlberg, Ricks, & Snarey, 1984; Roff, 1970), delinquency (Loeber, 1982; Spivack, Marcus, & Swift, 1986), alcohol and substance abuse (Smith & Fogg, 1979), and indeed all three (O'Neil & Robins, 1958). Although the risk status of withdrawn behavior is less clear, recent data suggest that extreme withdrawal that persists over several years increases risk for internalizing problems such as depression (Rubin, 1985).

Longitudinal data indicated that, by the third grade, up to one third of the children in the Philadelphia public schools exhibited poor coping skills and that behaviors in kindergarten defined high-risk patterns for subsequent special placement, grade retention, academic problems, and behavioral maladjustment (Spivack & Swift, 1977; Spivack, Rapsher, Cohen, & Gross, 1978). Because ICPS-deficient youngsters are more likely than ICPS-competent ones to display the behaviors that predict more serious problems later, it seems desirable to implement ICPS training programs as early in life as possible.

Issues of Implementation

Several important implementation issues of our program may differ from those of other interventions; these issues set the stage for a description of the program itself.

Four issues that concern every program implementer are (a) when to intervene, (b) with whom,

(c) how, and (d) for how long. For us, strategies in these matters were guided by our initial testing of children, by what we observed that children actually do and say, and by the theoretical position that served as a springboard for our approach.

When. The earliest age that our measures of problem-solving thinking skills could distinguish behavior groups was age four (Shure & Spivack, 1970). Although measured verbal skills (e.g., ability to talk in complete sentences) did not relate to the number of solutions or consequences a child could offer, many 3-year-olds in urban settings at or below the poverty level did not have enough language for us to measure their problem-solving abilities.

Who. Although the ICPS approach is applicable to anyone and is associated with behavioral adjustment in diverse populations (Spivack, Platt, & Shure, 1976), we chose to implement our interventions with urban, poor children. Because of community or childrearing circumstances, these children are at relatively greater risk for behavioral dysfunction and interpersonal maladjustment than are higher income youngsters.

Should such training be targeted only to those who are already showing deficits that predict later dysfunction, or would mass targeting (in our case, training the whole classroom) ultimately be more effective? In our school-based program, we chose mass targeting because (a) more youngsters can be reached in shorter time periods; (b) it can provide help for unidentified false negatives—those incorrectly identified as not being at risk; (c) as a child-responding program, initially ICPS-competent youngsters help to avoid group silence; and (d) no one would feel left out. On the assumptions that ICPS intervention would do no one harm and that no matter how good a problem solver one is, one can always get better, we included everyone in the class. The children were trained by the teacher in small groups.

How. In our initial testing of children, we learned that adjusted children could think of negative, forceful ways to obtain a toy from another child just as the poorly adjusted children could, but adjusted children could also think of more nonforceful ways (Shure & Spivack, 1970). Our goal was not to take away what poorly adjusted children already knew but to help them think about what they can do, how what they do might affect themselves and others (consequences), and then to discover that there is more than one way to solve a problem (alternatives). We believe that teaching children to think of their own solutions to problems and consequences to acts enhances their understanding of what to do in interpersonal situations. If our theoretical view of interpersonal problem solving is correct, children's social adjustment and interpersonal competence should be guided more by how, than by what, they think.

ICPS-trained children are guided to problem solve during the day when real problems occur. The transition from formal teaching of key program concepts to use in real situations is an advantage of having the teacher as trainer, rather than having a person who comes to the child for a limited amount of time (e.g., a school psychologist or counselor).

How long. The preschool and kindergarten formal curricula take 4 months to complete if conducted daily. The informal use of the approach during the day should be continued as long as the children are in school.

How the Program Works

The format of the nursery program is a script (Shure & Spivack, 1971b; Spivack & Shure, 1974), upgraded in sophistication for use in kindergarten (Shure & Spivack, 1974a). Teachers work with small groups of 6–10 children for about 20 minutes per day. It is best to mix talkative with quiet youngsters. The formal program script includes both prerequisite thinking skills and key substantive, problem-solving skills to be learned.

Formal Didactics

Certain basic language concepts must be understood before a child can perceive alternative solutions and consequences to a problem. These prerequisite concepts are the precursors to thinking of alternative solutions and consequences and to the final ICPS skills to be learned.

Language, thinking, and paying attention. (approximately 10–12 lessons) During the 1st and 2nd weeks, depending on the class' pace, consider basic word concepts integral to alternative-solution and consequential thinking.

Teaching the concept of negation, through the use of the word *not,* is important: A child can later decide what and what not to do and whether something is or is not a good idea. With games centered on interpersonal relationships, one game a kindergarten teacher plays with the children is to say, "If I tap my knee, sit still. If I do not tap my knee, raise your hand." With variations on body movements, teachers also play games with various combinations of "Your name is not Rochelle"; sometimes the teacher tries to trick a child by pointing to Rochelle.

The words *some* and *all* help children to learn to recognize that particular solutions may succeed with some people but not succeed with all people. Thus, they come to appreciate that friends like to play with them some of the time but not all of the time, and that they can have or do what they want some of the time. The word *or* helps youngsters learn to think about more than one way to solve a problem: "I can do this or I can do that." Inherent in problem solving is the idea that there may be more than one element about a person to consider before taking action. When children learn that a teacher is simultaneously angry at a child *and* busy talking to that child, they can recognize that it would be a bad time to ask the teacher for something. After introducing these word concepts one at a time, a teacher may say "I am thinking of Allan, Robert, William, and Paul. Am I thinking of all of the boys or some of the boys in this room?"

To enhance the child's ability to reason in terms of cause-and-effect and appreciation of consequences, including people's feelings, the teacher introduces the concept of *if . . . then*. "If I do this, then he might feel sad," or "If I do that, then he might not play with me." To introduce this concept the teacher may say "If I am thinking of a girl, then I am not thinking of ———. Children would respond, "a boy" or "Steven."

The words *same* and *different* can help children to develop the habit of thinking of a variety of solution categories: "I can think of something different to do." The child can also learn to recognize, for example, that hitting and kicking are the same idea; they are both hurting. Asking is different from hurting. To teach these words, the teacher can use a popular game having the group perform various body movements. First, they are encouraged to do the same thing such as clap their hands, then to think of something different such as stomp their feet. In addition to helping the child think about whether an idea is or is not a good one and then think of something different to do, these games also serve as a precursor to sensitivity to others, because they require each child to notice what others around them are doing.

How people feel. (approximately 20 lessons) The next couple of weeks, again depending on the class' pace, focus on identification of, and sensitivity to, feelings about self and others. Building on the first set of games, children learn to identify a youngster who is and is not smiling and who is and is not crying. Using *if . . . then* logic, the child learns to identify and label emotions; for example, "if he is crying, then he is sad." Earlier concepts further help the child to identify emotions by recognition of who is and is not smiling (i.e., happy) and crying (i.e., sad), and that happy and sad are different feelings. If people's feelings are considered in decision making, it is necessary to identify and to be able to verbalize them.

After children can identify another's feelings in a problem situation, they must learn to be sensitive to those feelings. In addition to recognizing that different people can feel differently about the same thing, becoming sensitive to the preferences of others is also important in deciding what to do. "I like to swim, but he does not." The ability to evaluate with perspective helps a child who wants a toy from his friend to think about what would make that friend happy and what would not. Children learn that different people can like different things, and that is acceptable. Children learn that they can think about what people like and about how people feel by watching what people do, hearing what people say, or by asking people if they are not sure. Learning that everybody does not choose the same thing is important because many young children assume others would choose what they would like, which often leads to faulty conclusions and therefore unsuccessful solutions. Using pictures of foods, forms of transportation, animals, or places, a child is first asked what he or she would choose if given the choice of playing in the park or being sick in bed. Then, that child is asked what he or she thought another child might choose. Some choose being sick in bed because "Mommy brings me presents." To discover things about others, the child is asked "How can you find out?" and then encouraged, if necessary, to ask.

Beyond recognizing and finding out about others' feelings, children begin to think about ways to influence them. A new concept, *maybe* is introduced. "Maybe he likes to paint and maybe he does not." Using previously learned concepts, the child thinks about the idea that it is possible to like more than one thing such as blocks and running; if one way to make someone happy is not successful, it is possible to try a different way.

To understand that consequences are in direct relationship to cause-and-effect, that is, "Sarah hit Jimmy *because* Jimmy hit Sarah first," children must not only learn to understand cause-and-effect, but also to think in such a way that they will see the causal connection between an act and its consequence(s). The words *might* and *maybe* are important in cause-and-effect in human relations. Preceding causes may not be a certainty. The *why* and *because* connectives are also useful in situations where a problem can be avoided (e.g., "I fell because I ran too fast."). Emphasis is also placed on thinking about why a child might be feeling happy, sad, or mad, and what another child might or could have done or said to make that child feel a particular way.

In one game a picture is shown of a child crying and the teacher says, "How is this boy feeling?" After the child says, "sad," the teacher follows with "He might be sad because . . . ." Pointing to another child in the picture, the teacher asks, "What can this boy do to make him feel happy again?" When the child answers, the teacher says, "That might make him happy," and then asks, "Can you think of something different he can do?"

Other word concepts help children learn to think: "I can play with that toy *later*, not *now*"; "I can wait till *after* you're finished"; or "If you will not play with me now, maybe you will play with me later." Children enjoy these word games and sometimes make up silly time sequences. "I do not brush my teeth *before* I get out of bed."

Problem solving. (approximately 15 lessons) After having mastered the word concepts and other prerequisite problem-solving skills, children can relate to games and dialogues needed to acquire the programs' major interpersonal problem-solving thinking skills. Interspersed with stories and simple role-playing games to maintain interest, this section (one third of the program) is divided into three parts: (a) alternative solutions, (b) consequences, and (c) solution–consequence pairing. Solutions and consequences are elicited from, not given to, the children. As the children grasp and generate program concepts, they can decide and evaluate for themselves what to do and what not to do when confronted with an interpersonal problem.

The goal for the first section, alternative solutions (i.e., there's more than one way), is to stimulate children to think of as many different solutions as possible to everyday interpersonal problem situations presented to them. Excerpts

from the kindergarten program may communicate the flavor of a typical lesson.

Script Narration for Alternative Solutions.

Problem: Girl wants her brother to let her push the grocery cart.

[Have the children repeat problem as stated]

Teacher: "O.K. Who can think of something this girl (*point*) can do so she can get a chance to push the cart?" (*response*) "That's one idea. She can . . . (*repeat child's idea*). Now the idea of this game is to think of lots of different ideas, lots of different ways this girl can get her brother to let her push the grocery cart. One way was to . . . (*again, repeat first response*). Can anyone think of a different (another, new) idea (way)?"

Avoid saying, "That's a good idea." The children will evaluate ideas themselves in later sections of the scripts. Instead say, "Good, you gave a different idea."

"That's a different idea! She can (*repeat first idea*) or she can (*repeat second idea*). Now we have two ways (*show two fingers*). I'm going to write all of your ideas on the board. Let's fill up the whole board (*a good motivating technique*). Who has another idea? (*If necessary, repeat the problem.*) O.K., now we have three (*show three fingers*) ideas! Way #1 was . . . or Way #2 was . . . or Way #3 was. . . . What else can she do?"

When children run out of ideas, proceed as follows:
"She can . . . " Repeat each solution given thus far, classifying enumerations. For enumerations (e.g., "give him candy, give him presents") repeat the solutions, classify them as "giving something" and ask for an idea that is different from giving something. "Or she can (*continue to repeat response*) or she can. . . ." (*when children are out of ideas, ask*) "What can she say? Let's fill up the whole board!"

Hints

Consistent Nonresponder

Children who have responded only minimally, often begin to parrot others' ideas. Such youngsters should not be pushed for a new idea. It is more important to praise them for having said something with a comment such as "Good, you told us too!" Another useful technique is to let the child hold a puppet, and ask the puppet for an idea instead of the child. Or, just tell the child to whisper his or her idea into the puppet's ear.

Disruptive Behavior

Concepts taught in the lesson can be applied to disruptive behaviors that occur during a lesson. Such behaviors should be assessed for whether the act is or is not provoked by another child, intentionally or not. For example, if Child A is genuinely blocking the view of Child B, and B pushes A out of A's chair, ask B, "How does that make A feel? What else can you do or say so A will get out of your way?" On the other hand, if B pushes A for no apparent reason, ask, in a nonthreatening way, why B did that. If the child says, "I don't know," or gives no reason, just ask, "How do you think A feels when you do that? Can you think of something to do or say now so A won't feel that way?"

Dominating Behavior

A child dominating the group can be asked, "How might we feel if one child has all the turns and some children do not have any?"

The goal for the second section, consequential thinking, is to guide children to think about what might happen next if a particular solution is carried out. Children are encouraged to identify all the consequences that they can to their own solutions, and then to decide whether their idea is or is not a good one. A concrete example of how children learn to evaluate their own ideas follows.

Script Narration for Consequential Thinking.

Problem: Girl wants children to let her play with them.

Teacher: "O.K., let's make up a different kind of story; a story about 'What might happen next?' Pretend that the girl pushed him. That's something the girl can do. I'm going to put that over here. (*Write the solution on the left side of the board, then draw a line down the middle.*) "Now listen carefully. This is a new question. If the girl pushes him what might happen next in the story?

O.K., Tanya, the boy might push her back. I'm going to write all the things that might happen next over here." (*Point to the right side of the board and write the consequence last given.*)

"Now let's think of lots of things that might happen next if the girl pushes the boy. Good, Steven told us what might happen next. The boy might cry."

Write his answer on the right side of board. Draw an arrow now from the solution to the two consequences given thus far. For example:

She could   ⟶ He might push her back.
push him.   ⟶ He might cry.

When no further thoughts are offered, switch to: "What might this boy (*point to boy*) do if this girl pushes him?"
"O.K., Greg, that's something he might do. He might tell his mother." (*Add this to the list.*)

She could   ⟶ He might push her back.
push him.   ⟶ He might cry.
              ⟶ He might tell his mother.

"Can anyone think of something different the boy might do?"
(*If not already offered, ask*), "What might the boy say to the girl if she (pushes him out of the way)? How might the boy feel if the girl (pushes him)? Do you think she might feel happy, sad, or mad?"

Add the response to the list on the board. When all thoughts have been completed, follow with:
"Maybe some of us think (pushing him) is a good idea. Maybe some of us think (pushing him) is not a good idea. If you think (pushing him) is a good idea, raise your hand.
Susan, why is (pushing him) a good idea?" (response) "O.K., Susan, maybe it is a good idea because. . . ." (*Repeat reply.*)
Ask each child with a raised hand, Why is it not a good idea? Have children evaluate nonforceful solutions such as "say please," "give her candy," etc., as well as forceful ones such as grabbing and hitting.

The goal for the final section, solution-consequence pairing, is to encourage children to offer a solution to a problem, follow it up with a consequence, return to the same problem for a second solution and its possible consequence, and so on. Such exercises provide experience in linking pairs of solutions and consequences. "If I do this, that might happen; If I do that, this might happen." For example, in trying to get help in putting toys away, a child might say, "Punch him if he won't help" (solution), "but he might punch me back" (consequence). "If I ask him" (solution), "he might help" (goal).

Informal Problem-Solving Dialogue Techniques

In addition to the formal didactics, the trainer is taught to extend the approach from helping children think about hypothetical people and their problems to helping them think about actual problems that arise during the day. An illustration of this dialoguing follows, based on an incident involving Billy, who pushed Michael off a bike.

> Teacher: Billy, why did you push Michael off that bike?
> Billy: I want it.
> Teacher: What *might* happen if you push him like that.
> Billy: He might fight.
> Teacher: Is pushing him off a good idea?
> Billy: Yep!
> Teacher: Why?
> Billy: He won't give it to me.
> Teacher: Pushing is one way to get the bike. Can you think of a *different* way to get him to let you ride the bike?
> Billy: (*turns to Michael*): Can I have it when you're finished? (Spivack & Shure, 1974, p. 60)

This conversation, although carefully guided by the teacher, still enhances prerequisite language skills and problem-solving cognition on the part of the child. First, the child (Billy) was communicating at a level at which he was capable. The dialogue used words and concepts that were taught in the program such as *not, might,* and *different.* Second, by using these words Billy was able to do his own thinking. Billy was asked why he pushed Michael off the bike (causal thinking). Then, he was asked if he thought that was a good idea because of his own understanding of what might happen next (consequential thinking). When it was clear that Billy was more interested in getting the bike than in the fact that Michael might fight, the teacher did not tell him what to do. Instead the teacher agreed casually that pushing is one way and guided him to think of a different solution to the problem (alternative thinking).

This example of problem-solving communication, which we call dialoguing, ended up with Michael suggesting, "Let's ride together." Although the final solution ended with Michael

continuing to ride the bike, Billy was satisfied with riding together. Instead of feeling dissatisfaction or frustration, these children felt good about their own decision.

Outcomes and Research Evidence

We tested the impact of repeating the curriculum with content variations in kindergarten and compared the impact of that with nursery school only, kindergarten only, and no training at all. What did the formal didactic program plus informal dialoguing do for the thinking and behavior of the children?

When Trained by Teachers

1. As measured by the Preschool Interpersonal Problem Solving test (PIPS) (Shure & Spivack, 1974b), trained youngsters, as compared to the control group, gave more relevant solutions to hypothetical problems (e.g., problems concerning one child wanting a toy from another and how to avert mother's anger after having damaged an object) after training than before it. As measured by the What Happens Next Game test (WHNG) (Shure & Spivack, 1974c), trained children also gave more potential consequences to acts such as grabbing a toy, and taking an object from an adult without first asking. In behavior, overimpulsiveness and inhibition were significantly reduced in trained youngsters, compared to the control group. Prosocial behaviors were significantly enhanced, as measured by the Hahnemann Pre-School Behavior Rating Scale (HPSB; Shure & Spivack, 1971a). In both nursery school and kindergarten, these gains were independent of IQ.

2. One year of training was sufficient for significant ICPS and behavior gains. If training did not occur at the nursery school level, kindergarten was not too late.

3. A significant link was found between ICPS skill gains, especially solution skills, and behavior gains that supported the view that ICPS abilities are significant mediators of overt behaviors.

4. At the 1- and 2-year follow-up points, gains were maintained. Trained youngsters who had not previously shown behavior problems were less likely than controls to begin showing them during the follow-up periods. The latter findings

highlight ICPS' preventive impact on inner city children before they enter the more demanding constraints of the primary grades. That non-trained youngsters began to show behavior difficulties in kindergarten or first grade confirms the designation of this population as high risk. These findings are consistent with Spivack and Swift's (1977) finding of increased maladaptation as inner city children move through the early grades. ICPS intervention significantly reversed that trend.

When Trained by Mothers

In addition to using teachers as trainers, the nursery school script was modified for use by mothers with a single child at home (Shure & Spivack, 1975; 1978). That project yielded the following major findings:

1. Replicating teacher-training research, mother-trained children improved significantly more than controls in both ICPS skills and behaviors, with the strongest link occurring between the trained solution skills and measured social adjustment and interpersonal competences.

2. Inner city mothers, many with little education, functioned effectively as trainers after having been given ICPS training of their own. Mothers' increased ability to think about and to solve hypothetical problems about children (e.g., two of her children are fighting) was closely related to how mothers guided their children to solve actual problems that arose (i.e., dialoguing). The combination of these two parenting skills had a direct impact on the child's ICPS skills. Research showed it was a change in the child's ICPS skills that had the most significant direct impact on behavior. Another group of children had been trained by mothers who administered the program lessons but who were not given ICPS training of their own. Those children also improved more in ICPS skills and behavior than did non-trained controls, but their improvements were not as great as the ones shown for children instructed by the group of mothers who had been trained. These findings suggest that greater benefit accrues to the child when both mother and child are taught to solve problems.

3. The improved behavior of children trained at home generalized to the school suggests that the benefits of acquiring ICPS mediating skills are not situation specific.

The body of findings cited thus far (Shure & Spivack, 1978; 1982b) demonstrated that ICPS training fosters mental health by building coping strategies in high-risk, but relatively normal, children. Both teachers and parents, many of the latter ICPS-deficient at the start, became effective training agents in relatively short time periods; this is important for preventionists to know when making choices about what to implement and who is trained to do such work.

Program's Positive Aspects and Limitations

Consideration of ICPS' positive and limiting factors can help to put this strategy into a more realistic perspective for potential users.

Positive Aspects

In addition to the encouraging research findings reported earlier, the program is a proactive solution for children at risk. The intervention goes beyond helping the trainer merely to understand children, in the hope that such understanding will lead to more effective communication. Rather, it actively engages the child to learn ICPS skills and how to use them.

The approach is a generic one, applicable to diverse racial, ethnic, and age groups. It applies to anyone who wants to think or learn to think for himself or herself. ICPS curricula have been created for youngsters through high school and young adulthood (Spivack, Platt, & Shure, 1976), as well as for youngsters in both lower and middle socioeconomic status groups (e.g., Camp & Bash, 1981; Elardo & Cooper, 1977; Weissberg, Gesten, Liebenstein, Schmid, & Hutton, 1979). They have also been created or adapted for abused youngsters and their parents (Nesbitt et al. 1980), for learning disabled youngsters (Weiner, 1978), and for emotionally disturbed children and their parents (Yu, Harris, Solovitz, & Franklin, 1986). On balance, evaluations of these programs are positive. Moreover, this diversity of program adaptations suggests that ICPS interventions are seen by people in mental health, education, and social welfare as having wide applicability and potential to prevent more serious behavioral dysfunction.

The program can be implemented without lengthy preparation. A trainer can use the curriculum as is or adapt it flexibly to present content (not concepts) in his or her own way. Moreover, the program's goals and relevance are quickly recognized by the user; its materials are readily available and have multipurpose potential at a modest cost with easy and natural integration into educational curricula, for example, in teaching colors, red is different from blue; in teaching numbers, 3 comes after 2 and before 4.

In addition to our formal research data showing that mother-trained youngsters generalized their behavior to school, informal interviews with parents of teacher-trained children suggested that ICPS training generalized to the home (Spivack & Shure, 1974). Parents reported, for example, that children used the words *same* and *different* at the dinner table (e.g., "A spoon is different from a knife." "We are all eating the same thing.") One mother reported that her son started to tell her how he felt. When given something he wanted he said, "That makes me happy." If he could not have what he wanted, he said, "I'm sad." Other parents reported their child's use of descriptive words in reference to their (the mother's) feelings. One girl, who never picked up her toys, said, "Are you happy, Mommy? I picked up all my toys." Another looked at his mother and asked, "Mama, why are you mad?" The mother said, "I'm not mad," and the boy responded, "You look mad." Several mothers noticed important changes in their child's behavior often toward their brothers or sisters. They shared more; they asked for things more, instead of grabbing or hitting; and they seemed to be more sensitive to how others feel. One mother told us that she found herself listening more to her child because "He talks to me more now."

Thus, the ICPS approach seems to be a program with potential for widespread dissemination. With the help of a 3-year grant from the (Pew) Glenmede Charitable Trust Foundation, Dr. Kathryn Healey, who has worked in ICPS-training programs with diverse populations, became project director for what is called the Incorporation Project. Four resource teachers who provide consultation and training to classroom teachers were trained with 16 kindergarten classroom teachers. After the 1st year, resource teachers trained both new resource teachers and new classroom teachers and their aides. The goal of this approach is to create a cadre of key trainers (resource teachers) and for the program ultimately to become self-sustaining (Healey, Brewer, Brock, & Swift, in preparation).

Evaluations from the first year program show significant improvements in positive behaviors (e.g., concern for others, being liked by peers) and decreases in negative behaviors (e.g., physical and verbal aggression, emotional outbursts, and impatience) in children. With less intense supervision than that provided during our initial research years, these results tell us the program is sufficiently robust to disseminate more widely, without major difficulties.

Perhaps most importantly of all, the overall response to the program by trainers and children is very positive. Our first personal thrill came when a teacher told us a mother reported that her 4-year-old child came home and said, "Mommy, I solved a problem in school today."

Limitations

What to expect, and when to expect it. For optimal program impact, children should be exposed to ICPS for at least 4-month periods. The behavioral impact of shortened programs (e.g., Dick, 1981) is reduced. Although most children apply the initial verbal concept skills outside the formal training in the early weeks, initially ICPS-deficient children do not begin to solve interpersonal problems on their own until later in the program. As primary problem-solving thinking skills are applied, behavior change can be seen in many children. Inhibited children begin to speak up after 2 or 3 weeks in the program, and many relate better to others after 2 months. Although impulsive behavior takes longer to affect, most children show signs of increased patience, less emotionality, and a readiness to talk things over before the program ends. At that time, they show signs of an ability to think by talking about what they do in ways suggesting that more appropriate overt behavior may follow, although some may still act aggressively or impulsively. ICPS training requires patience by the trainer. It is not a magic pill. It does not happen overnight. It takes time.

Dialoguing is not simple to learn. Problem-solving dialoguing cannot be a mechanical set of questions applied to any problem that arises. As one of our teachers insightfully noted, the concepts must be understood. Because such understanding takes time, a shortened program is less effective. Larcen (1980), for example, noted that in his 8-week program, trainers only began to dialogue toward the end of the program (Week 6)—the point at which they themselves absorbed the style and developed the techniques to dialogue. Because most adults are used to telling a child what to do and explaining why the adult's idea is a good one, the art of guiding children to tell us what to do and why is often difficult to learn. To overcome this initial difficulty, we train this technique one step at a time with simple applications of the initial word concepts (e.g., "Donna is painting. Is Sarah doing the same thing or something different? Terrence is crying. How does he feel? How can we help him feel happy again?"). With simple applications like those, both the children and the trainer can ease into the approach slowly and comfortably.

Dialoguing may run against one's natural reflexes. Were dialoguing entirely natural, more adults would guide a child to think through a problem without specific dialoguing training. Interviews with parents of 6- to 16-year-olds across social classes reveal how unusual the problem-solving approach is. Although the content of particular problems and what parents do and say may differ, the extent to which parents encourage children to think does not change simply because the children get older or because they are middle class.

Whether dialoguing seems natural to the user, it poses the threat of loss of control in handling children in problem situations, thus, making it both unnatural and anxiety provoking. Encouraging the child to tell the adult what she or he thinks is a good idea and why it is can be construed as giving the child license to do and say whatever she or he wants, including things that go against the values of the parent or teacher. One parent, expressing such a concern, protested, "My child is not going to manipulate me out of cleaning his room!" In fact, adult values need not change. Although the child is not given the choice about whether to clean his or her room, the child can be guided to think about his or her way of doing it.

Another misconception about dialoguing is that it is all right for children to always end up with what they want; this adds to the potential difficulty of using it. In reality, dialoguing helps children cope with frustration when a need or desire is unobtainable. For example, one 4-year-old wanted her mother to read her a story at an inconvenient time. Her ICPS-trained mother handled it this way:

Mother: Mary, I'm sewing right now. When I get this much done (*shows her*), then I can read to you.
Child: Why can't you read it now?

Mother: Because I promised your father I would have this done when he gets home, and I don't want to feel rushed.
Child: O.K.
Mother: Can you think of something different to do while I finish?
Child: I'll look at my pictures . . . and then I can watch TV. (Shure & Spivack, 1978, pp. 139–140)

Given that the child is more likely to carry out her or his own solution(s) than adult demands or suggestions, emotional confrontation can be avoided when both parent and child recognize the problem and each other's point of view. The child learns to accept what she or he cannot have and to wait for what she or he can have, when guided to think of the impact on parents of what she or he wants and of how waiting has meaningful consequences. Dialoguing is an approach that can advance this important objective.

Although it is possible that a formal didactic program without dialoguing can enhance behavioral adjustment (a speculation not yet researched), dialoguing introduces an in vivo quality by encouraging children to apply ICPS skills on their own when faced with real-life problems. In this regard, Weissberg and Gesten (1982) noted that teachers of school-aged children reported that dialoguing may be the key to independent problem-solving thought. Weissberg et al. (1981) attributed behavior change in their studies at least in part to the systematic incorporation of dialoguing into their overall training format. The real point to stress is that actually applying the program in real-life situations helps children to associate how they think with what they do, and how they behave.

Given the value of the ICPS approach, one teacher from our service incorporation project may have expressed the sentiments of many, "There are some teachers who seem to be set in their ways about teaching. Having to be receptive and to open themselves up to ICPS can be difficult for them" (Healey et al., in preparation). These limitations notwithstanding, we believe that behavior change will last longer and become a more natural part of the child's person when the child, not the adult, does the thinking.

Starting a New School-Based Program

Three sets of considerations are important in starting new school-based programs: (a) those actually implementing the program need the support, but not the pressure, from administrators in higher authority; (b) those starting the program must strike a balance between careful forward planning and flexibility for change to meet the needs of the users; and (c) those starting the program should have an initial consultation from people with program experience. Our experience suggests that effective handling of these matters maximizes chances for successful program implementation.

Support From Above

Our first contacts in obtaining support have been with highly placed administrators. For the preschool intervention, we met with the preschool's director and assistant director, and because preschool and kindergarten are under a single administrative umbrella, we also met with the director of early childhood education for both. Without the initial support of the directors, it does not matter who wants to do the program; with such support, middle-level administrators (e.g., field supervisors) and principals can better see the program's value, feel honored that their school was chosen, and transmit support and enthusiasm to their teachers. The latter, in turn, will likely enhance greater teacher commitment. Although the director may help to identify suitable schools, it is important that no principal, field supervisor, or teacher be made to feel obligated; programs are only as effective as the trainers who conduct them. Personal contact at all relevant levels of administration provide insights into people's feelings toward the program before the actual intervener, usually the classroom teacher, is ever contacted.

Planning and Flexibility Balance

Planning a school-based intervention is important both in terms of articulating its content and incorporating it into the classroom. If the program is to have real meaning for the implementer, she or he must have input concerning both program content and its means of implementation.

Program content. We have always stressed that, although the program's basic concepts are carefully planned and sequenced, literal program content and its manner of presentation can be flexible. Modes of presentation of program materials can change (e.g., pictures can be replaced with role playing); timing of lessons can change (i.e., the pace of some groups is faster than others); and specific materials can change (e.g., depending on budget, commercial or homemade puppets and pictures can be used). Indeed, teachers are free to create their own games to illustrate program concepts with materials already in the classroom. There is ample room for flexibility as long as basic program concepts and sequencing are honored and program content remains relevant to ICPS.

Classroom incorporation. No matter how carefully the process of implementation is planned, circumstances will inevitably create obstacles that will interrupt a program's flow. In school-based programs, a planning and flexibility balance is important for scheduling and teacher-training procedures. For example, in our program we had to reschedule our own preplanned research agenda because of an unanticipated school strike, and teachers, who were responsible for a certain amount of academic lessons, got behind. We had to recognize the simultaneous pressures from superiors on teachers to catch up on teaching demands as well as to implement ICPS. The latter was a luxury to them, not a necessity. Once the teachers recognized that we understood their dilemma and a new schedule was planned with their input, anxieties decreased and the job got done. We added personnel to complete the evaluation on time; the extra pressure was on us, not the teachers.

How teachers are trained is another important issue in balancing planning with flexibility. Although the initial training plan may call for weekly, after-school meetings for 2 hours each, teachers may be unable or may simply prefer not to meet that often. In such a case, it may be necessary to hold monthly ½-day workshops. Although we found the latter useful in specific situations, teachers most often preferred weekly meetings for four reasons: (a) they provided a "we" feeling, an important support system, and an exposure to teachers from other schools; (b) they provided an opportunity for trainees to role play program games to enhance familiarity with them; (c) they reassured trainees that problems as well as program gratification could be shared; and (d) they made it possible to concentrate on smaller program units, facilitating absorption of relevant information (Shure, 1979). How such meetings are spaced, or supplemented with in-class observations and demonstrations, vary with the staff involved. But for optimal impact on the ultimate recipients (i.e., the children), accommodations must be made to the needs of the implementer without compromising the integrity of the program.

Initial consultation with experienced personnel. We trained the first group of ICPS teachers ourselves. Whenever possible, it is desirable to have program developers or highly trained staff give at least a 1- or 2-day training workshop. Our first experience in starting a service program for kindergartens led us to develop the Incorporation Project model. We hope it will increase the likelihood that ICPS will be maintained and that it will lead to its ultimate ownership by the schools. Because we were on the scene to launch this service intervention, more teachers could be included than if the primary teacher trainer first had to learn the program himself or herself. If that is the case, it is advisable to start small, perhaps using only a soft process evaluation. A slow build-up allows key trainers and classroom teachers to become comfortable with the program and avoids undue pressures for success while people are first learning how to conduct the program.

ICPS After Age Five

Although important associations have been shown between ICPS skill and behavior in elementary school-aged children (Spivack & Shure, 1982), the impact of school-based ICPS training (Shure & Spivack, 1982a) on adjustment of older children has been less firmly established. Reports based on such programs suggest that either behavior did not improve (Allen, Chinsky, Larcen, Lochman, & Selinger, 1976) or behavior did improve but links between ICPS and behavioral gains were weaker than for younger children (Elias, 1980; Weissberg et al., 1981).

With urban fifth graders (Sure, 1986), the 4½-month ICPS program improved positive behaviors, but a program reexposure was needed in the sixth grade to reduce negative impulsive and inhibited behaviors. With further research needed, it seems thus far that earlier may indeed be better than later, at least in terms of obtaining more impact in less time. Whether overt behavior patterns of older children are more fixed and change resistant, whether teachers are slower to recognize changes in older children when they do occur, or whether it is more difficult logistically to incorporate new programs into the existing academic curricula, research suggests that, although it may take longer to do so, it is not too late for ICPS to have beneficial impact on children's mental health after age five.

What's Next?

We have been awarded a grant from the Prevention Research Branch, National Institute of Mental Health, to address some unanswered questions about ICPS interventions at the kindergarten level. Briefly, we plan to examine the effectiveness of (a) combined parent and teacher training of the same child versus teacher training only on reducing or preventing high-risk behaviors and on diagnosable disturbances and (b) ICPS training over a longer follow-up period (through fourth grade) than has been conducted to date.

The need for early intervention has been documented by Zax and Cowen (1976) who, in regard to the Rochester Primary Mental Health Project, noted that "children with early identified dysfunction, left alone, did poorly in the first several school years and were already quite impaired by third grade" (p. 531). Spivack et al. (1978) reported:

> How a child initially adapts to the interpersonal and task demands of the school environment gives indication of his likelihood to respond productively in subsequent situations he will face in the schools. . . . Early behavior patterns reflect the child's response to a new environment of peers and adults in a kindergarten, a response that apparently reflects a more general capacity to handle new situations which may bode ill unless something specific is done about it. (pp. 17–18)

We can now test whether, over time, ICPS intervention is one approach that might be taken to enhance children's adaptation to school and to the real world.

References

Allen, G., Chinsky, J., Larcen, S., Lochman, J., & Selinger, H. (1976). *Community psychology and the schools: A behaviorally oriented multilevel preventive approach.* Hillsdale, NJ: Erlbaum.

Asarnow, J. R., & Callan, J. W. (1985). Boys with peer adjustment problems. *Journal of Consulting and Clinical Psychology, 53,* 80–87.

Camp, B. W., & Bash, M. A. (1981). *Think Aloud: Increasing social and cognitive skills—A problem solving program for children, Primary level.* Champaign, IL: Research Press.

Cowen, E. L. (1980). The wooing of primary prevention. *American Journal of Community Psychology, 8,* 258–284.

Cowen, E. L., Pederson, A., Babigian, H., Izzo, L. D., & Trost, M. A. (1973). Long-term follow-up of early detected vulnerable children. *Journal of Consulting and Clinical Psychology, 41,* 438–466.

Dick, A. (1981). *The effects of training in social problem solving and verbal self-instruction on behavioral adjustment, social problem-solving cognition, and cognitive tempo in socially impulsive kindergarten children.* Unpublished doctoral dissertation, New York University.

Elardo, P. T., & Cooper, M. (1977). *Aware: Activities for Social Development.* Menlo Park, CA: Addison-Wesley.

Elias, M. J. (1980). *Developing instructional strategies for television-based preventive mental health curricula in elementary school settings.* Unpublished doctoral dissertation, University of Connecticut, Storrs.

Granville, A. C., McNeil, J. T., Meece, J., Wacker, S., Morris, M., Shelly, M., & Love, J. M. (1976). *A process evaluation of project developmental continuity interim report IV: Pilot year impact study—Instrument characteristics and attrition trends* (Vol. 1) (No. 105–75–1114), Washington, DC: Office of Child Development.

Healey, K., Brewer, P., Brock, L., & Swift, M. (in preparation). Issues in dissemination: Moving from research to widespread applications.

Kohlberg, L., Ricks, D., & Snarey, J. (1984). Childhood development as a predictor of adaptation in adulthood. *Genetic Psychological Monographs, 110,* 91–172.

Larcen, S. W. (1980). *Enhancement of social problem-solving skills through teacher and parent collaboration.* Unpublished doctoral dissertation, University of Connecticut, Storrs.

Loeber, R. (1982). The stability of antisocial and delinquent child-behavior: A review. *Child Development, 53,* 1431–1446.

McKim, B. J., Weissberg, R. P., Cowen, E. L., Gesten, E. L. & Rapkin, B. D. (1982). A comparison of the problem-solving ability and adjustment of suburban and urban third grade children. *American Journal of Community Psychology, 10,* 155–159.

Nesbitt, A., Madren-Braun, J., Bruckner, M., Caldwell, R., Dennis, N., Liddell, T., & McGloin, J. (1980). *Children's Resource Center: A problem solving approach. Final Evaluation.* Report to Law Enforcement Assistance Administration #77–2A (1)–36–52, Washington, DC: and Adams County Department of Social Services, Commerce City, Co. (Available from Draft Aid Reproductions, 1088 S. Gaylord, Denver, CO. 80209)

Olson, S. L., Johnson, J., Belleau, K., Parks, J., & Barrett, E. (1983, April). *Social competence in preschool children: Interrelations with sociometric status, social problem-solving, and impulsivity.* Paper presented at the meetings of the Society for Research in Child Development, Detroit.

O'Neil, P., & Robins, L. N. (1958). The relation of childhood behavior problems to adult psychiatric status: A 30-year follow-up study of 150 subjects. *The American Journal of Psychiatry, 115,* 961–969.

Richard, B. A., & Dodge, K. A. (1982). Social maladjustment and problem-solving in school-aged children. *Journal of Consulting and Clinical Psychology, 50,* 226–233.

Roff, M. (1970). Some life history factors in relation to various types of adult adjustment. In M. Roff and D. F. Ricks (Eds.), *Life history studies in psychopathology* (pp. 265–287). Minneapolis: University of Minnesota Press.

Rubin, K. H. (1985). Socially withdrawn children: An "at-risk" population? In B. H. Schneider, K. H. Rubin, & J. E. Ledingham (Eds.), *Peer relations and social skills in childhood* (Vol. 2): *Issues in assessment and training* (pp. 125–139). New York: Springer-Verlag.

Shure, M. B. (1979). Training children to solve interpersonal problems: A preventive mental health program. In R. E. Munoz, L. R. Snowden, J. G. Kelly (Eds.), *Social and psychological research in community settings,* (pp. 30–68). San Francisco: Jossey-Bass.

Shure, M. B. (1980). *Interpersonal problem solving in ten-year-olds.* Final Report No. MH–27741, Washington, DC: National Institute of Mental Health.

Shure, M. B. (1986). *Problem solving and mental health of ten- to twelve-year olds.* Final Summary Report No. MH35989. Washington, DC. National Institute of Mental Health.

Shure, M. B., & Spivack, G. (1970, April.) *Problem-solving capacity, social class and adjustment among nursery school children.* Paper presented at the meeting of the Eastern Psychological Association, Atlantic City.

Shure, M. B., & Spivack, G. (1971a). *Hahnemann preschool behavior (HPSB) rating scale.* Philadelphia: Hahnemann University, Department of Mental Health Sciences.

Shure, M. B., & Spivack, G. (1971b). *Interpersonal cognitive problem solving (ICPS): A mental health program for four-year-old nursery school children: Training script.* Philadelphia: Hahnemann University, Department of Mental Health Sciences (Revised, 1982; 1987).

Shure, M. B., & Spivack, G. (1974a). *Interpersonal cognitive problem solving (ICPS): A mental health program for kindergarten and first grade children: Training script.* Philadelphia: Hahnemann University, Department of Mental Health Sciences (Revised, 1978).

Shure, M. B., & Spivack, G. (1974b). *Preschool interpersonal problem-solving (PIPS) test: Manual.* Philadelphia: Hahnemann University, Department of Mental Health Sciences.

Shure, M. B., & Spivack, G. (1974c). *The What Happens Next Game (WHNG); Test and Scoring Instructions.* Philadelphia: Department of Mental Health Sciences, Hahnemann Medical College and Hospital (mimeo).

Shure, M. B., & Spivack, G. (1975). *Problem solving techniques in childrearing: Training script.* Philadelphia: Hahnemann University, Department of Mental Health Sciences.

Shure, M. B., & Spivack, G. (1978). *Problem solving techniques in childrearing.* San Francisco: Jossey-Bass.

Shure, M. B., & Spivack, G. (1982a). *Interpersonal problem solving (ICPS): A training program for the intermediate elementary grades.* Philadelphia: Hahnemann University, Department of Mental Health Sciences.

Shure, M. B. & Spivack, G. (1982b). Interpersonal problem solving in young children: A cognitive approach to prevention. *American Journal of Community Psychology, 10,* 341–356.

Shure, M. B., Spivack, G., & Jaeger, M. A. (1971). Problem solving thinking and adjustment among disadvantaged preschool children. *Child Development, 42,* 1791–1803.

Smith, G. M., & Fogg, C. G. (1979). Psychological antecedents of teenage drug use. In R. G. Simmons (Ed.), *Research in community and mental health,* Vol. 1 (pp. 87–102). Greenwich, CT: JAI Press.

Snyder, J. J., & Shanks, D. (1982). Social-cognitive skills in preschool children: Relationship to teacher and peer ratings and *in-vivo* behavior. *Behavioral Counseling Quarterly, 2,* 148–155.

Spivack, G., Marcus, J., & Swift, M. (1986). Early classroom behaviors and later misconduct. *Developmental Psychology, 22,* 124–131.

Spivack, G., Platt, J. J., & Shure, M. B. (1976). *The problem solving approach to adjustment.* San Francisco: Jossey-Bass.

Spivack, G., Rapsher, L., Cohen, A., & Gross, R. (1978). *High risk early signs for delinquency and related behavioral difficulties: The first nine years of a longitudinal study.* Interim Report I. Report to National Institute for Juvenile Justice and Delinquency Prevention, Law Enforcement Assistance Administration, Grant #76–JN–990024.

Spivack, G., & Shure, M. B. (1974). *Social adjustment of young children.* San Francisco: Jossey-Bass.

Spivack, G., Shure, M. B. (1982). Interpersonal cognitive problem solving and clinical theory. In B. Lahey & A. E. Kazdin (Eds.), *Advance in Child Clinical Psychology: Vol. 5* (pp. 323–372). New York: Plenum.

Spivack, G., & Swift, M. (1977). The Hahnemann high school behavior (HHSB) rating scale. *Journal of Abnormal Child Psychology, 5,* 299–308.

Turner, R. R., & Boulter, L. K. (1981, August). *Predicting social competence: The validity of the PIPS.* Paper presented at the meeting of the American Psychological Association, Los Angeles.

Weiner, J. A. (1978). *A theoretical model of the affective and social development of learning-disabled children.* Unpublished doctoral dissertation, The University of Michigan, Ann Arbor.

Weissberg, R. P., & Gesten, E. L. (1982). Considerations for developing effective school-based social problem-solving (SPS) training programs. *School Psychology Review, 11,* 56–63.

Weissberg, R. P., Gesten, E. L., Carnrike, C. L., Toro, P. A., Rapkin, B. D., Davidson, E., & Cowen, E. (1981). Social problem solving skills training: A competence-building intervention with second- to fourth-grade children. *American Journal of Community Psychology, 9,* 411–423.

Weissberg, R. P., Gesten, E. L., Liebenstein, N. L., Schmid, K. D., & Hutton, H. (1979). *The Rochester Social Problem Solving (SPS) Program: A Training Manual for Teachers of 2nd–4th Grade Children.* Rochester, NY: Center for Community Study.

Yu, P., Harris, G. E., Solovitz, B. L., & Franklin, J. L. (1986). A social problem solving intervention for children at high risk for later psychopathology. *Journal of Clinical Child Psychology, 15,* 30–40.

Zax, M., & Cowen, E. L. (1976). *Abnormal psychology: Changing conceptions* (2nd ed.). New York: Holt, Rinehart and Winston.

Mary Jane Rotheram-Borus

CHAPTER

7

Assertiveness Training with Children

Each day children are confronted with a variety of interpersonal problems that require assertiveness. For example, how does a child approach a teacher who grades a test incorrectly? Is a child who responds aggressively more likely to get the grade changed than the child who asks sheepishly? How does a child respond when a peer cuts in front of him in the cafeteria lunch line? When an adolescent girl wants to ask a boy to a dance, how should she approach him (i.e., should she say she likes him or is that pushy)? How does an adolescent convince a potential employer that she or he is right for the job?

Children who are socially skilled in resolving these problems are likely to be well adjusted in many areas of their life, particularly at school (Combs & Slaby, 1977; Van Hasselt, Hersen, Whitehill, & Bellack, 1979). For example, assertive social behavior has been shown to relate positively to IQ (Dorman, 1973) and to healthy adjustment in the classroom (Cartledge & Milburn, 1978; 1980; Deluty, 1984a). Conversely, children who have interpersonal difficulties, who withdraw from social interactions and who show little emotional expressiveness or social independence, have been found to be low achievers in school (Perkins, 1965). Because of these findings, it seems desirable to teach children to be assertive.

This chapter outlines an approach for assertiveness training with children—one of many potential models for increasing children's social competence. A literature search revealed 172 articles published during the last 10 years that evaluated the importance of children's social skills or at-

tempted to train children to be more competent socially. A number of studies with both socially isolated, unpopular children and aggressive, rejected children has suggested that increasing children's social competence can enhance their adjustment (Cooke & Appoloni, 1976; O'Conner, 1972; Patterson, 1972; Spence, 1983).

The assertiveness-training program that we implemented and evaluated in elementary classrooms was found to be an effective preventive intervention with nondeviant children as well. This model is based on the assumption that assertive and nonassertive behaviors are learned skills. Therefore, through an active, rewarding, educational experience, children can acquire new skills and can reduce maladaptive behavior patterns. The program attempts to expand children's repertoires for getting their needs met effectively in interpersonal interactions.

Competence, or assertiveness, is multidimensional (Anderson & Messick, 1974); it consists of many skills that children must modulate depending on the social setting and their individual goals. The training sensitizes children to their own feelings and thoughts and increases their awareness of how others are responding. Children are provided with a set of rules outlining the socially approved means to reach their goals and the nonverbal and verbal skills needed to

This chapter was written with support from the National Institute of Child Health and Human Development, HD 2084001 and Grant No. CDP 66458 from the Administration of Children, Youth and Families.

interact successfully with others. Given such training, we expect that children will experience fewer problematic interactions and receive more social rewards, which results in the child feeling better about himself or herself and others. Improved social adjustment can hopefully generalize to other areas of the child's life such as school achievement.

In this chapter, we review briefly the definition of assertiveness, describe the actual prevention program, consider the empirical evidence supporting its effectiveness, and suggest adaptations of the model.

Assertiveness

Assertiveness defines sets of thoughts, feelings, and actions that help a child to obtain personal goals in a socially acceptable manner (O'Malley, 1977). Although the definition of an assertive act can vary across settings, observers from the same culture are likely to agree on the behaviors that are generally classified as assertive, in contrast to either passive or aggressive. For example, in the United States, looking a teacher in the eye and answering a question in 1 to 3 seconds are considered assertive behaviors. A student who consistently interrupts, demands attention, and infringes on others' rights is labeled aggressive. Finally, a student who limits direct eye contact with others, and who waits 10 to 15 seconds before responding after another person has spoken, is behaving in an inhibited, self-effacing way; this person is likely to be seen as passive by others.

Deluty (1985) demonstrated that some children consistently act in assertive ways and others act

Table 7–1. Continua of Passive Assertive/Aggressive Nonverbal and Verbal Behavior

Nonverbal	Passive		Assertive		Aggressive
Eye contact	Looking at floor	20% eye contact 80% looking around room	Eye contact 70–80%, occasional break	95% eye contact	Glaring 100% eye contact, no breaks
Voice level	Inaudible	Low tone, weak	Audible, clear decibel range	Loud, not matching average	Yelling
Voice tone	Whining	Apologetic	Modulated, no meta-messages; matches request or refusal	Irritated, negative	Angry, demanding
Posture gestures	Hunched shoulders, hands behind back	Turned sideways, head at right angle to shoulders, weight directly on feet	Weight off balance, head and shoulders straight, hands raised	Fists clenched, arms folded across chest, resting on heels	Leaning forward, fists shaking, arms flailing
Personal Space	7 feet	4 feet	1½ to 3 feet	1 foot	6 inches
Verbal					
Requests	This is sure a mess.	If you aren't busy and think you might have time, maybe you'd like to clean this mess.	I would like you to clean this mess.	You should clean this up.	Clean up this.
Refusals	Well, I am pretty busy . . . Well, okay.	Well, I don't think I'll have time. I'll let you know, maybe.	I don't want to play ball with you now.	No way.	No, why would I play with a jerk like you.
Feeling range	Satisfaction	Hurt	Excitement, hurt, anger, ecstasy, irritation, scared.	Anger, excitement	Rage

aggressively across social situations. However, other researchers find that children vary in assertiveness in positive social encounters, in contrast to negative social encounters (Michelson, DiLorenzo, Calpin, & Ollendick, 1982). We define assertiveness as the socially competent response in most situations; Table 7–1 provides examples of the continua of passive, assertive, and aggressive behaviors.

Although it is true that assertive acts are more likely than passive or aggressive acts to result in rewarding interaction with others, it is still important that children have a range of social behaviors, including those that might be labeled passive and aggressive. From this range, a child can choose to act assertively (Rotheram, 1984). Children without a full range of behaviors in their repertoire are limited and unable to engage in assertiveness as defined by Lazarus (1971) (i.e., the full expression of oneself). For example, when approached by a stranger for a car ride, the opti-

mal response may be aggressive, not assertive. In other situations, passive behavior may better meet one's goals than assertiveness.

Furthermore, because evaluations of assertiveness depend on situational contexts, a given act can be simultaneously passive and aggressive. For example, three 8-year-old friends are playing in the schoolyard. One child states with assertive nonverbal behavior, "John, I would like *you* to come with me." Is this an assertive request toward John or an aggressive act towards the uninvited friend? In ongoing social networks, the definition of assertiveness depends on the perspective of the observer and often requires a functional analysis of the behavior, that is, what impact does this have on others?

Finally, assertiveness requires a coordinated interaction of cognitive, affective, and behavioral skills. Table 7–2 outlines some prerequisite skills needed to respond assertively. Based on social-learning theory (Bandura, 1969), we attempt to

Table 7–2. Model for Social Interaction Process With Associated Prerequisite Cognitive, Behavioral, and Emotional Responses for Effective Interpersonal Style

Model of Strategy for Social Interactions	Adaptive Skills Cognitive	Behavioral	Emotional
1. Problem orientation	1. Social inferential ability	— — — —	1. Self-monitoring of internal discomfort
2. Negative emotional response	2. Labeling of negative emotion (e.g., anxiety, depression, excitement) and assessing intensity of response	2. Ability to control behavioral response	2. Labeling of negative emotion (e.g., anxiety, depression, excitement) and assessing intensity of response
3. Cope with negative response	3. Identify covert self-punishment, catastrophic thinking, intervene with coping self-talk, self-reinforcement	3. Control of nonverbal responses, use of time out	3. Relax physiologically
4. Problem solve: (a) clarify goal (b) generate alternative (c) evaluate select alternative	4. (a) state one goal in one sentence (b) divergent thinking (c) social inferential ability to assess realistic consequences	4. (a) direct requests, refusals (b) behavioral repertoire to implement any alternative	4. Assessment and ability to control new emotional states that arise
5. Respond behaviorally	5. Belief you have the right to be assertive, self-esteem in ability to respond	5. Verbal skills, (disclosures, "I" statements, requests, refusals), nonverbal skills (eye contact, voice tone latency level, facial expression)	5. Relaxation techniques
6. Evaluate	6. Self-reinforce, goal set	6. Request feedback from environment	6. Monitor and assess internal state

teach children an interaction routine. Maladaptive habitual responses are eliminated as each aspect of an interpersonal interaction sequence is examined. The child's thoughts, feelings, and actions, and each component response necessary to be socially competent, are practiced. Building on earlier work by those who trained children in either behavioral (Bornstein, Belack, & Hersen, 1977; Evers & Schwarz, 1973; O'Conner, 1972; Oden & Asher, 1977; Whitehill, Hersen, & Coe, 1979) or cognitive skills (Allen, Chinsky, Larcen, Lochman, & Selinger, 1976; Spivack, Platt, & Shure, 1976), we emphasized the coordination of feelings, thoughts, and actions. Capitalizing on evidence that modeling, role playing, praising, behavioral rewards, peer support, cueing, and coaching are effective teaching strategies (Spence, 1983), we developed a simulation game that incorporated all of these techniques to maximize the impact of assertiveness training.

Assertiveness-Training Program

This specific assertiveness-training program is delivered as a time-limited preventive intervention in fourth and fifth grade classrooms over a 12–20 week period twice a week for 1 hour (Rotheram, 1980). Variations on this model are described later in the chapter. The training was divided into seven segments as outlined in Table 7-3. Each segment took three to four lessons to master. Although we evaluated this program based on a 24-session format, our clinical impression was that more practice would have benefited many children. The main program goals were to increase assertiveness, reduce the number of behavior problems, and hopefully find generalization to peer popularity and achievement.

Each session followed the same sequence, that is, didactic teaching regarding the components of assertiveness, presentation of problem situations, group problem solving, and behavioral rehearsal and feedback on performance. The program was delivered by undergraduate and graduate students who acted as group leaders. These leaders had less experience with children than the typical teacher. Leaders received training on the behavioral management of children, completed a 4-week course on assertiveness training with adults, and were closely supervised in the classroom throughout the project.

To help trainers better manage small groups of children and to ensure that training a group was a rewarding experience, the trainer (supercoach) delivered tokens to each child throughout the session whenever positive behaviors were observed. These tokens were small ($2'' \times 2''$) pieces of colored construction paper. Although the tokens were not exchanged for tangible rewards, children valued them greatly, counted how many they had received at the end of the session, and often kept a special box in their desk for their tokens. Although we tried to further enhance the reward experience by letting children distribute the tokens, we soon learned that the practice led to arguments and stealing, rather than encouraging assertive behaviors. Hence, ultimately, only the supercoach distributed tokens.

Sequence of Activities

Didactic presentation. At the beginning of each session, educational information for one skill, that is, acting assertively, was presented entertainingly for 5–10 minutes. Dressed in costumes depicting such characters as "El Jerko Deluxe," "The Mean Machine," and "Mr. Straight Arrow," leaders role played situations to help children define assertive behavior and to understand one new aspect of presenting oneself assertively. The sequencing of these elements is outlined in Table 7–3.

Presentation of problem situations. To enhance learning, a simulation game was developed. Following the didactic presentations, students in each class were divided into teams of 6–10 students for the remainder of the session. Students' roles varied as team members. For half of the period, students were assigned the role of actor; for the rest of the session, they were cast as directors. Supercoach, the paraprofessional leader, presented a series of problems (e.g., "You are standing in the lunch line, and the boy in front of you allows a friend to cut in line."). The team's task was to solve the problem by setting goals, generating alternative solutions, and evaluating the consequences of each alternative. This section of the training was similar to a television game show in which contestants try to solve problems cooperatively.

Behavioral rehearsal and feedback. Actors selected one alternative to role play. During the role play, directors evaluated the actors' assertiveness. Directors were assigned to monitor different verbal and nonverbal behaviors. For example, there was an eye-contact coach, a director who focused on the actors' facial expressiveness, a director who listened to and evaluated the spoken words, and a director who monitored ges-

Table 7–3. Agenda for Assertion Training Interventions

Section	Didactic Introduction	Role Play Sample	Nonverbal Behavioral Focus	Interpersonal Problem Solving	Thought Rehearsal
1.	Define passive, assertive, aggressive. Role play for class.	You took a permission slip home to your parents so you can participate in a special school program. Your parents have not signed it. What do you want?	Eye contact, voice loudness	Clarifying clear goals, 1 sentence	Verbalize cognitive states most people feel when behaving passive, assertive, aggressive (e.g., passive, "I'm not worth it.")
2.	Feeling Thermometer or SUDS. An anxiety scale from 0–100.	A boy crowds in front of you in a cafeteria line. You don't like it. What can you do? What else?	Posture, voice tone	Generating alternatives	Verbalize positive self-thoughts at low SUDS.
3.	"Strokes" giving and receiving compliments. Self-reinforcement.	Giving compliments to all group members, including yourself; you like your ballet lessons. What can you do? What else?	Facial expressions	Generating alternatives	Verbalize positive and negative self-thoughts. Intervene with positive after each negative.
4.	Making friends	Interviewing stars from TV, meeting someone on a bus, telling friend he hurt your feelings. What is likely to happen?	Personal space	Means and ends evaluation	Role play catastrophic fantasy or worst outcome of making a friend.
5.	"Playing Cool," controlling anger by taking time out.	You have been working hard on a test. Your teacher yells at you that you are cheating. What are you saying to yourself? What can you do? What is likely to happen?	Gestures	Evaluate consequences	Role play coping self-talk.
6.	"The Big Switch," accepting a negative from someone else and self-reinforcing.	You have forgotten to do your homework and your teacher's angry with you. What are you saying to yourself? What can you do? What will your teacher do?	Latency	Evaluate consequences	Role play coping self-talk.
7.	Strategy learning with new problems.	Request and refusal situations	Consolidate	Review	Consolidate

tures and body movements. Group members and the supercoach created the ambiance of a sound stage during this phase of the game. One child director would call out "Ready, hold it. Action!" Another would halt the role play with the command, "Cut!" After the rehearsal, directors provided their feedback, signaling whether the behaviors were assertive by touching a green card, passive (a blue card), or aggressive (a red card). The team then repeated the role play, role played another solution to the same problem, or worked on solving and rehearsing a new problem. Actors and directors switched roles for half of each session.

Training techniques

Assertiveness training is based on social-learning theory (Bandura, 1969, 1977). The following principles were used to guide the trainers' interactions with children and the structure of the material.

Emphasize and reward strengths. Rather than punish inappropriate behavior, leaders rewarded students frequently to enhance learning, to build peer support for appropriate behaviors, and to inform students of desired behavior. Leaders used tokens to cue children to appropriate group behaviors. For example, students did not always attend to the group activity. In such cases, leaders rewarded attending students by handing each a token and saying warmly, "I like the way you pay close attention to your job." Negative behaviors were ignored. Several students were highly aggressive in the small groups (e.g., they hit peers). Time-out was used with these students (i.e., each was asked to leave the group for 1 minute and was rewarded on their return to group activity).

Use the principle of successive approximation. Students gradually came to understand distinctions between assertive and nonassertive behaviors; they role played assertive behaviors, and their feelings were monitored after several sessions. Students' attempts to be assertive were rewarded. Trainers were instructed first to reward some aspect of the student's behavior whether nonverbal, verbal, or evidence of good intention and then to select one aspect of the child's performance and set a goal for the student's next attempt. For example, "John, I really liked the way you looked Susan in the eye. Next time, I would like your voice to be a little stronger." Inappropriate gestures or passive verbal behaviors were ignored until a later role play. No more than one goal was set at any one time. Each week, trainers were cued to emphasize a different nonverbal, verbal, and problem-solving skill.

Model assertive behavior. The trainer is a model of assertive behavior for children. Spivack and Shure's (1974) interpersonal problem-solving program strongly emphasized the importance of teachers *dialoging* with children. Dialoging is a process that the teacher uses to encourage the use of skills to deal with everyday classroom problems (Spivack, Platt, & Shure, 1976).

In our program, trainers and classroom teachers were encouraged to model appropriate assertive behaviors and techniques taught in assertion-training sessions throughout the day. Specific rehearsal with coping styles was encouraged. Using this approach, trainers demonstrated their own thought and coping processes to children, rather than modeling an assertive behavior automatically. For example, a trainer would say, "Johnny is acting up in the group. What am I going to do? I get very upset when Johnny acts up. First, take a few deep breaths. I can handle this. I am feeling calmer. I will ask Johnny not to hit and tell him he will take a time-out if he does hit again. I know what to do. I can handle myself." Rather than being a model with a perfectly pat assertive behavior, the supercoach demonstrates a coping model for the children.

Encourage independent thinking. To develop appropriate assertiveness, children must have opportunities to control their own behavior and to structure their environment. One technique used to encourage independence was the sequence of feedback delivered following a role play. Leaders were instructed to ask in sequence: (a) What does the child actor like about his or her own behavior, and what one feature would the child like to change; (b) what did each child director like about the actor's behavior; (c) what did the supercoach leader like about the behavior; and (d) what goal would the supercoach leader have for the next role play? Across sessions, the child directors increasingly assumed the role of the leaders. They came to ask the child actors questions automatically, such as, "What did you like about your job?"

Weekly Content

Phase 1. Weekly program content is summarized in Table 7–3. Trainers have four goals: (a) to familiarize students with the simulation game; (b) to teach discrimination among passive, assertive, and aggressive behaviors; (c) to build cohesion among group members; and (d) to teach goal clarification. Following a didactic presentation of definitions, with characters role playing passive, assertive, and aggressive interactions, students were divided into teams with a supercoach.

In each group session, the first task was to ask children to give compliments to themselves, for example, "What did you like about yourself today?" Beginning with compliments helps to build group cohesion and makes the training a rewarding experience for children. When a student makes a joke (e.g., "You think you are smart! Ho, ho"), children are instructed to ignore the laughing, and the teaser is asked how she or he is different from the target child.

Teams were then presented with a problem, and they practiced setting a goal for that situation. For example, supercoach said, "The classroom is noisy, and you cannot study your lesson. What can you do?" When children responded with negative goals such as, "Yell at the other children," "Ask my teacher to get angry with them," or "Look mean until they are quiet," they were asked to restate their goals in terms of positive ones. Positive goals are statements of desire such as, "What do you want more of?" For the situation cited, positive alternative goals include asking children to talk softly, to go into another room to talk, or to talk at recess or asking the teacher to move the student to another room. Positive goals are stated in one sentence. More than one sentence implies more than one goal.

In Phase 1, the leader presented one alternative to solve the problem (e.g., "Ask the children to be quiet."). The child actors role played one of the alternative solutions, and the child directors were asked to give feedback on the performance. After the role play, supercoach asked the actor, "What did you like about your eyes?" In early sessions, supercoach prompted for desired responses both before and after the role play.

Phase 2. Attention is next focused on children's feelings. Children are taught to use a "feeling thermometer," with a scale from 0 to 100, to identify their feelings. The concept is borrowed from Wolpe's (1958) Subjective Units of Discomfort Scale (SUDS) used with phobics. Children describe situations in which their own feelings vary in intensity from 100, 80, 60, 40, 20, and 0. For example, a feeling thermometer of 80 may be telling your father that you do not want to go to the basketball game with him.

The SUDS assessment is used as one way to practice assertiveness in monitoring the role plays; it also becomes part of the classroom routine as teachers interact with students. Before and after each role play, students are asked, "What are your SUDS? Where is your feeling thermometer?" Very simple relaxation techniques are used. For example, children practice spelling their name backwards and tensing and then relaxing muscles when their feeling thermometer gets high. Leaders help children to build a hierarchy of anxiety-provoking situations,

within which children assign SUDS scores and report their physiological reactions. For example, one child may get a stomach ache and a SUDS score of 60 when trying to make a new friend; another may experience shaking hands and have a SUDS score of 80 in the same situation. Homework assignments focus on identifying situations in which students have low and high SUDS.

Building on past successes, leaders move from focusing on eye contact to rewarding children's assertive posture and voice. Simultaneously, leaders encourage children to think of more than one solution for the problem after presenting the problem and setting goals. Unlike Spivack and Shure's (1974) program, however, children are rewarded specifically for assertive alternatives. Although generating passive and aggressive options are not punished, assertive options are chosen for the role plays. Leaders emphasize the importance of brainstorming; children are not allowed to ridicule or punish peers during this process.

Phase 3. Treating oneself well is emphasized during this phase. In addition to stating positives about oneself, children are encouraged to exchange compliments. Leaders structure these exchanges and ask for specific compliments to same-sex peers. Even at fourth and fifth grade, students are embarrassed to compliment opposite-sex peers.

Because facial expressiveness is one of the most important nonverbal behaviors associated with compliments, children play pantomime games to practice a wide range of facial expressions. One child chooses a specific feeling to pantomime, and peers attempt to guess the emotion. It is useful to use the stimulus photographs developed in McPhail, Middleton, and Ingram's (1980) Startline Program as a supplement to the didactic material. Children are shown these photographs, and they learn to identify the nonverbal cues that support their judgments about the emotional state being expressed. For example, viewing McPhail et al.'s (1980) photographs, a child may say, "The eyes tell me this person is sad. They go down at the end." For another photo, a child may accurately say, "The smile is happy, but the eyebrows are pinched together and make me unsure how this person feels." Children learn about nonverbal expressions both by practicing the identification of emotional states and by providing others with feedback.

The problem-solving section of each session highlights the statement of positive goals and generation of alternative solutions to various problems. During the role-playing sequence, child actors are halted early in the rehearsal and are asked, "What are you saying to yourself now?" Children role play positive coping instructions to themselves in problem situations. For example:

I am unsure of what to say. I want to get out of class early, even though the other students must stay. The teacher does not like me and probably will not let me go. That is okay. I can handle this problem. I can ask, even if it does not work. I will ask him. It does not matter whether he likes me. Even if the teacher says, 'No,' I can call my mother and ask her to tell my friends I will be late. I can handle this problem.

Leaders feed the actors lines to prompt self-enhancing statements.

Phase 4. Children practice making friends. Imitating adult social skills, children are taught to ask open questions (Lange & Jakubouski, 1977). Open questions are those that start with *how, why,* and *what about.* Such questions require more than one-word answers. To make this skill attractive, children imitated newscasters and interviewed their favorite movie star. Asking open questions was not a prerequisite skill for making friends in middle childhood. On the other hand, the interviewing helped children learn to generate alternatives (What would they ask these stars?), identified a positive image whom they could use as a model (e.g., What would my favorite star do with this situation?), and made the simulation game fun and interesting.

Children began to evaluate consequences of their actions during these role plays and problem solving. To facilitate the process, directors asked the actors, "What is the worst thing that could happen to you?" From practicing these worst-case scenarios, children came to recognize that they could survive, even if the catastrophic fantasy was actualized.

During one session, we conducted an exercise to assess children's personal space. A large *X* was placed on the floor with masking tape. From 10 feet away, children were slowly approached by a same-sex peer, an opposite-sex peer, and a friend from front, back, and each side. Children varied in their personal space, depending on the direction of approach and the nature of the peer relationship. Their reactions were used to discuss personal space and differences in personal space during role plays.

Phase 5. Learning to cope with criticism was the focus of this training segment. Children practiced talking to themselves when they received both justifiable and unjustifiable criticism. Tak-

ing a time-out was presented as one option for handling criticism. Children were taught to say, "I need some time to think this over. I will talk with you later." Although children neither used these behavioral options spontaneously in role plays nor did teachers see them used later in the classroom, the concept of "playing cool" and maintaining an image of self-pride when in trouble seemed useful. When unpleasant problem situations were later presented and children were asked to generate ridiculous consequences (e.g., "No one would ever talk to me again in my life," "I might grow black horns," or "My parents might put me up for adoption"), they laughed at them.

Role playing these options helped children to gain a broader perspective of their own negative thoughts in problem situations. This phase of training seemed to result in a decrease of the anxiety a child experienced when criticized. Children could imagine how a "cool" movie star might handle such a situation and could imitate this star.

Phase 6. This phase of the curriculum continued to emphasize responses to criticism. Whereas playing cool addressed children's feelings in negative interactions, this new segment emphasized behavioral responses. The "big switch," a version of Lange and Jakubouski's (1977) technique for responding to criticism, was taught. When criticized justifiably, children accepted the criticism and were taught to say self-positive statements such as, "Yes, I am late, but I usually try to be on time" or "I made a mistake, but it is not like me." Fourth and fifth graders realized spontaneously that if such statements were untrue, the big switch would be useless.

The didactic sessions focused on how children decide when to try to change their own behavior in response to criticism and when not to try. The curriculum clarified that parents and teachers often wanted changes that children did not want to make (e.g., being quiet in class). Each class group identified areas that the teacher wanted changed. A large group discussion focused on whether or not the students wanted to change these behaviors. In smaller teams, each child reported one behavior that others had asked her or him to change, after which the group discussed whether or not such a change should be made and the costs and benefits of changing for other people. The impression reported by supervisors was that children with behavior problems did not want to change their behavior; they either felt that others were wrong to request changes in their behavior or stated assertively or aggressively that they would "change for no one!"

This aspect of training was too brief to address adequately the issues of self-monitoring one's behavior. Group leaders recommended that more attention, role plays, and peer group support and feedback be focused on this topic. In the process of evaluating the consequences of different alternatives, children are articulating underlying value systems and areas in which they share or do not share the values of a teacher, peers, and parents.

Phase 7. In this phase, the integration of thinking, feeling, and acting assertively was practiced in a set sequence:

1. Identify the problem
2. Set a positive goal
3. Assess one's feeling thermometer
4. Get calm by encouraging oneself, spelling one's name backwards, or tensing and relaxing muscles
5. Generate ways to achieve one's goal, evaluate options, and select an alternative
6. Act
7. Identify one's successes
8. Decide what to do next time.

Each child rehearsed at least two problems following this sequence. Children broke into small groups of two each, and the supercoach role played with them two at a time. All sessions ended with children complimenting each other.

Impact of the Program

The program's effectiveness has been evaluated with a sample group of fourth to sixth graders ($N = 343$; Rotheram, 1982a; Rotheram, 1982b; Rotheram, Armstrong, & Booraem, 1982). Children were assigned to three conditions: assertiveness training, a no-treatment control, and an alternative intervention. The assertiveness-training program, previously described, was conducted for 2 hours a week for 12 weeks. Children in the alternative treatment participated in a self-confidence–training simulation game similar to the television program College Bowl (Flowers & Marston, 1972). Competing on 3-person teams, children answered questions on hobbies and academic classroom material. Students were assigned to teams with classmates of similar confidence levels. Confidence was operationally defined as attempting to answer the teacher's questions. Flowers and Marston (1972) found that low and average responders increased their participation rate when grouped with same-level–responding peers.

After a successful competition experience with peers at the same response level, children were gradually integrated into groups with higher level responders. Initially low responders were rewarded as they interacted with children whose initial response levels were higher. Flowers and Marston (1972) found that children who gained confidence in answering questions during this game answered teachers' questions frequently during regular class periods. Thus, assertiveness training was compared to an intervention that had already been shown to have positive effects on children's classroom participation and also to a no-program control group.

The first question our research addressed was, Did children acquire the skills targeted by the program? On a problem-solving measure, the quality of alternative solutions improved significantly for all participants in the assertiveness-training program, although the number of alternatives generated increased only for the fifth grade program. Program children generated significantly more assertive problem solutions and fewer passive and aggressive solutions than nonprogram children. Similarly, on a self-report inventory of assertive behaviors in the classroom, significantly more assertive choices were reported both immediately following the intervention and 1 year later than before the program. We also assessed children's ability to get a group of four peers to accept their individual choices of favorite foods and hobbies. Those receiving assertiveness training were better able to reach their goals; boys were better than girls at this task. Collectively, these results demonstrated that the program did achieve its first goal—teaching the program's targeted skills.

Given that program children's skills had improved more than other groups during the pre-post period, we next asked whether these changes related to other behavioral changes. To that end, students' question-asking and -answering behaviors were assessed in the classroom for 6 weeks before and after training. Similarly, we assessed changes in the teachers' rewarding and punishing statements to students. Although program children asked fewer questions following the intervention, they initiated contact with the teacher significantly more often than children in the other groups.

In contrast, students who had self-confidence training answered teachers' questions significantly more often and received more rewards from the teachers than did program children. Teachers also rated program children as better behaved than the other groups and as having higher achievement levels. Furthermore, there was significantly less variance in the teachers' ratings of peer popularity among program children than among other groups. More important, 1 year after the program ended, new classroom teachers rated program children as higher in achievement than children in other groups.

Because teachers' expectations could have unduly colored their ratings, children's grades were examined before, immediately after, and 1 year following the intervention. Immediately following the intervention, the grades of students in the self-confidence–training group improved significantly more than other groups. However, 1 year later, students who received assertiveness training had significantly higher grades than their peers.

The three groups did not change differentially in self-esteem. Although no differences were found in popularity shifts based on peer ratings, teachers reported significant group differences in classroom alliances. The greatest changes following the program were among those students who were doing well before the program started (i.e., students with high initial teacher ratings in comportment and achievement). These students improved more than students with initial behavior problems, academic problems, or both academic and behavior problems. Interestingly, 1 year later, program students who had initial behavior problems were found to have improved significantly in comportment.

We also found that differential program impact related to characteristics of the trainer (Rotheram, 1982b). Children in groups led by relatively more assertive leaders reported enjoying the group experience, trusting their peers, and wanting the group to continue more than those with leaders rated less assertive. Children trained by less assertive leaders, however, had higher scores on the problem-solving measures. Because the leaders as a group were reasonably assertive, program supervisors felt that the relatively less assertive leaders provided more opportunities for students to structure the group activity. Highly assertive leaders by contrast tended more often to control group activities, to reward students, and to direct group interactions. Rather than emphasizing peer interactions, these leaders functioned more as the hubs on a wheel, channeling information and feedback among group members.

This program was adapted and evaluated with 9th and 12th graders (Rotheram & Armstrong, 1980). Although trained adolescents were rated by observers as behaviorally more assertive in role playing situations, there were no significant differences in assertiveness on self-report measures. Cohesion, as measured by postgroup questionnaires (Lieberman, Yalom, & Miles, 1973), significantly affected assertiveness. Cohesion can be enhanced by leaders' structuring activities such as exchanging compliments, instructions to exchange tokens, and requests to restate negative goals in a positive manner (e.g., "I do not like jumping" becomes "I would like to spend time gathering apples instead of jumping."). Only youth in high cohesion groups increased in assertiveness. Similar programs were also conducted with suicide-attempting adolescents in a hospital-based clinic (Trautman & Rotheram, 1987) and suicidal runaways (Rotheram, 1987a; 1987c). The program's formats varied in those instances including such features as family groups or Saturday workshops.

In addition to our own work, researchers have used an assertiveness model to reduce aggressiveness among adolescents (Goldstein & Pentz, 1984; Pentz, 1980); to enhance comportment of youth in correctional settings (Beidleman, 1981; DeLange, Barton, & Lanham, 1981); preventively, with adolescents in school (Waksman, 1984); to reduce smoking (Del Greco, 1986; Glasgow & McCaul, 1985); with disturbed children (Carducci, 1980); and to reduce drug use (Battjes, 1985; Botvin & Wills, 1985; Hawkins, Catalano & Wells, 1986).

Opportunities and Limitations

Although the assertiveness-training program has many strengths, each strength identifies a potential problem for those who may seek to replicate this program. First, this program was conducted in a predominantly White, middle-class school setting. Its content was developed, implemented, and evaluated by researchers with predominantly White, middle-class backgrounds. Thus, the program described heavily reflects the norms and values of the dominant middle-class culture in the United States. Although that emphasis may be associated with later success in the U.S. labor market (Borus, 1984), it is not necessarily appropriate for all children.

Evaluations of assertive and nonassertive or socially competent and incompetent are based on culturally specific social norms (Rotheram &

Phinney, 1987). For example, casting one's gaze to the floor signals deference to authority for a Mexican-American child. Although most school teachers are likely to endorse deference, a White American teacher may misconstrue a Mexican-American child's downcast eyes as sullenness or withdrawal.

Conceivably, training children to be assertive might yield benefits in the school setting, while it could lead to punishment in a home with different cultural norms (Rotheram, 1987c). In conducting this assertiveness-training program with minority children, we are, to a considerable extent, teaching a style of approaching and solving problems; these expanding behavioral repertoires may differ importantly from the values of the child's cultural background (Rotheram, in press). To date there has been no evaluation of potential negative consequences of such school-based programs. Relatively few have monitored the program's effect on a range of classroom variables, let alone its impact across very different settings with different demand qualities.

Such research is needed. There is limited empirical evidence that *code switching*—using one set of behaviors at home and another at school—occurs in social acts (Gumperez, 1982, Gumperez & Roberts, 1980). Teachers and researchers need to increase their understanding of the cultural norms of those being trained and become sensitive to the potentially negative impact of preventive interventions, especially in nonschool settings. Such concerns raise issues similar to those voiced around the issue of bilingual education. Should the cultural norms of a minority be accommodated, or must minorities learn the social norms of the majority to succeed in the majority culture? What are the consequences of becoming bicultural and of adopting the norm of the dominant group?

Some programs that seek to build children's interpersonal coping have circumvented this problem by claiming to teach a process rather than specific behaviors. However, no program is value free, and most of the processes deemed to be necessary for success in U.S. school classrooms reflect White, middle-class values and norms of competence (Rotheram, in press). The assertiveness-training program that we have described makes these values explicit and encourages coping strategies aimed directly at minimizing conflict and simultaneously reaching one's goals. This strategy may be problematic when it violates the cultural norms of the child's reference group. Nonetheless, some researchers have shown that assertiveness training reduces problem be-

haviors of highly aggressive Black adolescents (Huey, 1983; Huey & Rank, 1984; Stewart & Lewis, 1986). Each of these evaluations, however, used White, middle-class indices of adjustment as outcome criteria.

There may also be some potential gender problems in increasing assertiveness. In our society, boys are generally encouraged to be more assertive than girls (Maccoby & Jacklin, 1974). In our study, girls became increasingly assertive from fourth to sixth grade—more assertive than boys. In adulthood, men are more assertive than women, which is a reverse of the pattern in childhood (Lange & Jakubouski, 1977). It is likely that the social rewards for assertiveness shift dramatically in adolescence. Girls are rewarded for passivity, while boys are given rewards and praises for assertiveness (Deluty, 1981).

Introducing class-based, assertiveness-training programs as part of the everyday school curriculum avoids stigmatizing children—a problem that takes on greater importance as children grow older. However, when such a program is used as a potentially therapeutic intervention for students, there can be negative consequences. For example, when piloting assertiveness training for high school students, teachers selected students whom they felt would benefit most from the training. These students attended a series of assertiveness-training classes. After 10 weeks, students continued to raise the question, "How was I selected? What is wrong with me?" When the entire class participates, children are able to engage enjoyably with children from different social groups. This opportunity allows relatively unpopular children to enjoy themselves and to experience success with more popular children. Teams can be structured so that each group includes some children who are positive models for assertiveness.

Another major limiting factor is that the program has not yet been evaluated when implemented by the classroom teacher. To be successful on a large scale, the training must be conducted by teachers, and workshop materials must be available to the teachers. The current evaluation is based on a class program conducted by several research assistants; in that program, all students had opportunities to practice assertiveness in small groups and were rewarded frequently. It may be difficult for a single-classroom teacher to distribute this amount of attention to all students in a class. One alternative is for teachers to use aides or interns to help in the training. Because the present program was delivered by fairly inexperienced students, it should be relatively easy for paraprofessional and professional staff to conduct such training jointly.

Teachers are likely to vary in their ability to implement the program. For example, we found outcome differences that related to the trainers' level of assertiveness (Rotheram, 1982b). The range of interpersonal skills among teachers is likely to be even greater than that of our student leaders. In any case, there is a need to identify the interpersonal skills and personal qualities of trainers that can facilitate learning program concepts and generalizing these skills to new settings.

Evaluation is a key component of any school-based program. In addition to the self-report assertiveness inventory we designed for our studies of elementary- and high-school students (Rotheram et al., 1982; Rotheram & Armstrong, 1980), several other instruments are relevant to the assessment of program skills. The Children's Action Tendency Scale (Deluty, 1979) is a 13-item inventory designed for fourth and fifth graders that asks children to choose between two sets of alternatives (e.g., passive vs. aggressive, assertive vs. aggressive, and passive vs. aggressive). Several studies have examined the reliability and validity of this instrument (Deluty, 1979; 1984a; 1984b). It seems important to use this instrument in the format originally designed by Deluty (1979), because role playing evaluations do not show high reliability when alternative methods of scoring the Children's Action Inventory have been employed (Deluty, 1984b; Williamson, Moody, Granberry, Lethermon, & Blouin, 1983). In addition, there are several other self-report assertiveness inventories used with children (Connor, 1982; Lee, Halberg, Selmon, & Haase, 1985; Reardon, Hersen, Bellack, & Foley, 1979; Wood & Michelson, 1978) and adolescents (Waksman, 1985). Less information is available regarding the reliability and validity of these scales.

Developmental challenges shift throughout the elementary and high school years. A skill-building prevention model creates opportunities to design educational modules aimed at specific, developmentally linked, high-risk behaviors. For example, drug and alcohol use often begins between seventh and ninth grades (Kandel, 1986). A programmatic assertiveness intervention at that level could build on the thinking, feeling, and behavioral skills taught in middle school. The big switch could be rehearsed in situations where preadolescents are likely to engage in drug use (e.g., at a party with no adult supervision). "Just say, 'No' to drugs" involves sophisticated skills in knowing one's own feelings, differenti-

ating one's personal goals from those of peers, having behavioral skills of looking others in the eye and saying in a confident voice tone, "No!", and self-rewarding in the face of peer rejection. The several weeks it would take to acquire such skills could easily be incorporated into a health class. The model proposed is in some ways similar to the life-skills training approach described by Botvin and Tortu (1988) for drug prevention.

Assertiveness training is also potentially relevant to prevention of life-threatening behaviors such as suicide attempts, unsafe sex, and drug use and to reduce the possibility of contracting Acquired Immune Deficiency Syndrome (AIDS; Rotheram, 1987b; Rotheram & Trautman, 1986; Trautman & Rotheram, 1987). Rotheram (1987b) has used the assertion model to develop a screening interview for adolescents in imminent danger of suicide. In addition to identifying suicidal risk factors related to demographic and background factors, for example, history of suicide attempts, family history of suicidal behavior, current depression, history of conduct problems, and drug and alcohol use, the screening procedure assesses youths' ability to engage assertively in behavioral tasks incompatible with suicidal behavior. Youths are asked to

• Generate three self-positives

• Identify and rate on a feeling thermometer high- and low-risk situations for suicide

• Write three nonsuicidal alternative actions that could be taken in high-risk situations

• Make a written commitment for no suicidal behavior

• Identify three persons who can be called on for help in suicide-eliciting situations. (Rotheram, 1987b)

Youths who can complete these tasks successfully are considered not to be in imminent danger of suicide and do not seem to need emergency psychiatric intervention (Rotheram & Bradley, in press).

Likewise, unsafe-sex and drug-use behaviors place adolescents at risk for AIDS. Current prevention programs seek primarily to increase adolescents' general knowledge of the definition and transmission of Human Immunodeficiency Virus (HIV), to identify high risk groups, and to be aware of safe behaviors (DiClemente, Zorn, & Temoshok, 1986). However, to change youths' behavior patterns successfully, assertive social behaviors in high-risk social settings must also be acquired (Mantell, 1987; Rotheram, 1987d). A modified assertiveness-training model offers a framework that can be used to reduce the risk of HIV infection among adolescents.

Helpful Hints

Making assertiveness training fun seemed to be one of the major reasons for this program's success. Given the program's structure, all children experienced some measure of success. Regardless of their competence level, children's strengths were noticed and rewarded by themselves, peers, and adult models. Generating easy-to-learn labels for various assertiveness techniques (e.g., playing cool, the big switch, feeling thermometer) seemed to facilitate children's acquisition of techniques. Teachers could cue children jokingly in interpersonal problem situations during regular classroom activities to use the big switch, thus enhancing learning and generalization.

The program was implemented in a school district using a top-down consultation model. Program support was gained first at the district level; then the staff at one school was approached. Even with support at the district level, the program was introduced gradually to the school. In the 1st year, the researchers and students conducted the training while classroom teachers observed the groups. A supervisor frequently spent the entire session talking, moving from group to group, and helping the leaders. The supervisor was training the teacher through this process to implement the program. She or he would emphasize the advantages and disadvantages of each intervention technique and highlight principles of behavioral management of children. Also during the 1st year, the researchers demonstrated that the assertiveness-training intervention was successful. In the 2nd year, teachers implemented the program as coleaders with the staff from the assertiveness-training program. Only following such training can teachers, in our view, institute the program.

Conclusion

Assertiveness training is an active, enjoyable, classroom-based program that combines components of numerous social skills, coping skills, and behavioral interventions to help children be more socially competent. This intervention package seems to be a promising prevention strategy that can be instituted programmatically across several school years. Offering programs of this type through the middle-childhood years can provide a solid foundation for prevention programs targeting specific, high-risk behaviors in junior high and high school students.

Further research is needed to evaluate the applicability of this prevention program with minority youth, to evaluate the efficacy of second generation programs implemented by teachers, and to assess the differential effectiveness of various program components.

References

Allen, G. J., Chinsky, J. M., Larcen, S. W., Lochman, J. E., & Selinger, H. V. (1976). *Community psychology and the schools*. Hillsdale, NJ: Erlbaum.

Anderson, S., & Messick, S. (1974). Social competence in young children. *Developmental Psychology, 10,* 282–293.

Bandura, A. (1969). *Principles of behavior modification*. New York: Holt, Rinehart and Winston.

Bandura, A. (1977). Self-efficacy: Toward a unifying theory of behavior change. *Psychological Review, 84,* 191–215.

Battjes, R. (1985). Prevention of adolescent drug abuse. *International Journal of Addictions, 20,* 1113–1134.

Beidleman, W. (1981). Group assertiveness in correctional settings: A review and methodological critique, *Journal of Offender Counseling, Services, and Rehabilitation, 6,* 60–87.

Bornstein, M. R., Bellack, A. S., & Hersen, M. (1977). Social skills training for unassertive children: A multiple-baseline analysis. *Journal Applied Behavioral Analysis, 10,* 183–195.

Borus, M. (1984). *Youth and the labor market*. Kalamazoo, MI: W. E. Upjohn Institute for Employment Research.

Botvin, G., & Tortu, S. (1988). Preventing adolescent substance abuse through life-skills training. In R. H. Price, E. Cowen, R. Lorion, & J. Ramos-McKay (Eds.), *Fourteen ounces of prevention: A casebook for practitioners* (pp. 98–110). Washington, DC: American Psychological Association.

Botvin, G., & Wills, J. (1985). Personal and social skill training: cognitive-behavioral approaches to substance abuse prevention. *National Institute of Drug Abuse Monographs, 63,* 8–49.

Carducci, D. (1980). Positive peer culture and assertiveness training: Complementary modalities for dealing with disturbed adolescents. *Behavior Disorders, 5,* 156–162.

Cartledge, G., & Milburn, J. (1978). Teaching social skills to children: A review. *Review of Educational Research, 1,* 133–156.

Cartledge, G., & Milburn, J. (1980). *Teaching social skills to children*. New York: Pergamon Press.

Combs, M., & Slaby, D. (1977). Social skills training with children. In B. Lahey & A. Kazdin (Eds.), *Advances in Clinical Child Psychology*. New York: Pergamon Press.

Conner, J. (1982). Self-report measure of assertiveness in young adolescents. *Journal of Clinical Psychology, 38,* 101–106.

Cooke, T. P., & Appoloni, T. (1976). Developing positive social-emotional behaviors: A study of training and generalization effects. *Journal of Applied Behavior Analysis, 9,* 65–78.

DeLange, J., Barton, J., & Lanham, S. (1981). The wiser way: A cognitive-behavioral model for group social skills training with juvenile delinquents. *Social Work With Groups, 4,* 37–48.

Del Greco, L. (1986). Four year results of a youth smoking prevention program using assertiveness training. *Adolescence, 21,* 631–640.

Deluty, R. H. (1979). Children's Action Tendency Scale: A self-report measure of aggressiveness, assertiveness, and submissiveness in children. *Journal of Consulting and Clinical Psychology, 47,* 1061–1071.

Deluty, R. H. (1981). Assertiveness in children: Some research considerations. *Journal of Clinical Child Psychology, 10,* 149–155.

Deluty, R. H. (1984a). Behavioral validation of the Children's Action Tendency Scale. *Journal of Clinical Child Psychology, 10,* 155–158.

Deluty, R. H. (1984b). On the proper use of the Children's Action Tendency Scale: Comment on Williamson et al.'s Study. *Behavior Therapy, 15,* 426–428.

Deluty, R. H. (1985). Consistency of assertive, aggressive, and submissive behavior for children. *Journal of Personality and Social Psychology, 49,* 1054–1065.

DiClemente, R., Zorn, J., & Temoshok, L. (1986). Adolescents and AIDS: A survey of knowledge, attitudes, and beliefs about AIDS in San Francisco. *American Journal of Public Health, 76,* 1443–1449.

Dorman, L. (1973). Assertive behavior and cognitive performance in preschool children. *Journal of Genetic Psychology, 123,* 155–162.

Evers, W., & Schwarz, J. (1973). Modifying social withdrawal in preschoolers. The effects of filmed modeling and teacher praise. *Journal of Abnormal Child Psychology, 1,* 248–256.

Flowers, J., & Marston, A. (1972). Modification of low self-confidence in elementary school children. *Journal of Educational Research, 66,* 30–34.

Glasgow, R., & McCaul, K. (1985). Social and personal skills training for smoking prevention. *National Institute on Drug Abuse Monograph Series, 63,* 55–66.

Goldstein, A., & Pentz, M. (1984). Psychological skill training and the aggressive adolescent. *School Psychology Review, 13,* 311–323.

Gumperez, J. (1982). *Language and social identity.* London: Cambridge.

Gumperez, J., & Roberts, C. (1980). *Developing awareness skills for interethnic communication.* Paper #12. Singapore: Seameo Regional Language Center.

Hawkins, D., Catalano, R., & Wells, E. (1986). Measuring effects of social skills training for drug abusers. *Journal of Consulting and Clinical Psychology, 54,* 661–664.

Huey, W. (1983). Reducing adolescent aggression through group assertiveness training, *School Counselor, 30,* 193–203.

Huey, W., & Rank, R. (1984). Effects of counselor and peer led assertiveness training groups for Black adolescents who are aggressive, *Journal of Counseling Psychology, 31,* 193–203.

Kandel, D. B. (1986). Processes of peer influence in adolescence. In R. Silberstein (Ed.), *Development as action in context: problem behavior and normal youth development* (pp. 203–228) New York: Springer-Verlag.

Lange, A., & Jakubouski, P. (1977). *A cognitive-behavioral approach to assertiveness training.* Champaign, IL: Research Press.

Lazarus, A. (1971). *Behavior therapy and beyond.* New York: McGraw-Hill.

Lee, D., Halberg, E. T., Selmon, A. G., & Haase, R. F. (1985). An assertive scale for adolescents. *Journal of Clinical Psychology, 41,* 51–57.

Lieberman, M. A., Yalom, I. D., & Miles, M. B. (1973). *Groups: First Facts.* New York: Basic Books.

Maccoby, E., & Jacklin, C. (1974). *The psychology of sex differences.* Stanford: University Press.

Mantell, J. (1987). *Prevention of HIV infection among women.* Women and AIDS Conference, National Institute of Mental Health, Washington, DC.

McPhail, P., Middleton, D., & Ingram, D. (1980). *Social education/communication.* Startline pupil materials, London, England, School Publications Council: Longman Group Limited.

Michelson, L., DiLorenzo, T. M., Calpin, J. P., & Ollendick, T. H. (1982). Situation determinants of the Behavioral Assertiveness Role Play Test for Children. *Behavior Therapy, 13,* 724–734.

O'Conner, R. (1972). *Social learning and communication: A psychological approach to mental health.* New York: Holt, Rinehart, and Winston.

Oden, S., & Asher, S. (1977). Coaching children in social skills for friendship making. *Child Development, 48,* 495–506.

O'Malley, M. (1977). Research perspective on social competence. *Merril-Palmer Quarterly, 23,* (1), 29–44.

Patterson, R. I. (1972). Time-out and assertive training for a dependent child. *Behavior Therapy, 3,* 466–468.

Pentz, M. (1980). Assertiveness training and trainer effects on unassertive and aggressive adolescents. *Journal of Counseling Psychology, 27,* 70–72.

Perkins, H. V. (1965). Classroom behavior and underachievement. *American Educational Research, 2,* 1–12.

Reardon, R. C., Hersen, M., Bellack, A. S., & Foley. (1979). Measuring social skills in grade school boys. *Journal of Behavioral Assessment, 1,* 87–105.

Rotheram, M. (1980). Social skills training with elementary school and high school students. In D. Rathjen & J. Foreyt, (Eds.), *Social Skills Throughout the Lifespan,* New York: Pergamon Press.

Rotheram, M. (1982a). Assertiveness training with underachievers, disruptive, and exceptional children. *Psychology in the Schools, 19,* 532–539.

Rotheram, M. (1982b). Variations in children's assertiveness due to trainer assertion level. *Journal of Community Psychology, 10,* 228–236.

Rotheram, M. (1984). Therapeutic issues in assertiveness training. *Psychology: A Journal of Research, 21,* (1), 28–33.

Rotheram, M. (1987a). Children's academic and social competence. *Journal of Educational Research, 80,* (4), 206–211.

Rotheram, M. (1987b). Evaluation of imminent danger of suicide in children. *American Journal of Orthopsychiatry, 47,* (1), 50–67.

Rotheram, M. (1987c). The child and the school. In L. Combrink-Graham, *The Child in Family Therapy* New York: Guilford Press.

Rotheram, M. (1987d). AIDS prevention among adolescents at high risk. In S. Blumenthal, G. Weissman, & A. Eichler, *Women and AIDS* Washington, DC: National Institute of Mental Health.

Rotheram, M. (in press). Social skills training: Applications and limitations. In S. Compass, L. Bond, & C. Swift (Eds.), *Prevention Research in the School.* Fontana, CA: Sage Publications.

Rotheram, M., & Armstrong, M. (1980). Assertiveness training with high school students. *Adolescence, 15,* 267–295.

Rotheram, M., Armstrong, M., & Booraem, C. (1982). Assertiveness training with elementary school children. *American Journal of Community Psychology, 10,* 567–582.

Rotheram, M., & Bradley, J. (Eds.), (in press). *Suicide Prevention Among Teens in Community Settings.* Tulsa, OK: University of Oklahoma Press. (Funded by the National Resource Center, Tulsa. Three chapters by M. Rotheram & J. Bradley.)

Rotheram, M., & Phinney, J. (1987). Ethnic behavior patterns as an aspect of identity. In J. Phinney & M. Rotheram (Eds.), *Children's ethnic socialization: Pluralism and development* Beverly Hills, CA: Sage Publications.

Rotheram, M., & Trautman, P. (1986). *Cognitive-behavioral interventions with adolescent suicide attempters and their families: A treatment manual.* Unpublished manuscript.

Spence, S. (1983). Social skills training with children and adolescents. In S. Spence, & G. Sheappard, *Developments in social skills training.* Norwich, England: Patson Press.

Spivack, G., Platt, J. J., & Shure, M. (1976). *The problem solving approach.* San Francisco: Jossey-Bass.

Spivack, G., & Shure, M. (1974). *Social adjustment of young children: A cognitive approach to solving real-life problems.* San Francisco: Jossey-Bass.

Stewart, C., & Lewis, W. (1986). Effects of assertiveness training on the self-esteem of Black high school students, *Journal of Counseling and Development, 64,* 638–641.

Trautman, P. D., & Rotheram, M. (1987). Cognitive-behavioral interventions with children. In A. Frances & R. Hales (Eds.), *Annual Review of Psychiatry, 1986,* Washington, DC: American Psychiatric Press.

Van Hasselt, V., Hersen, M., Whitehill, M., & Bellack, B. (1979). Social skills assessment and training for children: An evaluative review. *Behavior, Research, and Therapy, 17,* 413–442.

Waksman, S. (1984). Assertiveness training with adolescents. *Adolescence, 19,* 277–282.

Waksman, S. (1985). Development and psychometric properties of a rating scale for children's social skills. *Journal of Psychoeducational Assessment, 3,* 111–121.

Whitehill, M., Hersen, M., & Coe, T. (1979). Conversation skills for socially isolated children. *Behavior, Research and Therapy, 18,* 217–225.

Williamson, D. A., Moody, S. C., Granberry, S. W., Lethermon, V. R., & Blouin, D. C. (1983). Criterion-related validity of a role play social skills test for children. *Behavior Therapy, 14,* 466–481.

Wolpe, J. (1958). *Psychotherapy by reciprocal inhibition.* Stanford, CA: University Press.

Wood, R., & Michelson, L. (1978). *Assessment of assertive behavior in elementary school children.* Paper presented at the Annual Meeting of the Association for the Advancement of Behavior Therapy, Chicago.

Gilbert J. Botvin and Stephanie Tortu

CHAPTER

8

Preventing Adolescent Substance Abuse Through Life Skills Training

Despite Herculean efforts of schools, community organizations, and law enforcement agencies over the past two decades, substance abuse in the United States continues to be a significant problem (U.S. Public Health Service, [USPHS], 1986). Notwithstanding recent evidence of declines in the prevalence rates of some psychoactive substances, substance use seems to have become part of the normal rites of passage for many American youth. Unfortunately, experimentation and casual use of most psychoactive substances all too often lead to regular patterns of use characterized by both psychological and physical dependence.

The use of one psychoactive substance often precedes the use of others in a relatively predictable and well-defined sequence. Individuals generally begin with the use of tobacco and alcohol, progressing to the use of marijuana; some individuals may eventually progress to opiates and other illicit substances (Hamburg, Braemer, & Jahnke, 1975; Kandel, 1978). Clearly, not all individuals who experiment with a given substance will become regular users; nor will individuals who use tobacco, alcohol, or marijuana necessarily progress to the use of stimulants, depressants, opiates, or other illicit substances. However, psychological factors such as low self-esteem, depression, and poor coping skills are significant for predicting subsequent progression to problematic forms of substance use (Kandel, Kessler, & Margulies, 1978).

Although a great deal of emphasis is generally placed on the use of illicit substances, considerable concern has also developed more recently regarding the use of the "gateway" substances of tobacco, alcohol, and marijuana. This concern goes beyond the fact that individuals using these substances have been found to be at greater risk for using illicit drugs such as heroin and cocaine, which have traditionally been viewed as more dangerous. It is also based on the growing body of epidemiological, laboratory, and clinical evidence that indicates that the use of these substances may also have substantial health consequences. This is particularly true for cigarette smoking which, although legal for adults, has been identified as the number one preventable cause of mortality and morbidity in the United States (USPHS, 1979).

Conventional approaches to the prevention of tobacco, alcohol, and drug abuse have relied on the provision of factual information concerning the adverse consequences of using these substances. These approaches have been based on the assumption that individuals begin smoking, drinking, or using drugs because they lack the requisite knowledge for making a rational decision. In addition, many prevention programs have included fear arousal messages designed to scare adolescents into not using drugs. Although such approaches may have a certain intuitive and logical appeal, evaluation efforts designed to test their efficacy have consistently indicated that they are unable to deter substance use (Berberian, Gross, Lovejoy, & Paparella, 1976; Braucht, Follingstad, Brakarsh, & Berry, 1973; Schaps, Bartolo, Moskowitz, Palley, & Churgin, 1981; Thompson, 1978).

Consequently, the challenge confronting the field of substance abuse prevention has been to demonstrate that preventive interventions can be developed that reduce tobacco, alcohol, and drug abuse. Recent research has focused primary attention on the development and testing of prevention strategies targeted at the various psychosocial factors believed to promote substance abuse among adolescents (Botvin, 1986). The approaches tested differ from previous tobacco, alcohol, and drug abuse prevention approaches in several important ways. They are based on a more complete understanding of the causes of tobacco, alcohol, and drug use and abuse; are grounded in theory; use well-tested cognitive behavior-change techniques; and perhaps most important, have been tested using rigorous evaluation designs.

This chapter focuses on a substance abuse prevention program that we have developed and tested over the past decade. This approach, called Life Skills Training (LST), has been designed to be implemented with junior high school students. As in other psychoeducational approaches to substance abuse prevention, students are taught how to resist social influences to smoke, drink, or use drugs. A distinguishing feature of this approach, however, is that these resistance skills are taught within the context of a broader program designed to enhance generic personal and social skills.

In the first section, the background, underlying theory, and rationale for this approach are discussed. In the next section, the key components of the prevention program are described. This is followed by a brief section summarizing the results of our evaluation research. The final section, intended to assist service providers and practitioners, includes a detailed discussion of planning and implementation issues.

Background, Theory, and Rationale

Factors Promoting Substance Use

Evidence from a variety of sources suggests that social, cognitive, attitudinal, personality, and developmental factors may all promote the initiation of substance use (Blum & Richards, 1979; Braucht et al. 1973; Jessor & Jessor, 1977; Wechsler, 1976). Social influences to smoke, drink, or

use drugs can originate from the attitudes and behavior of family members (particularly parents and older siblings) and friends. They may also arise from the portrayal of substance use in the popular media as something that is both acceptable and an essential ingredient of popularity, sex appeal, sophistication, success, and good times. Furthermore, the initial use of most substances tends to occur in social situations, with solitary use being relatively uncommon (Friedman, Lichtenstein, & Biglan, 1985).

On an individual level, a number of psychological factors have been associated with substance use, including low self-esteem, a greater need for social approval, high anxiety, low assertiveness, an external locus of control, and an impatience to assume adult roles (Botvin & McAlister, 1981; Millman & Botvin, 1983). Researchers have also found that substance users differ from nonusers along several behavioral dimensions which suggests a difference with respect to value orientation. For example, individuals who use drugs tend to get lower grades in school, are less likely to participate in organized extracurricular activities such as sports or clubs, and are more likely than nonusers to engage in antisocial behaviors such as lying, stealing, and cheating (Demone, 1973; Jessor, Collins, & Jessor, 1972; Wechsler & Thum, 1973). Finally, evidence from a variety of sources indicates that certain substances tend to be used together. For example, adolescents who use opiates are also likely to drink excessively and to smoke.

Jessor (1982) argued that the association among various health-compromising behaviors is one of the clearest facts to have emerged from the past decade of research. The significance of this observation is that a number of problem behaviors seem to be caused by the same underlying factors. For this reason, as well as for practical reasons, we and others have argued that prevention programs should be developed which target the underlying determinants of several theoretically and empirically related problem behaviors (Botvin, 1982; Swisher, 1979). This postulate is the basis for the LST program which aims at increasing students' general personal and social competence, thereby affecting the factors that underlie many types of substance use and health-compromising behavior.

For most individuals, initial experimentation with tobacco, alcohol, and drugs, and the subsequent development of regular patterns of use typically occur during the preadolescent and adolescent period (Millman & Botvin, 1983). During this time, individuals typically experiment with a wide range of behaviors and lifestyle patterns as part of the natural processes of separating from parents, developing a sense of autonomy and independence, and acquiring some of the skills necessary for functioning effectively in the adult world. Profound cognitive changes occur during the beginning of adolescence that significantly alter the adolescent's thinking and view of the world. Furthermore, as students approach adolescence, there seems to be a progressive decline in the impact of parental influence and a corresponding increase in the impact of influence from peer networks (Utech & Hoving, 1969; Glynn, 1981). Finally, adolescents seem to have a natural proclivity for perceiving themselves as invulnerable to the hazards of risk-taking and health-compromising behaviors (Urberg & Robbins, 1983).

These and other developmental changes occurring during this period increase adolescents' risk of yielding to various direct and indirect pressures to smoke, drink, or use drugs. Increased reliance on the peer group tends to promote substance use in some individuals, particularly if they are part of a peer network that holds values supportive of substance use. At the same time, the cognitive developments occurring prior to and during this period can serve to increase vulnerability to substance use influences by undermining the credibility of knowledge related to the potential risk of using these substances. For example, adolescents' increased cognitive sophistication may enable them to discover inconsistencies or logical flaws in the arguments advanced by adults about the potential risks of substance use or may help them to formulate their own counter arguments and construct rationalizations for ignoring these risks, particularly if substance use is perceived as having social or personal benefits.

Theoretical Foundations

The theoretical foundations of the LST prevention program rest largely on social learning theory (Bandura, 1977) and problem behavior theory (Jessor & Jessor, 1977). Within this framework, the use of psychoactive substances is conceptualized as a socially learned and functional behavior which is the result of the interplay of both social-environmental and personal factors. Substance use behavior, like other types of behavior, is learned through a process of modeling and reinforcement which is mediated by personal factors such as cognitions, attitudes, and beliefs.

Some individuals may be motivated to smoke, drink, or use drugs in an effort to cope with expected failure or as an alternative way of achieving a desired goal. For example, some adolescents who are not successful academically or socially may begin to use drugs as an alternative means of achieving popularity, social status, or self-esteem. Similarly, tobacco, alcohol, and certain other drugs may be used in an attempt to cope with tension or anxiety, particularly social anxiety.

Other individuals may begin smoking, drinking, or using drugs after repeatedly observing high-status role models engage in these behaviors or as the result of the persuasive appeals of advertisers or peers. Differential susceptibility to social influence seems to be mediated by personality; youth with low self-esteem, low self-confidence, low autonomy, and an external locus of control are more likely to succumb to these influences (Bandura, 1969; Rotter, 1972).

One limitation of focused, pressure-resistance, prevention models that rely exclusively on the teaching of refusal skills is that even though students may learn the refusal skills, they might have little motivation to apply them. In fact, Friedman et al. (1983) found in an empirical study of students who began smoking in social situations that the majority had knowingly entered the situation with the specific intention to smoke. Thus, an argument supporting broader based programs like LST is that successful prevention strategies must not only provide students with the skills needed to resist social pressure to use tobacco, alcohol, or other drugs, but they must also reduce the motivation to use these substances.

For these reasons, the LST approach combines both training in the use of refusal skills and generic personal and social skills in an effort to enhance overall competence. Teaching social resistance or refusal skills should increase students' ability to resist social influences promoting substance use. Consequently, improving students' general personal and social competence should reduce their motivation to use drugs.

The Role of Information and Knowledge

As noted above, merely providing information about the extreme negative consequences of substance abuse is by itself of marginal value as a prevention strategy. This does not mean that such information and knowledge cannot play an important role in substance abuse prevention. To the contrary, some knowledge about the use of tobacco, alcohol, and drugs may be a useful component of substance abuse prevention programs. For example, because adolescents typically overestimate the prevalence of smoking and drinking, correcting normative expectations of high substance use can help to reduce the perceived social support for these behaviors.

It is important that the information and knowledge included in prevention programs be selected with an understanding of cognitive-developmental factors. Adolescents tend to have a "present-time" orientation. For many, the perceived short-term social benefits of smoking, drinking, or drug taking override concerns for potential negative consequences, especially distant, long-term ones. Thus, it may be more meaningful to focus on some immediate consequences of use, especially ones that adolescents might view as social liabilities. In the case of smoking, these immediate short-term consequences include nicotine stains on the teeth and bad breath.

The Importance of Personal and Social Competence

The acquisition of adequate social skills seems to play an important role in both psychological adjustment and psychosocial development. Basic interpersonal skills are necessary for the initiation and maintenance of friendship and other mutually beneficial relationships; they are among the most important skills that an individual must learn. A lack of social competence may lead to rejection and social isolation, which may in turn result in poor psychological adjustment.

Individuals begin to acquire basic social skills during childhood; as they mature, their social skills typically increase. By the time individuals become adolescents, many have acquired a repertoire of social skills such as initiating and maintaining conversations, giving and receiving compliments, refusing unreasonable requests, and expressing feelings. Social skills, like other behaviors, are learned through a combination of modeling and reinforcement. The development of these skills depends on having opportunities to observe and practice them. In addition to acquiring social skills, it is also important that adolescents learn the kind of refusal skills that will enable them to resist pressure to engage in behaviors that they might otherwise choose to avoid.

Social skills represent the largest collection of skills that people need to function effectively as adults. Additionally, the quality of life is enhanced by acquiring an array of personal skills including the abilities to make responsible decisions, cope with anxiety, and improve personal habits.

Program Description

General Overview

The LST program was developed after a careful consideration of many factors found to be associated with the initiation of adolescent substance abuse. The prevention program itself is in the form of a psychoeducational curriculum that focuses on the primary psychosocial determinants of substance abuse. This type of prevention strategy is designed to help young people develop basic personal and social skills and an increased sense of personal control. As a result, emphasis is placed on learning to apply and practice skills that are relevant to the problems confronting adolescents. Thus, the problem of substance abuse is addressed within the larger context of acquiring basic life skills and enhancing personal and social competence. Because the LST approach was designed for junior high school students, it focuses on the prevention of the use of tobacco, alcohol, and marijuana—the "gateway" substances.

Program Objectives

The main objectives of the LST program are to

• Provide students with the necessary skills to resist direct social pressures to smoke, drink excessively, or use marijuana

• Decrease students' susceptibility to indirect social pressures to use tobacco, alcohol, and other drugs by helping them to develop greater autonomy, self-esteem, self-mastery, and self-confidence

• Enable students to cope effectively with anxiety, particularly anxiety induced by social situations

• Increase students' knowledge of the immediate consequences of smoking, by providing them with accurate information concerning the prevalence rates of tobacco, alcohol, and marijuana use

• Promote the development of attitudes and beliefs consistent with nonsubstance use.

Program Components

The LST program includes five major components. Each component described consists of two to six lessons designed to be taught in sequence. Table 8–1 provides a brief overview of each topic in the program with the number of class sessions recommended to cover each topic. A more complete description of the program's content and activities is contained in the LST teacher's manual (Botvin, 1983).

Knowledge and information. This component is composed of four sessions. Session 1 provides general information about cigarette smoking, with emphasis on the prevalence of cigarette smoking among teenagers and adults, and the declining social acceptability of smoking. Session 2 focuses on the immediate physiological effects of smoking, using biofeedback apparatus to demonstrate the effect of cigarette smoking on heart rate, carbon monoxide in expired air, and hand steadiness. The third and fourth sessions are similar to the first session, with the emphasis on alcohol and marijuana respectively. Students are given the necessary information about alcohol and marijuana to counter common myths and misconceptions. The goal is to help them in making responsible, informed decisions about their own use of alcohol and marijuana.

Decision-making component. The second component consists of four sessions. The first two sessions concern making decisions effectively and responsibly. Students discuss how they make important decisions; a strategy for making decisions is suggested. This session also identifies tactics that others may use to influence one's decisions. Sessions 3 and 4 introduce students to the techniques used by advertisers to influence the decisions made by consumers. Students discuss the purpose of advertising and review the use of deceptive advertising techniques. Cigarette and liquor advertisements are highlighted as examples of how deceptive techniques may be used. Students are taught to identify these techniques and avoid falling prey to the appeals used to persuade them to smoke cigarettes and drink alcohol.

Self-directed behavior change. The third component of the LST program consists of two class sessions focusing on the understanding of self-image and the concept of self-improvement. An 8-week self-improvement project is begun during this component to help students improve one aspect of their lives. Session 1 explains what self-image is, how it is formed, and how it can be

improved through a self-improvement plan. During Session 2, each student selects a skill or behavior that he or she would like to improve or change and identifies a long-term (8-week) goal, as well as a series of short-term (weekly) goals. Students complete progress reports so that their weekly progress can be followed as they learn to shape their own behavior.

Coping with anxiety. The fourth component involves learning to cope with anxiety and consists of two sessions. It features explicit instructions on how to use specific anxiety-reduction techniques. Students are invited to discuss their own experiences with anxiety, the symptoms of anxiety, and the common situations that produce anxiety. Three anxiety reduction techniques are taught: a basic relaxation exercise, a deep breathing exercise, and the use of mental rehearsal. A 12-minute relaxation audiotape is used to introduce the students to the relaxation exercise in the classroom. Students are encouraged to practice these techniques at home and to integrate them into their everyday lives as active-coping strategies. They are also made aware of their own anxiety-producing thought sequences, shown how these sequences influence their reaction to anxiety-producing situations, and taught the importance of controlling them.

Social skills. This is the largest of the five components; it includes six sessions. Sessions 1 and 2 cover communication skills, define verbal and nonverbal communications, and present specific guidelines for avoiding misunderstandings. Session 3 is designed to help students overcome shyness. Students are taught skills needed to initiate social contacts, give and receive compliments, begin, maintain and end conversations. Session 4 focuses on skills needed to maintain boy–girl relationships. This session begins with a discussion of attraction. Students learn how to initiate and sustain conversations with the opposite sex and how to plan dates and social activities. The last two sessions in this unit are for assertiveness training. Students discuss the reasons for not being assertive and learn the benefits of appropriate assertiveness. General verbal and nonverbal assertive behaviors are taught, and students are asked to apply them to situations involving peer pressure to smoke, drink, or use marijuana.

Booster Sessions

Because the pressure and opportunity to use tobacco, alcohol, and marijuana remains, indeed of-

Table 8–1. Life Skills Training Program Description

Number of sessions	Topic	Description
I. Knowledge and information		
4	Substance use: myths and realities	Common attitudes and beliefs about tobacco, alcohol, and marijuana use; current prevalence rates of adults and teenagers; social acceptability of using these substances; process of becoming a regular (habitual) user, and the difficulty of breaking these habits; one immediate physiological effects of smoking
II. Decision making		
2	Decision making and independent thinking	Discussion of routine decision making; description of a general decision-making strategy; social influences affecting decisions; recognizing persuasive tactics; and the importance of independent thinking.
2	Media influences and advertising techniques	Discussion of media influences on behavior; advertising techniques and the manipulation of consumer behavior; formulating counter-arguments and other cognitive strategies for resisting advertising pressure; cigarette and alcohol advertising as case studies in the use of these techniques.
III. Self-directed, behavior change		
2	Self-image and self-improvement	Discussion of self-image and how it is formed; the relationship between self-image and behavior; the importance of a positive self-image; alternative methods of improving one's self and self-image; beginning a self-improvement project.
IV. Coping with anxiety		
2	Coping with anxiety	Discussion of common anxiety-inducing situations; demonstration and practice of cognitive-behavioral techniques for coping with anxiety; instruction on the application of these techniques to everyday situations as active coping strategies.
V. Social skills		
2	Communication skills	Discussion of the communication process; distinguishing between verbal and nonverbal communication; techniques for avoiding misunderstandings.
1	Social skills (A)	Discussion on overcoming shyness; initiating social contacts, giving and receiving compliments; basic conversational skills: initiating, sustaining and ending conversations.
1	Social skills (B)	Discussion of boy-girl relationships and the nature of attraction; conversations with the opposite sex; social activities and asking someone out for a date.
2	Assertiveness	Situations calling for assertiveness; reasons for not being assertive; verbal and nonverbal assertive skills; resisting peer pressures to smoke, drink, or use marijuana.

ten grows, during the middle or junior high school years, the creation of a health-promoting, school milieu is helped by booster sessions after the initial presentation of the LST curriculum. For this reason, a 10-session curriculum for the 8th grade and a 5-session booster curriculum for the 9th grade have been added to the original program package.

The booster sessions are designed to reinforce the main points of the LST program, but the emphasis is decidedly on the demonstration and practice of the social and personal skills that form the foundation of this prevention approach. Teacher's manuals have been developed for both the 9-session and 5-session booster curricula.

Evaluation Studies

Several evaluation studies have been conducted to assess the efficacy of the LST prevention strategy. These studies were also designed to obtain information about the effectiveness of different types of providers, of booster sessions, and with different target populations, different "gateway" substances, and with and without a formal teacher-training workshop and ongoing consultation. Throughout our research studies, a concerted effort has been made to maximize internal and external validity. Considerable attention has been paid to research design and measurement issues, and many refinements have been made over the years to strengthen the methodological rigor of the studies. Our research studies have progressed from small-scale pilot studies involving just a few hundred students to large-scale prevention trials involving several thousand students.

Pilot Study

The initial pilot study (Botvin, Eng, & Williams, 1980) was designed to assess LST's short-term efficacy in preventing the onset of cigarette smoking among 8th–10th graders ($N = 281$) from two comparable suburban New York schools. After randomly assigning schools to experimental and control conditions and pretesting students, the program was conducted in the experimental school. At the end of the program, the experimental group was found to have 75% fewer new cigarette smokers than the controls. Although a 3-month follow-up study (Botvin & Eng, 1982) found some erosion of the posttest effects, there were still 67% fewer new smokers among program students than controls.

Peer Leader Study

A second study assessed program efficacy when conducted by 11th and 12th grade peer leaders (Botvin & Eng, 1982). In this research, seventh graders in two comparable suburban New York schools were randomly assigned to experimental and control conditions ($N = 426$). In addition to self-report questionnaire data about smoking behavior, saliva samples were collected from students using the "bogus pipeline" technique (Evans, Hansen, & Mittlemark, 1977).

Posttest results indicated that there were 58% fewer new smokers among program students as compared to controls. Saliva thiocyanate (SCN) analysis confirmed that finding. Thus, although SCN levels increased significantly from pretest to posttest in controls (indicating increased cigarette smoking), there were no changes in SCN levels among program participants. The 1-year follow-up data indicated that there were 56% fewer LST students than controls who had become regular cigarette smokers since the pretest.

Scheduling Format and Booster Sessions

A third study (Botvin, Renick, & Baker, 1983), with 7th grade students from several suburban schools ($N = 902$), sought to assess the relative efficacy of (a) the LST program when implemented by regular classroom teachers according to two different implementation schedules (one class per week versus multiple classes per week), and (b) booster sessions. Self-report data were collected by questionnaire, and the "bogus pipeline" technique used in the previous study was repeated.

At posttest, there were 50% fewer smokers in the experimental groups than in the controls. No differences were found between groups receiving the LST program according to the two implementation schedules. At the 1-year follow-up, there were 55% fewer smokers among program students who had the more intensive implementation. Furthermore, there were 87% fewer regular smokers among the 7th grade program students who also had 8th grade sessions booster sessions compared to controls.

Alcohol Pilot Study

To assess the potential of this intervention strategy for other forms of substance use, we conducted a pilot study with seventh graders from two comparable New York City public schools ($N = 239$), randomly assigned to experimental and control conditions. Information was included in the LST program concerning the consequences of alcohol misuse and, where appropriate, the skills taught were applied to situations that might promote alcohol use.

All students were pretested by questionnaire during the 7th grade and tested again 9 months later. No program effects were evident at the initial posttest; however, at the 9-month follow-up point, 54% fewer program students reported drinking than controls during the past month, 73% fewer program students reported heavy drinking, and 79% fewer students reported getting drunk one or more times per month.

Substance Abuse Prevention Study

A study (Botvin, Baker, Renick, Filazzola, & Botvin, 1984), involving seventh graders from 10 public schools in suburban New York ($N = 1311$), was conducted to determine the relative efficacy of the LST approach for preventing tobacco, alcohol, and marijuana use. This study also assessed the relative efficacy of teachers and older peer leaders and of booster sessions conducted in both the eighth and ninth grades.

Initial postprogram effects for tobacco, alcohol, and marijuana were evident only for students in the peer-led condition. These effects were of roughly the same magnitude as those observed in prior studies. There were 40% fewer experimental smokers in the peer-led LST condition than in the control condition. The most interesting results were with respect to marijuana use; there were 71% fewer students in the peer-led LST condition reporting marijuana use compared with controls.

At the 1-year follow-up point, significantly fewer students in the peer-led booster LST group than controls were smoking and using marijuana. The 2-year follow-up data indicated that the strongest effects over time were for cigarette smoking. Retrospective analysis showed that teachers were more variable than peer leaders in the quality of their program implementation. Although some teachers followed the instructions in the intervention protocol in conducting the program, others clearly did not. Analysis of a restricted sample of teachers who implemented the program with reasonable fidelity yielded findings similar to those obtained by peer leaders. Although these results support the program's efficacy when implemented by both peer leaders and classroom teachers, they suggest the need to examine more closely potential barriers to successful implementation to ensure program effectiveness when conducted in the "real world."

Current Studies

In addition to the preceding studies, we are now conducting three large scale prevention trials. One study involves two cohorts of approximately 10,000 students each from 56 public schools in New York State. Using a randomized block design, schools were assigned to the following conditions: LST with a formal teacher-training workshop, LST with packaged (written and vidio) teacher training, and a no-contact control. Teachers will implement the LST program with 7th graders. Booster sessions will be provided in both the eighth and ninth grades.

Two other studies now underway are examining LST's efficacy with urban minority students. The first, still in a developmental phase, is with a predominantly Black sample ($N \cong 3,000$) from 30 public schools in northern New Jersey. The other study is being done with a predominantly Hispanic sample ($N = 5,000$) from 47 schools in New York City; the sample is equally divided between public and parochial schools. Although the prevention strategy in this program is essentially the same as that used in our previous research, the curriculum materials have been modified to maximize cultural sensitivity and appropriateness to the target population. Preliminary evidence from both the pilot phase and first year of the full-scale prevention trial offers support for the approach's efficacy with urban students in a multiracial environment.

Planning and Implementation Guidelines

Recent improvement in the quality of substance abuse prevention and other school health education programs has led to a greater emphasis on factors that facilitate dissemination, implementation, adoption, and diffusion of new health curricula (Basch, 1983; Bauer, 1980; Kolbe & Iverson, 1980). Introducing an innovative curriculum into a school system is a very complex process, often hindered by the fact that schools are structurally arranged to resist change (Sarason, 1982). While planning to implement a new curriculum, one must keep in mind that the process is fraught with psychological, sociological, political, and economic concerns. Each person who plays a role in bringing an innovative curriculum into the classroom moves through the change process with a different set of concerns. Although all parties involved may desire the change, each answers to a different set of constituents.

For example, school administrators are typically concerned about program costs, parental or school board reaction to the innovation, and how long it takes to train teachers adequately. Members of an evaluation research team are concerned with ensuring that teachers and other program providers understand the theoretical rationale for the new program and learn the skills needed to implement it with fidelity in the school environment. Teachers wonder if the new teaching strategies demanded by the curriculum will change the way in which they relate to students, and if people who know about the curriculum will be available for questions and advice once the implementation has begun.

Initial Planning

In our own evaluation research, we have had the opportunity to work with members of the educational community as they move to adopt the LST program. During the early stages of this process, it is necessary to identify, and communicate with, individuals or groups with the power to make decisions about adopting a new curricula. These decision makers include school superintendents, other district level administrators, and school board members. Although they may not have the power to adopt curricula, concerned parents, particularly when organized into groups, can have an enormous influence on decision makers.

Our experience suggests that the best way to initiate this process is to make the initial contact at the district level. If such district-wide support is present, we work our way down through the system, meeting next with principals and assistant principals, department heads, and eventually classroom teachers. During these meetings, the program is described, along with its background and rationale, and the results of our evaluation studies are briefly summarized. Without such support, the obstacles encountered in attempting to implement a new program may be insurmountable. Worthwhile programs may never get started or, once underway, may languish in subsequent years and eventually be discontinued if sufficient support does not exist for "institutionalizing" them.

Parent support is very valuable. We have found it helpful to have a letter from the district superintendent or principal sent home to parents, informing them about the new intervention program. Most schools do not routinely obtain parental approval for programs such as LST if they are incorporated into existing curricula. After the informational letter to parents, LST is treated like any other academic program. However, if data are being collected that identify students either directly (by name) or indirectly through the use of ID codes, parental consent or notification is necessary.

Scheduling Considerations

The LST curriculum was designed to be taught in the sequence presented in Table 8–1. The numbers of class periods required for each topic are also presented in Table 8–1. It is recommended that the LST program be started in the 7th grade because the pressures to use tobacco and alcohol intensify, and most experimentation begins at this time. It is also possible to begin the program in the 6th grade. However, the program is not recommended for use with a younger age group because it was specifically designed to teach psychosocial skills that junior high or middle school students most needed. The curriculum can be taught either once a week or as a concentrated minicourse over a 3- to 4-week period.

Program Materials

The materials needed to conduct the LST program include a teacher's manual and a student workbook. The teacher's manual contains detailed lesson plans describing both the content and activities to be included in each session. The student guide includes classroom exercises and homework assignments and some factual information and space to keep notes. A 12-minute relaxation audiotape designed to be used during the session on coping with anxiety is also part of the curriculum package.

Teacher Selection

The teachers who implement the program are very important to its success. Although LST fits naturally within a health or science curriculum, it has also been taught in English, social studies, home and careers, and earth science. Good student rapport, commitment to the program, and motivation to teach LST are important teacher qualities. These qualities are probably more important than the subject area in which the teacher has been trained. Ideally, someone familiar with the faculty at a particular school should be asked to nominate several teachers from that school who would be interested in teaching the program. Those teachers should be invited to review the program and to volunteer if they wish to teach it. To make it more attractive, school officials can provide teachers with professional recognition, release time, or other suitable incentives. During the planning stages in a particular school, all program teachers should play a role in its day-to-day management to enhance the sense of teacher control.

Teacher Training

Given the nature of the LST program, the teacher's role and even the classroom techniques differ from those used in most traditional tobacco, alcohol, and drug abuse prevention programs. The teacher's role can be conceptualized as partly facilitator and partly coach or trainer. As facilitators, teachers are responsible for initiating and directing class discussion and correcting any misinformation. As coaches or trainers, they are responsible for teaching an array of personal and social skills using a combination of techniques including instruction, modeling, behavioral rehearsal, feedback, and reinforcement.

In conducting LST evaluation research over the past 10 years, we have given increasing attention to teacher training (Tortu & Botvin, 1987). As several educational researchers have observed, quality teacher training and staff development are necessary components of any successful implementation of a curricular innovation (Fullan, 1985; McLaughlin & Marsh, 1978; Patterson & Czajkowski, 1979). Although supporting data are not available, it is likely that many innovative prevention curricula are not implemented in classrooms because teachers and other program providers feel both uncomfortable with new work demands and poorly equipped to use the new teaching techniques. Proper training ensures that teachers become comfortable with their new roles by providing a situation in which they can learn and practice new teaching techniques prior to classroom implementation.

The first step in the training process involves conducting a formal training workshop, designed to provide program leaders with a general understanding of the problem of adolescent substance abuse and a thorough grounding in the LST approach. Specifically, the training workshop is designed to

1. Provide participants with an understanding of the issues of substance abuse and with LST's theoretical rationale,

2. Provide a full description of the program and the curriculum materials needed to implement it successfully,

3. Familiarize participants with program content and activities,

4. Demonstrate the teaching techniques needed to implement the LST curriculum,

5. Provide participants with opportunities to practice the teaching techniques in a small group setting and receive feedback on their performance,

6. Provide guidelines for scheduling and implementation, and

7. Generate a sense of enthusiasm and commitment among individuals who will be teaching the program.

The format of a typical 1-day training workshop is shown in Table 8–2. The day's activities begin with the provision of a conceptual framework on which the rest of the day's training is based. The problem of teenage substance abuse is reviewed, and workshop participants are introduced to LST's background, theory, and rationale.

In the next section of the workshop, guidelines for the implementation of the program are introduced along with training in the use of techniques for facilitating skills acquisition. Teachers are also advised on the program scheduling format, how to maximize student involvement, how to set up the self-improvement project, and how to do classroom role plays.

The next portion of the training involves a detailed review of each session of the curriculum. Embedded in this review is the demonstration by workshop staff of essential LST teaching skills. Because the skills involved in the coach role are least familiar to teachers, they are emphasized the most. Curriculum review and skill demonstration occur in a small group setting. Finally, participants are given an opportunity to practice teaching selected program components using the techniques covered in the workshop.

Table 8–2. Life Skills Training Program Teacher Orientation Workshop

I.   Introduction
     A. Welcome
     B. Background and rationale for program

II. Presentation of program implementation guidelines
     A. The teacher's special roles: facilitator and coach
     B. Description of self-improvement project
     C. Tips for doing role plays
     D. Scheduling of program
     E. LST classroom ground rules
     F. Question and answer period

III. Review of the life skills training curriculum and demonstration of teaching techniques
     A. Smoking: myths and realities
     B. Smoking and biofeedback
     C. Alcohol: myths and realities
     D. Marijuana: myths and realities
     E. Decision making and independent thinking
     F. Advertising
     G. Self-image and self-improvement
     H. Coping with anxiety
     I. Communication skills
     J. Social skills (A)
     K. Social skills (B)
     L. Assertiveness

IV. Practice and feedback session

V.   Review and question and answer period

Ongoing Support and Consultation

The training process does not end with the formal training workshop. LST staff members continue to offer support, guidance, and consultation as teachers implement the program. Regular visits to the classroom by LST program staff are scheduled to provide feedback on teachers' classroom performance.

New concerns surface as the program is being implemented. As teachers begin to use the new curriculum, their early concerns center on how it will affect them and their routine teaching activities. Once these concerns are addressed and implementation is well underway, their focus generally shifts to concerns about student reaction to the new program (Loucks & Pratt, 1979). They may, for example, worry that some students are unwilling to participate in role plays or skill practice sessions, or that some students are not ready or capable of learning some of the curricular skills. LST staff work with individual teachers to solve these difficulties. By providing this ongoing guidance, teachers' sense of efficacy is enhanced, and the likelihood is decreased that they will abandon the program due to lack of support services.

Evaluation Guidelines

Although evaluation research has already shown that LST's primary prevention strategy is effective under well-controlled research conditions, an evaluation component in future applications can help to determine whether the program is being effectively implemented. Evaluation can proceed at several levels. Minimally, there should be a process evaluation to determine if the program has been successfully and completely implemented. This can be done by making up a list of session objectives and activities (taken directly from the teacher's manual) and using it as a simple checklist. The checklist is to be completed after each session.

We also recommend that an outcome study be done based on pretesting and posttesting of participating students with respect to tobacco, alcohol, and marijuana use (i.e., amount and frequency) for the past month, week, or day. Substance use status can be ascertained from dichotomous (*yes* or *no*) items (e.g., "Have you smoked one or more cigarettes in the past month?") or a general measure for each substance incorporating several categories of use into one item (e.g., "How often, if ever, do you generally smoke cigarettes?"). Response categories can range from *never* to *several times a day*. Additional information about useful outcome measures and data collection procedures is provided in several of our research reports (e.g., Botvin et al., 1983, 1984).

Special care should be taken in collecting data about illegal behaviors from students. It is essential to protect students' confidentiality. One solution is to collect anonymous data. However, in longitudinal research, where it is important to track individual students and examine changes over time, some means of linking data collected at different time points is necessary. This can be accomplished by the use of unique ID codes matched to students' names on a master list. The master list should be kept in a secure location (e.g., a locked filing cabinet in a locked room) controlled by the researchers. The original questionnaires and master list should be destroyed after data analyses have been completed.

Fundamental differences between primary prevention programs and treatment programs affect how these interventions are evaluated. Treatment program outcomes can be evaluated in terms of reductions in target behaviors. However, evaluation must proceed with respect to reduction in the rate of increase of a given target behavior or the proportion of individuals manifesting that behavior relative to an appropriate comparison group due to the nature of preventative interventions.

Thus, for example, in the case of cigarette smoking, a prevention program would be evaluated in terms of the extent to which it reduced the proportion of individuals who become occasional or regular smokers relative to some comparison group, rather than the proportion of individuals quitting. Outcome evaluation, therefore, must demonstrate that fewer individuals began to smoke in the intervention group relative to some comparison group (i.e., a nonintervention group or a group receiving a different intervention). Because the normal expectation among teenagers is that there should be an increase in new smokers, drinkers, and marijuana users (even in the group receiving a preventive intervention), meaningful evaluation cannot be accomplished without an appropriate comparison group. Simply assessing whether substance use increased in the intervention group alone would be entirely misleading, because it might lead to the erroneous conclusion that the intervention was not effective when, in fact, it may have substantially reduced the smoking onset rate.

Summary and Conclusions

Substance abuse among adolescents continues to be a major health problem in the United States. Conventional prevention approaches have relied either on providing factual information about the adverse consequences of using these substances or on fear-arousal messages designed to scare adolescents into not using drugs. Unfortunately, neither of these approaches has been found to be effective in decreasing substance use among adolescents. Recently, however, attention has been focused on the development and testing of prevention programs targeted to the psychosocial factors believed to promote substance abuse among adolescents. One such prevention approach is the LST Program.

Designed for junior high school students, the LST program teaches students how to resist social influences to smoke, drink, or use drugs. In addition, students learn generic personal and social skills to enhance their ability to make decisions, cope with anxiety, and have successful interpersonal relationships. Evaluation studies conducted over the past 10 years have shown that the LST program is successful in reducing the tobacco, alcohol, and marijuana use.

Despite the promising results obtained in our previous evaluation studies with this psychoeducational prevention strategy, considerable research is still needed to determine its long-term effectiveness, generalizability to other populations (particularly urban minority populations), and generalizability to other health-compromising or problem behaviors. In addition, potential barriers to dissemination and implementation must be identified and strategies for overcoming them must be developed and tested.

References

Bandura, A. (1969). *Principles of behavior modification.* New York: Holt, Rinehart and Winston.

Bandura, A. (1977). *Social learning theory.* Englewood Cliffs, NJ: Prentice-Hall.

Basch, C. E. (1983). Research on disseminating and implementing health education programs in schools. *Journal of School Health, 54,* 57–66.

Bauer, K. G. (1980). *Improving the chances for health: Lifestyle change and health evaluation.* San Francisco: National Center for Health Education.

Berberian, R. M., Gross, C., Lovejoy, J., & Paparella, S. (1976). The effectiveness of drug education programs: A critical review. *Health Education Monographs, 4,* 377–398.

Blum, R. & Richards, L. (1979). Youthful drug use. In R. I. Dupont, A. Goldstein & J. O'Donnell, (Eds.), *Handbook on drug abuse* (pp. 257–267). Washington, D.C.: U.S. Government Printing Office.

Botvin, G. J. (1982). Broadening the focus of smoking prevention strategies. In T. Coates, A. Petersen, & C. Perry (eds.) *Promoting adolescent health: A dialog on research and practice* (pp. 137–148). New York: Academic Press.

Botvin, G. J. (1983). *Life skills training: Teacher's manual.* New York: Smithfield Press.

Botvin, G. J. (1986). Substance abuse prevention research: Recent developments and future directions. *Journal of School Health, 56,* 369–374.

Botvin, G. J., Baker, E., Renick, N., Filazzola, A. D., & Botvin, E. M. (1984). A cognitive-behavioral approach to substance abuse prevention. *Addictive Behaviors, 9,* 137–147.

Botvin, G. J. & Eng, A. (1982). The efficacy of a multicomponent approach to the prevention of cigarette smoking. *Preventive Medicine, 11,* 199–211.

Botvin, G. J., Eng, A., & Williams, C. L. (1980). Preventing the onset of cigarette smoking through life skills training. *Preventive Medicine, 9,* 135–143.

Botvin, G. J., & McAlister, A. (1981). Cigarette smoking among children and adolescents: Causes and prevention. In C. B. Arnold (Ed.), *Annual review of disease prevention* (pp. 222–249). New York: Springer.

Botvin, G. J., Renick, N., & Baker, E. (1983). The effects of scheduling format and booster sessions on a broad spectrum psychosocial approach to smoking prevention. *Journal of Behavioral Medicine, 6,* 359–379.

Braucht, G. N., Follingstad, D., Brakash, D., & Berry, K. L. (1973). Drug education: A review of goals, approaches and effectiveness, and a paradigm for evaluation. *Quarterly Journal of Studies on Alcohol, 34,* 1279–1292.

Demone, H. W. (1973). The nonuse and abuse of alcohol by the male adolescent. In M. Chafetz (Ed.), *Proceedings of the second annual alcoholism conference* (pp. 24–32) (DHEW Publication No. HSM 73-9083). Washington, DC: U.S. Government Printing Office.

Evans, R. I., Hansen, W. B., & Mittlemark, M. B. (1977). Increasing the validity of self-reports of smoking behavior in children. *Journal of Applied Psychology, 62,* 521–523.

Friedman, L. S., Lichtenstein, E., & Biglan, A. (1985). Smoking onset among teens: An empirical analysis of initial situations. *Addictive Behaviors, 10,* 1–14.

Fullan, M. (1985). Change processes and strategies at the local level. *The Elementary School Journal, 85,* 391–421.

Glynn, T. J. (1981). From family to peer: Transitions of influence among drug-using youth. In D. Lettieri, J. Ludford (Eds.), *Drug abuse and the American adolescent* (pp. 57–81) (DHHS Publication No. ADM 81-1166). Washington, DC: U.S. Government Printing Office.

Hamburg, B. A., Braemer, H. C., & Jahnke, W. A. (1975). Hierarchy of drug use in adolescence: Behavioral and attitudinal correlates of substantial drug use. *American Journal of Psychiatry, 132,* 1155–1167.

Jessor, R. (1982). Critical issues in research on adolescent health promotion. In T. Coates, A. Petersen, & C. Perry (Eds.) *Promoting adolescent health: A dialog on research and practice* (pp. 447–465). New York: Academic Press.

Jessor, R., and Jessor, S. L. (1977). *Problem behavior and psychosocial development: A longitudinal study of youth.* New York: Academic Press.

Jessor, R., Collins, M. I., & Jessor, S. L. (1972). On becoming a drinker: Social-psychological aspects of an adolescent transition. *Annual of the New York Academy of Sciences, 197,* 199–213.

Kandel, D. B. (1978). Convergences in prospective longitudinal surveys of drug use in normal populations. In D. B. Kandel (Ed.), *Longitudinal research on drug use: Empirical findings and methodological issues* (pp. 3–38). Washington, DC: Hemisphere (Halsted-Wiley).

Kandel, D. B., Kessler, R. C., & Margulies, R. Z. Antecedents of adolescent initiation into stages of drug abuse. In D. B. Kandel (Ed.), *Longitudinal research on drug use: Empirical findings and methodological issues* (pp. 73–99). New York: Wiley.

Kolbe, L. J., & Iverson, D. C. (1980, August). *Implementing comprehensive school health education.* Paper presented at the National Conference on Promoting Health Through Schools, Denver.

Loucks, S., & Pratt, H. (1979). A concerns-based approach to curriculum change. *Educational Leadership, 37,* 212–215.

McLaughlin, M. W., & Marsh, D. D. (1978). Staff development and school change. *Teachers College Record, 80,* 69–94.

Millman, R. B., & Botvin, G. J. (1983). Substance use, abuse, and dependence. In M. D. Levine, W. B. Carey, A. C. Crocker, & R. T. Gross (Eds.), *Developmental-behavioral pediatrics* (pp. 683–708). Philadelphia: W. B. Saunders.

Patterson, J., & Czajkowski, T. (1979). Implementation: Neglected phase in curriculum change. *Educational Leadership, 37,* 204–206.

Rotter, J. B. (1972). Generalized expectancies for internal versus external control of reinforcement. In J. B. Rotter, J. E. Chance, & E. J. Phares (Eds.), *Application of a social learning theory of personality* (pp. 260–295). New York: Holt, Rinehart and Winston.

Sarason, S. B. (1982). *The culture of school and the problem of change,* (2nd ed.). Boston: Allyn & Bacon.

Schaps, E., Bartolo, R. D., Moskowitz, J., Palley, C. S., & Churgin, S. (1981). A review of 127 drug abuse prevention program evaluations. *Journal of Drug Issues, 22,* 17–43.

Swisher, J. D. (1979). Prevention issues. In R. I. Dupont, A. Goldstein, and J. O'Donnell, (Eds.), *Handbook on Drug Abuse* (pp. 49–62). Washington, DC: National Institute on Drug Abuse.

Thompson, E. L. (1978). Smoking education programs. *American Journal of Public Health, 68,* 150–157.

Tortu, S., and Botvin, G. J. (1987). *School-based smoking prevention: Factors influencing effective provider training.* Manuscript submitted for publication.

Urberg, K., & Robbins, R. (1983). *Adolescent invulnerability: Developmental course, antecedents, and relationship to risk-taking behavior.* Unpublished manuscript, Wayne State University, Detroit.

U.S. Public Health Service. (1979). *Smoking and health: A Report of the Surgeon General.* Washington, DC: Department of Health, Education and Welfare.

U.S. Public Health Service. (1986). *Drug abuse and drug abuse research: The second triennial report to Congress from the Secretary, Department of Health and Human Services* (DHHS Publication No. ADM 87–1486). Washington, DC: U.S. Government Printing Office.

Utech, D., & Hoving, K. L. (1969). Parents and peers as competing influences in the decisions on children of differing ages. *Journal of Social Psychology, 78,* 267–274.

Wechsler, H. (1976). Alcohol intoxication and drug use among teenagers. *Journal of Studies in Alcohol, 37,* 1672–1677.

Wechsler, H., & Thum, D. (1973). Alcohol and drug use among teenagers: A questionnaire study. In M. Chafetz (Ed.), *Proceedings of the second annual alcoholism conference* (pp. 33–46) (DHEW Publication No. HSM 73-9083). Washington, DC: U.S. Government Printing Office.

Robert D. Felner and Angela M. Adan

CHAPTER

9

The School Transitional Environment Project: An Ecological Intervention and Evaluation

Effects of Life Transitions

Individuals experiencing major life transitions are at increased risk for psychological and other adaptive difficulties. These same transitions, however, may also provide opportunities for relatively rapid enhancement of developmental outcomes and the growth of more adequate coping skills (Felner, Farber & Primavera, 1983; Felner, Rowlison, & Terre, 1986). In either case, the changes in functioning that take place as the individual attempts to meet the adaptive tasks of the transitions may have enduring consequences. Positive change can make the person more resilient in the face of future life stresses and discontinuities. Negative changes in functioning during transitions may endure and precipitate further downward spirals in psychological and behavioral functioning (Bloom, 1978; Felner, Farber, & Primavera, 1983). For these reasons, it is particularly appropriate to target preventive efforts to life transitions, especially frequently occurring ones that have clear adaptive consequences for those who experience them (e.g., Bloom, 1978; Felner, Primavera, & Cauce, 1981).

Whereas some transitions are a function of the organism's growth and maturation (Erikson, 1959), others reflect changes in the relationship between the person and the social environment. Bronfenbrenner (1979) called the latter "ecologi-

cal transitions"; they involve a change in role or environmental setting. Felner, Farber and Primavera (1983) and Felner, Rowlison, and Terre (1986) have noted that these transitions occur around marker-events in the person's life. Those authors occur proposed that the term *transitional life event* best captures the unique nature of these life events and their accompanying processes. How well people cope with the tasks and challenges of adapting to these transitions is influenced both by their own competencies and skills and by important characteristics of the settings in which the transition occurs (Felner, Farber, & Primavera, 1983; Felner, Rowlison, & Terre, 1986). The rest of this chapter focuses on one such transitional life event (i.e., normative school transition) and a prevention program for children and youth who experience this event. Our discussion stresses both student characteristics and elements of the school environment that must be considered in designing and implementing prevention programs.

School Transitions

At some point in their lives, nearly all children and adolescents in the United States experience predictable, normative school transitions, for example, when moving from elementary to junior high or from elementary grades or junior high to high school. Previous research has shown that such changes are often accompanied by significant shifts in psychological and academic adjustment. Specifically, recent research has shown that the transition to high school is often followed by significant decreases in academic performances and by increases in absenteeism, marked declines in psychological well-being, and increased potential for substance abuse, delinquency, and other behavioral or social problems (Felner, Adan, & Evans, 1987; Felner, Ginter, & Primavera, 1982; Felner et al., 1981). Similarly, Blyth, Simmons, and Carlton-Ford (1983), Simmons, Burgeson, Carlton-Ford, and Blyth (1987), and other researchers (e.g., Hirsch & Rapkin, 1987) have shown that the transition to junior high school may be accompanied by significant declines in psychological adjustment and increases in symptomatology.

Risks Accompanying School Transitions

Changes in adaptation accompanying school transition can also have broader, more enduring consequences. Both lower grades and absenteeism have been found to relate consistently to later school failure, premature school dropout (U.S. Department of Health, Education, and Welfare, 1975), and more serious forms of emotional dysfunction during adolescence and adult life (Bachman, Green, & Wirtanen, 1971; Cowen, Pederson, Babigian, Izzo, & Trost, 1973; Galloway, 1985).

Notwithstanding the consistent associations between normative school transitions and the development of academic and psychosocial adjustment problems, it must be noted that such transitions are not equally predisposed to risks for all students. Both personal characteristics and attributes of the school setting can influence the extent to which negative outcomes follow transitions. The Transitional Life Events model, which is guiding our work, offers a framework for predicting factors that may shape transition outcomes and help in understanding the mechanisms that predispose to or alleviate negative outcomes in transactional processes (Felner, Farber, & Primavera, 1983; Felner, Rowlison, & Terre, 1986). This model holds that transitional tasks accompany such life changes and that the difficulty experienced in attempting to master these tasks reflects both the environmental context and the person's history and current coping abilities. A person's vulnerability to dysfunction during a transitional life event is a function of each set of factors independently and the ways in which the factors interact to shape the adequacy of the person's coping efforts (Felner, Rowlison, & Terre, 1986).

Threshold of vulnerability. In seeking to identify personal characteristics that place a student at greater risk for dysfunction during school transitions and to understand the mechanisms underlying these effects, we have focused on students who were coping adequately before the transition (i.e., those who were above a threshold of vulnerability). This threshold is not static; rather, it varies at different points in peoples' lives as a function of their current coping resources and skills and the contexts and demands they confront. In the case of school transitions, students who will be well above their vulnerability threshold are those who have good coping skills, are doing well academically and socially, have low levels of prior school mobility, and are not experiencing other risk conditions (e.g., lags in physical growth and maturity, additional transitions, minority status, or being from disadvantaged families). Students above their vulnerability threshold are expected to have relatively less difficulty in negotiating school transitions. By contrast, students who are not clearly above the threshold and whose coping resources might be seriously taxed by change may be at heightened risk even if they have not previously displayed any signs of dysfunction.

Recent work supports this view of vulnerability during transitions and points to specific personal characteristics that may influence a person's vulnerability during a normative school transition. For example, Felner et al. (1981) found that disadvantaged and minority students, as well as students with high rates of prior school mobility, showed significant declines in school performance following the transition to high school. By contrast, nonminority students, especially those who had not experienced high levels of previous school changes, showed no such negative effects. The co-occurrence of other life transitions and stressors also increases the likelihood that a normative school transition will have negative outcomes (Simmons et al., 1987). Additionally, the adaptive impact of this transitional life event may vary systematically in terms of the areas of functioning affected and as a function of gender and associated risk factors (Felner et al., 1981; Felner et al., 1982; Hirsch & Rapkin, 1987; Simmons et. al. 1987). Thus, to understand the impact of this transition and to evaluate fully interventions for students who experience it, both the conditions associated with differential levels of individual and population vulnerability must be considered, and multiple areas of functioning must be attended to in the assessment of outcomes.

Individual's characteristics, though important, are not the only determinants of differential risk during transitions. The characteristics of the setting being entered and their concordance with those of the setting being left can also facilitate or impede students' adaptive efforts and, thus, affect their threshold of vulnerability.

School Settings Affecting Transition

Two critical features of the school setting that affect the difficulty students have in mastering the essential transitional tasks are the complexity of the school environment and the setting's capacity to respond to students' needs. These setting characteristics relate to the ease or difficulty students have when trying to understand a new school's expectations and regularities and trying to reorganize their formal and informal support networks. Schools in which there are high levels of flux and disorganization, that require high levels of new understanding, and that make more social and academic demands than one's previous school, are experienced as complex. Illustratively, schools fed by several different elementary or junior high schools may be more daunting to new students than schools in which students simply move from one building to another with the same peer group. In the latter case, the students are challenged by the need to adapt to a new environment with new older peers. However, when there are many feeder schools, students are also confronted by an entirely new peer system in their own grade cohort and higher levels of broad systemic flux. This also generally occurs in a much larger environment.

With the new demands placed on students traversing the normative life change of school transition, teachers and other school personnel frequently face the tasks of getting to know often large numbers of new students and providing information and support to them. Once again, the number of different schools from which students are entering the new setting, as well as the sheer size of the entering class and of the school, limits the ability of school personnel to accomplish these tasks. Thus, the student's ability to adapt to the new school environment is diminished by the limited capacity of school personnel to be responsive

to their needs or even to get to know them. Unfortunately, these conditions tend to be the worst in settings in which students most need support and assistance.

The School Transitional Environment Program

Target Populations and Settings

The School Transitional Environment Program (STEP) is designed to facilitate the adaptation of students making normative school transitions. Specifically, it is targeted to students entering school environments characterized by large numbers (i.e., several hundred or more) of entering students, usually coming from multiple feeder schools. For example, STEP can be applied appropriately in junior or senior high schools in which entering students come from two or more elementary schools and in senior high schools that are fed by several middle schools or junior high schools.

Although the program is appropriate for all students within these school contexts, STEP may particularly benefit students who are at greatest risk, that is, students whose coping resources are seriously taxed during the transition or who lack in their environments important support sources that might facilitate adaptation to this transition. It is particularly important for school personnel to note that STEP is targeted toward students who, in addition to the transition, are experiencing risk conditions that often are most strongly associated with academic difficulties. Examples of such risk factors include low socioeconomic or minority status, the occurrence of other life transitions or stressors, entering puberty, and lower levels of coping skills or family support.

We are not saying that STEP is inappropriate for students entering middle or high school from middle or upper middle-class backgrounds. The conditions taxing the resources of the latter groups can either be similar to (e.g., puberty) or quite different from (e.g., high levels of competition or pressure to succeed) those experienced by inner-city, disadvantaged youth. Although many middle-class students may also be just above their threshold of vulnerability, STEP's efficacy has not yet been fully tested with this population. Such work is currently underway, but program outcome data are not yet available. Because STEP is a primary prevention program, it is not intended for students who are already failing or have serious adjustment difficulties. Although such students can appropriately participate in STEP, we do not assume that their participation will alleviate existing problems.

STEP Program Elements

STEP seeks to reduce the difficulty of the transitional tasks and to increase coping resources available to students by modifying specific elements in the ecology of the school setting. By avoiding an overtaxing of students' coping skills and resources during normative school transitions, STEP strives to maintain levels of functioning of students who had previously been coping adequately (i.e. above their threshold of vulnerability). Thus, based on a transitional life-events view of the challenges confronting students at these times, students' vulnerability to the development of academic and emotional difficulties following school transitions is reduced, if STEP projects are successful in bringing about desired alterations in the school environment. Students can then maintain effective school functioning.

Project STEP has two primary elements: (a) reorganizing the regularities of the school environment to reduce the degree of flux and complexity of the social and physical setting that the student confronts, and (b) restructuring the roles of homeroom teachers and guidance personnel.

Reorganizing the social system. STEP's first element seeks to reorganize the social system the student is entering, including, when necessary, aspects of the physical environment that shape key social interaction patterns. The primary goals of this component are to reduce the degree of flux the student confronts on entering the new school and to facilitate reestablishment of a stable peer support system, especially with other STEP students. Toward these ends, STEP students are assigned to classes so that all primary academic subjects, such as English, mathematics, social studies, science, or other core subjects appropriate to the school district, and homeroom are taken only with other STEP students.

Thus, the students no longer need to adapt to, and cope with, continually shifting peer groups in each of the classes, as happens when classes are put together randomly from the full set of incoming freshmen. In STEP, there is a high degree of overlap and constancy among the students in at least four classes and their homeroom. This change in the social ecology of the system

seeks to reduce students' difficulty in mastering the essential transitional task of reestablishing and redeveloping a stable, satisfying peer-support system. Additional goals of this program element are to enhance the students' sense of belonging in the school and to foster perceptions of the school as a stable, well-organized, understandable, and cohesive place.

The reorganization of the social system occurs in another important way as well. Within the school building, STEP classrooms are located in close physical proximity to one another (e.g., the same part of one wing and floor of the building). Minimizing distances between classes further facilitates students' sense of being familiar with, and comfortable in, the school. It also results in more informal interactions among STEP classmates between classes. This change reduces the students' perception of the school as a forbidding environment that they cannot manage with their usual resources, especially in large schools whose sheer physical size is often overwhelming to incoming students. This change in physical environment may help to maintain or enhance students' initial sense of mastery and control. Finally, the reduced need for STEP students to pass through parts of the building in which there are more advanced, older students may lessen the extent to which they find the school experience frightening or intimidating. This type of physical rearrangement also reduces the exposure of younger students to difficult social pressures from older students, which is an important factor in the temporal association between school transitions and the onset of diverse problem behaviors (e.g., substance abuse).

A key structural note is pertinent here. Because of factors such as the need for students to take noncore classes, ability groupings, the economic use of building resources, and other setting regularities, schools may be obliged to remix subsets of students. Sometimes, it is simply not possible to keep the same homeroom students together in all core courses. In actual practice, STEP has typically involved the identification of subgroups of 65–100 students in the incoming class. These groups are assigned as STEP *units*. Hence, students in each STEP class are not exactly the same during each period; rather, all students in a particular STEP core class come from the full population of the STEP unit. In this way, if several hundred or more students enter a particular setting, the number of STEP units required is determined by the number of students assigned to each subunit divided into the total number of entering students.

Assigning students to a homeroom. The second STEP element involves assigning all incoming project students to a homeroom in which the role of the teacher has been redefined. STEP units of 65–100 students have typically had four to five homerooms resulting in approximately 20–30 students in each homeroom and other STEP core classrooms. Actual numbers of homerooms used can be varied to suit the size of the STEP units into which the school has been subdivided for the project.

The homeroom teacher's roles are modified in this element so that she or he serves as the primary administrative and counseling link between the students, their parents, and the rest of the school. In STEP, the homeroom teacher performs many of the guidance and administrative activities that are more typically carried out by guidance counselors and other school staff in transitional programs. For example, STEP teachers both help STEP students to choose classes and provide counseling for school and personal problems. When a STEP student is absent, the homeroom teacher contacts the family and follows-up on excuses. Before the school year starts, STEP teachers contact parents of STEP students to explain the nature of the program to them and to encourage contact with STEP teachers. Finally, STEP teachers meet briefly as a group, once or twice a week, to attempt to identify those students who need additional help or support from teachers or guidance counselors and those students for whom a family contact is needed. In implementing these changes and carrying out their new roles, teachers receive consultation and supervision, when necessary, from school guidance staff.

Teachers for each STEP unit are selected from among all instructors of incoming students' academic subjects who volunteer for the program. With few exceptions, eligible teachers express interest in participating. Thus, self-selection by teachers is not a factor either in the final selection of STEP teachers nor in the efficacy of the program. Instead, teachers are selected as a function of two program-relevant factors. First, for each STEP unit there is only one teacher for each of the primary academic core subjects, generally four to five subjects (e.g., math, social studies, English, science, and health) as defined by that school system. Second, because the minimal amount of disruption of the setting is a program goal, to the greatest extent possible, teachers are chosen whose assigned classrooms are in close physical proximity to each other. This reduces the degree to which teachers must forgo accustomed classrooms and move to unfamiliar settings. Teachers of the core academic subject classes also serve as the homeroom teachers for students in their STEP unit.

Homeroom counseling periods in STEP generally last 15 to 20 minutes. Each student has a counseling session approximately once every 4 to 5 school weeks. These sessions take place at the teacher's desk which has been placed in a corner of the classroom and separated as far as possible from other students. In some schools, homeroom periods must be extended to allow adequate counseling time; other students then use this time as a brief study hall. Because STEP units are self-contained through much of the day, such time shifting (i.e., extending the homeroom period) is readily accomplished.

Teacher preparation. Initial preparation of STEP teachers includes two elements that occur before the start of the school year. One full day is devoted to enhancing teachers' academic and social-emotional counseling skills. Particular emphasis is given to such issues as the development of basic listening skills, identification of emerging emotional or academic difficulties, understanding transitional and developmental tasks, strategies for helping students cope more effectively, ways of handling the issues and concerns of parents, and referral processes for troubled students or those with more extensive academic or personal counseling needs. Information about requirements for graduation, college admissions, and appropriate preparation for other career paths is also provided. This initial training is conducted by school guidance staff and school mental health professionals. If such personnel is not available in a school, the training can be done by qualified outside professionals who are familiar with the school settings.

A second ½ to 1 full day is devoted to team-building activities. The focus is on enhancing communication among team members and clarifying program expectations. Additionally, time is spent arriving at a consensus about team-meeting times, necessary coordination activities, and the clarification of roles. All STEP unit teachers and other relevant program personnel (e.g., counselors and social workers) participate in this second preparatory training experience. This aspect of training also highlights the nature of the changes in the STEP teacher's role and emphasizes that the intent of these changes is to enhance counseling available to students, not to replace counselors or other school mental health staff.

During the school year, team meetings of STEP teachers generally last 20–30 minutes. Depending on the school, they take place either during a free period scheduled during the school day or at the end of the day immediately after the school's instructional activities are over. Counseling staff members meet at least once a month with STEP teachers during these meetings to discuss particular problem students and general issues of counseling technique and procedures. They are also available to teachers for ad hoc group meetings and individual consultation at other times. STEP counselors and project teachers have reported that they have more informal and individual meetings about students than they did prior to STEP's implementation.

One qualifying consideration bears mention. STEP has been implemented in several settings in which minimal counseling and school mental health resources were available. In such settings, outside consultants (e.g., the senior author and his or her associates or staff from the mental health center) fulfilled many of the functions of school counseling staff. Because many school systems suffer from a shortage of counseling resources, such alternative solutions may be essential for the program to work effectively. Significantly, the STEP model enables such underresourced settings to extend counseling to deal with basic student needs in ways that are not otherwise possible.

An additional, unintended (but not undesired) aspect of this element was its effect on teacher satisfaction. Many teachers spontaneously reported greater satisfaction with teaching as a function of their involvement in STEP. Specifically, they reported feeling less overwhelmed by the demands posed by entering students. Perhaps even more important, they reported both a greater sense of influence over the positive outcomes obtained with students and feeling more connected to students personally. As one teacher said, "This is the first time in quite a while that I actually feel like I know what is going on with my students and that I have a real sense of them as people." Such responses from STEP teachers have facilitated the program's acceptance in schools that initially tried only one pilot program unit, as well as its expansion to new schools that visit operating STEP programs.

The changes comprising this element have four goals. The first is to make the transitional task of acquiring and reorganizing important sources of formal support less difficult than it might otherwise be or, more specifically, to increase the instrumental and affective social support students perceive as being available from school-based sources. The second goal is to reduce the difficulties students have in accessing important information about school rules, expectations, and regularities, thus, to facilitate their efforts to deal with the transitional task of reorganizing their own daily school-related routines. The third goal is to increase students' feelings of accountability and decrease their sense of anonymity; and the fourth is to increase teachers' familiarity with students and decrease the time it takes for such familiarity to develop. In addition to making teachers more effective sources of support to students, such familiarity reduces the extent to which they feel overloaded when confronted by the many new students entering the school. There is also some evidence to suggest that the extent to which teachers know students and are comfortable with them relates to the levels of adjustment problems that students display (Gesten, Cowen, & Wilson, 1979).

Major Program Findings

The initial experimental trial of STEP was conducted in a large urban high school in which entering ninth grade students were primarily from low socioeconomic and minority backgrounds ($N=65$). Of these, 59 completed all assessment measures and the full-year program. A matched control sample ($N=120$) that entered as part of the larger freshman class was identified; in that group, 113 completed all assessment measures. Felner et al. (1982) reported that whereas control students showed significant decreases in academic performance and increases in absenteeism by the end of the first period year, STEP students did not show such effects. Similarly, control students declined markedly in self-concept scores over the year, while STEP students had stable self-concept scores. Changes in the control students were similar to those seen in students who had made the transition to the same school setting in previous years (Felner et al., 1981), indicating that the effects found for that group were not atypical. Given that a primary goal of an effective prevention program is to keep negative changes from occurring, STEP seems to have realized that goal.

In addition to these outcome measures, several process measures were obtained to evaluate the extent to which hypothesized program elements were actually experienced as intended by STEP students and the degree to which these elements related to observed differences in academic or socioemotional adjustment. Overall, compared to control students, STEP students perceived the school environment as more stable, understandable, well-organized, involving, and supportive. They also saw teachers and other school personnel as providing higher levels of support, especially by the end of the school year. By contrast, control group students evidenced significantly greater declines in their evaluation of the school environment and their feelings about school and school personnel across the year than did STEP students.

Follow-up Study

A long-term, follow-up study using school records was recently completed on the samples in the initial STEP experimental trial (Felner, Weissberg, & Adan, 1987). Records were obtained for over 90% of the students in the initial samples; these records included sufficient data to establish whether students had graduated, transferred, or dropped out while failing. There were no systematic differences in the frequencies with which STEP and control subjects had transferred, nor were there systematic differences between transfers and remaining students on demographic characteristics and pretransition school adjustment levels. Thus, students from the two groups, for whom complete records were available, remained well matched on all relevant demographic and pretransition measures.

Dropout rate. The most striking finding from the follow-up study was the differential dropout rate for the two groups. The 43% dropout rate for controls was similar to that of students in the school in which the study was done the previous year as well to the dropout rates reported in high schools that serve similar populations. By contrast, the 21% dropout rate for STEP students was less than half that of the control group. Moreover, whereas several nondropout control subjects had been placed in alternative programs for students who are failing, no STEP student required such a placement. Thus, actual dropout and failure rate differences between the groups when these students are considered are somewhat greater than the figures cited.

Academic achievement and absenteeism. The follow-up study also provided evidence of the enduring effects of the STEP program on academic achievement and absenteeism and its effectiveness in keeping high-risk students above their threshold of vulnerability and in preventing the development of more serious problems. In both the first and second year of high school, STEP students had significantly higher grades and fewer absences than the control group. Although these differences were still in evidence directionally, the two groups began to approximate each other more closely by the third year a pattern that continued in the fourth year. The closing of the gap, however, was not because of poorer performance by STEP students nor because of better performance by controls; rather, it reflected differential dropout rates in the two groups.

Significant differences in grades and absences between the two groups in the first and second year reflect the fact that many more control students than STEP students did poorly after the transition. Many of these poorly performing students, especially controls, dropped out by the end of the second year (approximately 19% of all nontransferring controls vs. 4% of STEP students). Thus, by the third year, particularly among controls, there was an overall increase in grade averages of remainers. This differential attrition continued through the end of the third year; by then, 32% of nontransferring control students had dropped out.

Given the hypothesis that the STEP program would be particularly helpful to students nearest their threshold of vulnerability, one other finding bears special mention. Control students who were still in school at the end of the third year, and beyond, had significantly higher levels of pretransition academic adjustment indices than STEP students who remained in school. For example, control students who were still in school at the end of the third year were students who had significantly better grades in the eighth grade than the STEP students who remained, even though there were no initial grade differences between the full experimental and control groups). Thus, it seems that STEP did differentially help somewhat poorer students to remain above their thresholds for failure and dysfunction.

A point to consider in evaluating these findings is that STEP students participated in the program only during the first (transitional) year. After that, they returned to the general student population for all subsequent years. Thus, long-term positive program effects observed are due strictly to the enduring effects of the first-year STEP intervention and not to any kind of continuing program involvement.

Replications, evaluations, and generalization trials. There have been several STEP replications, further evaluations, and generalization trials; other such trials are in process. One major effort of this type (Felner, Adan, & Evans, 1987) was carried out in two high schools and three junior high schools or middle schools in rural and suburban communities. Students in these schools were primarily from lower-class and lower-middle class socioeconomic backgrounds. Their circumstances ranged from families receiving government assistance to working-class backgrounds (i.e., semi-skilled or skilled workers).

Given the assumption that primary prevention programs potentially can address conditions and antecedents that predispose diverse disorders (Felner, Rowlison, & Terre, 1986) and given that findings can identify links between academic problems and later socioemotional disorder (e.g., Bachman et al., 1971; Cowen et al., 1973; Galloway, 1985), a broader range of outcome measures was used to evaluate the new program's impact. These included measures of depression and other emotional problems (e.g., anxiety, conduct disorders), school behavior problems, delinquent and substance abuse problems, suicidal ideation, as well as grades, absences, and self-concept. Process data were collected again as were measures of individual differences in coping skills and stress experiences. This broad-based assessment battery was designed to provide a rich and comprehensive picture of program efficacy for the students served. The 2-year follow-up data have been obtained for an initial replication cohort, and 1-year follow-up data are available on a second cohort.

The preliminary results of these analyses, which are beyond the scope of this chapter, are generally consistent with findings for the initial STEP program. STEP students, entering both junior and senior high schools, showed significantly fewer decreases in academic performance or indices of positive mental health (e.g., self-concept) and fewer increases on measures of emotional and behavioral dysfunction and difficulties (e.g., depression, self-reported substance abuse and delinquent acts, and teacher ratings) compared to their respective controls. For the 2-year follow-up cohorts at the senior high school level, the academic performance and drop-out rate findings closely parallel those of the original study.

A second set of comparison groups in these same settings was used to evaluate the relative efficacy of STEP when compared to a more individually focused intervention (i.e., training in generic coping and social-problem-solving skills now directed toward the transitional tasks). Although findings for this second set of comparison groups

were somewhat superior to those for nonintervention controls, they did not adapt as well as STEP students to the new school environment, particularly in academic domains.

Discussion

Limitations and Benefits

Several program limits may be clear and are built in; others are less apparent. Among the former, STEP projects are intended for schools with particular characteristics. Large schools made up of students who enter from several different feeder schools appear to have the greatest potential to benefit from such a program. Among large schools, those that serve students other than those in the upper academic or socioeconomic levels stand to profit most from such a program, particularly when evaluated by dropout rates and academic failure.

STEP's benefits are less well documented for schools that serve predominantly high-achieving students with levels of intrinsic motivation. Based on the general model of transition used and the positive findings from STEP program evaluations, it may well be that STEP programs can benefit such students academically and adjustively, even if program benefits with respect to dropout rates and school failure are less sweeping than in STEP programs that serve less motivated and less successful students. Nonetheless, STEP should show substantial utility for reducing the emotional and behavioral upheaval and dysfunction that accompany transition, even for academically successful students. The needs that such students have for instrumental and emotional support from teachers and peers and reduced system setting demands, given the academic pressures and competition they may feel, can conceivably be as important for them as for students who experience a very different set of stressors associated with economic disadvantage.

One concern in generalizing STEP to other school settings is its potential for unintended negative consequences. Future program evaluation research should consider this issue. It is conceivable, for example, that for academically high-achieving students, STEP elements intended to enhance peer interactions might also intensify the level of competition that students experience. Hence, expanding the program to new situations and populations may require modifications to ensure that positive program elements are not undermined by interactions with different types of school regularities and attributes or student population characteristics.

Another limiting factor is that STEP may be less appropriate or less needed in small schools where, for example, one or two sixth grades may move to another building for seventh grade, with virtually no change in the peer group structure. In such schools, it may be helpful to modify homeroom teachers' roles to match the STEP model and to keep newly entering students together in one part of the building. The potential advantages of such changes, however, may depend on the building size, the number of other grades and classes in the building (e.g., only 7th and 8th graders vs. 7th through 12th graders), and related factors that make a school environment more complex and increase its stressors for entering students. Basically, however, to reach informed conclusions about STEP's generalizability and utility for small schools will require more focused research on this question than has been done.

Among STEP's positive features are the program's demonstrated efficacy, its low cost, and the fact that it places few demands on a school's resources. The program's efficacy has been previously described in some detail. Program costs are relatively minimal because STEP's primary elements focus on reorganizations of the school environment (i.e., rearrangement of classroom assignments for teachers and some preplanning vis a vis the students' course and classroom assignments). STEP requires no significant dollar expenditures beyond what is needed for a school's typical operation.

The reallocation of teacher homeroom time and roles is somewhat more complex. In this sphere, the time needed for meaningful counseling interactions to occur (15–20 minutes a day) requires that compensatory time be found elsewhere. One solution is to subtract a small amount of time (1–2 minutes) from each subsequent period. Other possible solutions include lengthening the school day by several minutes or shortening break periods and lunch. Although redefinition of the homeroom teacher's role requires the support and endorsement of teachers and counselors, small amounts of prior training, and some monitoring, the program needs few if any additional human or economic resources beyond these relatively low-cost inputs.

Another advantage of STEP is that it does not require either the diversion of classroom time or the disruption of teaching schedules. In contrast to life skill programs or other programs that seek to teach competencies, STEP does not depend on lessons or curricula during class time. With the many demands that teachers face and the pressure to take as little time as possible away from basic academic instruction for other activities, a program such as STEP that enhances academic performance and reduces emotional and behavioral difficulties without disrupting instruction is attractive.

Other potential advantages of STEP are less obvious and may require further research to document. One such advantage suggested by pilot data from previous program evaluations is that teachers share STEP student's view that they feel better about the school environment and their involvements in it because of the program. Although the sample of participating STEP teachers is still small, those teachers have shown significant improvement in their attitude toward teaching in general and toward students in particular. These findings are not surprising; indeed, they are consistent with the attitudes of teachers more generally who report knowing their students better (Gesten et al., 1979). STEP enables teachers to get to know students sooner and better. It also reduces the distance and lack of efficacy teachers often feel in trying to influence students' lives constructively. Presently these statements are based on strong impressions gained from our program experiences; more extensive and systematic research is needed before they can be made conclusively.

STEP also provides an intervention context in which other initiatives can function more effectively. For example, some school-based suicide prevention programs seek to enable teachers or peers to identity early signs of risk among the students in the school (Felner, Silverman, & Adan, 1986). A situation in which large numbers of students from different feeder schools enter a school in which teachers are unfamiliar with them, and they with each other, hampers identification of suicide risk behaviors specifically, and a range of other health risk behaviors more generally. This may be especially problematic during a period of heightened risk for such behaviors (i.e., the transitional year). In summary, STEP offers a context that can facilitate the identification of diverse other individual risk factors and behavior.

Two final limitations of STEP should be noted. First, the program is not designed to reverse existing dysfunction. Although it is possible that a student who was not well integrated in the peer group in elementary or junior high school will find it easier to become part of a meaningful peer group through STEP, maladjustment reversal effects are not anticipated for most students. There is nothing in our data, for example, to suggest that students who were failing and advancing only because of an automatic pass, based on age not achievement, become better students. Similarly, it should be stressed that STEP is a prevention program that focuses on a specific set of developmentally hazardous risk circumstances. Although students' competencies and feelings of efficacy may be enhanced by making a successful transition (Felner, Rowlison, & Terre, 1986) and continuing to do well in school may result in their ultimately becoming better prepared for life, such competency development is not a primary program focus. Although programs to teach life skills or competencies can be conducted within the STEP's framework, STEP's outcomes will not necessarily be influenced by them. Indeed, as some have noted (e.g., Cowen, 1987), such individually focused competency programs (at least the first exposure to them) may be best targeted toward younger students than toward those who go through normative school transitions.

*Awareness Development and
Practical Considerations*

Efforts to implement STEP can be enhanced by an awareness on the part of school personnel and the community of the program's (a) minimal costs, (b) efficacy in addressing hazardous conditions which often are antecedents of diverse academic and emotional problems, (c) potential for improved teacher morale, and (d) minimal disruption of instruction. Many of these concerns have hampered implementation of preventive programs in the ways that they were intended (U.S. Department of Education, 1987) and have detracted from the fidelity and continuity of more expensive programs that require extensive teacher or outside personnel involvements.

Discussions with teachers, parents, and administrators, emphasizing STEPs natural fit in the school and the fact that it does not interfere with the school's prime mandates are very important in rooting the program effectively. Our experience suggests that by following an initial program presentation emphasizing those points, these groups find STEP's goals and structure to be congruent with their goals and needs. In other words, when the changes in school routines and practices that are essential to the program are carefully explained, they make eminent good sense to potential consumers. Such preprogram dialogue with relevant groups facilitates the de-

velopment of a needed and helpful collaborative relationship in implementing STEP. The importance of such collaboration for the success of prevention programs is highlighted elsewhere (Felner, Jason, Moritsugu, & Farber, 1983). Moreover, developing an awareness not only of STEP's effectiveness as a prevention program but also its sensitivity to the competing demands and realities of the school system is particularly helpful in facilitating program acceptance.

STEP also offers policymakers an intriguing strategy for addressing difficult social problems (e.g., high school dropouts) that relate to later more serious problems (e.g., delinquency, unemployment) that cost the public millions of dollars annually. Although the program is by no means a complete answer to these problems, clarification of its potential human and economic savings for policymakers and their constituencies are important steps in gaining acceptance for the program.

STEP's further development can move in several congruent directions. One is to develop, as a program add-on, extracurricular activities that either extend existing STEP units or draw together students from several STEP units. Additionally, STEP units (perhaps with slightly different composition) could be developed not just for students in the transitional year but also for subsequent years. The intent of such a step would be to continue to minimize the risk-enhancing flux and disorganization of the school environment (Felner, Rowlison, & Terre, in press). Although the flux may be less acute after the transitional year, some of it remains, especially in high-mobility environments. Extension of STEP to later school years can maintain, indeed enhance, a user-friendly school environment. More generally, STEP efforts may result in schools paying greater attention to the nature of the unintended hazards that the school environment presents to children and adolescents.

Conclusion

STEP projects and their evaluations underscore the potential for developing inexpensive but effective prevention programs based on informed modification of school environments and practices. Given STEP's low cost versus the staggering costs to individuals and society of the problems that they seem to be effective in reducing, those concerned with developing effective mental health and academic enhancement programs should be encouraged by available program findings. The current work also highlights the important fact that STEP is minimally disruptive to its host setting—the school. Indeed, it fits well and unobtrusively in the school environment.

A key lesson of this work is that prevention programs need not focus either on changing individuals or on the deficit models and assumptions that underlie them. Rather, it confirms that theoretically derived, systematic environmental changes can be used effectively for prevention purposes. Indeed, such efforts may be no more difficult to mount and constructive change no more difficult to obtain than in individually oriented prevention programs. With regard to both naturalness and ease of program implementation and positive program effects, benefits from STEP seem to be at least as great, if not greater, than from more costly and time-consuming, individually focused enhancement programs. In our view, the collaborative stance taken in developing and implementing STEP was particularly helpful in achieving these conditions and outcomes.

At a more specific level, the STEP experience suggests that schools should pay greater attention to unintended, often unnoticed, developmentally hazardous circumstances that school environments may present for the children and adolescents who must function in them. The small costs that STEP entails seem to yield major benefits both to students and school personnel, resulting in a far more user-friendly environment. STEP's encouraging findings also draw attention to the possibility that ecologically based prevention programs modifying regularities and practices of the school environment may be more efficacious than programs focusing on individuals (e.g., programs based on an awareness of student's needs or problems by teachers and peers and curriculum-based efforts).

Hopefully, STEP's success can advance the potential of prevention efforts generally, as well as the ways in which the form and structure of such efforts can be conceptualized. Future research in this area can help to develop a clearer understanding of environmental conditions that lead to predictable deviations and dysfunction in development and that enable us to direct children and youth on a path toward more favorable educational and adaptive outcomes.

References

Bachman, J. G., Green, S., & Wirtanen, I. D. (1971). *Youth in transition* (Vol. 3). Ann Arbor: Survey Research Center, Institute for Social Research.

Bloom, B. L. (1978). Marital disruption as a stressor. In D. G. Forgays (Ed.), *Primary prevention of psychopathology (Vol. 2): Environmental influences* (pp. 81–101). Hanover, NH: University Press of New England.

Blyth, D. A., Simmons, R. G., Carlton-Ford, S. (1983). The adjustment of early adolescents to school transitions. *Journal of Early Adolescents, 3,* 105–120.

Bronfenbrenner, U. (1979). *The ecology of human development: Experiments by nature and design.* Cambridge: Harvard University Press.

Cowen, E. L. (1987, May). *Community psychology and routes to psychological wellness.* Presentation to the first biennial Community Research and Action Conference, Columbia, SC.

Cowen, E. L., Pederson, A., Babigian, H., Izzo, L. D., & Trost, M. A. (1973). Long-term follow-up of early detected vulnerable children. *Journal of Consulting and Clinical Psychology, 41,* 438–446.

Erickson, E. H. (1969). Identity and the life cycle. *Psychological Issues Monographs 1,* New York: International Universities Press.

Felner, R. D., Adan, A. A., & Evans, E. (1987). *Evaluation of school-based primary prevention programs.* Unpublished manuscript.

Felner, R. D., Farber, S. S., & Primavera, J. (1983). Transitions and stressful life events: A model for primary prevention. In R. D. Felner, L. A. Jason, J. N. Moritsugu, & S. S. Farber (Eds.), *Preventive psychology: Theory, research and action* (pp. 199–215) New York: Pergamon Press.

Felner, R. D., Ginter, M. A., & Primavera, J. (1982). Primary prevention during school transitions: Social support and environmental structure. *American Journal of Community Psychology, 10,* 227–240.

Felner, R. D., Jason, L. A., Moritsugu, J. N., & Farber, S. S. (1983). Preventive psychology: Evolution and current status. In R. D. Felner, L. A. Jason, J. N. Moritsugu, & S. S. Farber (Eds.), *Preventive Psychology: Theory, research, and action,* (pp. 3–10). New York: Pergamon Press.

Felner, R. D., Primavera, J., & Cauce, A. M. (1981). The impact of school transitions: A focus for preventive efforts. *American Journal of Community Psychology, 9,* 449–459.

Felner, R. D., Rowlison, R. T., & Terre, L. (1986). Unraveling the Gordian knot in life change inquiry: A critical examination of crisis, stress, and transitional frameworks for prevention. In S. M. Auerbach & A. L. Stolberg (Eds.), *Crisis intervention with children and families* (pp. 39–63). Washington, DC: Hemisphere Publishing.

Felner, R. D., Rowlison, R. T., & Terre, L. (In press). A life transition framework for understanding marital dissolution and family reorganization. In S. A. Wolchik & P. Karoly (Eds.), *Children of divorce: Perspectives on adjustment.* New York: Gardner Press.

Felner, R. D., Silverman, M. M. & Adan, A. M. (1986, June). *Primary prevention: Relevance of principles to prevention of youth suicide.* U.S. Department of Health and Human Services: National Conference on Prevention and Intervention in Youth Suicide, Oakland, CA.

Felner, R. D., Weissberg, R. P., & Adan, A. M. (1987). *Long-term follow-up of a school transition program.* Unpublished manuscript.

Galloway, D. (1985). *Schools and persistent absentees.* New York: Pergamon Press.

Gesten, E. L., Cowen, E. L., & Wilson, A. B. (1979). Competence and its correlates in young normal and referred school children. *American Journal of Community Psychology, 7,* 305–313.

Hirsch, B. J., & Rapkin, B. D. (1987). The transition to junior high school: A longitudinal study of self-esteem, psychological symptomatology, school life and social support. *Child Development, 58,* 1235–1243.

Simmons, R. G., Burgeson, R., Carlton-Ford, S., & Blyth, D. A. (1987). The impact of cumulative change in early adolescence. *Child Development, 58,* 1220–1234.

U.S. Department of Education (In press). Report to Congress and the White House on the nature and effectiveness of federal, state, and local drug prevention/education programs.

U.S. Department of Health, Education, & Welfare. (1975). *Dropout prevention.* Washington, DC: Educational Resources Information Center (ERIC Document Reproduction Service No. ED105 354).

William S. Davidson II and Robin Redner

CHAPTER

10

The Prevention of Juvenile Delinquency: Diversion From the Juvenile Justice System

Background Considerations

Concern over adult crime and juvenile delinquency is prominent in American society. In annual surveys conducted from 1972 through 1984, United States citizens were asked "Is there more crime in this area than there was a year ago, or less?" In each year except one, the most frequent response was *more crime,* which indicates the belief that crime has been increasing (Gallup, 1984). In similar surveys from 1965 through 1984, respondents were asked, "Is there any area right around here—that is, within a mile—where you would be afraid to walk alone at night?" Over the last 17 years, the proportion of respondents indicating fear in their own neighborhood has steadily increased from one third to nearly one half (Roper Organization, 1985).

Although the rising concern over crime is not debatable, contemporary approaches to aiding troubled youth have been characterized by disagreements over where and when to direct ameliorative efforts. There has been a continuing tension between the desire to prevent crime and the need to protect society from convicted offenders (Elliot, Huizinga, & Ageton, 1985; Empey, 1982; Krisberg & Austin, 1978). As early as the 1800s, social reformers suggested houses of refuge as an alternative to adult prisons. More recent debates have been between those who sup-

port early identification of potential offenders as a basis for preventive interventions (e.g., Hawkins & Lishner, 1985; Loeber, Dishion, & Patterson, 1984) and those who support selectively incapacitating career criminals (e.g., Greenberg, 1977).

The major argument for early identification has been that youthful antisocial behavior produces adult antisocial behavior; therefore, preventive intervention holds promise of reducing adult crime (Fareta, 1981; Loeber & Loeber-Stouthamer, 1987; Patterson, 1986; Robins, 1981). Furthermore, juveniles are viewed as the group most amenable to intervention because they are believed to be more malleable. Thus, the focus on early identification of, and preventive interventions with, troubled youth allows the possibility of remedying a major social problem. Although proponents of early identification have argued that our prediction ability is sufficient to warrant intervention, others have argued that the rate of inaccuracies (particularly false positives) is too high to justify these interventions (Loeber & Loeber-Stouthamer, 1987).

Another factor in the debate has been the ineffectiveness of traditional treatment with criminal populations. This lack of demonstrated ability to rehabilitate is cited as a primary justification for preventive models, as well as an argument against implementing widespread preventive interventions (e.g., Lipton, Martinson, & Wilks, 1975; Trojanowicz & Morash, 1987).

The Prevention Model and Its Theoretical Base

If a preventive model is conceptually valid, the major issue it presents is effective implementation. What should be included in an intervention? Major theories of juvenile delinquency have been drawn on in response to this question (Elliot et al., 1985). One rich source of ideas has been the concept of individual differences, reflected in the early work of Glueck and Glueck (1951). Their classic study compared 500 institutionalized delinquent youths with 500 noninstitutionalized "normal" youths on over 400 characteristics including a variety of personal, physical, and social variables. From the large number of observed, statistically significant differences, prediction schemes were developed to identify delinquents.

Subsequent studies consistently reported differences between delinquents and nondelinquents (Andrew, 1981; Waldo & Dinitz, 1967). Similar comparisons have been made in terms of socialization (Smith & Ausnew, 1974), moral development (Prentice, 1972), family communication patterns (Alexander & Parsons, 1973), learning disabilities (Broder, Dunivant, Smith, & Sutton, 1981), social skills (Gaffney & McFall, 1981), interpersonal contingencies (Stuart, 1971), intelligence (Mednick & Christiansen, 1977), and problem-solving skills (Spivack & Shure, 1982). Not surprisingly, most of this research has documented differences between delinquents and nondelinquents.

This paradigm has been very influential in the prevention area because most intervention attempts draw heavily on established differences between delinquents and nondelinquents. The specific forms of intervention programs have varied widely and have focused on psychological, educational, medical, vocational, recreational, or other presumed deficits present in predelinquents (Mayer, Gensheimer, Davidson, & Gottschalk, 1987).

Theories focusing on environmental variables as the source of delinquent behavior have also been used as a basis for prevention programs. Cultures, social structures, social opportunities, social-control mechanisms, and social institutions have all been cited as causally related to delinquency.

In the reverse sense, for example, Viniaminov reported no cases of murder in the 20 years he spent living among the Aleuts (Pelto & Pelto, 1976). That type of observation (i.e., that some societies are remarkably lacking in aggression) led to the recognition of cultural factors as the source of antisocial behavior.

It has been suggested that the social conflict inherent in complex materialistic societies, such as the United States, fosters crime because of anomie (Cloward & Ohlin, 1960; Merton, 1957). Anomie, or normlessness, is thought to be produced by social disorganization and differential opportunity for achievement. To oversimplify, if a youth cannot earn enough money to buy a car legitimately, then the pressure to steal a car is increased. Social-control theory specified the processes through which macrolevel, theoretical variables actually affect delinquent behavior, that is, a variety of conditions lead to the situation in which the youth's ties to the conventional order are weakened thus producing delinquent behavior (Hirschi, 1969).

A final theoretical position (i.e., social-labeling theory) suggests that delinquency can only be understood in the context of individual behavior and society's response to that behavior. This theory assumes that society defines deviant behavior and that environmental labeling, in response to a perceived deviant act, makes deviants deviant (Becker, 1963). It has been argued that deviance, and hence delinquency, is created by people's reaction to an act (Glaser, 1975; Matza, 1969). Certain behaviors were "designated as crimes when they were repugnant to persons with sufficient political power to have the law impose their standards of conduct on others" (Glaser, 1975, p. 59). Typically, both the actor and the act are labeled deviant.

Many prevention programs are based on environmental theories of criminal behavior. One example would be many community-based interventions that seek to alter the opportunity structure for youthful offenders (Empey, 1971). Many particular therapeutic models seek to capitalize on the social-control aspects of behavioral contingencies, families, or peer groups (Emshoff, Davis, & Davidson, 1981). Furthermore, the rise in diversion programs for juvenile offenders can be attributed directly to the influence of social-labeling theory (Davidson, Gensheimer, Mayer, & Gottschalk, 1987).

The Specific Context of the Adolescent Diversion Project

In addition to the social influences and theoretical developments described, many specific events provided the impetus for the delinquency prevention program described in this chapter. Two facts in particular highlighted the need to consider preventive alternatives. First, the ineffectiveness of traditional treatments for adjudicated delinquents (Davidson et al., 1987; Lipton et al., 1975; Romig, 1978) led to the hope that preventive alternatives could have constructive impact on juvenile delinquency and, ultimately, on adult crime. Preventive alternatives that address problems before they become entrenched can avoid the stigmatizing effects of legally ordered treatment.

Second, even if traditional approaches were effective, they tended to be prohibitively expensive. Current cost estimates of institutional treatment for youthful offenders consistently run over $40,000 per year, and existing institutions are overcrowded (Davidson et al., 1987; National Institutes of Justice, 1987). Because of the expense of traditional approaches to the treatment of offenders, lower cost-preventive alternatives are very appealing.

The decision to design a juvenile delinquency prevention program raised several issues. The first was when in the developmental sequence of delinquent behavior to intervene, that is, before delinquent behavior was formally labeled (i.e., primary prevention) or after such formal labeling (i. e., secondary or tertiary prevention). The decision was made to intervene at a midpoint along this continuum, that is, after the appearance of official juvenile delinquency, but before the point of formal adjudication. The intervention-targeted youth had been formally apprehended by the police and referred to juvenile court but had not yet been judged guilty or innocent by a juvenile court judge.

This intervention point was selected to minimize the potential negative-labeling effects of court adjudication, and because, notwithstanding the appeal of intervening as soon as possible with troubled youth, the delinquency literature offered no support for choosing an earlier intervention point. There was no evidence of primary prevention efforts affecting later delinquent behavior. Identification of high-risk groups or individuals was espoused in the prevention literature, but the inability to accurately predict delinquent behavior argued against the feasibility of a demonstrably successful intervention (Kahn, 1965; Loeber & Loeber, 1987). Indeed, the best available evidence suggested that starting such a delinquency prevention program based on predictors of delinquency would identify two youngsters inaccurately for every accurately identified youth. For these reasons, it was decided to pro-

vide the intervention to youth in immediate risk of involvement with a formal, juvenile justice system.

The second major decision involved who should deliver the preventive intervention. Strong arguments based on effectiveness and cost considerations were being made for the use of nonprofessional change agents within the prevention and delinquency literature (Durlak, 1973; Rappaport, Chinsky, & Cowen, 1971). More recent evidence (Berman & Norton, 1985; Durlak, 1979) presented an even more convincing case for the effectiveness of nonprofessionals. The decision to use college students as nonprofessional service providers in our program also reflected that the change agents would be developmentally close to the adolescent youth. We hypothesized that the developmental similarity would enhance the effectiveness of the nonprofessionals.

The third important implementation decision concerned the content of the intervention. At the time the project was being developed, there were no unequivocal research findings on which to base a specific juvenile delinquency intervention (Davidson & Seidman, 1974). Therefore, the most promising models were selected and compared during the years of the prevention project. Generally, relatively intense, time-restricted intervention models based on social-learning theory were implemented. The one-on-one interventions were carried out in the youths' natural environments and focused on the critical life domains of family, school, and employment. The interventions were designed to be relatively brief (i.e., 16 to 18 weeks) and included structured implementation steps to ensure the attainment of specific program goals.

A final important aspect of the intervention's development, the Adolescent Diversion Project (ADP), was the action-research concept that guided its progress. The ADP model (Fairweather & Davidson, 1986) went through four systematic studies before its dissemination. Briefly stated, the concept involves four phases: (a) program development, (b) evaluation, (c) replication, and if warranted, (d) dissemination. The ADP went through the stages of development, evaluation, and replication from 1974 to 1986. That work is the focus of the rest of this chapter. More detail is available in a recent volume (Davidson, Redner, Amdur, & Mitchell, 1988).

Developing the Original Model

The first developmental phase of the ADP took place during 1973 to 1975 in Champaign-Urbana,

Illinois. The original research on the effectiveness of the ADP was done as part of a larger project studying the effectiveness of nonprofessional-change agents (Seidman & Rappaport, 1974).

Because ADP was to be a preventive intervention for youth in legal jeopardy, arrangements for referrals were made with the juvenile divisions of the two local police departments. Youths participated in the project prior to their formal involvement with the juvenile justice system. Administrative agreements were made with the police who, surprisingly, also sought an alternative to the juvenile court and the consequences of probation or institutionalization.

The two police departments (Champaign and Urbana) were in contact with 1,200 to 1,500 youthful law violators annually. The vast majority of violations involved minor legal infractions that were typically disposed of by talking with the youth. Approximately 10% of those contacted or arrested were considered for petition to the local circuit court. Project referrals were drawn from this latter 10%.

Following initial planning activities with the two police departments, considerable effort was devoted to implementation of the ADP model. Plans were discussed for referral procedures, intake and termination assessment, random-assignment procedures, the assurance of the participant's voluntary involvement, protection of the youths' constitutional rights, and specification of the intervention methods. After a period of negotiation, it was agreed that the referral decision would be left to the discretion of individual juvenile officers in the two participating cities. Referral decisions were to be based on the following guidelines:

> Since the project does not want to become involved with youth who have been charged with only a single minor offense and are not likely to find themselves in further legal difficulty, only refer youth for whom court referral is being seriously considered.

During ADP's first 2 years, only fall referrals were accepted because the change agents were college students; therefore, the program had to be coordinated with the academic calendar. Seventy-three youths were referred during these 2 years. Following formal referral, an interview was held with the offender and one parent. At that time, an ADP staff member explained the program and reviewed participants' rights both from a legal perspective and as voluntary participants in a prevention project. Participation and confidentiality agreements were signed at this time.

Following intake assessment, the delinquent youth and his or her parents were informed of the random-assignment outcome. Participants were assigned to the ADP or control group. This control group completed the preassessment, and a termination assessment 4 months later, but had no other contact with the project. All preassessment was done with participants naive as to experimental- or control-group assignment. ADP's first phase compared participants with no-treatment control participants. Police and court records were followed on all 73 youths while they were involved in the ADP and for a 2-year follow-up period.

Participant Youth

The 73 youths in Phase 1 (61 male, 12 female) averaged 14.3 years of age; 49 were White and 24 Black. On the average, they had completed 8 years of school. In the year prior to referral to ADP, they had been arrested an average of 2.16 times, for a variety of offenses, of which the two most common were larceny and breaking and entering.

Student Volunteers

Undergraduate student volunteers, most of whom majored in psychology, sociology, and related social sciences, were assigned to participating youths within 48 hours of intake. Every effort was made to match students and youths on the basis of mutual interests, race, and sex. Students received academic credit for their participation.

Intervention Model

The ADP operated on the educational pyramid model (Seidman & Rappaport, 1974). Volunteers received 6 weeks of training based on a six-unit training manual that included reading assignments, homework assignments, and practice role plays. Advanced graduate students trained students weekly in groups of six to eight. After training, there were weekly supervisory meetings. Graduate student trainers in turn were supervised weekly by two faculty members.

Each volunteer worked with his or her youth 6–8 hours a week for the 18 weeks. Intervention techniques included developing a good relationship with the youths (Goodman, 1971), behavioral contracting (Stuart, 1971), and child advocacy (Davidson & Rapp, 1976). The contracting component involved the assessment and modification of the interpersonal contingencies in the lives of the youths (i.e., modifying relationships between the youths and their parents or teachers). This technique was based on written interpersonal agreements between the youths and significant others.

In addition, most youths required access to community resources. Resource mobilization maximized the durability of desired changes and provided legitimate avenues for youths to attain their goals. The model of child advocacy used in the ADP involved specifying areas of need, locating individuals or organizations with needed resources, selecting and using strategies to gain access to the needed resources, and transferring advocacy skills to the youths (Davidson & Rapp, 1976).

Results

Davidson et al. (1977) described the diverse findings that emerged from ADP's first developmental phase. The model's effectiveness in preventing delinquency was the major concern. Table 10–1 presents the simple recidivism rates for the first phase of operation of the ADP. The tables include the simple recidivism rates (defined as one or more police contacts) for the cumulative period of the project, the 1-year follow-up period, and the 2-year follow-up period. The ADP model produced significantly lower recidivism rates than the control group, whose participants were released with no further intervention. In summary, the ADP project services were effective in reducing delinquency.

Table 10–1. Phase 1 Project: Simple Recidivism Cumulative 2-Year Follow-up

Condition	n	No petitions	One or more petitions
Behavioral contracting/ child advocacy	49	27	22
Control	24	1	23

Note. Chi Square = 17.68; df = 1; $p < .001$

Conclusions From the Phase 1 Project

Relative to the literature on interventions with delinquents, the ADP produced positive results. The observed impact on official delinquency was unusually strong, and the durability of the results over a 2-year, follow-up period was encouraging. The positive nature of these early findings highlighted the needs for (a) replication and (b) more careful examination of the model's components to identify the specific factors responsible for delinquency reduction.

Two major questions emerged from the Phase 1 model development. How much did the type of intervention contribute to the results? How much did the type of service provider (i.e., college students) contribute to the results? These questions were examined in Phases 2 and 3.

Phase 2 of ADP Development

ADP's second phase replicated and extended the initial work and addressed the questions raised by the Phase 1 findings. To examine the effectiveness of intervention content, we constructed variations on the original model. The original model was labeled the action condition. To separate its components and examine their relative contributions to reducing delinquency, we compared four separate components to the prototypical model.

First, a specific intervention and training model was developed around a family-focused behavioral program (e.g., Alexander & Parsons, 1973; Gross, Brigham, Hopper, & Bologna, 1980; Stuart, Jayaratne, & Tripodi, 1976). This variation was labeled the action condition family focus.

Second, because the original ADP involved relationship development, a relationship-therapy intervention and training model was constructed (e.g., Goodman, 1971; Robin & Foster, 1984; Shelley, 1971). The relationship component of the model was named the relationship condition.

Third, administrative setting (i.e., within vs. outside the setting, Kushler & Davidson, 1981), rather than treatment content, was studied in relation to program outcomes. Toward that end, the intervention was administered within the juvenile court setting. This group was named the action condition court setting.

The fourth and final component examined whether the Phase 1 findings were because of nonspecific attention. This group was labeled the attention placebo condition. Isolating the effects of nonspecific attention or differential record keeping is not often done in outcome studies; yet, it is critical to causal inferences about effects (Smith, Glass, & Miller, 1980). Accordingly, student volunteers were given brief, nonspecific training in relying on their natural helping skills as the basis for intervention. Phase 2 of ADP development compared these delinquency intervention models.

Youth Involved in Phase 2

Phase 2 took place in Lansing, Michigan. From the fall of 1976 through the spring of 1980, 228 youths were referred to the project; 8 refused to participate. Of these youths, 83% were male; 26% were minorities; and the mean age was 14.2 years. In the year prior to referral, the 220 participants had been arrested an average of 1.46 times and petitioned to court an average of 1.54 times. Youths had been charged with a wide variety of crimes including person, property, and status offenses; however, the two most common crimes again were larceny (34%) and breaking and entering (24%). No other crime category reached a frequency of 10%.

Youths were referred from the local juvenile court following a preliminary hearing. Referral criteria excluded youths the court would otherwise release, such as youths charged with serious person crimes or youths already on probation.

The court's intake referee provided the youths and parents with a brief description of the diversion alternative. Youths and parents interested in participating met with project staff who explained the project and obtained permission for participation. Youths were then randomly assigned to one of the alternative ADP models described in this chapter. Randomization was stratified for sex, race, court referee, and order of referral. Seven youths dropped from various conditions; no more than two youths dropped from any one condition ($N=213$).

Project Operation in Phase 2

Because of administrative and pragmatic considerations, not all intervention conditions were implemented during each year of Phase 2's 5-year period. This resulted in a different number of youths being assigned to each condition. Each ADP model, however, involved college students working one-on-one in the community with youths. The 8 weeks of training was followed by the 18-week intervention period, during which

students worked 6–8 hours per week under supervision. Specifically, all youth and volunteer interventions took place in the youth's home, at recreational locations, or in any other mutually agreed upon community setting.

There were important variations in training and supervision across conditions. Training groups for the action, action-family focus, and action-court setting and relationship groups consisted of six to eight volunteers trained and supervised by two individuals 2 hours per week for 26 weeks. The attention placebo group by contrast had 8 to 15 volunteers supervised by two individuals 2 hours per month for 26 weeks. Notwithstanding the structural similarity of the several models, their training and supervision differed.

The action group ($n=76$), essentially a replication of Phase 1, was implemented each year for 5 years. This condition used the techniques of behavioral contracting (Douds, Engelsgjerd, & Collingwood, 1977; Stuart, 1971) and child advocacy (Davidson & Rapp, 1976; Melton, 1983) to intervene in problem areas of the youth's life. Behavioral contracting was based primarily on social learning theory; child advocacy was based on the propositions of differential opportunity theory.

The 80 hours of student training in this condition was guided by an 8-unit manual consisting of written material, homework assignments, and role plays. Ten psychology graduate students worked in pairs as volunteer supervisors. They, in turn, received 2 days of training and 2 hours of supervision per week throughout the entire intervention by PhD psychologists. All supervisors served in multiple conditions to avoid confounding supervisor and treatment effects.

The intervention model involved four phases: (a) assessment of desired behavior change and needed community resources, (b) initiation of behavioral contracts and advocacy efforts, (c) assessment and revision of intervention efforts, and (d) preparation for the end of service. Throughout the intervention, it was the volunteer's responsibility to use advocacy and contracting techniques to meet the youth's individual needs. Youths and parents were also trained in these techniques to facilitate their use after the project ended.

The action-family focus group ($n=24$) was implemented during the 4th ($n=12$) and 5th ($n=12$) years of the project. In this condition, principles of advocacy and contracting were applied exclusively with family members. During the 80 hours of volunteer training, an 8-unit manual similar to the action condition model was used; however, the importance of family relationships as determinants of delinquency was emphasized (Patterson, 1985). Five senior graduate students in psychology worked in pairs as supervisors. They received 2 days of training with 2 hours of supervision per week by doctoral-level psychologists. As with the action condition model, the emphasis was on a behavioral approach rather than on any form of psychotherapy. The advocacy and contracting efforts were applicable to parents or siblings depending on specific circumstances.

The action-court setting group ($n = 12$) occurred during the 5th year as a preliminary attempt to assess the contribution of supervisor and supervision setting to treatment effectiveness. The key question at stake was the extent to which the program's efficacy depended on its independence from the court system (Rappaport, Seidman, & Davidson, 1979; Vincent & Trickett, 1983).

Student volunteers were trained in the action model of intervention by an advanced psychology graduate student and a caseworker from the juvenile court selected to be a representative of the juvenile court staff. The caseworker had a master's degree in criminal justice and 17 years of juvenile justice experience. The 8 weeks of volunteer training were conducted by both supervisors in classrooms at the university; this was also true for all other groups. The doctoral-level staff provided 2 days of training to both the graduate student and court caseworker. At the end of training, however, the weekly supervision sessions were moved to the caseworker's office, and the caseworker assumed sole responsibility for supervision.

The major differences between this condition and other action-model interventions were using the juvenile court member, rather than a graduate student, as supervisor and using the court setting for volunteer supervision.

In the relationship group ($n = 12$) of the 3rd year, intervention procedures were derived from the interpersonal theory of human behavior (e.g., Goodman, 1971; Robin & Foster, 1984; Rogers, 1957; Sullivan, 1953; Truax & Carkhuff, 1967), which emphasized the importance of interpersonal relationships as determinants of delinquency. Therefore, relationship group training focused on the development of empathy, unconditional positive regard, communication skills, and genuineness (Egan, 1975). Student volunteers were trained with an 8-unit manual for a total of 80 hours. Four different senior graduate students in psychology worked in pairs as supervisors. The graduate student supervisors received 2 days of

training with intervention supervision 2 hours per week from the doctoral-level staff.

Thus, the relationship group emphasized the development of a strong relationship between the youths and volunteers. It was distinctly different from all other conditions because it did not involve significant others in the intervention and did not use either behavioral contracting or advocacy techniques.

The attention placebo group ($n = 29$) was implemented during the 3rd year of Phase 2. Because this group was an attempt to control for the effects of nonspecific attention, it provided minimal training and supervision and emphasized the volunteers' natural skills (Durlak, 1979; Korchin, 1976). Student volunteers' training consisted of three 2-hour lectures, covering the history of the juvenile court, prominent theories of delinquency, and the importance of the helping relationship; the lectures were given by two members of a university-operated volunteer organization. The two lecturers had experience as human service workers and as volunteer supervisors for various projects; both had completed college credits in psychology and social work. The lecturers received 2 days of training and 2 hours of monthly supervision. The intervention consisted primarily of recreational activities such as athletics and was intentionally atheoretical.

There was a separate control group for each project year. Participants in this group were returned to the local juvenile court for normal processing. It should be recalled that youths were randomly assigned to conditions using a stratification procedure that controlled for sex, race, court referee, and order of referral. In contrast to Phase 1, which involved a comparison between treatment and no treatment or legal intervention, the comparison in Phase 2 was between treatment and typical court processing.

Results from Phase 2

Phase 2 program effectiveness findings, based on a complex set of process and outcome measures, are reported in detail in Davidson, Redner, et al. (1987). Our discussion concerns only the impact of the several models of the ADP on future delinquency.

Table 10–2 shows the results of the cumulative recidivism rates for the 2-year follow-up period. There were a number of interesting results. First, there were no differences in recidivism among the action group, the action-family focus group,

Table 10-2. Phase 2 Project: Simple Recidivism—Cumulative

Condition	n	No petitions	One or more petitions
AC	76	47	29
ACFF	24	13	11
ACCS	12	4	8
RC	12	8	4
APC	29	14	15
CC	60	23	37

Note. AC = action condition; ACFF = action condition-family focus; ACCS = action condition-court setting; RC = relationship condition; APC = attention placebo condition; CC = control condition, Chi Square = 10.29; $df = 5$; $p < .07$.

and the relationship group. Together, these three treatments were superior to the combined action-court setting group, the attention placebo group, and the control group. Second, taken individually, the action group was superior to the attention placebo group in a statistically reliable sense. Although the relationship group and action-family focus groups also demonstrated average recidivism rates lower than the attention placebo condition group, when they were individually compared to the attention placebo condition group, the differences were not statistically reliable. Finally, the action-court setting group was the least effective in reducing delinquency. Although not statistically different than the control group, the action-court setting group was different from all other groups in a statistically reliable way.

These results led to the following conclusions. The Phase 1 results were replicated, which supported the conclusion that the program helped prevent delinquency. It seemed that the intervention may need a well-specified model to be effective. Several specific intervention models that we compared were not differentially effective in reducing delinquency. Unstructured attention was not as effective as any of the systematic interventions in reducing delinquency. These conclusions led to the design of the Phase 3 study that examined the differential effectiveness of three volunteer types.

Phase 3 of ADP Development

This study addressed a major question arising from Phase 1: How much did the type of service provider or change agent contribute to the effect of reduced delinquency? Clearly, the interventions were effective when university student vol-

unteers were the change agents; however, many prevention programs use nonuniversity community members as change agents.

The research literature on the effectiveness of nonprofessionals provides evidence that college students may be particularly successful as service providers (Durlak, 1979). The credit that college students often receive for their participation serves to sustain motivation and commitment. College students often have the enthusiasm and idealism needed to develop special rapport with their clients. This rapport then can increase the chances of success with difficult populations. The demographics and social status of college students are frequently more similar to their clients than are the demographics of professional change agents. This role similarity has been proposed as a mechanism for the greater success of indigenous nonprofessionals with their clients (Durlak, 1979). Because of the above evidence, it seemed reasonable to examine experimentally the generalizability of the ADP when noncollege students were used as service providers.

Because there were few differences in the efficacy of Phase 2's three structured intervention groups, the decision was made to use the action group model in Phase 3. In Phase 2, Kantrowitz (1979) found that action group volunteers reported greater enjoyment of and satisfaction with the intervention than either the action-family focus or relationship volunteers. This finding, in combination with the greater role flexibility that the action group model allows, resulted in a decision to implement the behavioral contracting and advocacy model. In summary, Phase 3 of ADP development experimentally evaluated the action intervention model when implemented with university college students, community college students, or community members as change agents. The control group again consisted of youths who received typical court processing.

Youths Involved in Phase 3

Phase 3 took place in Lansing, Michigan, from the fall of 1979 to the spring of 1981. All 134 youths, who were referred to the project following Phase 2 referral procedures, agreed to participate. Criteria for youth selection and random assignment to groups were also identical to Phase 2. Five youths were dropped from various conditions ($N = 129$). The mean age of the youths was 14.10 years; 83.9% were males; and 29.8% were minorities. In the year prior to referral, the 129 juveniles had been arrested an average of 1.5

times and petitioned to court an average of 1.32 times. As in the previous study, youths had been charged with diverse crimes, the two most common of which were larceny and breaking and entering.

Project Operation in Phase 3

The three intervention groups all involved volunteers working individually with their assigned youth. Each intervention group used the behavioral contracting and child advocacy techniques described for the action-condition group in Phase 2. Training and supervision procedures were similar to those used in the previous programs. The difference among Phase 3 intervention groups was the type of volunteer used to implement the model. The new project operated on the same schedule as the earlier ones (i.e., 8 weeks of volunteer training and 18 weeks of intervention with case supervision).

The university volunteer group ($n=47$) consisted of students recruited from a large midwestern university. Volunteers were randomly selected from a large pool of interested students and were allowed to enroll in a psychology course for credit. The students' average age was 21 years; 52% were female; 91% were single; 4% had children; 91% were White; 44% were Catholic; and 70% had some previous human service experience.

The community college group ($n=35$) volunteers were recruited from a midwestern community college in the same city as the prevention program. Similar to the university volunteer group, these volunteers were allowed to enroll in a psychology course for which they received course credit and grades. Their average age was 26 years; 70% were female; 67% were single; and 33% had children; 91% were White; 70% were Protestant; and 67% had some previous human service experience.

The community volunteer group ($n=18$) differed from the other two groups. Although their training, supervision, and intervention model were identical to the other conditions, these volunteers did not receive course credits or grades for their participation.

It was difficult to recruit and retain community members. They were recruited through a variety of methods including presentations to service clubs, public service announcements in the electronic media, newspaper ads, posters, and word of mouth. Over 200 potential volunteers made contact with the project. All but 18 dropped out prior to the completion of training. In fact, the vast majority dropped out before training started. Because the volunteer pool was small, the project could not select volunteers randomly; rather, each person who volunteered was accepted. The average age of community volunteers was 35 years; 67% were female; 36% were single; 43% were married; 21% were divorced or separated; 40% had children, 100% were White; 60% were Protestant; and 93% had some human service experience.

The control group ($n=25$) consisted of delinquent youths who, in Phase 2, were returned to the juvenile justice system for normal court processing.

Results from Phase 3

Table 10–3 presents the results of the analysis of simple recidivism for Phase 3. Recidivism rates are again presented cumulatively from the point of intake through 2 years of follow-up. Collectively, the three groups that had interventions involving a volunteer, regardless of type, had significantly lower recidivism rates than the control group. There were, however, no statistically dependable differences among the three volunteer intervention programs. The results from Phase 3 demonstrated that the action model (i. e., behavioral contracting and child advocacy), as implemented by several different volunteer groups, was far more effective in reducing delinquency than traditional court processing.

Thus, Phase 3 provided another replication of the action-condition model's effectiveness. In addition, it allayed suspicions that the program was effective, in large part, because of the characteristics of the university volunteers. Although there were numerous reasons to believe that college students contributed something special to the program, Phase 3 indicated that somewhat older,

Table 10–3. Phase 3 Project: Simple Recidivism—Cumulative 2-Year Follow-up

Condition	n	No petitions	One or more petitions
University volunteers	47	30	17
Community college volunteers	35	26	9
Community volunteers	17	13	4
Control	25	8	17

Note. Chi Square = 13.38; $df = 3, p < .01$

more experienced individuals could also be effective change agents.

Phase 4 of ADP Development

The fourth phase of ADP development involved a more extensive replication of the model program than had occurred in Phases 2 and 3. The goal was to replicate the ADP action model in a large urban setting and assess its generalizability using paid staff as service providers. In many respects, Phase 4 was a preliminary examination of the model's potential for dissemination. Phase 4 also involved an experimental comparison of the ADP action model with an outright release group and a court-processed group.

Youth Involved in Phase 4

Phase 4 took place in Detroit, Michigan. During its operation (1982–1983), 521 eligible youths were referred by the juvenile divisions of four precincts of the Detroit metropolitan police department. The eligibility criteria specified that the youths had to be: (a) between 12 and 16 years of age, (b) residents of one of the four precincts, and (c) charged with an offense that would normally have been referred to court. Additional restrictive criteria stated that youths could not be on probation, receiving services from a juvenile court program, or involved in pending juvenile court cases.

Of the 521 referrals, 395 agreed to participate in the project. These youths were randomly assigned to one of three alternatives: (a) participation in the diversion program (ADP group); (b) release to parents with no further intervention (release to parents group); and (c) traditional court processing (court-processed group). The average age of the participants was 14 years; 84% were male; 91% were Black; and 58% came from a single-parent household. They had completed an average of 7.4 years of formal education at the time of referral. Most (65%) were referred for property-related offenses such as breaking and entering, larceny, and auto theft.

Project Operation in Phase 4

Referrals were made by 15 youth officers from four different Detroit (city) precincts. All were given a written copy of the referral procedures and a brief overview of the project. After review-

ing the initial complaint usually made by a street officer, youth officers determined eligibility and made referrals. The intake worker contacted the parents of youths who met initial criteria via phone or house call to arrange the intake interview.

The intake interview occurred within 2 days of referral. The youth and one or both parents met with the intake worker. The interview consisted of a description of the project, the voluntary nature of participation, the random assignment procedures for the three dispositional alternatives, and the responsibilities of both the family and the project. After the completion of the intake interview, the youths were randomly assigned (stratified for sex) to the ADP group, the release to parents group, or the court-processed group.

Project staff were hired after screening approximately 400 résumés and conducting 16 interviews. The screening and interviewing were conducted by the research staff and an employee of the local agency. The project was staffed by a project director, an assistant project director, two family workers, and an intake worker.

Staff participated in an intensive 2-week training program that included an introduction to the project, an overview of local and national juvenile justice issues, and eight training units presenting the conceptual framework for the ADP intervention model. Each unit included specifics in assessment, behavioral contracting and advocacy techniques, methods to monitor the intervention, and case-termination procedures. Also included were individual case-planning exercises, role playing of intervention situations, and exercises on assessment procedures.

After intake, ADP group members ($n=137$) were contacted by a family worker within 48 hours of random assignment. The ADP intervention combined child advocacy (Davidson & Rappaport, 1978) and behavioral-contracting techniques (Karoly & Steffen, 1984; Patterson, 1982; Stuart, 1971). The goal was to develop participating families' advocacy and behavioral-contracting skills.

Initially, the family worker provided training and experience in behavioral contracting and advocacy. Subsequently, the family worker encouraged the parents and youth to pursue advocacy and contracting activities on their own. The family worker's initial responsibility was assessment of behavioral changes desired by youth and parent(s) and surveying the family's unmet needs. After the assessment process was completed, the family worker and family agreed on a plan of action, using the techniques of advocacy and contracting. These sessions occurred either in the home or in another mutually agreeable setting other than the worker's office. During the first 12 weeks, the family worker was involved with each family 3 hours per week. During the final 4 weeks, the family worker acted as a consultant to the family for 1½ hours per week. Contracting and advocacy efforts by the family were encouraged during this stage to facilitate transfer of these skills.

After intake, youths in the release to parents group ($n=134$) were sent home without further intervention for the referring offense by the police or the court. All referring (instant) charges were dismissed.

Youths in the court-processed group ($n=124$) were returned to the police for petitioning to Juvenile Court after intake. During the intake meeting, the intake worker explained that the youth would have normally been petitioned to court and had, as a result of random assignment, a one in three chance of still being petitioned to court. The intake worker submitted to the referring police officer a form that identified the youths who needed formal handling by the juvenile justice system.

Results from Phase 4

The complex process and outcome measures used to evaluate Phase 4 of ADP, as well as program findings, have been reported in detail in Davidson & Johnson (1987). Table 10–4 shows the impact of the project on delinquent behavior through the 1-year follow-up on simple recidivism. The results in terms of recidivism indicated that the action model was superior to either the release to parents group or the court-processed group. The difference between the action group and both other conditions were statistically dependable. Thus, it seems that the action model can be used effectively by paid professional staff in a major urban setting. It is also important to note that there was no statistical difference in the recidi-

Table 10–4. Phase 4 Project: Simple Recidivism—Cumulative 1-Year Follow-up

Condition	n	No petitions	One or more petitions
Juvenile court	124	82	42
A.D.P.	136	107	29
Release to parents	135	92	43

Note. Chi Square = 5.87; $df = 2$; $p < .06$

vism rates of the release to parents group and the court-processed group.

Key Issues in Disseminating Prevention Programs

The major purpose of this chapter is to provide information about effective prevention programs that can facilitate dissemination. The field of prevention has often assumed that dissemination is an easy or automatic set of events following the demonstration of effectiveness (Havelock, 1976). This "better mousetrap" approach to dissemination has tremendous appeal. It posits that the demonstration of effectiveness will motivate widespread dissemination of the effective model and ensure the reliable reproduction of the prototype.

The dissemination of social programs has become a major field of study (e.g., Blakely et al., 1987; Tornatzky, Fergus, Avellar, Fairweather, & Fleischer, 1981). The general finding from this research is that the dissemination process is anything but automatic. Rather, a highly proactive approach is needed to ensure the spread of effective alternative programs. Replicating effective programs is a complex, often unreliable, process. Indeed, replications of effective programs sometimes bear little resemblance to the original model (e.g., Blakely et al., 1987; Hall & Loucks, 1978; Rappaport, Seidman, & Davidson, 1979). These findings are particularly troublesome because of the positive relationship between the integrity of program replications and their efficacy (Blakely et al., 1986; Tornatzky et al., 1981).

Suggestions for Program Dissemination

In this section, we comment on the key ingredients of the ADP model, including suggestions for its successful adoption and for the adoption of other prevention programs. To accomplish this, we draw on broader dissemination literature as well as our specific experiences in conducting ADP over a 15-year period.

At the level of social systems, each phase of the ADP model required intense involvement with local juvenile justice institutions. Typically, ADP staff spent 2 days per week working directly with the staff of the juvenile justice system. In the Phase 4 project, for example, the intake worker spent one morning per week in each of the four precinct stations. During this time, the intake worker was available for referrals, attended roll call, met with precinct leadership, and checked on future referrals. Similarly, in Phases 2 and 3, ADP staff spent two half-days per week with the intake staff of the local juvenile court. A critical aspect of this time was the social contact between project and juvenile justice staff. The shared cups of coffee were as important as the required staff meetings. In our experience, an active approach to interagency relationships is vital to ensure successful project adoption and replication.

As important as the informal relationship is the more formal need to convince local justice officials that the project will not be "here today and gone tomorrow." A critical ingredient in the success of the ADP was that local officials viewed the project as a continuing dispositional alternative. In the past, programs involved juvenile courts in prevention efforts for 1 or 2 years after which programs were denied funding and disappeared. Such unstable commitments, which were particularly true during the era of prolific federal seed money, created suspicion of prevention program promises.

In the case of the ADP, there were two positive side effects of our long-term commitment to the court. First, local officials who were opposed to dispositional alternatives could not ignore us and wait for the project to fade. The ADP became a relatively stable entity that could not be denied by its opponents. Second, our continuing commitment during times of few referrals or court administrative turmoils demonstrated that we were as sincerely concerned with juvenile delinquency as the police or the juvenile court staff.

Another critical ingredient in ADP's success was the setting for the intervention (i.e., the youths' natural environments). For years, it has been argued that an understanding of environmental variables was crucial to understanding juvenile delinquency. Adolescents' involvement with families, schools, and peers are core factors in most contemporary explanations of juvenile delinquency. All of ADP's structured interventions involved change agents participating in the youths' natural environments as opposed to the change agents' office or center. This was also a critical issue in selecting change agents. Over-professionalized staff or those trained in restrictive professional roles often express ambivalence about entering the environments of delinquent youths. It is essential to select change agents who are willing to work in the youths' natural settings. Only then can the major causes of delinquency be addressed.

Other issues relate more directly to the intervention model itself. Both experience and the dissemination literature (Rappaport et al., 1979) indicate that close adherence to the original ADP model is necessary for the results to be replicated. The ADP model emphasizes youths' strengths rather than their weaknesses. Various theoretical positions use different language to describe this perspective. The behaviorists refer to behavioral accelerators, advocates refer to youth rights, and community psychologists refer to empowerment. These perspectives share a view of youths as individuals with assets and abilities rather than repositories of environmental and personal pathologies. Third, the ADP model had specifiable components and a limited intervention period. Our experience was that both of these ingredients were important to successful adoption and dissemination. A detailed plan of action maximizes the chances of accurate replication.

ADP's underlying philosophy was that it be a true alternative to justice system processing for all appropriate youths. Accordingly, our administrative agreements with the juvenile court stated that we would not return difficult youths to the police or court system. This decision produced positive effects for the program's operation. Change agents and supervisors were completely aware that their task was to make the intervention work for both easy and difficult cases. This is not to imply that ADP is a panacea for all adolescents in trouble. Rather, what we learned is that the program made it possible to deal successfully with cases that would otherwise have been identified as impossible. This was because of the original decision not to return difficult cases to the legal system. We believe that this decision is an important operating principle that must be incorporated in dissemination efforts.

Our experience, confirmed by the Phase 2 research, was that change agents required close supervision. Weekly case supervision was important in at least two ways. First, it kept change agents faithful to the intervention model. There is a tendency for all change agents to drift from intervention models in the face of real world frustrations. Our experience and the research literature indicate that this tendency degrades the integrity of the intervention model (Sechrest & Redner, 1979). Second, we found that weekly supervision required less time than monthly supervision. In Phase 2 research, Kantrowitz (1979) found that supervisors who met monthly with their change agents spent more total time supervising than those supervisors who met weekly with their change agents because frequent contacts were needed outside of supervisory sessions.

Conclusions

There are several potential obstacles to implementing prevention programs. Alternative prevention programs often compete with existing agencies for clients. More importantly, successful prevention programs can make existing agencies superfluous. Although the hope is that effective prevention efforts will allow existing systems to deal more effectively with youth who are not suited for such programs, one immediate result of an effective prevention program may be to reduce an agency's client flow. Such potential competition for cases needs to be anticipated, especially in the case of the justice system, which is very sensitive to caseload issues. In the case of the ADP, the agency responsible for our referrals was the agency most likely to be threatened by the program's success. Our experience proved that this situation is a tightrope that requires constant balancing.

Change agents are often reluctant to work in their clients' natural environments. Creating a change-agent role that demanded close involvement with youths while maintaining close supervision were effective strategies to deal with these issues. In our intervention, professional staff were more difficult to train than nonprofessional volunteers because of the restrictive role behaviors they had adopted.

Replicating the ADP model required intense community activity to initiate and maintain the source of referrals. Mental health professionals often use relatively passive referral modes. Our early experiences with ADP demonstrated the futility of a passive approach to the juvenile justice system. If one waits in the office for referrals, one will spend a lot of time waiting. An active mode of interacting with the juvenile justice system is necessary.

A final major issue is funding. The original ADP projects (Phases 1 through 3) were supported by federal research grants. In all phases, the ADP was committed to continuation of the project contingent on positive results. To keep this commitment, we sought nonfederal sources of support. Our experience has been that state and local sources offer excellent opportunities for funding prevention alternatives. Local and state officials are particularly interested in any potential fiscal savings offered by prevention programs. They also will understand the chronically overloaded situations facing many criminal justice and mental health systems.

The task of creating and maintaining prevention programs is neither simple nor quick. These programs require long-term commitments from program developers, researchers, community agencies, and funding sources. This commitment must be firm at the initial stages of the program because definitive results take time, reasonable numbers of clients, and continued funding. Finally, replication and dissemination of prevention programs must operate systematically; they must be developed with a specifiable set of operations and clearly defined goals. Only when all these conditions have been met can any prevention program have some hope of success.

References

Alexander, J. F., & Parsons, B. V. (1973). Short term behavioral intervention with delinquent families. *Journal of Abnormal Psychology, 81,* 219–225.

Andrew, J. M. (1981). Delinquency: Correlating variables. *Journal of Child Clinical Psychology, 10,* 136–140.

Becker, H. S. (1963). *Outsiders: Studies in the sociology of deviance.* New York: Free Press of Glencoe.

Berman, J. S., & Norton, N. C. (1985). Does professional training make a therapist more effective? *Psychological Bulletin, 98,* 401–407.

Blakely, C. H., Mayer, J. P., Gottschalk, R. G., Roitman, D., Schmitt, N., Davidson, W. S., & Emshoff, J. G. (1986). *Salient processes in the dissemination of social technologies.* Washington, DC: National Science Foundation.

Blakely, C. H., Mayer, J. P., Gottschalk, R. G., Schmit, N., Davidson, W. S., Roitman, D., & Emshoff, J. G. (1987). The fidelity-adaptation debate: Implications for the implementation of public sector social programs. *American Journal of Community Psychology, 15,* 253–268.

Broder, P. K., Dunivant, N., Smith, E. C., & Sutton, L. P. (1981). Further observations on the link between learning disabilities and juvenile delinquency. *Journal of Education Psychology, 73,* 838–850.

Cloward, R., & Ohlin, L. (1960). *Delinquency and opportunity.* Glencoe, IL: The Free Press.

Davidson, W. S., Gensheimer, L. K., Mayer, J. P., & Gottschalk, R. G. (1987). Current status of rehabilitation programs for juvenile offenders. In C. Hampton (Ed.), *Antisocial behavior and substance abuse* (pp. 68–75). Washington, DC: U.S. Government Printing Office.

Davidson, W. S., & Johnson, C. (1987). *Diversion in Michigan.* Lansing, MI: Department of Social Services, Office of Children and Youth Services.

Davidson, W. S., & Rapp, C. (1976). A multiple strategy model of child advocacy. *Social Work, 21,* 225–232.

Davidson, W. S., & Rappaport, J. (1978). Towards a model of advocacy. In G. Weber & G. McCall (Eds.),

Advocacy and the disciplines (pp. 66–97). New York: Sage.

Davidson, W. S., Redner, R., Amdur, R., & Mitchell, C. (1988). *Alternative treatments for troubled youth*. New York: Plenum.

Davidson, W. S., Redner, R., Blakely, C. H., Mitchell, C. M., & Emshoff, J. G. (1987). Diversion of juvenile offenders: An experimental comparison. *Journal of Consulting and Clinical Psychology, 55,* 68–75.

Davidson, W. S., & Seidman, E. (1974). Studies of behavior modification and juvenile delinquency. *Psychological Bulletin, 81,* 998–1011.

Davidson, W. S., Seidman, E., Rappaport, J., Berck, P., Rapp, N., Rhodes, W., & Herring, J. (1977). Diversion programs for juvenile offenders. *Social Work Research and Abstracts, 13,* 40–49.

Douds, A. F., Engelsgjerd, M., & Collingwood, T. R. (1977). Behavior contracting with youthful offenders and their parents. *Child Welfare, 56,* 409–417.

Durlak, J. A. (1973). Myths concerning the nonprofessional therapist. *Professional Psychology, 4,* 300–304.

Durlak, J. A. (1979). Comparative effectiveness of paraprofessional and professional helpers. *Psychological Bulletin, 86,* 80–92.

Egan, G. (1975). *The skilled helper.* Belmont, CA: Brooks/Cole.

Elliot, D. S., Huizinga, D., & Ageton, S. S. (1985). *Explaining delinquency and drug abuse.* Beverly Hills, CA: Sage.

Empey, L. T. (1971). *Explaining delinquency.* Lexington, MA: Heath.

Empey, L. T. (1982). *American delinquency: Its meaning and construction.* Homewood, IL: Dorsey.

Emshoff, J. G., Davis, D. D., & Davidson, W. S. (1981). Social support and aggression. In A. P. Goldstein, E. G. Carr, W. S. Davidson, & P. Wehr (Eds.), *In response to aggression: Methods of control and prosocial alternatives* (pp. 402–443). New York: Pergamon.

Fairweather, G. W., & Davidson, W. S. (1986). *An introduction to community experimentation.* New York: McGraw-Hill.

Fareta, G. A. (1981). A profile of aggression from adolescence to adulthood. *American Journal of Orthopsychiatry, 51,* 439–453.

Gallup, G. (1984). *The Gallup Report.* Princeton, NJ: Gallup.

Gaffney, L. R., & McFall, R. M. (1981). A comparison of the social skills in delinquent and nondelinquent adolescent girls using behavioral role-playing inventory. *Journal of Consulting and Clinical Psychology, 49,* 959–967.

Glaser, D. (1975). *Strategic criminal justice planning.* Washington, DC: U.S. Government Printing Office.

Glueck, S., & Glueck, E. (1951). *Unraveling juvenile delinquency.* Cambridge, MA: Harvard University Press.

Goodman, G. (1971). *Companionship therapy.* San Francisco: Jossey-Bass.

Greenberg, D. (1977). The incapacitive effects of imprisonment: Some estimates. *Law and Society Review, 9,* 541–580.

Gross, A. M., Brigham, T., Hopper, C., & Bologna, W. (1980). Self-management and social skills training: A study with predelinquent and delinquent youths. *Criminal Justice and Behavior, 7,* 161–183.

Hall, G. E., & Loucks, S. F. (1978, March). Innovation configurations: Analyzing the adaptation of innovations. Paper presented at the annual meeting of the American Educational Research Association, Toronto, Ontario, Canada.

Havelock, R. G. (1976). *Planning for innovation through dissemination and utilization of knowledge.* Ann Arbor, MI: University of Michigan.

Hawkins, J. D., & Lishner, D. M. (1985). Childhood predictors and the prevention of adolescent substance abuse. In C. L. Jones & R. D. Battjes (Eds.), *Etiology of drug abuse: Implications for prevention* (pp. 117–131). Washington, DC: National Institute on Drug Abuse. (ADM85–1385)

Hirschi, T. (1969). *Causes of delinquency.* Los Angeles: University of California Press.

Kahn, A. J. (1965). A case of premature claims. *Crime and Delinquency, 20,* 233–240.

Kantrowitz, R. E. (1979). *Training nonprofessionals to work with delinquents: Differential impact of varying training/supervision/intervention strategies.* Unpublished doctoral dissertation, Michigan State University, East Lansing.

Karoly, P., & Steffen, J. J. (1984). *Adolescent behavior disorders: Foundations and contemporary concerns.* Lexington, MA: Lexington Books.

Korchin, S. (1976). *Modern clinical psychology.* New York: Basic Books.

Krisberg, B., & Austin, J. (1978). *The children of Ishmael.* Palo Alto, CA: Mayfield Press.

Kushler, M., & Davidson, W. S. (1981). Community and organizational level change. In A. P. Goldstein, E. G. Carr, W. S. Davidson, and P. Wehr (Eds.), *In response to aggression: Methods of control and prosocial alternatives* (pp. 346–401). New York: Pergamon.

Lipton, D., Martinson, R., & Wilks, J. (1975). *The effectiveness of correctional treatment.* New York: Praeger.

Loeber, R., & Loeber-Stouthamer, M. (1987). Prediction. In H. C. Quay (Ed.), *Handbook of juvenile delinquency* (pp. 325–382). New York: Wiley & Sons.

Loeber, R., Dishion, T. J., & Patterson, G. R. (1984). Multiple gating: A multistage assessment procedure for identifying youths at risk for delinquency. *Journal of Research in Crime and Delinquency, 21,* 7–32.

Matza, D. (1969). *Becoming deviant.* Englewood Cliffs, NJ: Prentice-Hall.

Mayer, J. P., Gensheimer, L. K., Davidson, W. S. & Gottschalk, R. G. (1987). Social learning treatment within juvenile justice: A meta-analysis of impact in the natural environment. In A. Goldstein & S. Apter (Eds.), *Youth violence* (pp. 24–38). New York: Pergamon.

Mednick, S., & Christiansen, S. O. (1977). *Biosocial basis of criminal behavior.* New York: Gardner Press.

Melton, G. B. (1983). *Child advocacy.* New York: Plenum Press.

Merton, R. K. (1957). *Social theory and social structure* (2nd ed.). New York: Free Press.

National Institutes of Justice. (NIJ) (1987). Juveniles in institutions. *NIJ Reports.* Washington, DC: U.S. Department of Justice.

Patterson, G. R. (1982). *Coercive family interactions.* Eugene, OR: Castalia Press.

Patterson, G. R. (1985, August). *Performance models for antisocial boys.* Paper presented at the annual meeting of the American Psychological Association, Los Angeles.

Patterson, G. R. (1986). Beyond technology: The next stage in developing an empirical base for parent training. In L. L'Abate (Ed.), *Handbook of family psychology and therapy.* (pp. 432–444). Homewood, IL: Dorsey.

Pelto, G. H., & Pelto, P. J. (1976). *The human adventure.* New York: Macmillan.

Prentice, N. M. (1972). The influence of live and symbolic modeling on prompting moral judgment of adolescent delinquents. *Journal of Abnormal Psychology, 80,* 159–211.

Rappaport, J., Chinsky, J. M., & Cowen, E. L. (1971). *Innovation in helping chronic patients: College students in a mental institution.* New York: Academic Press.

Rappaport, J., Seidman, E., & Davidson, W. S. (1979). Demonstration research and manifest versus true adoption: The natural history of a research project to divert adolescents from the legal system. In J. Kelly, L. Snowden and R. Munoz (Eds.), *Social and community interventions* (pp. 101–144). San Francisco: Jossey-Bass.

Robin, A. L., & Foster, S. L. (1984). Problem-solving communication training: A behavioral family systems approach to parent-adolescent conflict. In P. Karoly & J. J. Steffen (Eds.), *Adolescent behavioral disorders: Foundations and contemporary concerns* (pp. 195–240). Lexington, MA: Lexington Books.

Robins, L. N. (1981). Epidemiological approaches to natural history research. *Journal of the American Academy of Child Psychiatry, 20,* 566–580.

Rogers, C. R. (1957). The necessary and sufficient conditions of therapeutic personality changes. *Journal of Consulting Psychology, 21,* 95–103.

Romig, D. A. (1978). *Justice for our children.* Lexington, MA: Lexington Books.

Roper Organization. (1985). Opinion roundup. *Public Opinion, 5,* 12.

Sechrest, L. B., & Redner, R. (1979). Strength and integrity of treatments. In L. B. Sechrest, R. Redner, & S. Martin (Eds.), *Review of criminal evaluation results* (pp. 19–62). Washington, DC: National Criminal Justice Reference Service, U.S. Department of Justice.

Seidman, E., & Rappaport, J. (1974). The educational pyramid: A paradigm for research, training, and manpower. *American Journal of Community Psychology, 2,* 119–130.

Shelley, E. (1971). *Volunteers in probation.* Boulder, CO: National Center for Volunteers in Juvenile Court.

Smith, P. M., & Ausnew, H. R. (1974). Socialization as related to delinquency classification. *Psychological Reports, 34,* 677–678.

Smith, M. L., Glass, G. V., & Miller, T. I. (1980). *The benefits of psychotherapy.* Baltimore: Johns Hopkins University Press.

Spivack, G., & Shure, M. B. (1982). The cognition of social adjustment. In B. B. Lahey & A. E. Kazdin (Eds.), *Advances in child clinical psychology* (pp. 139–164). New York: Plenum Press.

Stuart, R. B. (1971). Behavioral contracting within the families of delinquents. *Journal of Behavior Therapy and Experimental Psychiatry, 2,* 1–11.

Stuart, R. B., Jayaratne, S., & Tripodi, T. (1976). Changing adolescent deviant behaviour through reprogramming the behaviour of parents and teachers: An experimental evaluation. *Canadian Journal of Behavioural Science, 8,* 132–144.

Sullivan, H. S. (1953). *The interpersonal theory of psychiatry.* New York: Norton.

Tornatzky, L. G., Fergus, E. O., Avellar, J. W., Fairweather, G. W., & Fleischer, M. (1981). *Innovation and social process: A national experiment in implementing social technology.* New York: Pergamon.

Trojanowicz, R. C., & Morash, M. (1987). *Juvenile delinquency: Concepts and control* (4th ed.). Englewood Cliffs, NJ: Prentice-Hall.

Truax, C. B., & Carkhuff, R. (1967). *Toward effective counseling and psychotherapy.* Chicago: Aldine.

Vincent, T. A., & Trickett, E. J. (1983). Preventive interventions and the human context. In R. D. Felner, L. A. Jason, J. N. Moritsugu, & S. S. Farber (Eds.), *Preventive psychology* (pp. 67–86). New York: Pergamon.

Waldo, G. P., & Dinitz, S. (1967). Personality attributes of the criminal: Analysis of research studies from 1950–1965. *Journal of Research in Crime and Delinquency, 4,* 185–202.

SECTION
III
Prevention Programs for Adults and the Elderly

The programs described in this section make it clear that prevention is not just for children. Effective prevention programs can and have been developed for people throughout the entire life span.

Health and mental health risks in adulthood are frequently associated with major life transitions. Three of the four programs described in this section focus on such transitions—birth of a child, divorce, and widowhood—and the fourth focuses on health behaviors that increase the risk of cardiovascular disease.

In chapter 11, "The Perceived Personal Control Program," Tadmor focuses on pregnant women undergoing caesarean birth. This experience can be traumatic, particularly if it is unanticipated. Tadmor's program mobilizes natural and organized supports for these women, provides information, and uses anticipatory guidance sessions to help couples anticipate and cope with the emotional and physical stress they will experience in the birth process. The program produces earlier hospital discharges, reduces the need for medication, and improves mother–infant attachment as well as promoting a more rapid rate of psychological recovery.

Divorce has reached nearly epidemic proportions in the United States. The divorce process creates a variety of psychological problems and poses new coping challenges. Bloom and Hodges' describe their 6-month program in chapter 12, "The Colorado Separation and Divorce Program."

The program was developed for divorcing adults and implemented by paraprofessionals and subject matter experts to provide social support and facilitate confidence building in child rearing, social interaction, single parenting, and career planning. The impact of their preventive program remains evident 4 years later, in terms of significantly better adjustment for participants and fewer separation-related problems.

In this century, we have conquered a variety of acute infectious diseases such as typhoid and smallpox, and yet as a nation we remain at high risk for chronic diseases, particularly cardiovascular diseases. Many cardiovascular diseases are preventable. The health behaviors needed for prevention include dietary changes and exercise as well as smoking cessation. Maccoby and Altman have developed a program of community education aimed at stimulating and maintaining changes in life-style that will result in a community-wide reduction in risk for cardiovascular disease. The "Stanford Heart Disease Prevention Program," described in chapter 13, is aimed at smoking cessation, nutrition, exercise, and reduction of hypertension and obesity. The program involves mass media, community organization, and social marketing of health programs. Thus far, their research indicates that when mass media campaigns are supplemented with face-to-face instructions, they indeed succeed in reducing behavioral and physiological indicators of cardiovascular risk.

The later stages of the life cycle are not without risk as well. Silverman's "Widow-to-Widow" program (chapter 14) is aimed at recently widowed persons still experiencing bereavement and the problems of coping with the loss of a loved one. In this program, widows contact newly bereaved women to offer one-to-one support. Telephone calls, home visits, and small group meetings are used to provide social support and mutual help. Research on widow-to-widow programs indicates that participants show improved mood, lower anxiety, and better social integration and progress more rapidly in the course of adaptation than do widows who do not participate in the program. Social isolation and the loss of social support is a major issue in the later years of life, and the widow-to-widow program has shown that it is capable of reducing that isolation and enriching the lives of bereaved women.

These programs share several interesting, common features. All have an educative component and are aimed at enhancing skills and knowledge to help cope with life transitions or health behaviors. Similarly, all seek to enhance social support. This is particularly true for the caesarean birth, divorce, and widowhood programs and is at least implicit in some techniques used in the community health education project.

Finally, all programs also provide a rich description of the details of actual program implementation. Broad strategy issues as well as specific techniques for implementation are described in ways that provide practitioners and researchers a fund of useful knowledge for actual program implementation.

Ciporah S. Tadmor

11

The Perceived Personal Control Preventive Intervention for a Caesarean Birth Population

The Perceived Personal Control Crisis Model

Crisis is a temporary period of disorganization in the functioning of an open system that is precipitated by ordinary stressful life events that are significant for the individual and temporarily beyond his or her capacity to cope with them. Furthermore, it is assumed that the quality of the crisis outcome may have a significant impact on the individual's mental health (Caplan, 1963, 1974).

The Perceived Personal Control Crisis model is a theoretical model of crisis. It explains the locus and intensity of crisis as a function of the perceived personal control (PPC) of the individual. The notion of PPC is a synthesis derived from Lazarus' (1968) notion of idiosyncratic perception of the stressor and Caplan's (1964, 1974, 1976, 1977; Caplan & Killilea, 1976) notion of availability of a coping response that mediates between the individual's appraisal of the event and his or her response to it. Perceived personal control is defined as the availability of a response to modify a stressor or its threatening characteristics (Averill, 1973). It involves the availability of perceived control on the emotional, cognitive, and behavioral levels that are assumed to be the mediating, buffering factors between the individual's perception of a stressful life event and the

quality of the crisis outcome. Hence, the PPC construct provides a generalized measure of resistance, irrespective of the specific threat or the precrisis personality of the individual. It is assumed that the potential benefit of PPC is derived from the combination of perceived control on the cognitive, emotional, and behavioral levels, with the understanding that individual differences may determine the importance of the various sources of control.

The PPC model has significant implications for crisis intervention. It calls for manipulation of situational variables, such as natural and organized support systems, information, anticipatory guidance, and the person's share in the decision-making process, as well as task-oriented activity, geared to enhance emotional, cognitive, and behavioral control. The PPC model is designed to

The author gratefully acknowledges the collaboration of Professor J. M. Brandes in the preventive intervention program for caesarean birth population and the collaboration of Y. A. Bar-Maor, J. Birkhan, and J. M. Hofman, and Dr. G. Shoshany in the preventive intervention program for pediatric surgery patients and their parents. The author wishes to thank the medical and nursing staff in the obstetric, pediatric surgery, and anesthetic departments, and the operating room, who were actively involved in the implementation of the preventive intervention programs. Last but not least, the author wishes to express her appreciation to Professor Gerald Caplan for his support and guidance throughout this work.

tackle high-risk factors for populations in key community institutions in order to minimize the emotional sequelae encountered following crisis. Furthermore, it is geared to assist individuals in accomplishing specific psychological tasks through the mediating services of natural and organized support systems.

The PPC model adheres to the goals of primary prevention and implies intervention on two distinct and yet complementary levels: (a) crisis intervention administered by a network of natural and organized support systems referred to as personal interaction; and (b) introduction of changes in policies, structures, and services conducive to positive mental health, referred to as social action (Caplan, 1964).

The PPC crisis intervention model has been implemented successfully for the following high-risk populations: (a) mothers of premature infants (Tadmor & Brandes, 1986), (b) mothers who encounter neonatal death (Tadmor, 1986), (c) medical staff dealing with terminally ill patients (Tadmor, 1987), and (d) children undergoing elective surgery and their parents (Tadmor, Bar-Maor, Birkhan, Shoshany, & Hofman, in press). In this chapter, an illustrative account of the implementation of the PPC model in the personal interaction and social action domains is discussed with respect to a caesarean birth population.

Objectives of the Perceived Personal Control Crisis Model

General objectives. The promise of the crisis intervention approach envisioned by the PPC model is not in the elimination of stressful events or in the reduction of an individual's exposure to life hazards. Its implementation by the individual's regulating support network is aimed at reducing the threatening characteristics of the event by augmenting the individual's emotional strength, familiarizing the person with the nature of the impending hazard, involving the person in the decision-making process, and equipping the person with task-oriented activities to master the predicament to minimize its emotional sequelae.

The short-term objective of the PPC model is the resolution of the immediate crisis and the restoration of the person to the precrisis state. The broader hope is to promote personality growth beyond the crisis level by enhancing the individual's adaptive potential to deal successfully with similar situations in the future. The long-term objective is to develop a crisis interven-

tion model that can serve as a generic model to be applied by professional caregivers to populations at high risk of encountering emotional crisis in fields such as health, education, and the military. Moreover, the inherent characteristics of the PPC model allow for the formulation of a system by which the mental health professional can achieve wider community coverage through the mediation of a regulating network of natural and organized support systems.

Specific objectives. The PPC crisis intervention model implemented in the obstetrics department of the Rambam Medical Center, Haifa, Israel, is designed to cater to the specific needs of a caesarean birth (CB) population. The CB population is defined as those women who deliver through caesarean section (5 to 15% of all deliveries). The objective is to enable the CB mother to accomplish the specific psychological tasks of caesarean birth so that the crisis has a positive outcome for her; her repertoire of coping skills is enhanced; and she is able to deal successfully with repeat CB in the future. Furthermore, the mental health professional attempts to implement a personal interaction program by working with the medical caregivers in the obstetrics department to enrich their understanding of the PPC model and to enhance the quality of their intervention with the CB population.

Rationale for the Formulation of Preventive Intervention for Caesarean Birth

The rationale for preventive intervention is derived from studies that indicate that women who deliver children by caesarean section have an increased likelihood of developing postnatal depression compared with the control population (e.g., Kendell, Rennie, Clark, & Dean, 1981). Our concern is also derived from reports of CB mothers who have unveiled their plight and the emotional difficulties they encountered. Intensive study of a CB population at the Rambam Medical Center indicates that there is a typical psychological experience of the CB mother that is totally different from that encountered by mothers experiencing spontaneous delivery. The experience of the CB population at Rambam Medical Center mirrors emotional difficulties encountered by CB mothers elsewhere (e.g., Cohen, 1977; Donovan, 1977). The special emotional difficulties of the CB mothers are accentuated by hospital practices and the attitudes of the medical staff, who perceive and treat the CB mother as a "section," a surgical patient rather than a new mother, reinforcing an impaired self-image in women already incapacitated by postoperative pain.

Reports of CB mothers suggest that even when CB is anticipated, the woman still hopes for a spontaneous delivery. This highlights the special plight of the unanticipated CB mother who has attended childbirth classes preparing for a shared spontaneous delivery with the father. The initial reaction is one of shock, reminiscent of the impact phase of generic crisis.

Whether the CB is elective or unanticipated, there is a high probability that the mother will be unprepared for the event, as well as ignorant of the reason a CB is needed. She thus remains prey to unrealistic fears and distorted interpretations. Without an explanation of the physiological sensations, she is likely to experience a sense of panic coupled with intense fears about the safety of the surgery and anesthesia for herself and the baby. The obstetricians' attempt to "spare" the CB mother by withholding information about the impending operation until the last moment only aggravates the situation. Lack of explanation with respect to the timing of an unanticipated CB may trigger blame, usually directed toward the medical staff, either for postponing the CB and consequently exhausting her or else for performing the CB prematurely and thus preventing the possibility of actively participating in delivery of the baby.

The hospital procedures and practices reinforce the surgical patient role likely to be internalized by the CB mother, affecting her self-image and role performance within and outside the hospital setting. The elective CB mother is likely to be admitted the day before the operation for tests and a restful night in the hospital. The following morning, she is taken to the operating room of the hospital on a stretcher, separated from the father, and placed in the reception room with surgical patients awaiting surgery. If the CB mother receives general anesthesia, the chances are that she will not see her baby until the next day; however, even if regional anesthesia is administered, the CB mother is not likely to benefit from the psychological advantages of this kind of anesthesia. In most instances, if she gets an opportunity to see her baby, it is going to be a quick glance, leaving her to deal with the social isolation encountered and the awesome feeling of being awake and aware that an operation is being performed on her body. Her fears are aggravated by the strangeness of the environment, with its peculiar sounds and unidentified odors, and by

unexplained physiological arousal. Her social isolation stands out in contrast to the otherwise noisy and crowded setting.

After surgery in the recovery room, she is likely to be exposed to moans and cries of other surgical patients that heighten her anxieties about her own condition and that of her baby. After a few hours in the recovery room, she is brought to the maternity ward. Her initial adjustment is likely to be hindered, since her return is likely to coincide with postoperative pain, the intensity of which comes as a total surprise to the vast majority of CB mothers who have not previously experienced a CB. For the next several days, the CB mother is likely to focus on her pain, secretions, and physical limitations. Conformity to a "sick role" is reinforced by hospital practices that exclude the baby from her care on the assumption that she is incapacitated by surgery and needs her rest. The vicious cycle of egocentric behavior perpetuated by the hospital practices, and the mother's own impaired role performance, is likely to yield a lowered self-esteem, adding to the already impaired self-image and resulting in a self-fulfilling prophecy.

By the time the baby is brought to them on the fourth day, many CB mothers are likely to refuse to take care of their babies, feeling incapacitated by the pain. This initial rejection of the baby is likely to trigger guilt feelings, heightened by a lack of bonding and a sense of alienation from the baby because of prolonged separation. These emotional difficulties encountered by the CB mother, characteristic of most of the CB population (e.g., Donovan, 1977), are aggravated in some women by ambivalence with respect to the identity of the baby. By the fourth day, a mother is also likely to encounter difficulties with nursing, because of engorgement and the lack of the suckling reflex in the babies accustomed to bottle feeding. For a great many CB mothers who view breast-feeding as an alternative way of facilitating attachment to the baby, this is a final blow to self-image, one that only a few women committed to nursing can overcome.

In the first few days after surgery, a mother is likely to share a room with other CB mothers for the convenience of the nursing and medical staff. After the initial intensive follow-up, she is moved to another room, most likely with women who have undergone spontaneous delivery. This practice is likely to reinforce the CB mother's lowered self-esteem and feelings of personal failure, since she is forced to witness their fast recovery and rapid turnover and their ability to care for their babies, as well as their endless reminiscing about their natural childbirth experience. The plight of the CB mother is further complicated by the predicament of the father, who may also experience feelings of helplessness and inadequacy, as well as the frustration of being deprived of the chance to support the mother and to share the birth of their baby.

These traumatic events and their accompanying negative feelings of guilt, personal failure, denial, blame, anger, helplessness, grief, inadequacy, and anxiety may trigger future failures and precipitate a full-blown crisis episode with each additional CB. Some CB mothers, ignorant of the reason they required a CB, are likely to attribute the need to the lack of physical or emotional effort on their part, necessitating a compensation for "letting the baby down." Futile attempts to make up to the baby may lead them to embark on maladaptive child-rearing practices. Notable exceptions to the pattern described above are women with bad obstetric histories, whose main concern is the end result, namely the baby. In these cases, the emotional sequelae of CB are minimized.

The Specific Psychological Tasks of the Caesarean Birth Population

Investigation of the typical experiences described above allows the formulation of the following psychological tasks that need to be accomplished by the CB mother to secure a healthy mother–child relationship as well as to achieve positive crisis outcome.

1. To acquire a realistic appraisal of the objective reasons for the performance and timing of CB to counterbalance guilt and blame. The prerequisite for the accomplishment of this task is acquisition of information as to the reasons, nature, and timing of CB, as well as to share in the decision-making process.

2. To deal with the loss of the natural childbirth. The accomplishment of this psychological task, more important in cases of unanticipated CB, requires dealing openly with the frustration, sense of personal failure, and grief in losing control over the childbirth, while simultaneously attempting to restructure the mother's perception of childbirth within the context of her capabilities.

3. To deal with the negative feelings triggered by the CB. The prerequisites for the accomplish-

ment of this task are acknowledgment and expression of feelings such as disappointment, anger, inadequacy, and fear.

4. To establish attachment to the baby. The accomplishment of this task requires dealing with ambivalence about the baby's identity and with the separation from the baby imposed by the physiological limitation as well as initiating early nursing and prolonged contact with the baby.

5. To deal with the physiological limitations imposed by the CB. The CB mother is required to resume task-oriented activities and start caring for herself and the baby (rooming-in) in spite of the postoperative pain.

Perceived Personal Control Preventive Intervention for the Caesarean Birth Population

Personal Interaction

The intervention based on the PPC model is geared to answer the specific needs of CB population before, during, and after CB. The model is applied by the medical caregivers in charge of the CB mother, such as obstetricians; anesthetists; midwives, pediatric, obstetric, and operating room nurses; pediatricians; a lactation counselor, as well as a veteran CB couple who have experienced shared CB. The intervention model is designed for both unanticipated and elective CB mothers and fathers. The former receive information close to the time of the CB, while the latter are invited to the obstetric department a few weeks before the scheduled CB for an anticipatory guidance session that includes audiovisual presentation of CB.

Anticipatory guidance session. The anticipatory guidance session serves to familiarize the CB couple with the department and to introduce them to the medical caregivers in charge. This is particularly important in the Israeli medical system of semisocialized medicine, which offers no continuity of medical care between the community and the hospital. The expectant mother attends a family health clinic in the community monthly in the first and second trimesters and weekly in the last month. In this community facility, she is likely to be cared for by obstetricians and nurses different from the ones she is likely to encounter in the hospital. Moreover, in the hospital she is likely to be admitted by one obstetrician, operated on by another, and cared for during her delivery by still another obstetrician. Consequently, a preliminary visit to the maternity ward and a meeting with the medical staff partly alleviates the difficulties stemming from the inherent characteristics of the multiagency medical system provided in Israel.

Furthermore, the summoning of natural and organized supports for the CB mother allows for the establishment of a semiautomatic regulating context that is seen not only as prerequisite for the accomplishment of the crisis work but also as an institutionalized setting for involving the future parents in the decision-making process (Hansell, 1976).

In the anticipatory guidance session, the CB mother is provided with detailed information with respect to the nature, course, safety, and duration of the CB; anesthesia; and the anticipated emotional and physiological reactions. Since her own emotional and physiological reactions are likely to be very similar to the ones described, she is more likely to believe the other information provided and to be less anxious about the safety of the CB. The medical team provides realistic estimates of how painful the experience will be and how long it will last, a procedure that facilitates the initiation of the "worry work" and generates a hopeful expectation while at the same time providing the woman with task-oriented activities to alleviate the postsurgical pain. The CB mother receives guidance about advantages of breast-feeding and instruction in nursing techniques and is encouraged to assume an active role in helping herself and other CB mothers on the floor. In this process, the mother gains some mastery in advance that will serve her when confronted with the real difficulty.

The anticipatory guidance session provides an opportunity for the open expression and ventilation of past childbirth experiences. It also allows for the stimulation of the reminiscence process, bringing forth the realization of what has been lost against a background of that which remains relatively stable, as well as for the sharing of common concerns and feelings with other CB couples, bringing forth the realization of the commonality of the predicament. The session provides a unique opportunity to assist the CB mother to restructure her perception of childbirth in a supportive atmosphere enhancing her personal worth.

Following the anticipatory guidance session, the CB couples are invited by the CB veteran parents to a support group meeting for purposes of guidance and support and for first-hand information about the physiological and emotional reactions anticipated and the ways of dealing with them.

The birth process. The elective CB mother, accompanied by the father, is admitted to the obstetrics department on the day of CB, and accompanied to her room to meet her roommate. Following initial introduction by the floor nurse, the CB future parents are accompanied to the reception room for tests and preparation for CB. Subsequently, they walk to the operating room located in the delivery suite.

After administration of regional anesthesia and initial preparations and introduction of medical caregivers to the CB mother, the gowned and masked father is called in by the midwife to join the mother. He sits on a low stool behind the anesthesia screen and can hold her untied hand. The father provides the mother with emotional support to counterbalance her loneliness and isolation. He reinstates her sense of confidence and control in interactions with the medical personnel. This allows the father to become a full partner in the birth of the baby, allows early and extended contact between the CB parents and the newborn, and diverts the attention of the CB mother from the surgery.

Once the baby is born, the anesthesia screen is lowered by the anesthetist to allow the parents to see the baby and resolve ambivalence with respect to the baby's identity. After initial examination within the parents' view, the pediatrician brings the naked baby to the parents and supplies initial information with respect to the baby's health in order to reduce anxiety. Subsequently, the wrapped baby is brought to the parents to hold and initiate bonding and enjoy for the remainder of the surgery. Thus, the anesthesia screen serves as a physical device to separate the professional and the emotional teams. The elimination of the surgeons' small talk gives the occasion a festive and inspiring touch. Once the surgery is completed and before the anesthesia screen is lowered, the father, accompanied by the midwife, is led outside the operating room, to be joined shortly by the mother.

Postpartum. Following the CB, the mother is brought directly to her room in the obstetrics department under the close supervision of the obstetric nurses. Within the first few hours, when the mother still enjoys the benefits of the analgesia from the regional anesthesia, the pediatric nurse or the lactation counselor brings the baby for the first nursing encounter to encourage close and early contact and secure continuity and success of breast-feeding. The baby is brought to almost all feedings until the mother feels ready and willing to accept full care of the baby. Active participation in the baby's care is seen as encouraging mastery and helping to overcome the sick role. The father is encouraged to take an active role in caring for the baby under the guidance and supervision of the nurses.

The pediatrician provides the mother with a full account of the baby's health, and the obstetrician prepares the mother to anticipate the sensations expected during the postpartum stay. Additional information about the CB side effects is obtained from the "Booklet for Caesarean Birth Mothers," aimed at reducing uncertainty and preventing disconfirmation of expectancies.

During the postpartum stay, a veteran CB mother, a member of the local CB support group, visits the new mother for purposes of guidance and support and to provide her with a role model who has successfully mastered the predicament. The new mother is encouraged by the obstetric nurses to serve as a veteran for new CB mothers on the floor, thus encouraging the recipient of help to become a dispenser of help, thereby initiating task-oriented activity in the service of generating hope and mastery.

Discharge from the hospital. Prior to the discharge, the CB parents are invited by the obstetrician to discuss relevant issues such as contraceptives, prospects of future pregnancies, sexual relationship following CB, and so forth.

A few weeks after CB, the parents are invited by the local mutual-help group to a support meeting for the purposes of sharing, assimilating, and integrating the CB experience. Occasionally, medical caregivers are invited to attend to participate in mutual feedback and enhance the understanding of CB parents on relevant issues on invited topics.

Social Action

As a result of implementation of the PPC model, a large number of changes have been introduced in the obstetrics department, geared to meet the specific needs of the CB population. Anticipatory guidance sessions are scheduled regularly for CB parents in the department, evoking the participation of the CB couple in the decision-making process with respect to kind of anesthesia, analgesia, breast-feeding, rooming-in, and discharge from the hospital. A detailed protocol of operative interventions is attached to the medical record of the CB in the outpatient clinic, outlining the spe-

cific activities to be performed by the medical caregivers in charge of CB. The protocol admitting the elective CB mother on the day of CB and the use of the operating room in the delivery suite have become institutionalized procedures in the department. In addition, not only is the father allowed to attend the CB when the mother is administered regional anesthesia, but his presence is welcomed at all times.

Provisions have been made for rooms designated for CB mothers as well as for the distribution of the "Booklet for Caesarean Birth Mothers." A new professional role, that of a lactation counselor, designed to help CB mothers with breast-feeding, has been introduced. Initiation of early nursing, within a few hours after CB, as well as bringing the baby to subsequent feedings until the mother is willing to accept full care, is made possible by the combined efforts of the pediatric nurses and the lactation counselor. Regular scheduled visits by CB veterans, members of the local CB support group, have become an integral part of the services provided by the obstetrics department. Medical consultation for CB parents is provided before discharge, and an appointment is scheduled for a follow-up examination in the outpatient clinic after 6 weeks.

Major Program Outcome Findings

The PPC crisis intervention model was implemented in obstetrics department "A" in the Rambam Medical Center while obstetrics department "B," a twin department in the center, served as a control group. The evaluation of the PPC model was done on a sample of 35 CB mothers matched on relevant variables. All CB mothers were administered regional anesthesia, all had a healthy baby delivered by caesarean section, and neither they nor their infants experienced medical complications during delivery or the postpartum period.

Each of the CB mothers completed a series of questionnaires on the fourth or fifth postpartum day that were designed to assess (a) psychological recovery (PR), defined as accomplishment of the specific psychological tasks of CB; (b) physiological recovery (PHR), designated by subjective and objective measures of the recovery process and independent functioning; (c) documentation of the implementation of the PPC crisis intervention model by the medical caregivers; and (d) the beneficial effects of the PPC model, yielding an individual PPC score. In addition, a questionnaire was designed to measure the duration of full breast-feeding and Halpern's (1975) Crisis Scale was administered at 6 to 12 months after the CB. The Community Mental Health Ideology Scale (Baker & Schulberg, 1967) was administered to the obstetricians of both departments before and after a series of workshops to measure preventive orientation.

The evaluation of the PPC model focuses on two distinct and yet complementary levels. Assessment on the theoretical level focuses on the underlying factors of the PPC theoretical construct, as well as on the determinants of the beneficial potential of the PPC model. Assessment on the applied level focuses on the effectiveness of the PPC crisis intervention in assisting the CB population in the accomplishment of the specific psychological tasks, as well as bringing forth attitude change in the medical and nursing caregivers in charge.

It was hypothesized that psychological recovery and physiological recovery would be enhanced as a function of PPC. The following dependent variables were analyzed: duration of hospitalization; use of narcotics, analgesics, and tranquilizer agents during and after the CB; initiation of individual care of the baby; duration of full breast-feeding at home; crisis score; PPC; PR; and PHR.

The research was undertaken to explore whether recovery from caesarean birth could be enhanced by the application of the PPC method, one that involves the systematic preparation of medical staff and parents alike. By present evidence, the outlook is indeed encouraging. The experimental manipulation yielded results that attest to both its factorial (internal) and its predictive (external) validity.

The factors that emerged from PPC item intercorrelations are the situational variables of organized support, information, sharing in the decision-making process, anticipatory guidance, and task-oriented activity. This agrees with an underlying theory of a tripartite division into emotional, cognitive, and behavioral control and provides empirical verification to the underlying factors of the PPC construct.

Furthermore, although no individual factor scale made a statistically significant contribution to the recovery criteria, cumulatively they did. Clearly, the beneficial potential of the PPC preventive intervention is contingent on its implementation as a whole. In sum, results accord with an integrative approach to preventive intervention that highlights structural and functional aspects of network connectedness. Correlational evidence between PPC scores and psychological and physiological recovery outcomes of the CB mothers regardless of group affiliation, experimental or control, seems to suggest that recovery outcomes are linearly dependent on PPC scores and that these scores distinguish between CB mothers in the experimental and control groups. These findings seem to support the underlying assumption of the PPC theoretical model that the PPC construct serves as a buffering, mediating factor between the appraisal of the stressor and the quality of the crisis outcomes.

In terms of practical application to be derived from the positive outcome attained by CB mothers in the experimental group, the following results were found. CB mothers in the experimental group as compared with CB mothers in the control group were released sooner from the hospital, initiated independent care of the baby (rooming-in) sooner, and continued nursing longer. After Day 1, mothers in the experimental group requested less analgesic agents, their psychological and physiological recovery was more rapid, and they reported enhanced PPC scores. Last but not least, fathers in the experimental group exhibited more attachment behavior to the baby.

It would seem that attitude change among experimental obstetricians toward a more preventive orientation was not solely the result of the training program, which certainly played its part, but also of the actual implementation of the PPC program. There is further evidence for this in the apparent change of perception among obstetric nurses. Traditionally known to focus on CB mothers, in this context they broadened the range of their concern to include the baby as well. Aside from increasing mention of the baby in the medical report card of the CB mother, they proceeded to help mothers with nursing, to visit more frequently in the intensive care unit, to bring the baby for nursing to the mother, and so forth.

Evidence for the success of PPC preventive intervention is to be seen not only in the greater effectiveness of the medical caregivers in the experimental department but also in the interest shown by medical staff in the control ward. "Contamination," minor as it was, may have ruffled the experimental design, but it also serves as a kind of testimonial. One of the advantages of the model is that it seems that it can be adapted to a great variety of individual skills and professional preparation.

A more detailed account of the PPC theoretical and applied model, materials used, the experimental procedure, and findings can be found elsewhere (Tadmor, 1984; Tadmor & Brandes, 1984; Tadmor, Brandes, & Hofman, in press).

Limitations of the Perceived Personal Control Preventive Intervention

Evaluation of the PPC model is limited by the same factors that limit evaluation of other primary prevention programs. Primarily these limitations stem from the fact that most of these programs are future oriented, offering at best "limited promise for quick feedback" (Zax & Cowen, 1972, p. 494), as well as from methodological difficulties. The difficulties arise since the goals of preventive intervention are multiple and complex and no single evaluation method can encompass all the variables in the study (Haggerty, Roughman, & Pless, 1975). Yet rigorous research using adequate controls and methodology aimed at modest, specified, operationally defined goals is long overdue.

Primary prevention programs may also be subject to moral criticism, on the grounds that preventive efforts invade human privacy on one hand and may arbitrarily withhold beneficial intervention from the control group on the other (Zax & Cowen, 1972). The mental health specialist called to deal with these issues will find it no easy undertaking.

Furthermore the PPC preventive intervention is designed to be implemented only in a key community institution such as the general hospital, school, army, or industry, and not in the community at large. It is imperative that one can identify (a) a target population, (b) the caregivers in charge, and (c) the policies and services in the institution geared for the target population.

The greatest potential of the PPC preventive intervention is also its major limitation since the preventive intervention is designed to be implemented by the medical and nursing staff. This promises to substantially augment the impact of the mental health worker, but at the same time it requires that the medical and nursing staff internalize the preventive intervention. Yet, it is well known that it is very difficult to secure attitude and behavior change. This difficulty is even greater in view of the fact that inherent in the underlying assumption of the PPC preventive intervention is that its potential benefit is derived from a combination of perceived control on the emotional, cognitive, and behavioral levels. The implication is that the preventive intervention has to be implemented in its entirety as a complex network of interlocking events. This imposes an additional burden on the staff as well as on the mental health worker. Furthermore, continuous training has to be provided for new physi-

cians and nurses joining the department. However, the preventive intervention is disseminated in part by the caregivers who have internalized it. These caveats can serve as a guide and a word of caution to those who would become involved in this type of work in the future.

The Positive Aspects of Perceived Personal Control Intervention in the General Hospital

The major questions of prevention of all sorts include *what* intervention is suitable for *which* population, as delivered by *whom* under *what* conditions. The PPC preventive intervention attempts to provide a comprehensive conceptual framework to deal with these issues.

The major contribution of the PPC preventive intervention model is its applicability in key community institutions in general and in the general hospital in particular. This formulation rests on the following considerations. The general hospital is perceived as a potential location where a crisis may be triggered because of the nature of the predicament, prolonged separation from family members, loss of control, and the detrimental effects derived from the dehumanizing aspects inherent in the structure of total institutions (Goffman, 1961). The PPC preventive intervention attempts to enhance the quality of the interaction between the individual in distress, the hospital, and her significant others. This is especially important in view of a theoretical orientation that emphasizes the role of this interaction in the etiology of mental disorder.

Intensive study of the structure of the general hospital setting reveals that its inherent need to be a smooth-running operation promotes the fallacy that identifies maladaptive coping behavior with positive mental health. Consequently, the isolated patient who passively surrenders to the authority and treatment of the medical caregivers, inhibits expression of negative feelings, and abstains from demanding information and participation in the turn of events is perceived by the medical caregivers as a model patient, coping well with his or her predicament. The inevitable outcome is that the feedback from the medical caregivers reinforces sick role behavior with its detrimental corollaries.

The dangers inherent in the structure and operation of the system are accentuated by physician's professional persona (Caplan, 1974), which dictates the withholding of information about the patient's condition unless the patient takes the initiative. This problem is aggravated by the fact that most patients operate on the premise that information should be volunteered. This break in communication has significant consequences for the mental health of the patient population. Lack of information impedes cognitive control, which is instrumental in attaining a realistic appraisal of the situation, which is in turn a prerequisite to an adaptive coping. The PPC model advances the case for the active, demanding patient surrounded by her spouse or equivalent. It also requires patients to take an active part in the decision-making process and openly expresses their concerns. This behavior, which exemplifies adaptive coping, may facilitate psychological growth beyond the specific stressor encountered.

The importance of focusing preventive intervention in the general hospital is highlighted by another concern. Since it is assumed that the hospitalized individual is manifesting a crisis identity, the danger lies in the fact that the medical caregivers relate to the impaired self-image as the authentic identity of the individual, consequently perpetuating the crisis identity beyond the hospital setting. Providing information to the medical and nursing staff with respect to the expected patterns of crisis behavior as well as the specific psychological tasks of their patient population deepens their understanding, increases their satisfaction from their job, and enhances the quality of their intervention by timing adequate intervention to coincide with the peak of the individual's susceptibility for maximal results.

In addition to reducing the psychological cost, PPC preventive intervention has been shown to be effective also in reducing the financial cost by shortening hospitalization and reducing the use of analgesia.

The choice of the medical and nursing staff as implementers of preventive intervention is indicated by additional concerns. This approach promises to help reduce the shortage of mental health professionals by focusing on target populations and employing nonpsychiatric professionals in the prevention of mental disorder. Furthermore, preventive intervention implemented by the medical and nursing staff is devoid of the stigma associated with intervention offered by mental health professionals and consequently is more readily accepted. This is particularly true of individuals of low socioeconomic status who are used to interpreting their difficulties in moral or medical terms.

The intention is not to turn the medical caregivers into quasi-psychologists or to interfere with their effectiveness. Instead, the goal is to strengthen their hand and allow them to choose strategies of intervention compatible with their professional orientation and personal intervention styles.

Sequence of Steps in Developing a Perceived Personal Control Program

The Role of the Mental Health Professional in the Personal Interaction Realm

Before implementing the PPC model, the mental health specialist must undertake an intensive study of the obstetrics department through personal involvement in patient consultation, doctor's visits, seminars, surgery, and high-risk consultation. The worker should also accumulate information to identify (a) populations at high risk of developing emotional dysfunction and (b) policies, structures, and services detrimental to the mental health of the CB population.

Preventive intervention in the personal interaction realm consists of the following activities undertaken by the mental health specialist.

1. The mental health professional participates in on-the-job training of the medical and nursing staff. The training workshops focus on (a) the underlying assumptions of the PPC crisis model, (b) the principles and strategies of the PPC preventive intervention model, (c) the specific psychological tasks of the CB population, (d) adaptive and maladaptive coping patterns, and (e) preventive intervention protocols. Workshops for the medical and nursing caregivers are conducted for obstetricians, obstetric nurses, midwives, medical students, pediatricians, anesthetists, and operating room nurses.

2. The mental health worker studies the CB population in the obstetrics department to identify the common difficulties encountered and formulates the specific psychological tasks of the CB population. This task rests on the assumption that crisis follows an identifiable sequence of phases characterized by common regularities of crisis behavior irrespective of the nature of the hazard or the precrisis personality of the individual.

3. The mental health professional establishes a task force composed of obstetricians and nurses. The function of the task force is to discuss tenta-

tive preventive intervention protocols and incorporate their recommendations in the final plan of action. The significance of the collaborative effort is that the value of the preventive intervention depends on its being feasible and applicable. Furthermore, the mental health specialist should never underestimate the need to obtain full approval of the house doctors and nurses. It is a mistake to think that as long as the head of the department has sanctioned the program, the medical staff will comply. If the staff are not convinced of the trustworthiness and potential helpfulness of the specialist, the specialist will soon find that his or her efforts will be blocked.

4. Gradually, detailed operational protocols can be formulated to answer the specific needs of the CB population. The preventive program is implemented by the medical and nursing caregivers in charge of the CB population, such as obstetricians, anesthetists, midwives, obstetric nurses, pediatric nurses, neonatologists, and lactation counselors, as well as additional sources of support such as the father and veteran CB parents.

5. The mental health professional convenes family members, the father in particular, to assist the CB mother. This activity is performed initially by the mental health worker and subsequently by the medical and nursing caregivers. Once the ritual of convening is initiated, the person who arranged the meetings should initiate the coping process by defining tasks, pacing them, and establishing an atmosphere conducive to activity and mastery. Furthermore, the convener, who generates movement from describing problems to defining tasks with the expectation of positive outcome, serves as a role model for the CB couple.

6. The mental health expert organizes a caesarean support group as an additional resource for the CB mother. This effort is facilitated by the heightened susceptibility and enhanced affiliation needs that passing through the medical service create. Strong attachment ties are established and endure beyond the hospital, providing the CB mothers with a continuous source of support and frame of reference.

The mental health professional is seen as instrumental in organizing the CB support group. Once the self-help group has been organized, the mental health specialist keeps the intervention to a minimum and does not attempt to supervise, train, or interfere with the genuine interest of the members of the group. Their firsthand knowledge and expertise is critical to support the person in distress.

The impetus for the establishment of the CB support group was derived from discontent with the prevailing medical practices before preventive intervention was introduced. It originated from the need to find an answer to personal problems and the need to reminisce and ventilate the difficulties encountered. As disclosures were shared, CB mothers derived emotional strength from the commonality of the experience, coupled with motivation to support other CB mothers. Gradually, the focus of the activity of the self-help group moved from the private to the public domain by helping other CB mothers. This objective is achieved by (a) providing support and guidance to the CB mothers in the obstetric department and in the community and (b) raising the awareness of the medical and nursing staff with respect to the legitimate needs of the CB population. The political objective of the CB group is to secure the changes in other obstetric departments in Israel that are provided for the CB mother in obstetric department "A" at the Rambam Medical Center.

7. Convening and organizing a network of natural and organized support systems for the CB mother may be the single most significant aspect of preventive intervention performed by the mental health profession. This is true because it establishes a semiautomatic regulatory context that is a prerequisite for the accomplishment of the adaptational work.

8. At this point, the mental health worker supervises the implementation of the preventive intervention by the regulating network. However, at times he or she may be required to implement key aspects of the preventive intervention alone. This is because it is important to (a) serve as a role model to the medical and nursing staff and (b) elicit feedback from the CB population, which in turn reinforces activity by the medical and nursing caregivers. The crux of preventive intervention is the persistence and perseverance of the mental health specialist that gradually erodes the resistance of the medical caregivers. Once the preventive intervention has been internalized by the medical and nursing staff in their professional orientation, it will be disseminated by modeling to new physicians and nurses as well as to medical and nursing students.

9. The mental health worker has to accompany the process of internalization with continuing mental health consultation and support in situations that overtax the resources of the staff (Caplan, 1970). *Helping the Helpers to Help* (Caplan, 1972) is thus a cardinal point of the whole preven-

tive intervention approach. The incorporation of the mental health professional as an integral part of the staff of the obstetrics department is important in promoting this end. The mental health professional can be assured that preventive intervention has been internalized when the head of the department is instrumental in dissemination of preventive intervention. This individual may do so by presenting the preventive intervention program at the staff meeting of the general hospital, in other hospitals, and in national and international conferences.

10. Finally, the mental health expert has to submit the effectiveness of the preventive intervention to rigorous scientific evaluation with respect to the CB population and the medical and nursing caregivers in charge of the target population. Subsequently, the findings can be presented to the caregivers involved in the preventive intervention and relevant changes introduced.

11. It is important that the mental health professional use media such as television and press to gain public exposure. The purpose of this public exposure is twofold: (a) to make the public aware of the benefits of preventive intervention and (b) to encourage consumer demand. Thus the momentum created from within is reinforced and extended from without. At this point, the mental health professional may start a new preventive intervention program for a new target population in the same department or may move to a new department altogether.

The Role of the Mental Health Professional in the Social Action Realm

Before implementing of the PPC preventive intervention, an intensive system analysis of all the departments that serve the CB population is needed. This goal is accomplished through personal involvement of the mental health expert in all activities of the system, such as patient consultation, doctors' rounds, surgery, and staff meetings. Initially the mental health expert has to identify policies, regulations, services, structures, and allocation of resources detrimental to the mental health of the target population. Subsequently, the individual has to introduce policies and services designed to promote the mental health of the CB population. It is also important that the mental health professional offer a course in crisis theory and intervention for populations

at high risk of encountering emotional dysfunction in the general hospital to students in medical and nursing schools prior to their entering the clinical field.

Conclusions

The PPC preventive intervention for a CB population is a novel preventive intervention approach based on a theoretical model of crisis. It is implemented by medical and nursing caregivers trained in the principles of the preventive intervention model in a general hospital setting. This preventive program tackles risk factors in the environment by manipulating such situational variables as natural and organized support systems, information, anticipatory guidance, sharing in the decision-making process, and development of task-oriented activity geared to enhance emotional, cognitive, and behavioral control. The specific objective is to help the CB mothers to accomplish specific psychological tasks and attain a positive crisis outcome. The general objective is to develop a generic preventive intervention model to be implemented by caregivers of other populations at high risk of encountering emotional dysfunction in the general hospital and other key community institutions.

The PPC preventive intervention falls in the realm of primary prevention and consists of an integration of the support system and crisis intervention fields (Caplan, personal communication, May 13, 1984). It implies intervention on two complementary levels. At the personal interaction level, the focus is on the target population and intervention is accomplished through the mediating services of a network of natural and organized support systems. At the social action level, the focus is on the system within a key community institution and the intervention introduces changes in the system conducive to a positive mental health.

The PPC model calls for a redefinition of the role of the mental health professional and presents a challenge for the field in setting up innovative action. In the personal interaction realm, the mental health specialist is responsible for studying the specific psychological tasks of high-risk populations and for identifying, recruiting, and training nonpsychiatric caregivers, family members, and self-help groups. In the social action domain, the mental health worker engages in analysis of systems in key community institutions and identifies policies and structures detrimental to mental health of the target population. He or she then introduces desired changes geared to answer the specific psychological needs of a normal population who are grappling with an ordinary stressful life event but are at high risk of encountering emotional dysfunction.

References

Averill, J. R. (1973). Personal control over aversive stimuli and its relation to stress. *Psychological Bulletin, 80,* 286–303.

Baker, F., & Schulberg, H. C. (1967). The development of a community mental health ideology scale. *Community Mental Health Journal, 3,* 216–225.

Caplan, G. (1963). Emotional crises. In A. Deutsch & H. Fishbein (Eds.), *The encyclopedia of mental health* (Vol. 2, pp. 521–532). New York: Franklin Watts.

Caplan, G. (1964). *Principles of preventive psychiatry.* New York: Basic Books.

Caplan, G. (1970). *The theory and practice of mental health consultation.* London: Tavistock Publications.

Caplan, G. (1974). *Support systems and community mental health: Lectures on concept development.* New York: Behavioral Publications.

Caplan, G. (1976, May). *Crisis theory and crisis intervention.* Paper presented at a seminar at Harvard University, Boston.

Caplan, G. (1977, February). *Support systems and community mental health.* Paper presented at a seminar at Harvard University, Boston.

Caplan, G., & Killilea, M. (1976). *Support systems and mutual help: Multidisciplinary explorations.* New York: Grune & Stratton.

Caplan, R. (1972). *Helping the helpers to help.* New York: Seabury Press.

Cohen, N. W. (1977). Minimizing emotional sequelae of caesarean childbirth. *Birth and Family Journal, 4,* 114–119.

Donovan, B. (1977). *The caesarean birth experience: A practical, comprehensive and reassuring guide for parents and professionals.* Boston: Beacon Press.

Goffman, E. (1961). *Asylums: Essays on the social institutions of mental patients and other inmates.* New York: Anchor Books.

Haggerty, R. J., Roughman, K. J., & Pless, I. B. (1975). Summary and implications. Where do we stand? In R. J. Haggerty, K. J. Roughman, & I. B. Pless (Eds.), *Child health and the community* (pp. 312–330). Toronto: Wiley & Sons.

Halpern, H. A. (1975). The crisis scale: A factor analysis and revision. *Community Mental Health Journal, 11,* 295–300.

Hansell, N. (1976). *The person-in-distress: On the biological dynamics of adaptation.* New York: Behavioral Publications.

Kendell, R. E., Rennie, D., Clark, J. D., & Dean, C. (1981). The social and obstetric correlates of psychiatric admission in the puerperium. *Psychological Medicine, 11,* 341–351.

Lazarus, R. S. (1968). Emotions and adaptations conceptual and empirical relations. In W. J. Arnold (Ed.), *Nebraska Symposium on Motivation.* Lincoln, NE: University of Nebraska Press.

Tadmor, C. S. (1984). *The perceived personal control crisis intervention model: Training of and application by physicians and nurses to a high risk population of caesarean birth in a hospital setting.* Unpublished doctoral dissertation, Hebrew University, Jerusalem.

Tadmor, C. S. (1986). A crisis intervention model for a population of mothers who encounter neonatal death. *Journal of Primary Prevention, 7*(1), 17–26.

Tadmor, C. S. (1987). Preventive intervention for the medical staff dealing with terminally ill patients. *Journal of Preventive Psychiatry.*

Tadmor, C. S., Bar-Maor, J. A., Birkhan, J., Shoshany, G., & Hofman, J. E. (in press). Pediatric surgery: A preventive intervention approach to enhance mastery of stress. *Journal of Preventive Psychiatry, 3*(4).

Tadmor, C. S., & Brandes, J. M. (1984). The perceived personal control crisis intervention model in the prevention of emotional dysfunction for a high risk population of caesarean birth. *The Journal of Primary Prevention, 4,* 240–251.

Tadmor, C. S., & Brandes, J. M. (1986). Premature birth: A crisis intervention approach. *The Journal of Primary Prevention, 6,* 244–255.

Tadmor, C. S., Brandes, J. M., & Hofman, J. E. (In press). Preventive intervention for a caesarean birth population. *Journal of Preventive Psychiatry, 3*(4).

Zax, M., & Cowen, E. L. (1972). *Abnormal psychology: Changing conceptions.* New York: Holt Rinehart-Winston.

Bernard L. Bloom and William F. Hodges

CHAPTER

12

The Colorado Separation and Divorce Program: A Preventive Intervention Program for Newly Separated Persons

The University of Colorado Separation and Divorce Program rests on three conceptual and theoretical supports: (a) social epidemiology, or formulations of how social factors play a role in determining the prevalance of disease or dysfunction; (b) primary prevention, that is, the importance of intervention programs that can prevent disorders in otherwise healthy populations; and (c) stressful life event theory—those theories that link stressful life events with the subsequent precipitation and perpetuation of physical and mental disorders.

Social Epidemiology

The general field of epidemiology concerns itself with the study of the distribution and determinants of disease prevalence (MacMahon & Pugh, 1970). Thus, the field of *social* epidemiology is specifically concerned with the identification of social factors that are associated with those distributions and determinants and with the development of social methods for reducing disease prevalence or dysfunction. That is, social epidemiologists are interested in identifying social factors that are associated with how disorders develop (their predisposition and precipitation) and with how long disorders last (their perpetuation).

There is substantial evidence that marital disruption plays a significant role in each of these aspects of the disease process. Indeed, there is probably no social factor that is more highly associated with the development and perpetuation of dysfunctional conditions (physical as well as emotional) than marital disruption.

Primary Prevention

The term *primary prevention* refers most generally to activities that can be undertaken with a healthy population to maintain or enhance their health. It is the focus on healthy populations and on health maintenance that distinguishes primary prevention from early case finding, treatment, and rehabilitation. Much has been written in the past decade about primary prevention (e.g., Bloom, 1984; Klein & Goldston, 1977) and its importance in the health service delivery program. Within the last several years, interest in the prevention of disease and dysfunction has grown, in

This project was funded, in part, by the National Institute of Mental Health Grant No. MH 26373 (Preventive Intervention for Newly Separated Persons, Bernard L. Bloom and William F. Hodges, co-principal investigators). We are pleased to acknowledge this support.

part as a response to the spiraling cost of medical care and in part as a consequence of gradual changes in social ideology and public policy.

Social epidemiologists have contributed to the interest in primary prevention by identifying social factors that appear to be associated with illness and that might be modified as a way of preventing illness. For example, recent studies have shown that persons who are socially isolated are at excess risk of becoming ill and that strengthening ties with other persons can reduce the risk of illness (e.g., Bloom, 1985; Gottlieb, 1982).

Stressful Life Event Theory

Among social factors that appear to play unusually important roles in the precipitation of illness (physical as well as mental), none seem more significant than what have come to be known as stressful life events. These events (e.g., death of a spouse, marital disruption, losing one's job, retirement, geographic mobility) appear to have the potential for bringing about illnesses among people who are healthy but vulnerable. Accordingly, there is a growing interest among people concerned with the prevention of illness in identifying stressful life events that might be unusually prevalent in a given community, in the hope of reducing the negative consequences of those events (Bloom, 1985).

The importance of marital disruption as a stressful life event can be understood in the context of the consistent relationship that has been found between marital status and health. Four explanatory hypotheses have been advanced to account for this relationship. First, the *premarital disability* hypothesis suggests that persons with physical or emotional disorders marry less frequently and those who do marry are less likely to maintain a successful marriage than persons without preexisting disabilities. Second, the *postmarital disability* hypothesis asserts that marital disruption may be significantly increased as a consequence of disabilities arising after marriage. Third, the *protective marriage* concept holds that the status of being married reduces the vulnerability to a very wide variety of illnesses. Finally, as has already been suggested, the *stressor* hypothesis asserts that marital disruption constitutes a significant stressful life event that exacts its toll on the physical and psychological well-being of the person.

These hypotheses are not mutually exclusive, of course, and there is no reason why they all cannot share in validity. What is striking, in general, is the consistent and powerful relationship between marital disruption and general health. To cite one remarkable example, in an earlier epidemiological study conducted in Pueblo, Colorado (Bloom, 1975), it was found that the annual admission rate into psychiatric inpatient facilities among men was 75 per 1,000 for men in disrupted marriages compared with 6 per 1,000 among men in intact marriages—a relative risk of 12 to 1. No other social characteristic has ever been found to be as dramatically associated with a dependent measure of psychological adjustment.

The clear association between marital disruption and physical and emotional disorders appears to have two interdependent components. First, illness (physical or emotional) or other forms of severe stress can precede and help precipitate marital disruption. Second, marital disruption can serve to precipitate physical and psychiatric difficulties in some persons who might otherwise not have developed such problems.

These two presumed components of the marital disruption and illness association lead to two different courses of action. First, as was the case in the Colorado Separation and Divorce Program, one can choose to work with persons undergoing marital disruption to lessen the stress and subsequent maladaptation associated with it. Alternatively, one can work with the married ill—emotional or physical—or with married persons undergoing severe stress in order to reduce the impact of the illness or stress on their marital adjustment. Interestingly, no study has been designed yet to implement and evaluate this latter program strategy.

Marital disruption, as a stressful life event, has three compelling characteristics. First, it is very common. Three million people are directly involved in a marital disruption in any given year—approximately the same number of people as are born (Bloom, Asher, & White, 1978; National Center for Health Statistics, 1987; Rankin & Maneker, 1985). Second, by common agreement, marital disruption has been judged as one of the most stressful life events that occurs, exceeded in severity by perhaps only one other event, the death of a spouse. Third, virtually no communities have any systematic and comprehensive services available for this at-risk population.

Problems Faced by Persons Undergoing Marital Disruption

A review of the literature regarding marital disruption (Bloom et al., 1978) indicates that marital disruption is a stressor of the first magnitude and that the time of greatest stress surrounds the time of physical separation. Reports of five specific problems keep recurring in the literature:

1. Socialization, including the need to strengthen what often has become a generally weakened social support system;

2. Child rearing and single parenting, whether the parent is custodial or noncustodial;

3. Legal and financial issues, including the need to have information about parental rights and responsibilities;

4. Housing and homemaking problems that are the consequence of the physical separation; and

5. Educational and occupational problems, most prominently for the spouse (usually the wife) who is joining or rejoining the labor force.

Program Objectives and Design Principles

The objective in developing the University of Colorado Separation and Divorce Program was to make available to a randomly selected group of newly separated persons a reasonably comprehensive program designed to help them cope with marital separation and its aftermath. It was our hypothesis that to the extent that the program achieved its objectives, we could find evidence of improved psychological and physical well-being in program participants in contrast with newly separated persons who served as no-treatment controls.

The basic principles guiding the design of the intervention program were as follows:

1. The program should maintain a clear rationale, in terms of the currently existing knowledge base.

2. The intervention program should be designed to provide services to newly separated persons, rather than, for example, to persons already divorced.

3. The program should have a specified duration rather than being indefinite in length.

4. The program should have a clearly specified set of eligibility requirements.

5. In order to permit a careful evaluation of the program, persons who met these eligibility requirements should be randomly assigned to ei-

ther an experimental intervention program or to a control group.

6. The program should be based at the university rather than in any community service agency such as the local mental health center. Marital disruption was not to be conceptualized or implicitly defined as an illness.

7. Careful attention had to be paid to keeping the program economical, since if it were established that it had demonstrable effectiveness, it should be able to be implemented in other settings without research grant support.

8. The program had to be fundamentally educational and competence enhancing in nature rather than psychotherapeutic, although it could have advertently therapeutic components.

9. The program should be comprehensive insofar as marital disruption is concerned, without at the same time overextending itself into other domains.

10. Since evaluation of the program would require the collection of follow-up information from program participants, special attention had to be directed to minimizing subject loss.

Program Overview

The University of Colorado Separation and Divorce Program accepted applicants for a 16-month period of time between April 1978 and August 1979. The intervention program itself ended in February 1980, and the process of follow-up data collection and evaluation continued until mid-1984. All program offices were located in the Department of Psychology on the campus of the University of Colorado. To be eligible to participate in the program, an applicant had to be (a) a resident of Boulder County, (b) in a legal first marriage, (c) living in a household separate from that of his or her spouse because of marital discord, and (d) separated no longer than 6 months.

Although these eligibility requirements were specific, they do not, even today, seem unreasonable. Yet, as it turned out, fewer than half of the people who expressed interest in the program were eligible. Of the total of 327 people who telephoned the program office to inquire about the project, 174 were ineligible. Of these 174 ineligible people, 49 (28%) were separated too long, 41 (24%) had had multiple marriages, 5 (3%) were both separated too long and had had multiple marriages, 24 (14%) resided outside of Boulder County, 38 (22%) had never been or were no longer married, and 17 (10%) were married but not separated.

By the end of the intake, 153 people had been accepted into the separation and divorce program who met all of the eligibility requirements. Upon acceptance into the program, the participants were randomly assigned on a 2:1 ratio into the intervention program and control group, respectively. Ultimately, we assigned 101 people into the intervention program and 52 people into the control group. Statistical analyses contrasting the intervention and control groups indicated that there were no differences between the two groups beyond those that would have been expected by chance (Bloom & Hodges, 1981).

Study participants were generally representative of young married adults in Boulder County. Half of the participants were parents, and more than 40% were males. Parents had an average of 2.2 children. In cases in which custody had been agreed upon, mothers were nearly always the custodial parent. The age range was 21 to 58. An average of 8 weeks had elapsed since the separation. It was the first separation for more than two thirds of the sample. Length of marriage averaged about 10 years, with parents being married significantly longer than nonparents. The sample had completed an average of nearly 16 years of education (equivalent to college graduate), and men had completed significantly more years of education than women. Nearly 85% of the entire sample was employed at the time of the first interview, with no differences in employment rate attributable to gender or parent status.

Identification of Study Participants

Since marital separation is not ordinarily a legally reportable event, there is no way of identifying the eligible population by means of any kind of document search. Accordingly, continuing attention had to be devoted to finding eligible people in the community. Our decision was to use all appropriate available avenues of publicity and, because of our interest in establishing a no-treatment control group, to describe the program in deliberately ambiguous terms, making no mention of services that might be available. The program announcement asked people who were newly separated to contact the office of the separation and divorce program and provided the telephone number.

Study participants included people in severe distress as well as those who were functioning well and who wanted only to share their experiences. The ambiguously worded program announcements were necessary in order to be fair to the comparison group for whom no program services would be provided. A waiting list control group strategy was not thought suitable since we wanted to follow people for an extended period of time.

We printed short attractive brochures describing the University of Colorado Separation and Divorce Program and distributed them from time to time to every public and private human service agency; to every psychiatrist, pediatrician, obstetrician, gynecologist, family physician, attorney, psychologist, and social worker in private practice; and to the clergy in Boulder County.

We posted the brochures on supermarket bulletin boards, in laundromats, and on public kiosks, and left brochures in the offices of the County Clerk who handled divorce filings and motor vehicle registrations. We inserted announcements in the personal columns, and small display ads regarding the program in every daily newspaper in Boulder County, and contracted for brief (less than 30 seconds) announcements to be made several times each week on the major AM and FM radio stations that served the county. At the time of the initial interview, study participants were asked how they heard about the separation and divorce program. Far more people mentioned the daily newspapers than any other source of information.

General Program Approach

Study participants assigned to the intervention program were told that the services available as part of the program would be available for the next 6 months. The literature on marital disruption suggested that 6 months was the appropriate duration of the program, in that most studies had indicated that that was the average duration of the greatest period of postseparation stress.

We designed a trial preventive intervention program that represented our best judgment about what was needed to be of help to a particular high-risk group. We had no evidence that the program would be effective and that persons assigned to the control group would be denied any services that had been shown to be useful. Indeed, it was conceivable that such a program, concentrating on a special stressed population and refusing to let "sleeping dogs lie" could do as much harm as good. At the same time, we had to be very careful that being assigned into the control group did not deny any services in the community that were already freely available to newly separated persons. Accordingly, the staff who were associated with the study participants who were not assigned to the intervention program were instructed to pay strict attention to the needs of the people they interviewed and to make full use of existing information and referral procedures to call people's attention to community services that were available and make referrals as seemed appropriate.

Program Staff: The Program Representatives

In order to make sure that the different components of the Separation and Divorce Program were well integrated, we designed the program so that every study participant assigned to the intervention group would have one staff member who would be responsible for coordinating all program components. We called this staff member the "program representative," and employed three such people. Each full-time program representative was responsible for providing direct service and for coordinating all other services for a caseload of 20 newly separated study participants.

Program representatives had two principal responsibilities. First, they were to contact (ordinarily by telephone) each newly separated person in their caseload at least every 2 weeks. Second, the program representatives were to serve as the link to the rest of the program as well as to resources in the community. The intervention program was designed to provide comprehensive services to newly separated persons with three exceptions—legal services, long-term psychotherapy, and medical care. Thus, it was in these three areas that we envisioned most referrals would be made.

Insofar as the biweekly contacts were concerned, the program representatives were to be sensitive to preexisting or emerging needs related to the marital disruption and to ways in which they, or other components of the intervention program, could be helpful. They were to be proactive without being a nuisance. It must be remembered that awareness of the need for help was not a requirement for participation in the intervention program. Many newly separated persons expressed interest in the study because they assumed that it was a research project and thought that they might be helpful. Others, of course, were interested in getting help, although

they had no reason to believe that any form of help was to be provided.

Program representatives were very creative in developing effective ways of working with their caseloads. They developed a number of social opportunities in collaboration with each other and saw themselves as having an important role to play in creating and providing sources of social support.

Regarding linking study participants with the rest of the intervention program as well as with appropriate community agencies, program representatives had a good understanding about services that were provided in the community by other agencies, and they knew how to make effective referrals to those other agencies. Similarly, they were very aware of the other major component of the intervention program and knew how to make referrals to that component.

Since, as it turned out, nearly all of the intervention group participants, men as well as women, were gainfully employed, one issue that came up quickly was when program representatives could meet with their newly separated caseload. One appealing possibility quickly arose—meetings over breakfast or lunch. Since this possibility seemed like an excellent time for program representatives to get together with their clients, program funds were rebudgeted to reimburse program representatives for expenses they themselves incurred in these meetings. Expenses associated with social activities planned by the program representative were also covered by research grant funds, although it should be noted that these expenses were all very modest.

Experiences with the program representatives were uniformly positive. The concept of the program representative was enthusiastically accepted and endorsed by intervention group participants. The program representatives clearly enjoyed their responsibilities and opportunities to be helpful, and intervention group participants gave the program representatives very high marks.

Program Staff: Subject Matter Specialists

The second major component of the intervention program was subject matter specialists. The plan, in designing the program, was to employ five subject matter experts on a part-time basis to provide expert consultation and education to the intervention program participants. The intention was to have these experts provide help in a group setting, perhaps meeting 2 hours weekly with groups of program participants who felt the need to discuss issues pertinent to that subject matter specialist's area of competence. As it turned out, these subject matter specialists provided considerably more help in individual contacts with intervention program participants than in group settings.

Subject matter specialists were recruited in the five areas that had been identified in a review of the literature as common problem areas for newly separated persons: (a) socialization and resuming the world of the single, (b) child rearing and single parenting, (c) housing and homemaking, (d) employment and education, and (e) legal and financial issues. Each recruitment posed a challenge in terms of finding the right part-time person for each position.

The socialization specialist was thought of as someone who would likely deal with the complex problems around reentry into the world of single persons—meeting people, dating, sexual issues, moral issues, loneliness, and so on.

The specialist dealing with child rearing issues was expected to help with issues regarding child rearing and single parenting, both from the point of view of the custodial as well as the noncustodial parent.

The housing and homemaking specialist would, we thought, be of more help to men than women, and could be someone specially skilled in homemaking, for example, a home economist already employed in the community. We anticipated that such a person could be helpful regarding such problems as budgeting, shopping, meal preparation, and other homemaking skills, as well as apartment and home rentals and purchases.

We thought that the career planning and employment subject matter specialist would probably work primarily with women since problems associated with this topic might commonly occur in the case of newly separated women who have not recently been gainfully employed and who must resume an interrupted career or build a new one. The specialist would be someone skilled in career development and employment and able to link study participants with representatives of public and private employment agencies and personnel directors of large employers in the metropolitan Boulder–Denver area.

Finally, the specialist in legal and financial problems would be an attorney or a paralegal with special skills in such areas as the establishment of credit eligibility for loans and bill consolidation and general legal issues pertinent to newly separated persons such as child custody,

visitation, maintenance, and child support. If we hired an attorney, we had already decided that that attorney would disqualify himself or herself from representing any intervention group participant at any time in any legal action related or unrelated to the marital disruption. Indeed, this was a general principle invoked regarding all subject matter specialists. As a condition for affiliation with the program, the subject matter specialists were not permitted to serve any program participant in a professional capacity outside of the program.

We budgeted enough funds to employ subject matter specialists between 2 and 4 hours per week and had little difficulty finding people in the Boulder community who were interested in these positions. We ultimately located and hired a social worker in private practice who had had considerable experience working with newly separated persons around the issues involved in being single again; another social worker with a number of years of experience working with single parents around child rearing issues was selected; a home economist employed by the local public utility company was hired to be of help in the areas of housing and homemaking; the director of a counseling center was enlisted to provide help to intervention group participants in the areas of employment and education; and finally, an attorney was hired to provide help in the areas of legal and financial problems. (Interestingly, before we could mention it, the attorney himself suggested that it would not be appropriate for him to ever represent any of the study participants in a divorce action at any time.)

The part-time nature of the subject matter specialist involvement in the project created unavoidable problems because of limited accessibility to the intervention program participants. Study participants and program representatives had to spend more time trying to arrange appointments with specialists than they had anticipated. It would have been desirable for the subject matter specialists to have been more easily available, but it was not possible to arrange a way of functioning that did not ultimately involve the common complexities of scheduling appointments among busy people.

Day-to-Day Operation of the Program

Study participants who were assigned to the intervention group were given appointments with the program representative who would be responsible for their overall case management. Study participants who were assigned to the control condition were given appointments with one of the advanced graduate students in the doctoral-level clinical psychology program at the University of Colorado who served as research assistants on the project. All follow-up interviews, conducted after the intervention program had terminated, were done by advanced clinical psychology graduate students.

The initial interview for the members of the intervention program provided an opportunity for the program representative to become acquainted with the study participant. At the end of the interview, the participant was told that certain services were available on demand for a 6-month time period and that the program representative would contact the study participant from time to time to see how things were going. The initial interview was thus envisioned as a start to the helping process.

In the case of study participants assigned to the control condition, at the conclusion of the interview the interviewers discussed, as seemed appropriate, the desirability of one or more referrals to community agencies. When the interview and referral process was completed, participants were told that they would be contacted in about 6 months in order to come in again for a follow-up interview so that the project staff might learn how they were getting along and what issues they were facing. For additional information about the day-to-day functioning of the separation and divorce program, see Bloom (in press).

Program Evaluation

As can be seen from the general description of the study, this was a two-group pre–post design with random assignment. Initial assessments were made in both groups, and then an intervention program was made available to one of the two groups. The original plan was to collect follow-up data 6 months after the initial interviews took place, that is, immediately after the time limit for participation in the intervention program had arrived in the case of the intervention program participants; and to begin a second follow-up interview 1 year later, that is, 18 months after entrance into the program.

Subsequent additional funding from the National Institute of Mental Health made it possible to complete the 18-month interviews and to add a 30-month follow-up interview. After completion of the analysis of the 30-month inter-

views, it became apparent that it would be very desirable to conduct one more follow-up assessment. By this time, grant funds were no longer available, so a less expensive brief telephone interview was conducted with all participants we could locate. This final interview was conducted about 4½ years after entrance into the program. Thus, by the time the study was completed, we had data from the initial interview and from four follow-up interviews available for analysis.

In spite of the fact that newly separated persons are a very mobile group, there was remarkably little subject loss. Of the original group of 153 study participants, we interviewed 150 at the time of the 6-month follow-up interview. Because the interest was in obtaining complete data sets, it was decided that once we failed to locate that person at any data collection point, the search for that person would not continue. Thus, at the time of the 18-month interview, of the 150 people we had interviewed 1 year earlier 145 were located and interviewed. At the time of the 30-month interview, 143 of the 145 people who had been interviewed a year earlier were located. Finally, at the 4-year interview, 134 of the 143 people who had been interviewed at the 30-month interview were found. Thus, we had a complete data set on 134 (88%) of the original group of 153 study participants. The low attrition rate was virtually identical in the control and experimental groups.

Marital Status Transitions

Divorce was nearly always the final outcome in this sample of newly separated individuals. Of the 143 study participants on whom complete 30-month data were available, 136 (95%) were ultimately divorced. The vast majority of these divorces took place within the first 18 months of separation. Reconciliations were not common and not often successful in the sense of sustaining an intact marriage. Of the 13 study participants who had reconciled by 6 months, only 9 were still reconciled at 18 months. Of these 9 persons, only 6 were still reconciled at 30 months, and only 4 of the 6 were still reconciled at 4 years. Through the first 30 months of the study, there were a total of 15 reconciliations, of which only 4 (27%) were still in effect at the final 4-year follow-up interview. Remarriages to new spouses were not very common and only slightly more successful than reconciliations. Of the 26 remarriages that took place within the first 30 months, 9 (35%) had already ended in divorce by the time of the 4-year follow-up interview.

Empirical Evaluation Study Results

Published reports are available regarding the evaluation of the intervention program as of each of the follow-up interviews (Bloom, Hodges, & Caldwell, 1982; Bloom, Hodges, Kern, & Mc-Faddin, 1985; Hodges & Bloom, 1986). Dependent measures of adjustment at the 6-month evaluation included composite self-report measures of anxiety and neurasthenia (Bloom & Caldwell, 1981), a measure of distress and maladjustment, and five measures reflecting the five areas in which difficulties had been reported in the literature—career and employment, legal and financial, single parenting, housing and homemaking, and socialization.

Principal dependent measures of adjustment at the 18-month evaluation included the same self-report measures of anxiety and neurasthenia; self-report rating scales of problem severity in the areas of feelings of guilt or failure, socialization, parenting, career or job-related issues, financial problems, housing or homemaking, health-related problems, drinking, drugs, or excessive smoking, legal problems, sexual problems; and an overall measure of life quality.

At the 30-month follow-up interview, dependent measures of adjustment included a repeat of the life quality measure as well as the measures of anxiety and neurasthenia, ratings of 11 problem areas in terms of problem severity, and estimates of the benefits associated with the separation. At the final 4-year follow-up interview, dependent measures were largely the same as those that had been employed at the previous evaluation.

Summary of Findings

At 6 months, the members of the intervention group were doing significantly better than those in the control group on five of the nine measures of adjustment that were developed. At 18 months, the differences between the intervention and control group had increased slightly. At 30 months, the differences between the two groups had continued to increase. At the final 4-year interview, the magnitude of the differences between the intervention and control groups had decreased, but significant differences consistently favoring the intervention group were still found. In contrast to the rapid, steady, and continuous improvement in the intervention group, the control group improved more slowly and tended to reach plateaus on several measures after which improvement

ceased. Thus, the effects of this 6-month intervention program have been shown to have a duration of at least 4 years.

Three factors contribute to the credibility of the general conclusion regarding intervention program effectiveness. First, members of the control group as well as of the intervention group reported that their participation in the study had been helpful to them. Thus, it was not only being part of the intervention program that resulted in reported improvement. Second, gains as a consequence of program participation were persistent and appeared over a far longer time period than could be accounted for on the basis of any response bias. Finally, gains in the intervention group, when contrasted with those in the control group, increased over time and then diminished. This time-related phenomenon is consistent with the conclusion that the program had some significant impact, as opposed to findings that did not change over time.

Closer examination of the nature of the reported improvement indicates that they were rarely linear. In one category were those measures of adjustment that showed rapid and significant improvement within the first 6 months of intervention program participation. Included in this group were symptoms of psychological well-being and reports of personal growth and increases in self-knowledge. Virtually none of the specific problem areas frequently identified by newly separated individuals demonstrated any significant improvement during the first 6 months of program participation.

A second group of changes were those that occurred more slowly to members of the intervention group, that is, significant improvements that were reported between the 6-month and 30-month interviews. Included in this group were many of the specific problem areas in which earlier improvement had not been found—development of new social relationships, lessened financial difficulties, increased sexual satisfaction, diminished feelings of guilt and self-blame, reduced feelings of loneliness, lessened sense of incompetence, improved physical health, and improved adjustment and sense of satisfaction in the work setting.

A third group of changes were those that occurred late in the follow-up evaluation sequence, that is, between the time of the 30-month and 4-year evaluations, regardless of earlier changes. This set of measures included all three components of the symptom checklist (that is, total symptomatology as well as measures of anxiety and neurasthenia), the quality of life scale, and reported job satisfaction.

Modifying the Separation and Divorce Program

In the course of the several years of active involvement in the Separation and Divorce Program, a number of ideas occurred to the staff and to the program participants regarding ways the program might have been conducted differently. Some of the proposed changes represent significant modifications of program design; others constitute ideas about carrying out more effectively the program as originally envisioned. Although most of the suggestions for program modification came from the experiences of staff or program participants, many came from the results of the periodic evaluation studies.

Identifying Program Participants

In some ways, the single most serious problem in implementing the Separation and Divorce Program was finding eligible subjects. It has already been noted that in spite of the fact that the eligibility requirements were very modest, a majority of people who contacted the program office were found to be ineligible for program services. But even if everyone who had contacted the program were to have been eligible, the total number represented but a small proportion—perhaps as small as 10%—of people who were eligible to apply.

The decision to publicize the program in the entire community and obtain eligible participants from this publicity was not, in retrospect, the easiest way of finding the largest proportion of newly separated persons. Although the program was publicized in every way thought possible, it is entirely possible that large numbers of newly separated persons did not hear of the program. Many people who heard of the program may very well have chosen not to participate. Because of the need to evaluate this pilot program, description of the nature of the intervention program was not possible in this publicity, and this ambiguity may have caused certain potential participants to choose not to involve themselves. For other potential participants, the notion of seeking help might have been unacceptable, if only because they might have considered themselves doing well.

At any event, a more targeted approach to locating eligible program participants would have been more appropriate, and agency personnel who are interested in implementing a separation and divorce program should include a variety of methods for locating intervention program participants. Two such targeted approaches seem especially useful to explore.

First, a program of this kind can be implemented through a health maintenance organization (HMO), much as was done by Wertlieb, Budman, Demby, and Randall (1982) in the Harvard Community Health Plan, an HMO in metropolitan Boston. Because there is reason to believe that an effective preventive intervention program for people undergoing this stressful life event may result in reduced use of medical services, an HMO might be willing to implement such a program for its subscribers, if only on a trial basis, without additional cost to HMO members.

Second, program participants can be located through work-related employee assistance programs or personnel offices. As is the case with HMOs, there is reason to believe that it would be to employers' advantage to provide help to their employees who are undergoing marital disruption. As the proportion of people of working age in the labor force is increasing, particularly in the case of women, employment settings represent an important source of intervention program participants.

With such a large proportion of study participants gainfully employed and the evidence that some of the negative consequences of the stress associated with marital disruption are seen in the work setting, a program based in the workplace might attract a larger proportion of eligible adults, as well as being more successful in achieving its objectives insofar as work-related personal disruption is concerned.

Program Duration

Some intervention program participants wished that their eligibility for program services was not time limited. Because the Separation and Divorce Program was a pilot study, some limit on the duration of the program was necessary. The 6-month limit on program eligibility that was established appeared to be appropriate in length and acceptable for the vast majority of program participants. But not for all. Furthermore, employing subject matter specialists on a very part-time basis (2 to 4 hours per week) limited their availability to intervention program participants. By increasing the number of people who could be responsibly helped at any given time, and by expanding the duration of the program, it would be possible to employ subject matter specialists for significantly longer proportions of their work week and thus increase their involvement in the program as well as their accessibility.

Assuming that a full-time program representative can work effectively with a caseload of 20 newly separated persons, as the present experience suggests, then the formula for adding to the total number of intervention program participants at any given moment is clear—one program representative for every 20 participants. Adjustments in this formula could be made on the basis of the demand for continued help. Similarly, it would be possible to add to the hours per week of subject matter specialists as a function of the total number of persons actively involved in the intervention program.

Use of Subject Matter Specialists

Our experiences have led us to believe that the concept of the subject matter specialist was a valid one in the context of the Separation and Divorce Program, but there were problems in implementing the concept. First, as to the selection of the competencies, the present results suggest that it would have been useful to have added a work-related specialist, that is, someone who could have been helpful in dealing with work-related problems that were associated with the marital disruption. That specialist could not only have provided help to participants directly, but also might have begun the process of working with employers in the Boulder County area in thinking about the implementation of the intervention program in the work setting. In addition, the intervention group seemed to have little need for a housing and homemaking specialist, although had the present approach been more proactive, that specialist could have made a greater contribution to the overall objectives of the program.

Second, as has already been mentioned, the usefulness of the subject matter specialists was limited by the fact that they were involved in the project so few hours per week and that at any given moment, few program participants had needs that were clearly relevant to the specialists' competencies. Both of these problems could have been dealt with by increasing the number of program participants, that is, by expanding the program.

Finally, making optimal use of the subject matter specialists would have taken a far higher level of ongoing monitoring. In an expanded program, it would be useful to employ a program manager whose responsibilities would include monitoring the work of both the program representatives and the subject matter specialists.

Increasing the Precision of the Program

In the case of those substantive problems in which little improvement was found, more precise services need to be designed. These problems include, first, legal and financial difficulties, for which improved competency-building skills could be developed. In addition, there was little evidence of increased happiness or relief from conflict on the part of intervention group participants. Although it is possible that these failings are simply evidence of the stressful nature of marital disruption, greater attention to the psychological components of the stress might result in a more successful intervention.

This longitudinal study has shown that neither improvement nor problems occur in both sexes in all areas at the same time. Accordingly, sensitivity to the experiences of this intervention program should make it possible to emphasize certain aspects of the intervention at certain times. Thus, for example, immediate improvement followed by a long flat plateau has been noted in certain aspects of the adaptation process. Program staff could be alert to the fact that additional efforts need to be undertaken in order to reduce the length of that plateau. In other areas, improvement was not noted for a rather long period of time. In these domains, program efforts could be concentrated earlier in the intervention process.

The importance of fostering social competency in coping with such stressful life events as marital disruption appears to have been demonstrated. Combined with a more intrapsychic approach, when indicated, and with attention to the nature and strength of the social support network, a multifaceted cognitively-oriented preventive intervention program can play a significant role in reducing the risks to both psychological and physical well-being associated with marital disruption, and perhaps with stressful life events in general.

Making the Program More Proactive

Improving the level of success in this kind of preventive intervention program may require a more proactive approach than was employed in this initial attempt. For example, it is possible to identify study participants who appear to be at unusually high risk by their scores on the various dependent measures of adjustment obtained at the initial interview. Program representatives could flag those persons and offer special or more frequent services to them.

Examination of the characteristics of persons who made greatest use of the various components of the preventive intervention program revealed that they had two characteristics in common. First, they were aware of difficulties in some particular area; second, they were above average in terms of psychological well-being. This finding underlines the potential importance of a more proactive approach in working with intervention group participants.

Many intervention program participants consciously used the program as a way to meet new people, in part to reaffirm their own self-esteem and worthiness and in part to deal with loneliness and social isolation. That is, the program not only provided help in how to meet new people in general, but also provided a vehicle for meeting other newly separated people who were in the intervention program.

Study participants provided a number of useful suggestions for program modification, for example, adding to the housing and homemaking service an organized cooperative for exchanging baby-sitting or other services. It would be very useful in a program of this kind to solicit suggestions for program modification in a proactive, ongoing way and to implement as many of those suggestions as seem appropriate and feasible.

Special Population Needs

The University of Colorado Separation and Divorce Program provided preventive intervention services to a very narrow demographic spectrum—relatively young, well-educated, gainfully employed, white, middle-class Boulder County residents who were newly separated from a first marriage. Some of these demographic characteristics were chosen deliberately as eligibility requirements that constituted part of the research design, whereas others simply reflected the demographic characteristics of the community served. There is no firsthand information about the suitability of this intervention program for a group that would be significantly different demographically. Thus, there are important limitations to the generalizability of the present findings.

For example, little is known about the special needs of widows or widowers, of people who are ending a second or third marriage, of people who are separated not because of marital discord but rather because of work-related responsibilities that keep them apart from one another, or of people who are ending a cohabiting relationship. Furthermore, we know little about special needs of non-White populations, of people who are dealing with other stresses (e.g., chronic unemployment) at the same time, or of the growing number of older persons who are ending marriages of 20 or more years in length.

We do know that there is very little in the literature of any systematic nature about the special needs of demographic subsamples of newly separated persons. Accordingly, if a human service agency were interested in serving a special group of persons undergoing marital disruption, it would be important to begin the project by conducting careful interviews with representatives of the group to be served in order to learn more about their special needs.

Local need assessment studies and analyses of public records of divorce filings and divorce decrees can play a supplementary role by identifying special groups who might make appropriate targets for programs designed to be of help to persons undergoing marital disruption.

Creating an Advisory Board

In some ways, the only real disappointment of the University of Colorado Separation and Divorce Program was in its failure to continue in the community when the pilot phase was over, in spite of its demonstrated success. This failure is not uncommon among federally funded projects that are pilot studies. Two suggestions are offered here for reducing the likelihood of such failures in the future, and both represent activities that would have been advantageous to undertake from the beginning of the present intervention program.

First, the local media provide an excellent resource for keeping the community in touch with the project and its findings. Our experiences were uniformly pleasant in working with local reporters, and we received a good deal of publicity about the program and about our general research activities in the field of marital disruption. On the other hand, we needed to be more proactive ourselves in calling the attention of the media to what we were learning, and to what the "news" was in what we were learning.

Second, a local professional advisory group to the project should have been established. The group could have been comprised of representatives of local human service agencies, among whom might have been those who would ultimately have continued the program after its pilot phase was concluded. The program would have been greatly assisted by the consultation and suggestions of such an advisory panel, and ideally the advisory group members would have known enough about the project throughout its existence to have been able to consider its continued existence in the event that it was successful in achieving its objectives.

References

Bloom, B. L. (1975). *Changing patterns of psychiatric care.* New York: Behavioral Publications.

Bloom, B. L. (1984). *Community mental health: A general introduction* (2nd ed.). Monterey, CA: Brooks/Cole.

Bloom, B. L. (1985). *Stressful life event theory and research: Implications for primary prevention* (DHHS Publication No. (ADM) 85-1385). Washington, DC: U.S. Government Printing Office.

Bloom, B. L. (In press). *The University of Colorado separation and divorce program: A program manual.* Washington, DC: U.S. Government Printing Office.

Bloom, B. L., Asher, S. J., & White, S. W. (1978). Marital disruption as a stressor: A review and analysis. *Psychological Bulletin, 85,* 867–894.

Bloom, B. L., & Caldwell, R. A. (1981). Sex differences in adjustment during the process of marital separation. *Journal of Marriage and the Family, 43,* 693–701.

Bloom, B. L., & Hodges, W.. F. (1981). The predicament of the newly separated. *Community Mental Health Journal, 17,* 277–293.

Bloom, B. L., Hodges, W. F., & Caldwell, R. A. (1982). A preventive program for the newly separated: Initial evaluation. *American Journal of Community Psychology, 10,* 251–264.

Bloom, B. L., Hodges, W. F., Kern, M. B., & McFaddin, S. C. (1985). A preventive intervention program for the newly separated: Final evaluations. *American Journal of Orthopsychiatry, 55,* 9–26.

Gottlieb, B. (1982). Mutual-help groups: Members' views of their benefits and of roles for professionals. *Prevention in Human Services, 1,* 55–67.

Hodges, W. F., & Bloom, B. L. (1986). A preventive intervention program for the newly separated: One year follow-up. *Journal of Preventive Psychiatry, 3,* 35–49.

Klein, D. C., & Goldston, S. E. (1977). *Primary prevention: An idea whose time has come* (DHHS Pub. No. (ADM) 80-447). Washington, DC: National Institute of Mental Health.

MacMahon, B., & Pugh, T. F. (1970). *Epidemiology: Principles and methods.* Boston, MA: Little, Brown.

National Center for Health Statistics. (1987). Annual summary of births, marriages, divorces, and deaths: United States, 1986. *Monthly Vital Statistics Report, 35, No. 13* (DHHS Pub. No. (PHS) 87-1120). Hyattsville, MD: Public Health Service.

Rankin, R. P., & Maneker, J. S. (1985). The duration of marriage in a divorcing population: The impact of children. *Journal of Marriage and the Family, 47,* 43–52.

Wertlieb, D., Budman, S., Demby, A., & Randall, M. (1982). The stress of marital separation: Intervention in a health maintenance organization. *Psychosomatic Medicine, 44,* 437–448.

Nathan Maccoby and David G. Altman

CHAPTER

13

Disease Prevention in Communities: The Stanford Heart Disease Prevention Program

There now exists a large literature on cardiovascular disease (CVD) epidemiology that links personal characteristics and life-style to subsequent CVD. The key predictors of CVD are family history, elevated arterial blood pressure, cigarette smoking, elevated plasma cholesterol, obesity, physical inactivity, and Type A behavior. Of particular relevance to psychologists is the fact that behavior is implicated in all of these, with the exception of family history. Similarly, other health problems such as cancer, lung disease, accidents and injuries, and substance abuse have behavior as the root of the problem. Clearly, there are a variety of ways to change behavior. Since chronic disease risk is widespread, the Stanford Heart Disease Prevention Program (SHDPP) hypothesized that community health education would be the most effective way to change behavior and the surrounding environment influencing behavior.

A variety of perspectives and theoretical formulations were blended to design and carry out the SHDPP education programs. In addition to community organization, which created a receptive environment for educational materials and programs, communication–behavior change theory, social marketing, and diffusion theory were used. A brief description of these theoretical perspectives is presented below.

Community Organization

The SHDPP education programs were conducted in a manner that encouraged involvement and ownership and control by local community groups. The following assumptions were made:

• Mass media education alone is powerful, but its effects may be augmented by community organization and development.

• Interpersonal behavior change programs can be enhanced relatively inexpensively through activation of community organizations.

• Community organizations can enhance the delivery, reach, and effectiveness of educational programs.

This research was designed and carried out by a large number of researchers from a variety of disciplines. Some of the key researchers in this group are John W. Farquhar, Peter D. Wood, William L. Haskell, Stephen P. Fortmann, C. Barr Taylor, June A. Flora, Byron W. Brown, Paul Williams, Doug Solomon, and Janet Alexander. The material reported in this chapter is a distillation of information published in other articles and chapters. Readers interested in the work of the Stanford Heart Disease Prevention Program should refer to the reference section of this chapter for a partial list of these publications.

• Community organizations can increase the community-wide adoption of programs and thereby the likelihood of maintaining these programs long term.

• Formation of new community organizations can be catalyzed by external (university-based) efforts by increasing the array of groups concerned with health education and health promotion.

Thus, the central theme of the community organization and development efforts was that collaboration between community organizations and SHDPP researchers would enhance the adoption of healthful behaviors and ultimately lead to the long-term institutionalization of health promotion programs in the community.

Communication–Behavior Change

The communication–behavior change (CBC) framework offered the SHDPP a perspective on how individuals and groups change knowledge, attitudes, and behavior. Concepts from this framework are drawn from social learning theory (Bandura, 1977), the hierarchy of learning model (Ray, 1973), the communication–persuasion approach of McGuire (1969), the attitude change formulation of Ajzen and Fishbein (1980), and others.

The CBC framework provided a step-by-step approach to achieving community-based education and behavior change and a guide to breaking down program objectives, messages, and materials into manageable and effective steps. In short, it forced SHDPP program planners to develop a rational basis for making intervention selections and for sequencing these selections over time. The CBC steps generally are as follows: (a) become aware (gain attention), (b) increase knowledge (provide information), (c) increase motivation (provide incentives), (d) learn skills (provide training), (e) take action (model), and (f) maintain change (provide support and guidance).

Social Marketing

The concept of social marketing (Kotler, 1984) is that many of the principles and techniques used to market commercial products can be applied to community health behavior change programs. In social marketing, the focus is on transactions whereby something of value is exchanged among parties. The social marketing process begins with an understanding of the consumer, leading to the creation of products and services with price, promotion, and distribution channels organized to attract the consumer. The Four P's of marketing management (i.e., the right product backed by the right promotion in the right place at the right price) can help guide the design and implementation of health communication campaigns. Although there are similarities between social marketing and the elements of CBC theory described previously, it is also evident that social marketing can help explicate the constraints of marketing health promotion in the complex environments of modern America.

Diffusion Theory

A central theme of diffusion theory that is applicable to community health education is that communication, persuasion, and learning in community systems flow through identifiable social networks. In order to achieve adequate adoption of the health innovations (behaviors) being advocated, therefore, opinion leaders within the community system should be recruited as collaborating educators. In operational terms, this led in the Five City Project (FCP) to the identification of community opinion leaders who were perceived by residents as credible sources of information. These opinion leaders included powerful community gatekeepers (e.g., physicians, government officials, wealthy businesspeople) as well as indigenous grassroots leaders (e.g., neighborhood activists, housewives, retired persons). These community opinion leaders were critical players in the design and implementation of the FCP. Their contributions to the long-term maintenance of the FCP after the Stanford researchers leave is at this point an unknown.

With this as background, the next section describes the components of the Stanford Three Community Study (TCS; implemented from 1972 to 1975) and the Stanford Five City Project (implemented from 1978 to 1992).

The Stanford Three Community Study

At the time the TCS was designed, the effects of combining extensive mass media with face-to-face instruction in community education programs were untested. In particular, three elements typically ignored in health campaigns were used:

1. Mass media materials were devised to teach specific behavioral skills, as well as to perform the more usual practice of offering information and influencing attitudes and motivation.

2. Both mass media and face-to-face instruction were designed to embody many previously validated methods of achieving changes in behavior and self-control training.

3. The campaign was designed on the basis of careful analysis of the specific needs and media consumption patterns of the target audience.

Three roughly comparable communities in northern California were selected. The town of Tracy was chosen as a reference community because it was relatively distant and isolated from media in the other communities. Gilroy and Watsonville, the two intervention communities, shared some media channels (e.g., some television and some radio), but each town had its own newspaper. Watsonville and Gilroy received different strategies of health education over a period of 2 years. Gilroy and Watsonville received health education through the mass media, and in Watsonville, a randomized experiment with a sample of persons at higher levels at risk for CVD was developed. This experiment used intensive face-to-face instruction for two thirds of the Watsonville high-risk group, with the remaining one third used as a control. All were exposed to health education through the media as a control against intensive face-to-face instruction. The basic sequential strategy of the face-to-face intervention was to present information about behaviors that influence risk of coronary heart disease (CHD), stimulate personal analysis of existing behavior, demonstrate desired behavioral skills, (e.g., food selection and preparation), guide the individual through tentative practice of these skills, and finally, gradually withdraw instructor participation.

In order to assess the effects of the TCS interventions, baseline and yearly follow-up data from surveys composed of interviews and medical examinations of a probability cohort (longitudinal) sample of 35 to 59-year-old men and women were completed. The overall risk of CHD for each of the participants in the study was estimated from a multiple logistic function of risk factors predicting the probability of developing CHD within 12 years. The logistic takes into account age, sex, plasma cholesterol concentration, systolic blood pressure, relative weight, smoking rate, and electrocardiographic findings (Truett, Cornfield, & Kannel, 1967). Developing a valid model of CHD

risk requires attention to the independent and interdependent relationships between variables contributing to risk. The multiple logistic technique accomplishes this modeling.

The intervention was intended to produce awareness of the probable causes of CHD and the specific behaviors that may reduce risk. The campaign also provided the knowledge and skills necessary to accomplish recommended behavior changes and helped individuals become self-sufficient in maintaining new health habits and skills. Diverse and integrated health communication messages were delivered through a variety of media channels (e.g., television spots, bus cards, newspaper advertisements, billboards, pamphlets, booklets, radio programs). Because of the sizeable Spanish-speaking population in the communities, the campaign was presented in both Spanish and English. The media campaign began 2 months after the initial baseline survey and continued for 9 months during 1973, stopped during the second survey, and then continued 9 more months in 1974 and on a reduced basis in 1975 (Farquhar et al., 1977; Maccoby, Farquhar, & Wood, 1977). Thus, the total TCS campaign could be seen as a set of phased media events—the information obtained for monitoring was used to refocus priorities, reset directions, and modulate the course of the campaign in the desired direction.

Findings of the Three Community Study

Overall, the results of the TCS suggest that community health status can be improved by an educational program delivered through media and interpersonal channels. Changes in health knowledge, health behaviors (e.g., diet, nutrition, exercise), CHD risk factors (e.g., high blood pressure, high cholesterol, smoking), and overall CHD risk (e.g., based on the Framingham multiple logistic function) were all found (Farquhar et al., 1977; Fortmann et al., 1981; Fortmann, Williams, Hulley, Maccoby, & Farquhar, 1982; Maccoby et al., 1977; Maccoby, in press; Meyer, Nash, McAlister, Maccoby, & Farquhar, 1980).

The TCS demonstrated that mass media, when used appropriately, can increase knowledge and help people improve their health habits. The results led the SHDPP to believe, however, that the power of this method could be enhanced considerably if it employed the media to stimulate and coordinate face-to-face instructional programs in natural community settings (e.g., schools, workplaces, community organizations). Thus, the TCS study stimulated further investigation designed to test these ideas.

The Stanford Five City Project

The FCP began in 1978 and will continue well into the 1990s. The FCP differs from the TCS in that the two communities selected for education are much larger, the health education campaign is aimed at benefiting the entire population, the communities are more complex socially, the education program is more extensive, and there are three reference cities rather than one. In the FCP, the education program is running for 6 to 8 years rather than 3, the effects of the intervention are being monitored in a wider age range (e.g., 12 to 74), changes in CVD event rates (i.e., morbidity and mortality) are being measured, and a community organization devised to create a cost-effective and lasting program of community health promotion is being fostered.

There are two major hypotheses to be tested in the FCP. The first is that community-wide education can achieve a lasting reduction in the prevalence of CVD risk factors within a general population, leading to a substantial decline in the Framingham multiple logistic measure of risk in a representative sample of persons ages 12 to 74. The second hypothesis is that this risk decline will lead to a decline in CVD morbidity plus mortality in persons of ages 30 to 74 that is significantly greater in the education cities than in the reference cities.

The education program of the FCP was introduced after completion of a baseline population survey. The effects of education on reducing risk factors are being assessed by comparing the results of the four independent sample surveys (i.e., cross-sectional) and cohort sample surveys (i.e., longitudinal) in the two treatment communities with the results of these surveys in two of the three reference communities. Epidemiologic surveillance of cardiovascular disease morbidity and mortality occurs in all five cities and is continuing beyond the education program.

The education program had three goals. The first was to generate an increase in the knowledge and skills of individuals and in the educational practices of organizations such that risk factor reduction and decreased morbidity and mortality were achieved. A second goal was to carry out the education program in a way that created a self-sustaining health promotion structure embedded within the organizational fabric of the communities that continued to function after the project ended. A third goal was to derive a model for cost-effective community health promotion from the experiences and data accumulated in this study and the TCS that would have general applicability to other American communities (Altman, Flora, Fortmann, & Farquhar, 1987). An additional purpose of the FCP was to analyze the secular trends in CVD risk factors, morbidity, and mortality during a time of declining CVD mortality, the cause of which is uncertain. Also, the rich survey data collected enabled testing of numerous hypotheses relating to CVD, epidemiology, behavioral medicine, psychology, community organization, physiology, and communication science.

The ideal study design for evaluating the efficacy of comprehensive community-based health education is to randomly assign a large number of communities to treatment and control conditions. The simpler design of five not randomly assigned cities was chosen because of limited resources and the extensive overlap of media markets in California. Selection of cities was subject to several constraints: location in northern California; populations exceeding 30,000; total populations of the five cities exceeding 300,000 to provide sufficient statistical power; reasonable similarity of ethnic, social, economic, and demographic characteristics; relative independence from other cities (thereby eliminating suburbs of larger metropolitan areas); no shared newspaper or electronic media markets between treatment and control cities; shared media markets between treatment cities (thus decreasing costs); and relative independence of the two treatment cities, despite some shared media services. The next section reviews the components of the education program.

Education Program of the Five City Project

Broadcast media programs. A wide variety of broadcast media strategies including public service announcements, television news series, radio series and talk shows, and television shows were used in the FCP. The goals of using these broadcast media included setting the community agenda (e.g., bringing a health issue to the attention of the community through public service announcements), encouraging the adoption of health-promoting attitudes and behaviors (e.g., a television series teaching people how to make and enjoy heart-healthy meals), and ultimately influencing people to modify risk factors and reduce premature morbidity and mortality. Some broadcast media products were hybrids; broadcast media were used to promote awareness of community programs and of print media (e.g., a radio series instructed people on how to quit smoking and also directed listeners to other programs and materials in the community that could support their cessation efforts).

Print media programs. Print media materials (e.g., newspapers, books, pamphlets, self-help kits) were also used widely in the FCP. Compared with broadcast media, print media can usually provide more information (if read and understood), messages of higher information density, and better skills training. Because print media can be read and reread at the users' own pace, it can provide information in a user-oriented format.

Print media products were distributed in the FCP through direct mail and existing organizations such as work sites and medical care providers. A variety of print media strategies was used in the FCP. These included print designed to promote a community event, to reinforce knowledge and skills being taught in an educational program, to raise general awareness about a health issue, or to change attitudes and behaviors.

Because of the large Spanish-speaking population in the intervention communities, mass media included Spanish language. Radio production, for example, was concentrated on Spanish-language stations because this is a major information source for this target group. In addition, weekly newspaper columns in both English and Spanish were a major component of the print media program. English materials were both translated directly into Spanish and also modified to be culturally relevant (through changes in content, style, and format).

Community interpersonal programs. The FCP community interpersonal programs were delivered through a variety of organizations including health departments, community colleges, schools, voluntary organizations, health professionals, work sites, hospitals, and other nonprofit health service agencies. These programs included traditional strategies such as classes and lectures as well as more innovative efforts such as incentive-based contests and use of lay neighborhood opinion leaders. In addition, several environmentally based interventions were implemented including a program that labeled heart-healthy items (e.g., chicken, fish, salad) in restaurants and a program in grocery stores that encouraged

checkers and baggers to add health education flyers to grocery bags.

Evaluation of the Five City Project

Formative and process evaluation methods. There are at least seven specific topics in which formative evaluation can assist in the design, development, production, and distribution of educational programs. These include

1. Audience needs analysis (e.g., understanding audience attitudes, beliefs, self-efficacy, and knowledge);

2. Audience segmentation (e.g., identifying subsections of the community with factors in common such as needs, risk, demographic characteristics, and media use);

3. Program design (e.g., addressing questions such as the proper name, location, and time for program and use of appropriate educational methods and materials;

4. Program testing (e.g., testing an early version of an intervention with relevant audiences);

5. Message design pretesting (e.g., to improve the effectiveness of specific mass media messages);

6. Community event analysis (e.g., investigation of the factors that motivate participants to attend an event, how they learn about an event, what they thought about an event, and how this experience will influence their future participation and behavior change attempts); and

7. Media event analysis (i.e., analysis of community media events).

A variety of process evaluation strategies was used. It is essential to identify a number of steps in the process of community change and to measure each of them. For example, although the ultimate outcome variable in these studies may be a change in morbidity and mortality due to heart disease and stroke, it is also important to measure intermediate stages such as knowledge and attitude change, skills learning, performance and maintenance of these skills, and success in community organization. Thus it is important to know who changed in response to interventions and how these individuals accomplished the change. It is also important to evaluate the success of achieving stable and meaningful change in community practices and institutions as a measure of success in leaving behind a program that runs partly or totally on its own energies. Although one cannot guarantee a totally clear explanation of success or failure, the use of process evaluation strategies will provide some important clues for understanding change or its absence as well as ideas for future research and intervention.

Summative evaluation methods. The population surveys of health behavior on CVD risk factors were conducted by full-time FCP staff at permanent survey centers in four of the five cities. City directories of households published by R. L. Polk were found to provide a relatively complete listing of households in each community (approximately 97% complete) and were revised every 2 years. All individuals ages 12 to 74 who resided in randomly selected households at least 6 months of the year were eligible for the surveys, invited to participate, and included in the denominator for calculation of participation rates.

There were two main types of samples: a cohort or longitudinal sample and an independent or cross-sectional sample. City directories of households published by R. L. Polk were used to obtain a listing of households in the target communities. These directories were updated every 2 years. All individuals ages 12 to 74 who resided in randomly selected households at least 6 months of the year were invited to participate in the survey. In the initial year of the survey, approximately 650 people from each community, selected randomly, were seen by survey center staff and constituted the first independent sample. These individuals were invited to participate in subsequent surveys every 2 years in order to study the process of change in CVD risk and related behaviors over time. Second, third, and fourth independent samples were conducted over the last 6 years of the project to study cross sections of the community without the potential confounding effects of repeated measurements.

The chief sources of data on health-related behaviors were questionnaires and dietary measures. The core questionnaire consisted of demographic measures, attitude and opinion measures, health knowledge assessment related to prevention of heart disease and stroke, stress behavior, diet, nutrition, weight behavior, smoking behavior, physical activity behavior, communication media use and interpersonal communication network analysis, and medical history including medication use. Finally, a random 50% of the participants were given a 24-hour dietary recall aided by food models to illustrate size, weight, or volume of foods.

A variety of physiologic measures was obtained including weight, nonfasting venous samples (e.g., for lipid, lipoprotein, plasma thiocyanate analysis), expired air carbon monoxide as a measure of cigarette use, blood pressure, urine samples (e.g., for urinary sodium, potassium, and creatinine measures), a low-level exercise test, and pulse rates.

The purpose of the community epidemiologic surveillance method was to allow for the calculation of comparable, city-specific rates for total and CVD mortality, fatal and nonfatal myocardial infarction, and fatal and nonfatal stroke in each of the five communities included in the study. Each community was defined with the use of census tracts so that accurate estimates of the population at risk and its age and sex structure could be extrapolated from the 1980 census. Only nonfatal CVD events that resulted in hospitalization were monitored, and identification of fatal cases was obtained through county death certificate files. Access to all coroner's records was obtained, as were copies of autopsies. All nonhospital deaths, both coroner's cases and others, were investigated further by contacting the decedent's family for the medical history and the circumstances of death. A questionnaire was also sent to the decedent's physician to obtain medical information (Fortmann et al., 1986).

Results of the Five City Project

At the time of this writing, only interim results are available. Main interim results from the cohort (i.e., longitudinal) sample indicate significant improvements in health-related knowledge of cardiovascular risk factors, reductions in blood pressure, and a reduction in pulse rate. After 28 months of education, the multiple CVD risk logistic for total mortality and for CHD events was less in treatment than in reference cities by 10.4% and 11.1%, respectively; at 52 months of education, these indices favored treatment by 13.4% and 7.4%, respectively. Similar results were obtained in the independent samples.

At the height of the education program, the number of exposures per adult of radio and television messages was close to 600 per year. The number of exposures to direct educational programs was about 1.5 per year at the height of the program. Overall then, the interim results from the FCP suggest that many of the goals of the project were achieved. It should be noted that changes in the community environment were also a goal of the study and worked synergistically with individual health behavior change efforts. For example, cigarette machines could be kept from minors or abolished; smoking could be banned in work sites and public places; cigarette advertising could be banned or heavily restricted; more healthful foods could supplant disease-promoting ones in schools and restaurants, in fast food places, and in food dispensing machines; and exercise opportunities could be made more readily available. Although the evaluation was not designed to explicitly assess these changes in the environment, evidence suggests that changes have occurred, particularly in terms of food labeling and smoking policies.

Future Challenges

The design and implementation of community-based disease prevention programs like the TCS and the FCP inevitably require balancing methods typically used in controlled laboratory research with the realities of conducting research in community settings. For a full discussion of these issues, see Farquhar (1978).

Community-based health interventions like the TCS and FCP could influence both individual-level factors (e.g., behavior, risk factors, health status) and community-level factors (e.g., structure and delivery of community health services, community traditions influencing individual community structure, involvement of community agencies with health programs, influence of community decision makers in health services, availability of health services, political milieu, physical environment in which health programs operate, and social norms about health). To date, more attention has been focused on influencing individual-level factors. In the future, our understanding of how community-based efforts can contribute to influencing community-level variables needs to be increased.

Even so, the conclusion is inescapable that compared with earlier decades, more effective educational methods in public health and psychology are available and thus should be applied extensively in community settings. To achieve the full potential of community health promotion, however, researchers and practitioners should become more proficient in using mediated and face-to-face education methods, collaborating effectively with community leaders and organizations, using qualitative evaluation methods such as ethnography to gain insights into the process of community change, and using communication channels natural to community systems (Far-

quhar et al., 1985,; Farquhar, Maccoby, & Wood, 1985). For example, it is unclear how emerging information systems such as home computers, cable television, and video technology influence the ways people acquire good and bad health habits. There is also a need to counteract institutional activities and practices that promote ill health (e.g., tobacco promotion and advertising, youths' easy access to tobacco, use of high-fat foods by restaurants, and government taxation practices with respect to tobacco). These latter variables have not been the explicit focus of community-based heart disease prevention programs.

A crucial challenge to community education programs is the extent to which the programs are adopted and maintained by the community when the research phase ends and the researchers obtain new grants and pursue other interests (Altman, Flora, & Farquhar, 1986). The long-term maintenance of interventions developed in community-based research programs, to be sure, is especially difficult to achieve. Because of the high absolute costs of these interventions, it is unreasonable to expect community groups to be able to adopt elaborate protocols conceived in university research programs. What typically happens is that a community adopts individual program elements from the larger intervention. For example, most communities would not have adequate resources to replicate the entire FCP smoking control program. What is likely, however, is that a community would adopt an element or elements of the smoking control program to maintain or replicate (e.g., a self-help quit smoking series, a smoking cessation course curriculum, or an incentive-based smoking cessation contest). The point is that community interventionists should plan carefully for their eventual departure from communities by promoting empowerment of community organizations and leaders and by relinquishing control over program design and implementation.

The following questions about the long-term social relevance of community heart disease prevention programs are essential to assessing the overall usefulness of these programs and the extent to which community empowerment is promoted:

1. How long are research-initiated programs able to maintain their influence on community health?

2. What programs are most easily adopted by the community?

3. How much and what type of assistance do community groups need from researchers to

maintain programs originally designed and implemented by researchers?

4. How do programs change when they are taken over by the community?

5. Do research-based programs increase the development of community-initiated programs?

Extending the Projects: The Next Generation

In 1986, the SHDPP was folded into the Stanford Center for Research in Disease Prevention (SCRDP). The SCRDP was developed to reflect the interest of the professional staff in extending the results of the SHDPP to other health problem areas and target audiences. Along these lines, in 1986 the SCRDP was funded by the Kaiser Family Foundation, as part of their National Health Promotion Program, to establish a Health Promotion Resource Center (HPRC) for the 13 western United States. The general mission of the HPRC is to provide technical assistance to communities throughout the west interested in designing, implementing, and evaluating community-based health promotion programs. The HPRC provides assistance to communities interested in preventing CVD, cancer, substance abuse, injuries, and adolescent pregnancy.

By the late 1980s or early 1990s, the Kaiser Family Foundation will have funded HPRCs throughout the United States, thereby developing a technical assistance network of health promotion professionals. In addition, the Foundation expects to award community health promotion grants to communities throughout the country.[1]

As noted previously, one of the challenges of the TCS and the FCP was developing materials and programs that could be adopted readily by interested communities and professionals around the country. A primary goal of the HPRC is to do just this—to transfer broadly the technology of community-based health intervention.

The HPRC is involved in the production of print and electronic media and computer technology as well as participation in a variety of outreach activities (e.g., face-to-face consultation, phone and mail consultation, delivery of workshops/confer-

ences, and availability of computer health information databases and a clearinghouse). By working closely with communities in the West, the HPRC hopes to extend the work of the SHDPP and other related projects. If successful, the concept of a linkage between research and development groups (in this case, a university) and community groups holds great promise for improving the health and well-being of citizens in this country.

An important goal of the HPRC is to encourage the development of innovative health promotion programs and materials, encourage the use of existing and effective materials and programs (e.g., promote replication), and tailor existing programs and materials that are effective or hold promise to the unique needs of individuals, organizations, and communities. Through processes of innovation, replication, and adaptation, the technology of community-based health promotion and disease prevention can reach its full potential. The focus in this regard is to work *with* communities, not *to* or *for* them. In addition, the intent is to demonstrate the possibilities of community health promotion.

Summary

Beginning in the early 1970s, large-scale community-based disease prevention programs were begun with the expectation that broad-based community intervention would result in lasting and cost-effective individual and community change. Some of the potential advantages of this type of intervention are its relevance to the everyday environments of people, the increased likelihood of community-wide exposure to the intervention through diffusion of innovations, generally high external validity, utility to public health policy, and its potential for cost-effectiveness.

Findings from the Stanford studies and others suggest that these programs have been successful in improving community health. They have also shown that via the use of an interdisciplinary staff of physicians, epidemiologists, behavioral scientists, biostatisticians and communication specialists it is impossible to mount large-scale community-based studies aimed at reducing the incidence and prevalence of chronic disease. Methodologically, quasi-experimental designs involving the collection of a variety of demographic, physiologic, and behavioral data can serve as a basis for both furnishing baseline infor-

---

[1]Additional information about the Health Promotion Resource Center and the Kaiser Family Foundation National Health Promotion Program can be obtained by writing David Altman, Stanford Center for Research in Disease Prevention, Stanford University School of Medicine, 1000 Welch Road, Palo Alto, CA 94304-1885.

mation for prospective intervention studies and assisting in the formulation of long-lasting interventions and evaluations of their effectiveness.

On the basis of experiences derived from the TCS, the FCP, and other similar community research, the Stanford group has developed a general set of guidelines with which to evaluate whether community health promotion efforts are likely to succeed. The two key components of these guidelines are that community interventions should attempt to be (a) comprehensive and (b) integrated for maximal effectiveness. Comprehensive refers to addressing multiple health problems, multiple health change goals (e.g., awareness, knowledge, beliefs, motivation, skills, behaviors, maintenance, and environmental/policy change), multiple targets of change (e.g., individuals, organizations, and environments), multiple channels of communication (e.g., face-to-face and mass media), multiple strategies for change (e.g., educational, community organization and development, environmental, and regulatory), and multiple evaluation methodologies (e.g., formative, process monitoring, summative, and cost analysis). Also important is integrating interventions within the community and integrating the efforts of community organizations. Thus, integration refers to coordinating efforts, collaborating with others, and sequencing implementation plans according to a predetermined plan (one that should be based on extensive formative research).

The TCS provided substantial indications that risk factors in CVD could be reduced through community-wide education. The FCP is an attempt to replicate and extend these findings by additional means of intervention. Through these programs, it is hoped not only that changes can be accomplished during the period of study but also that community and environmental change as well as behavior changes can be maintained in the long-term with sufficient magnitude and duration to provide a means for reducing both CVD risk and morbidity and mortality. A great deal has been learned since the early 1970s when the TCS was launched. Even so, a great deal still needs to be learned about the efficacy of community approaches. We remain optimistic that community-based change will be an important strategy in the armamentarium of technologies available to biomedical and social scientists. Through comprehensive and integrated community intervention, the health status of individuals and communities can undoubtedly be improved.

References

Ajzen, I., & Fishbein, M. (1980). *Understanding attitudes and predicting social behavior.* Englewood Cliffs, NJ: Prentice-Hall.

Altman, D. G., Flora, J. A., & Farquhar, J. W. (1986, August). *Institutionalizing community-based health promotion programs.* Paper presented at the annual meeting of the American Psychological Association, Washington, DC.

Altman, D. G., Flora, J. A., Fortmann, S. P., & Farquhar, J. W. (1987). The cost-effectiveness of three smoking cessation programs. *American Journal of Public Health, 77*(2), 162–165.

Bandura, A. (1977). *Social learning theory.* Englewood Cliffs, NJ: Prentice-Hall.

Farquhar, J. W. (1978). The community-based model of life-style intervention trials. *American Journal of Epidemiology, 108*(2), 103–111.

Farquhar, J. W., Fortmann, S. P., Maccoby, N., Haskell, W. L., Williams, P. T., Flora, J. A., Taylor, C. B., Brown, W. B., Jr., Solomon, D. S., & Hulley, S. B. (1985). The Stanford Five City Project: Design and methods. *American Journal of Epidemiology, 122,* 323–343.

Farquhar, J. W., Maccoby, N., & Wood, P. D. (1985). Education and communication studies. In W. W. Holland, R. Detels, & G. Knox (Eds.), *Oxford textbook of public health* (Vol. 3, pp. 207–221). Oxford, England: Oxford University Press.

Farquhar, J. W., Maccoby, N., Wood, P. D., Alexander, J. K., Breitrose, H., Brown, B. W., Jr., Haskell, W. L., McAlister, A. L., Meyer, A. J., Nash, J. D., & Stern, M. P. (1977). Community education for cardiovascular health. *Lancet, 1,* 1192–1195.

Fortmann, S. P., Haskell, W. L., Williams, P. T., Varady, A. M., Hulley, S. B., & Farquhar, J. W. (1986). Community surveillance of cardiovascular diseases in the Stanford Five City Project. *American Journal of Epidemiology, 123,* 656–669.

Fortmann, S. P., Williams, P. T., Haskell, W. L., Hulhey, S. B., Farquhar, J. W. (1981). Effect of health education on dietary behavior: The Stanford Three Community Study. *American Journal of Clinical Nutrition, 34,* 2030–2038.

Fortmann, S. P., Williams, P. T., Hulley, S. B., Maccoby, N., & Farquhar, J. W. (1982). Does dietary health education reach only the privileged? The Stanford Three Community Study. *Circulation, 66,* 77–82.

Kotler, P. (1984). Social marketing of health behavior. In L. W. Frederiksen, L. J. Solomon, & K. A. Brehony (Eds.), *Marketing health behavior: Principles, techniques, and applications* (pp. 23–39). New York: Plenum Press.

Maccoby, N. (In press). The community as a focus for health promotion. In S. Spacapan & S. Oskamp (Eds.). *The social psychology of health: The 1987 Claremont symposium on applied social psychology.* Newbury Park, CA: Sage Publications.

Maccoby, N., Farquhar, J. W., Wood, P. D., & Alexander, J. (1977). Reducing the risk of cardiovascular disease: Effects of a community-based campaign on knowledge and behavior. *Journal of Community Health, 3,* 100–114.

McGuire, W. J. (1969). The nature of attitudes and attitude change. In G. Lindzey & E. Aronson (Eds.),

The handbook of social psychology: Vol. 3. The individual in a social context (pp. 136–314). Reading, MA: Addison-Wesley.

Meyer, A. J., Nash, J. D., McAlister, A. L., Maccoby, N., & Farquhar, J. W. (1980). Skills training in a cardiovascular health education campaign. *Journal of Consulting and Clinical Psychology, 48,* 159–163.

Ray, M. (1973). Marketing communication and the hierarchy of effects. In P. Clarke (Ed.), *New models for communication research* (pp. 147–176). Beverly Hills, CA: Sage.

Truett, J., Cornfield, J., & Kannel, W. (1967). A multivariate analysis of the risk of coronary heart disease in Framingham. *Journal of Chronic Disease, 20,* 511–524.

Phyllis R. Silverman

CHAPTER

14

Widow-to-Widow: A Mutual Help Program for the Widowed

The Widow-to-Widow program has served as a model for programs for the newly widowed since the initial demonstration project was first reported on in 1969. In this program, other widowed persons are the primary caretakers, providing services to the newly widowed. These programs usually offer outreach that typically involves an unsolicited offer of help to the newly widowed. The names are obtained from death notices or by referral from funeral directors or clergy. In addition, programs provide small group discussions, lectures, and social activities for those who have been widowed longer (Silverman, 1986).

Programs have developed several organizational models to sustain themselves. Some follow the model of a voluntary organization, or club, with an elected president and various committees responsible for the group's program. This is probably closest to the intent of the original model, which emphasized voluntary mutual help efforts of the widowed on behalf of each other, with particular emphasis on the outreach component. Other programs have developed an agency structure with a paid executive and outreach workers who may be volunteers or who receive a small stipend. The name has also been adopted by agency bereavement programs that offer support groups convened by a mental health professional on the agency staff. This model is furthest from the intent of the original program.

In this chapter, the history of this program is presented and evidence is provided for why it was so effective as a preventive intervention model for meeting the needs of the newly widowed. In addition, guidelines for developing a program are described as well as dilemmas created for the mental health professional by this kind of program.

Overview and History of the Widow-to-Widow Program

The idea for the Widow-to-Widow program developed in response to an assignment the author received in 1964 from Gerald Caplan to develop a program of preventive intervention that would meet the needs of the newly widowed. Psychiatric wisdom at the time suggested that men and women experiencing conjugal bereavement were at risk of developing serious emotional difficulties (Marris, 1958; Parkes, 1965). Caplan, then director of the Laboratory of Community Psychiatry at Harvard Medical School, was interested in applying public health principles of primary prevention to mental health problems. At the time, preventive programs were often associated with early case findings by mental health clinicians. In contrast, the focus in this new initiative was on a population at risk in order to reduce or eliminate the risk before any treatment would be needed.

It was understood that psychological illness was certainly not the fate of every bereaved person. But given the variable nature of the human condition, it did not seem possible to identify in advance those individuals who were most at risk. In order to reach those with special needs, it seemed necessary to reach every newly widowed person in a given population. This process is not unlike a vaccination program in which everyone is immunized, even those who might have a natural immunity.

Before a program could be developed that would put this approach into practice, several questions had to be addressed. The first had to do with the needs of the widowed: Which of these needs would lead to subsequent problems if they went unmet? The second question was, How could such a service reach the entire newly widowed population in any given community and be accepted by them?

Needs of the Widowed

What was it that would be prevented? It was clear that we could not prevent widowhood, and therefore we could not prevent people from experiencing grief. At the time, the primary focus in most formulations about bereavement was on the extreme feelings that mourning evoked in the bereaved: sadness, despair, anger, and guilt. Psychological interventions were focused on helping the bereaved face these feelings and deal with them. However, data from the widowed themselves revealed that more was involved than these expressions of profound and disruptive feelings (Silverman, 1966). As the widowed talked about the death of their spouse, they focused on the changes in the way they lived their lives that resulted from the loss. They saw death as so disruptive of their way of living that they would never be the same. They lost not only their spouse but also the role of husband or wife and all that meant to them (Lopata, 1973; Silverman, 1970). This was consistent with Rappaport's (1963) finding that in every critical life cycle transition, a role shift was involved.

Bowlby (1961) and Tyhurst (1958) suggested that bereavement be viewed as a transition state. As Bowlby and Tyhurst characterized transitions, they provided a language for describing change over time. They suggested that this time of change can be divided into stages. Tyhurst talked about impact, recoil, and recovery, while Bowlby used the word *accommodation.* At each stage, the individual has different needs and different tasks with which to deal. Any help offered to someone in transition would need to facilitate the movement from one phase of the transition to the next (Silverman, 1966, 1969, 1970, 1972, 1986).

This conceptual framework became the basis for planning the Widow-to-Widow program. The framework made it possible to identify the unmet needs of the widowed by matching existing services to the needs suggested by each stage of the transition. For example, during the initial stage, immediately after the death, the needs of the bereaved center around arranging for burial of the deceased. This involves bringing the family together for the funeral. Religious beliefs and customs guide the way the funeral is arranged and the ways in which early mourning behavior is expressed. Funeral directors and clergy are critical caregivers during this period. Family and friends are available. It may be necessary to involve lawyers, insurance companies, banks, and the deceased's employers to deal with financial and legal matters. Social security applications have to be filed. If there are dependent children, help may be required with their care. This is a period when the widowed may feel numb and not believe the reality of their loss, only feeling the full impact of it for brief periods of time. They are often grateful for all the concrete tasks that need their attention to provide a framework for carrying on in that moment. The needed help and support are usually available (Silverman, 1966, 1986).

This help is rarely sustained over time. During the next phase of the transition, the pain of the loss may increase rather than decrease, and widowed individuals are often on their own. Friends and family have gone back to their own lives with the hope that the widowed person will be able to carry on. At this point, the nonwidowed seem eager for the widowed individual to be done with "it" quickly and do not want to hear their continuing pain. Women with limited financial resources begin to worry about work, others worry about how to live as a single parent or how to manage their lives alone. They need job counseling, help with understanding their children, assistance with financial management, and someone to talk with who understands what they are feeling. They do not know how to find these services.

We found that when the bereaved were referred for mental health counseling, they interpreted this to mean there was something wrong with them, reinforcing their worst fear that the acute pain they were experiencing was a symptom of a mental illness. In addition, mental health counseling could not meet all their needs, which seemed to be three things: someone to listen to their grief, someone to legitimate their feelings as appropriate, and someone to help them network to additional resources they required.

This view of widowhood as a period of transition provided the language for talking about intervention. In addition, it led to an end of talk about preventing emotional or mental stress. Stress seemed to be an appropriate reaction to the death of a loved one. It seemed more reasonable to focus on promoting people's ability to cope with their pain and to deal effectively with the changes in their lives.

The time of greatest need for the widowed seemed to be 6 weeks or 2 months after the death rather than immediately afterward. Their needs for someone to listen to them and to help them deal with the changes they were experiencing were not being met by existing caretakers in the community with whom the widowed would normally have contact. Nor was it clear that these needs could have been met by these caregivers, who seemed to have difficulty appreciating the widowed person's grief.

Developing the Widow-to-Widow Service

The need had been identified, and it was clear when help might be most meaningful. However, it was still not clear who would provide the service and how it would be possible to reach every member of the target population.

In a survey of widowed people, Maddison and Walker (1967) found that the most helpful person during the first year of bereavement was another widowed individual. There were several organizations for the widowed developing in the United States at that time, as well as one in England. They all emphasized the value of other widowed people as helpers. The experience of being in a group with others with similar experiences was one explanation offered for the success of these organizations. As one way of trying to replicate the group experience and the finding that another widowed person was most helpful, it was suggested that group therapy might be tried with the newly widowed. This did not seem appropriate. It would not meet the range of identified needs, and it would depend on a professional therapist to convene and lead the group. Wid-

owed individuals would not be the primary helpers. In addition, this approach would not be appropriate for a preventive trial because therapy usually depended on the client's asking for help, and the goal was to reach an entire population at risk. A preventive approach would require that this helper take the initiative.

In the early 1960s, New Career Programs for the poor were flourishing in New York as well as in other parts of the country (Pearl & Riessman, 1965). In these programs, residents of target communities were employed to reach out to identify people in need and connect them with needed services. This suggested a model that could be adapted to the needs of the widowed. Instead of matching people by race or common economic status, widowed residents in a community could be used to reach out. They could appropriately befriend the widowed, identify people in need, and help them find appropriate services.

At the same time, I heard about a local cemetery that provided services to the families they served. They employed a widow who reached out, 6 months after the death, to women whose husbands were buried at this cemetery. She offered them a listening ear, made referrals when necessary, and invited them to an annual educational meeting. Eighty percent of the women served accepted some contact with her.

Using these programs as models, an outreach program staffed by widowed people was proposed. They would be seen as neighbors, with no stigma attached to accepting this kind of help. This offer of assistance could be seen not as a verification that something was wrong but as an opportunity to talk with someone, as one might with a neighbor who really understood. The basis of the help would be a widow-to-widow relationship. At a time of great need, the widowed recipient would not have to bear the burden of deciding if he or she needed help and what kind of help to seek.

Implementing the Program

The steps followed in implementing this program would apply today for anyone starting a new program (Silverman, 1980, 1986).

Choosing a community. The community chosen for the initial implementation of the Widow-to-Widow program had recognized geographic boundaries with defined ethnic, racial, and religious populations. It offered a sufficient population of bereaved (approximately 250 per year or 2 per 1000) to warrant a program of the size proposed. A sufficiently large population was needed to test and evaluate the feasibility of the model. A section of the city of Boston with a population of 250,000 was chosen. A new outreach program should choose a population to match their resources in a specific geographic area to be sure that they can identify the target population.

Establishing the program in the community. To legitimate the service in the community and to guide policy setting, a community advisory board was established. This group was composed of representatives of the major religious and ethnic groups in the community. They also helped develop the criteria for choosing helpers and procedures for recruiting them.

Recruiting widowed aides. Helpers had to be attractive, engaging people whom the newly widowed would want to invite into their homes and who saw value in talking with other widowed persons about their grief. They had to have some perspective on their own grief so that they could share their own experience in order to help others. In addition, they had to be able to listen to other people's stories without getting unduly upset or needing to use the occasion to deal with their own grief at that moment. On the basis of what was known about timing in transition states, we assumed that persons widowed for at least 2 years should have reached such a point in their accommodation. We preferred that they live in the community in which they would be working. The widowed helpers were recruited by word of mouth, through local community action programs, and through a program for the widowed sponsored by a local Catholic Order.

Although the project initially hoped to reach both widows and widowers, it seemed impossible to find widowers as helpers. Men were, for the most part, working full time and had little energy for this kind of community activity. The advisory committee believed that widows reaching out to widowers would be misunderstood in this community. They advised that until men could be found to help, only widows be served. In programs developed since, men have been successfully involved as outreach volunteers; however, most men are still reluctant to get involved (Campbell & Silverman, 1987). The advisory committee also recommended that because younger women were considered at greater risk and the community already had a range of services available for the elderly, only women whose husbands were under age 65 when they died be included in the project.

Five women—three Catholics, one Jew, and one Black—were recruited as helpers. All of them had been involved in some type of volunteer community work and lived in or very near the target community. They took the job title "widow aide." Since the project would require a greater involvement in this work than any of them could provide as volunteers, we paid them a small salary based on what they could earn without jeopardizing their Social Security benefits. The advisory committee was very clear that the salary be kept small so that if this program proved successful and others wanted to replicate it using paid outreach workers, they could afford to do so.

In subsequent programs widow aides were recruited from among the ranks of those who were helped in the initial program. They have served without any remuneration (Widowed Person's Service, 1986). Programs in which aides were paid have had difficulty raising money to sustain themselves over time (M. L. S. Vachon, personal communication, June 20, 1985). In addition, this became a job for them, and there was danger of burnout and professionalization of the intervention (Abrahams, 1976).

Identifying the newly widowed. Because this was a research project associated with Harvard Medical School, the Department of Public Health, Bureau of Vital Statistics, was willing to provide death certificates for all men who resided in this target community and who were age 65 or less when they died. Black and Jewish families could be identified from the names of the funeral homes they used. Since religion is not on the death certificate and both Protestant and Catholic families are served by the same funeral homes, the funeral director was asked for this information. In the end, the information about religion was unimportant because the Catholic aides comfortably served both religious groups.

This contact with the funeral directors was the beginning of a long and fruitful relationship that lasted over the lifetime of the project and eventually led to grants from the funeral directors to pay the aides' salaries. This association also led to funeral directors in various parts of the country becoming involved in programs as sponsors and serving on the advisory boards (Silverman, 1977).

Because of the current emphasis on protecting people's privacy, health departments are reluctant to open their records, although they are public documents. Programs now rely more on newspaper obituaries and referrals from clergy or funeral directors.

Procedures for reaching out. Orientation meetings with the aides (Silverman, MacKenzie, Pettipas, & Wilson, 1974; Silverman, 1977, 1980, 1986) were held to the following procedures for reaching out to the newly widowed:

1. The first contact with the new widow would be 2 months after the death. Until this time, the aides did not think that a new widow would be able to begin to think of herself as a widow.

2. The aides designed stationery to be used to make the initial contact with the new widow. On the stationery, the advisory board was listed with no mention of Harvard Medical School or the Department of Psychiatry. They thought this information would intimidate people. In the letter, they said that they too were widowed and knew the value of meeting another widowed woman. They gave a time when they would come by the house to visit and provided their phone number in case the widow wanted to change the time.

The role of the professional. As the primary professional in this project, the author's main task was to monitor and document the work of the aides. In addition, the author had to create an atmosphere that allowed the aides to take charge of their work and build on their own experience as widows in designing the intervention. This required knowing when to step back and recognize the limitations of my own expertise. The author's professional knowledge was not as relevant as the knowledge they had gained from experience (Borkman, 1976).

Weekly staff meetings were occasions to reflect on their efforts with individual widows as well as to plan additional activities. The author served as a consultant to provide another perspective on what they were doing and as a sounding board when they were working with a difficult woman. The author provided information about community resources and was a liaison when a referral was in order. Gradually, the aides gained in confidence so that they were able to provide this type of consultation for each other and to do their own long-term planning.

For professionals to work successfully with this kind of mutual-help effort, they need to be able to relinquish control and accept the value of experiential knowledge (Silverman, 1977, 1978, 1980). They need skills as a consultant, and they need to understand organization development and process (Silverman, 1982). The typical clinician does not have these skills and should learn them before working with mutual-help efforts. For adult educators and community development and social group workers, learning these skills is part of their basic training. Several of the most successful efforts, that were not started by the widowed themselves, have been initiated by professionals with this kind of background (Ruth Lowensohn, personal communication, May, 1987; Anne Arsenault, personal communication, June, 1987; Trudy Freedman, personal communication, May, 1985).

The program as it evolved. Many widows were at home to receive the aide when she visited, but others called the aide sometimes to ask her not to come. Once verbal contact was made, even the most reluctant widow, to her surprise, found talking to be very helpful. The aide found that she was maintaining contact with the new widow about twice a month over the year, and most often this contact, often at the widow's initiative, was on the telephone. The aide was available, at any time of day or night, whenever the new widow had a need to talk. Social visits involved sharing meals, going to a movie, and sometimes taking the children out for ice cream.

Although the initial one-to-one contact was essential, it soon became clear that many of the women shared similar problems, for example, being single parents. Other women needed to extend their friendship network. They needed to meet other new widows. Until they were introduced by the aides, they were unaware of the other widows living within walking distance of their homes. Group discussions were set up in local churches or in people's homes to discuss common problems. Cook-outs and social activities provided the opportunity for them to meet socially and to begin to repeople their lives from within their own neighborhood (Silverman, 1969). This progression mirrored their changing needs as they moved through the stages of the transition (Silverman, 1978).

Some women were eager to become involved as helpers. When an aide felt she could not offer a widow what she needed, she introduced her to another aide. However, she could also introduce her to another widow, and she frequently did. The helping relationship was not exclusive, nor did the widow have to remain in the role of recipient to stay involved. The program was in effect generating the next generation of helpers.

As funding for this initial trial of the Widow-to-Widow model ended, a telephone hot line, known as the Widowed Service Line, was started to try to reach a larger population (Abrahams, 1972). This service was available not only to the newly widowed, but also to those who had been widowed for some time and to widowers as well. Three aides from the original program coordinated this project and trained and supervised the volunteers, some of whom had been helped in the original program (Silverman, 1986).

In 1971, the feasibility of an outreach program with an elderly population was demonstrated in a storefront program sponsored by the Jewish Welfare Federation in Boston (Silverman, 1986; Silverman & Cooperband, 1975). Adele Cooperband, one of the widow aides, reached out to newly widowed women from the Jewish community whose husbands were over 65 years of age at the time of their death.

In programs developed subsequently, as noted in the introduction, there have been many variations on these themes. Many programs provide a progression of services from outreach, to group discussions, to social activities, to becoming involved as helpers in turn. Some have hot lines instead of outreach efforts and advertise actively in local newspapers and with the funeral directors and clergy, so that the newly widowed know of their existence. A one-to-one relationship is established in these programs only at the newly widowed person's initiative. Other programs involve the widowed in group discussions from the very beginning, with most of their energy devoted to expanding the widowed persons' opportunities to repeople their lives and develop new social networks.

Outcomes

The Widow-to-Widow program was experimenting with an idea. It was unclear, initially, how people would react to this offer of help. It was unknown whether the newly widowed persons would allow the aide to visit or if they would even talk with her on the phone. It would have been premature to have considered a controlled experiment for this field trial because it first had to be worked out what it was the program was doing. Therefore, research associated with the project focused on documenting who accepted and who refused and on how the program unfolded to see if this was an intervention that could work. It was research in process, using a qualitative, descriptive approach (Silverman, 1988).

It could not be demonstrated empirically that risk among the widowed of developing serious emotional problems had been reduced, except in very crude terms (Silverman, 1986). It could be

demonstrated that this was an idea for an intervention that worked. Reports were published as we went along so that there was constant input into the professional, and to a limited extent, the popular literature of what we were learning. The nature of the intervention was reported as well as what we learned about the bereavement process (Abrahams, 1972; Silverman, 1966, 1967, 1969, 1972; Silverman & Cooperband, 1975; Silverman & Englander, 1975). This meant that others could, and did, adapt this model and put it to work in their communities. A measure of the merit of this model is reflected in the success of these new efforts.

In 1976, the Community Mental Health Center Act mandated that widow-to-widow programs be developed as part of Community Mental Health Center's Consultation and Education Programs. The American Association of Retired Persons adapted this model in 1974 in what is now known as the Widowed Person's Service, with programs all over the United States.

Who Accepted the Widow-to-Widow Service

The first woman the program served was widowed on May 26, 1967. The program continued for 2½ years, during which time the aides reached out to 300 women, with 60% of them accepting the offer of help. The program with the elderly had a higher acceptance rate. The idea was already established in the elderly community, and 75% of these women accepted. Neither race nor religion affected the response rate. However, having children at home made a difference. Women with dependent children at home were most likely to accept the offer of help at the time it was offered, 2 months after the death. Older women no longer concerned with child rearing and who were working deferred meeting the aide for a long time or were more likely to refuse.

Almost all the widows were embedded in extended family networks that they saw as helpful and supportive. Most of them were living in the same community in which they had been born and raised. Although they could count on their family and neighbors, with time this help became less relevant and the widows were eager for additional assistance. Twenty-eight percent of those who had refused said in follow-up interviews 3 years later that they would have accepted had they understood more about what the program offered.

In the first 7 months that the Widowed Service Line was in existence, 750 people called; 90% of them women. Most of these were people who had been widowed for some time, and this was the first time they found a place where they could talk about their grief.

Almost all (81%) of those who wanted help accepted because they needed to talk with another widow who would understand their feelings. Twenty-eight percent mentioned problems with their children (adult as well as minor); 25% simply needed reassurance that they would weather the crisis successfully. Some were concerned about inadequate income (24%), some specifically mentioned difficulties with relatives or family who did not understand their current situation (23%), some wanted advice or support in getting a job or going back to school (22%), and some wanted specific financial advice such as with benefit claims (19%).

Because the aides continued to call women who were initially reluctant about seeing them, many women only became involved as their needs changed over the first year. They are included in the profiles of those who accepted. Only those (91 women, or 39%) who never became involved were considered to have refused help. They gave the following reasons for refusing, in descending order of frequency: (a) They were too busy with job, family, or setting affairs in order; (b) they already had plenty of support from family and friends; (c) their grown children refused to allow the aide to talk with their mother; and (d) they were independent and had no need for support.

It was antithetical to the intent of the program to screen families in advance to determine their suitability. The aide, as a result, met a wide variety of women with different strengths, weaknesses, family situations, and abilities to cope. Nine women who accepted the offer of help had prior histories of serious psychological problems. Four were alcoholic, and this was quickly apparent to the aides. The problems the other women experienced were not immediately apparent to the aides. In time, the aides learned that two of the women had been diagnosed as schizophrenic, two had been hospitalized for depression, and for the fifth woman, no diagnosis was available. Only one of these women, who had experienced a depression several years before for which she was hospitalized, did not become ill again. She attributed this to the aide's intervention. The others developed symptoms in the course of their contact with the aide. These women were simultaneously involved in psychiatric treatment. Not only did

the aide's intervention not make a difference, but the other interventions did not help either. There were no new cases of major mental illness in the widows who accepted.

It would be nice to attribute this finding to the success of the intervention, but without a controlled study this conclusion could be easily challenged. It does, however, raise a question about the nature of the risk associated with widowhood. It may be that the risk of developing major emotional problems is greater after the death of a spouse only for those with prior histories or in communities in which the expressions of grief are defined as symptoms of an illness.

Vachon and her colleagues replicated this project in Toronto, Canada (Vachon, 1979; Vachon et al., 1980, 1982). They randomly assigned newly widowed women to control and experimental groups. From their work, we can be more explicit about the preventive capability of the widow-to-widow program. Widows who participated in the program were more apt to have begun new relationships and activities and experienced less distress than women who were not in the program. This was particularly true for women who experienced high stress immediately after the death. Over the 2 years of this study, most women recovered with or without help. However, those who were in the program seemed to do this in a shorter period of time.

Vachon et al.'s (1982) findings supported the idea that widowhood may be a time of great stress but not necessarily be sufficient to cause mental illness. Other factors such as lack of social support or a prior history of mental illness may need to be present before the risk is increased. Most women who accepted help felt that they were involved in a supportive network. The quality of the support may be the discriminating factor and would explain the power of the Widow-to-Widow intervention. Many of the women who refused in the original project and were managing well (Silverman, 1974, 1986) felt that they were already involved with others who were widowed and therefore the help offered was redundant. This supports the original supposition on which the Widow-to-Widow program was built—that another widow is the most effective helper. What is it in this experience that is so unique?

Facilitating Change

It is not possible to characterize a good outcome in simple terms that permit saying that one mode of accommodation is better than another. What became apparent was that those widows who were doing well displayed an ability to get on with their lives that seemed to involve a shift in identity, from wife to widow to woman (Golan, 1975). In addition, they developed an ability to allow the past to inform the present.

To adapt to her loss, the widow forged links among the past, the present, and the future. She integrated her past into the present; that is, she honored and remembered the past but did not live in it. She no longer felt that her loss had made her a person who had no role to play in society, and she began to develop confidence in her ability to control her present and future life, sometimes to the point that she did not recognize herself as the person she had been (Silverman & Cooperband, 1975). Accommodation ultimately meant discovering that her identity existed independently of the lost relationship and other relationships as well. Although relationships were still central to her life, they were based on a different level of mutuality and respect for her own competence and individuality (Lopata, 1979; Silverman, 1981, in press).

Vachon (1979) found that this type of movement was more evident in those who participated in the widow-to-widow group than in those who did not. These findings are also supported by the findings of Lieberman and Borman (1979) in their extensive study of the work of mutual-help groups. Videka-Sherman and Lieberman (1985) studied Compassionate Friends, an organization for bereaved parents. They compared professional help with mutual help and found greater positive change in those who participated in the mutual-help experience. Lieberman and Borman (1979) compared the members of 71 THEOS (They Help Each Other Spiritually) groups for the widowed with widowed people who did not join the organization. They found that the more intense a person's involvement with the group, the better the outcome with regard to self-esteem and absence of depressive symptoms. The evidence points to something special in the experience of sharing with someone with similar problems that makes possible this kind of change.

Mutual Help and Linking Relationships

A mutual-help exchange involves people who share a common problem, which one of them had previously coped with successfully. The helping person has expertise based on personal experience in solving this particular problem. There is a special mutuality in these relationships so that the help can go both ways. Therefore the term *mutual help* seems more appropriate than the more commonly used designation *self-help* (Silverman, 1978).

A mutual-help model may be particularly suitable for facilitating change in the widowed. It offers learning and growth opportunities through the medium of linking relationships. A linking relationship is one that helps a person bridge the gap between one phase of life and the next. When faced with a critical transition, there is a good deal of learning that needs to take place in order for people to know how to cope. In the widow-to-widow project, this learning comes largely from the linking relationships with other widows (Silverman, 1986). Through these relationships, the widow sees options for other roles for herself and gains additional perspectives on how to organize her life given the change that has occurred. She can practice new ways of relating to herself and to the world in a supportive and nourishing relationship with a peer. Learning is also made easier when the teacher is a peer (Gartner & Reisman, 1982; Hamburg & Adams, 1967).

As children grow, they need to learn from peers who serve as role models and with whom they can explore their common dilemmas. Children who have role model peers do not feel alone, unusual, or isolated; they feel legitimated. The need for this type of relationship probably holds true over an entire lifetime and not just to childhood or adolescence. For those who did not have such relationships in their own networks, the widow-to-widow programs fulfilled this need.

This linking relationship, by its nature, is temporary. As the new widow moves through the phases of transition, the help offered progresses from a focus on one-to-one assistance to help through involvement in a new community. Initially, as she identifies with the widow helper, the new widow finds it easier to accept the fact that the role of widow applies to her as well. This assists her in getting through the initial numbing and disbelief, which is often expressed in emotional denial. When friends find it difficult to hear her pain, another widow is able to stay with her and knows better than to offer platitudes such as "time will heal," or "by now you should be feeling better," as if grief were finite and could be easily disposed of. Finally, the widow has mobility in the system. She can move from recipient to helper; being able to reciprocate is affirming and builds her self-confidence.

The ability to shift roles in the system and the sharing of personal experiences are the fundamental factors that distinguish mutual help from other helping exchanges and, in large part, account for the success of this type of program.

Current Programs

There is no way of knowing all the programs that have come and gone over the years based on the Widow-to-Widow model. Most were local groups, meeting in people's homes, in synagogues and churches, or in community centers such as the YWCA. The model was straightforward, providing the widowed people with what they needed to know to develop helping programs on their own.

Councils on aging have also sponsored programs. An exemplary program in Arlington, Massachusetts, served people over age 65. They received names from the obituary columns and called all those who were over 65 and newly widowed. In consultation with a clinical social worker, these volunteers learned how to lead group discussions and planned the program's other activities as well. Other centers in nearby communities offered groups led by professionals and called this Widow-to-Widow. There is no way of controlling the use of the name to ensure the consumers that they are participating in a mutual-help experience rather than one run by a professional in which they do not learn to take charge of their life in the same way as in the Widow-to-Widow program.

Many programs have been started by professionals and successfully continued by the widowed themselves. For example, Anne Arsenault, an adult educator, saw a need and responded to it. With a group of widows involved with her from the beginning, she developed the Widow's Outreach Network in Kingston, Ontario, Canada. She helped them draft bylaws requiring regular election of officers, with a board of directors who acted as advisors and helped raise money. The membership learned organizational, leadership, and helping skills. Although the membership does not always accomplish things the way a professional might, drawing on their life experience and experience in the organization, they have carried on long since Arsenault left the community. They did not want to do outreach, feeling this was much too intrusive. Instead, they advertise extensively and are listed in services available in their community. They have a 24-hour hot line and a small office. The majority of these women did not finish high school. There are no paid staff; all volunteers take turns being in the office and on the hot line. They support themselves, covering out-of-pocket expenses and rent for the office with an annual Widow's Attic Sale, bake sales, and craft shows. In addition, they get a very small grant from the Canadian government (A. Arsenault, personal communication, June 1987).

The use of bake sales and the like is an important way of supporting programs. In the Pacific Northwest, there is a network of programs for the widowed that supports itself with a thrift shop they operate. The Canadian government, as well as other countries such as Great Britain, routinely provide volunteer neighborhood programs with small grants. Little like this exists in the United States. Nonetheless, none of these sources provides enough money to run an agency or program with a paid staff. As long as the group does not attempt to pay salaries and does not try to do more than their volunteer resources can sustain, they are likely to succeed.

There is no specific documentation of what programs began in response to the Community Mental Health Center Act initiative. However, it did raise the consciousness of professionals working in this area to the value of mutual-help programs and to the needs of the widowed. Since there was no funding associated with this mandate, few agencies could really afford to implement this initiative as a true mutual-help effort. Mutual-help programs, by their nature, do not generate income for agencies. Funding pressures require agencies to focus on services that generate income such as fee-for-service counseling. This focus on a mutual-help program may have influenced the recommendations of the Mental Health Task Force, convened by President Carter in 1978, which acknowledged the importance of social support for mental health and the value of mutual help as a source of social support.

The Widowed Person's Service, in some ways, has taken up where the original Widow-to-Widow program ended. It is sponsored by the American Association of Retired People (AARP) and has grown to a nationwide effort consisting of over 200 affiliated programs. The Widowed Person's Service has a national office in Washington, D.C., in the AARP headquarters. Their operating costs are paid for by AARP. A small staff, employed by the parent association, coordinates these programs. They develop training manuals for outreach volunteers and materials to help with the organization and operation of local groups. These professionals provide support to 35 organizers and 28 national trainers but do not themselves initi-

ate new programs. This task is left to the organizers. In turn, the outreach volunteers are
trained by the national trainers.

In some mutual-help organizations, the national office establishes standards that every local group must follow. If an individual went to an
Alcoholics Anonymous meeting anywhere in the
United States, he or she would find the same
format and program. The Widowed Person's Service has not made this requirement of local
groups. They allow for the local board to develop
its program to meet local needs with the resources available to them. Some groups do systematic outreach using obituaries or working
with the funeral directors and clergy to obtain
referrals. Other programs advertise in the newspapers and have volunteers available to talk on
the telephone. Most offer discussion groups and
social activities.

All of the Widowed Person's Service trainers,
organizers, and helpers do this work as volunteers. Nonwidowed people may volunteer as
trainers or organizers, but only widowed people
can do outreach work. All the boards of local programs must have widowed people on them as well.
The national office also publishes a directory of
widowed groups in the United States and Canada. This is updated regularly and includes any
voluntary organization run by the widowed for
the widowed. Each program or organization listed
is coded to provide the reader with information
on the services offered.

The Widowed Person's Service is dealing with
several problems. One of the most immediate is
the need to recruit more widowed volunteers as
people move in and out of the program. This is a
problem every volunteer program faces. The other
problem is how to involve widowers. A task force
has been convened to examine this problem and
make recommendations to staff and organizers
on what to do about it. Often programs that would
like to include an outreach component are not
doing so for lack of widowed workers. In some
communities where they are doing outreach,
there is a very low acceptance rate, for reasons
that are unclear. A third problem for the organization involves the differing needs of the widowed
themselves. Older widowed members find permanent friendship networks in their local program, and this can prevent the program from
remaining open for the newly widowed and
younger widowed persons. Younger widowed people tend to remain in an organization for a
shorter period of time, choosing to find their new
friendship networks in other places. Some pro-

grams are considering two networks, one for older
members and another for younger members.

Since the original program for the widowed began in 1967 and since the work of Kubler-Ross
(1969), there has been an increase in interest in
the needs of the dying. This led to the development of the hospice movement, which at this time
has more than 1,500 programs in the United
States alone. For many years the needs of the
bereaved were not attended to by people working
in this movement. They were guided by a hypothesis that by saying good-by and helping the dying
to have an appropriate death the needs of the
bereaved would be met. However, the needs of the
bereaved are different during the dying period
and emerge in different dimensions once the
death has occurred and emptiness has to be faced.
Hospice is now interested in the needs of the bereaved and is mandated to provide bereavement
counseling for 6 months to the surviving families
they serve. This is changing services available
for some bereaved in their communities and in
particular is making professionals more alert
to the needs of the survivors. It is not clear if
this professional effort will influence mutual
help programs for the good, or replace them.
Ideally, hospice programs serve as a link to
mutual-help programs and organizations in their
communities.

Programs for the widowed are now listed in
self-help and mutual-help directories being published by self-help clearinghouses throughout the
country (Madera & Reese, 1986). Interest in the
bereaved and in mutual help was further stimulated by the recent study by the Institute of Medicine of the National Academy of Science
(Osterweis, Solomon, & Green, 1984). Everyone,
Osterweis and her colleagues pointed out, needs
some help following a bereavement. Bereavement
should not be considered a psychiatric condition
requiring treatment. For many people, effective
help will come more appropriately and naturally
from family, friends, and existing social support
networks. They focus on the power of the mutual-
help experience for meeting the needs of the bereaved in a nonjudgmental, community context.

Conclusions

The Widow-to-Widow program was conceived as
a means of preventing mental illness in the newly
widowed. The program was successful in achieving this goal to the extent that it helped people
through this time of distress; showed them how

they could carry on with some joy, pleasure, and excitement; and supported them as they met the problems of daily living, pointing to alternative ways of managing their lives. Because the person reaching out was another widow who came to call informally, the new widow felt herself in the positive role of neighbor in need of temporary assistance. Had this help been offered by any professional person, except perhaps a member of the clergy, the new widow probably would have found herself in the position of being someone with a deficit, someone who needed treatment to make her whole. At a time when a woman is already feeling weak and disabled, becoming a professional person's client or patient would be yet another experience in which she discovers that she is not in full control of her own life.

This is not intended to degrade professional help, but rather to suggest that other types of help may be more effective in certain circumstances. There are several concerns about professional help with the bereaved. First, professional people and their agencies are products of their societies and so reflect many of the values and attitudes of their communities, including the values, attitudes, and taboos surrounding death and grief. Regardless of the recent educational emphasis on death and dying, most professionals still have difficulty in coping with grief and understanding and in facing the profound disruptions brought on by death itself. Of at least equal importance is the culture of professional help itself. Traditional clinical treatment programs and professional help are typically based on the underlying assumption that there is a deficit, a disease, or a dysfunction in the client. When bereavement and grief become the targets of therapies, they take on the image of aberrations to be exorcised. Grief and bereavement are more properly seen as basic universal human experiences. Disruption and pain are normal and appropriate. All of us must learn to deal with this experience.

Institutions for caring tend to honor professional expertise as the basis for all practice and to segregate people from each other, routinizing human interactions around professional experts. Organized in this way, they are remote from the social context, making knowledge necessary to all of us available from a small and select population. They tend to denigrate the experiential learning that fosters personal growth at such times in the life cycle. The Widow-to-Widow program organized itself around the needs people have for each other and the value of sharing the

expertise that people gain from this experience in living.

The development and growth of the Widow-to-Widow program has shown that mutual help generally has an advantage over professional help in that it does not treat people as ill and has an image-enhancing emphasis on learning from peers. In the end we are talking about not only a particular program or service, but also a way of helping people to create more caring communities. It has been the essence of this work that through mutual help an environment is created that minimizes barriers between people. This type of environment legitimizes people's need for each other and their ability to use their experience on each other's behalf.

Suggested Resources

Widowed Person's Service, 10–NC. 1909 K Street NW, Washington, DC, 20049.

References

Abrahams, R. B. (1972). Mutual help for the widowed. *Social Work, 17,* 55–61.
Abrahams, R. B. (1976). Mutual helping: Styles of caregiving in a mutual aid program—The Widowed Service Line. In G. Caplan & M. Killilea (Eds.), *Support systems and mutual help* (pp. 245–259). New York: Grune and Stratton.
Borkman, T. (1976). Experiential knowledge: A new concept in the analysis of self-help groups. *Social Service Review, 50,* 445–456.
Bowlby, J. (1961). Processes of mourning. *International Journal of Psychoanalysis, 44,* 317.
Campbell, S., & Silverman, P. R. (1987). *Widower: When men are left alone.* New York: Prentice-Hall.
Gartner, A., & Reissman, F. (1982). *Self-help in the human services.* San Francisco: Jossey-Bass.
Golan, N. (1975). Wife to widow to woman. *Social Work, 20,* 369–374.
Hamburg, D. A., & Adams, J. E. (1967). A perspective on coping: Seeking and utilizing information in major transitions. *Archives of General Psychiatry, 17,* 277–284.
Kubler-Ross, E. (1969). *On death and dying.* New York: MacMillan.
Lieberman, M., & Borman, M. (Eds.). (1979). *Self-help groups for coping with crisis.* San Francisco: Jossey-Bass.
Lopata, H. Z. (1973). Self-identity in marriage and widowhood. *The Sociological Quarterly, 14,* 407–418.
Lopata, H. Z. (1979). *Women as widows: Support systems.* New York: Elsevier.
Maddison, D., & Walker, W. L. (1967). Factors affecting the outcome of conjugal bereavement. *British Journal of Psychiatry, 113,* 1057–1067.
Madera, E. J., & Reese, A. (1986). *The self-help sourcebook.* Denville, NJ: St. Clares-Riverside Medical Center.

Marris, P. (1958). *Widows and their families.* London: Routledge and Kegan Paul.

Osterweis, M., Solomon, F., & Green, M. (1984). *Bereavement: Reactions, consequences and care.* Washington, DC: National Academy Press.

Parkes, C. M. (1965). Bereavement and mental illness: Part 2. A classification of bereavement reactions. *British Journal of Medical Psychology, 33,* 14–15.

Pearl, A., & Riessman, F. (1965). *New careers for the poor.* New York: Free Press.

Rappaport, R. (1963). Normal crisis, family structure and mental health. *Family Process, 2,* 68–80.

Silverman, P. R. (1966). Services for the widowed during the period of bereavement. In *Social work practice* (pp. 170–189). New York: Columbia University Press.

Silverman, P. R. (1967). Services to the widowed: First steps in a program of preventive intervention. *Community Mental Health Journal, 3,* 37–44.

Silverman, P. R. (1969). The Widow-to-Widow Program: An experiment in preventive intervention. *Mental Hygiene, 53,* 333–337.

Silverman, P. R. (1970). The widow as a caregiver in a program of preventive intervention with other widows. *Mental Hygiene, 54,* 540–547.

Silverman, P. R. (1972). Widowhood and preventive intervention. *The Family Coordinator, 21*(1), 95–102.

Silverman, P. R. (1974). Anticipatory grief from the perspective of widowhood. In B. Schoenberg (ed.), *Anticipatory grief* (pp. 320–330). New York: Columbia University Press.

Silverman, P. R. (1977). *If you will lift the load: A guide to the creation of widowed-to-widowed services.* New York: Jewish Funeral Directors of America.

Silverman, P. R. (1978). *Mutual help: A guide for mental health workers* (Department of Health, Education and Welfare Publication No. ADM 78-646). Washington, DC: U.S. Government Printing Office.

Silverman, P. R. (1980). *Mutual help groups: Organization and development.* Beverly Hills, CA: Sage.

Silverman, P. R. (1981). *Helping women cope with grief.* Beverly Hills, CA: Sage.

Silverman, P. R. (1982). The mental health consultant as linking agent. In D. Beigel & A. Naparstek (Eds.), *Community support system and mutual help: Building linkages.* New York: Springer.

Silverman, P. R. (1986). *Widow-to-Widow.* New York: Springer.

Silverman, P. R. (1988). Research as process: Exploring the meaning of widowhood. In S. Reinhaarz & G. Rowles (Eds.), *Qualitative gerontology.* New York: Springer.

Silverman, P. R. (In press). In search of new selves: Accommodating to widowhood. In L. A. Bond & B. M. Wagner (Eds.), *Families in transition: Primary prevention programs that work.* Beverly Hills, CA: Sage.

Silverman, P. R., & Cooperband, A. (1975). Mutual help and the elderly widow. *Journal of Geriatric Psychiatry, 8,* 9–27.

Silverman, P. R., & Englander, S. (1975). The widow's view of her dependent children. *Omega, 6*(1), 3–20.

Silverman, P. R., MacKenzie, D., Pettipas, M., & Wilson, E. W. (Eds.). (1974). *Helping each other in widowhood.* New York: Health Sciences.

Tyhurst, J. (1958). The role of transition states—including disasters in mental illness. In *Symposium on preventive and social psychiatry* (pp. 149–169). Washington, DC: U.S. Government Printing Office.

Vachon, M. L. S. (1979). *Identity change over the first two years of bereavement: Social relationships and social support in widowhood.* Unpublished doctoral dissertation, York University, Toronto, Canada.

Vachon, M. L. S., Sheldon, A. R., Lancee, W. J., Lyall, W. A. L., Roger, J., & Freeman, S. J. J. (1980). A controlled study of self-help intervention for widows. *American Journal of Psychiatry, 137,* 1380–1384.

Vachon, M. L. S., Sheldon, A. R., Lancee, W. J., Lyall, W. A. L., Roger, J., & Freeman, S. J. J. (1982). Correlates of enduring distress patterns following bereavement: Social network, life situation and personality. *Psychological Medicine, 12,* 783–788.

Videka-Sherman, L., & Lieberman, M. (1985). The effects of self-help and psychotherapy intervention on child loss: The limits of recovery. *The American Journal of Orthopsychiatry, 55,* 70–72.

Richard H. Price, Emory L. Cowen, Raymond P. Lorion, and Julia Ramos-McKay

Model Prevention Programs: Epilogue and Future Prospects

The reader who has examined the model programs described in this volume may have become curious about important issues that these programs, and others like them, raise. Although the programs seem on the surface to be quite diverse, are there elements that successful programs share? Are there special issues that practitioners should keep in mind in implementing these programs in their local communities? Do these programs meet the needs of ethnic and minority groups? What questions of public policy and what benefits and costs to program recipients and to society are associated with effective prevention programs?

Common Denominators of Success

The programs presented in this volume share several common features that can guide future prevention efforts. First, these programs are targeted. Their focus, in each case, is shaped by a reasonable understanding of the risks and problems encountered by the target group.

Second, all programs are designed to alter the life trajectory of the people who participate in them. They are aimed at long-term change, setting individuals on a new developmental course, opening opportunities, changing life circum-

stances, or providing support. The Houston Parent–Child Program developed by Johnson and his colleagues is a good example. Carefully designed experiences involving parent participation and education seem to change the family as a social system and increase the likelihood of developmental and school success.

In addition, successful programs give people new skills to cope more effectively and provide social support in the face of life transitions. For example, the substance abuse prevention program developed by Botvin, Tortu, and colleagues provides junior high school students with new coping skills to resist peer pressure to smoke, drink excessively, or use marijuana and to deal with other social challenges as well.

Another common denominator of successful programs is that they strengthen the natural support from family, community, or school settings. The outreach program developed by Olds for low income single mothers was designed to mobilize the social support of friends and relatives in the new mother's community.

Finally, although it may seem obvious, successful programs have managed to collect rigorous research evidence to document their success. Indeed, in a variety of different ways, each of the model programs in this volume has been successful in providing evaluation evidence of its effectiveness.

Program Evaluation and Indicators of Effectiveness

Strong research documentation is one distinguishing feature of the prevention programs reported in this volume. Each program offers objective evidence that behaviors reflecting central program goals were positively affected and that those gains endured over time. Such documentation, it has been suggested, separates effective primary prevention programs (of which there are relatively few) from aspiring primary prevention programs (of which there are many).

Confirming program evaluation data is a necessary precondition for program dissemination. Such data tell us that, at least under certain conditions and for certain groups, a prevention program works. Application, including assessments of a model's generalizability, is the next essential step in bringing a program's potential benefits to the many who stand to profit from it. Indeed, the prime objective of this volume is to stimulate this process by coalescing descriptions of demonstrably effective prevention programs for practitioners.

Continuing, sound program evaluation research is a needed link in the program dissemination chain. The notion of literal program replication is largely a fiction. Aspects of the program are modified or tailored to the resources and predilections of new settings. New target groups have their own special defining qualities. What works perfectly well under one set of conditions cannot be presumed to work equally well under all conditions. Hence, evaluating prevention programs under the inevitable circumstances of changing realities is an important gateway to assessing an intervention's power and generality.

Program evaluation research does more than just answer the question of whether or not a prevention program works. By also offering important clues about program strengths and weaknesses, it can help to shore up a program and pave the way toward more effective future programs. Program outcome research should be seen as part of a transactional process from which the ongoing processes of program enhancement and extension to new groups and circumstances is fashioned, rather than as an absolute.

Evaluating primary prevention programs is not a simple task. For one thing, most are conducted in natural community contexts under far less than antiseptic laboratory conditions. Target groups may be disrupted during the program, attendance often presents problems, appropriate control or comparison groups may be difficult to find, and day-to-day observations of a program's workings may necessitate in-process modifications in a program's original plan. In addition to the special problems of research in live community contexts, primary prevention evaluation studies face problems similar to those that program evaluation studies in other areas must surmount. Are the criterion measures reliable? Do they validly reflect the program's key outcome variables? Are the measures suited, socioculturally and developmentally, to the population being studied? Is there an appropriate control and comparison group? To what extent do findings across data sources converge? How robust are the outcome findings? How enduring?

Neither this volume in general nor this section in particular is intended as a primer in primary prevention program evaluation research. Fortunately, several excellent, practically oriented primers are available for those who conduct primary prevention programs in community settings (Bloom, 1979; Price & Smith, 1985). The point to be highlighted here is that outcome evaluation is an essential aspect of primary prevention programming. A continuing, serious commitment to such research is a necessary precondition for the field's wholesome growth.

In a very real sense, program evaluation research findings importantly shaped both the Task Force's procedural steps and its decisions about final contents of this volume. In its early stage, the Task Force adopted an idealized framework for proceeding. The members of the Task Force hoped that the exemplary prevention programs selected would fully and evenly represent (a) life stages of target populations (i.e., from infants through the elderly); (b) outcomes to be promoted or prevented (i.e., mental health, physical health, criminal justice, substance abuse); and (c) settings (i.e., schools, work sites, hospitals, HMOs, etc.). But they were also firm in the insistence that the programs selected have sound research documentation.

In moving from those abstract ideals to the world of reality, it became clear that the goals of a well-filled matrix and sound research documentation could not simultaneously be met. Given that the Task Force's foremost goal was to assemble practitioner-ready prevention programs, research documentation was accorded a higher priority than filling the matrix. As a result, the volume is overweighted to prevention programs for children and youth, thin within the adult age-range, and empty in several pockets (e.g., the elderly). Although there is some diversity in the terms of the types of outcomes that these programs promote or prevent and the settings in which they are conducted, there are gaps at those levels as well. Although some will find that distribution of programs disappointing, it reflects the types of documented primary prevention programs available. In that sense, it points clearly to directions in which future programming is needed.

The Task Force reviewed more than 300 program submittals. Although some were not seriously considered because they were not viewed as primary prevention programs, the single most important reason for excluding a program was the absence, or insufficiency, of program outcome data. It should be emphasized, however, that a number of programs that were not selected seemed very promising, although they were not far enough along in program evaluation to warrant inclusion in this casebook.

The field of primary prevention is in rapid, dynamic evolution. There are promising programs in the pipeline beyond those included in this volume. Some of those programs will eventually fill the matrix that the Task Force originally created. Represented in this volume is a set of today's exemplary, well-documented primary prevention program models. We hope that this form of presentation will serve both to accelerate the dissemination of these programs and to pave the way for a richer, more representative casebook of this type in the future.

Implementation and Dissemination Issues

Even highly effective model prevention programs are not always easily or automatically transformed into local program replications that will produce the intended preventive effects. Price and Lorion (1987) argued that the successful implementation of a model prevention program is a form of organizational reinvention (Rice & Rogers, 1980). The term *organizational reinvention* captures the process because the implementation of a model prevention program is inherently organizational in nature. The process involves the orchestration of both internal and external organizational resources, scanning the organizational and community environment, focusing program goals and objectives, and, finally, implementing the program and monitoring it for fidelity to its original goals. The success of these activities depends heavily on how receptive the host organization, whether it is a school, hospital, or social service agency, is to the new program.

Practitioners who wish to implement local versions of these model programs will have to be goal-oriented, entrepreneurial, sensitive to external relationships, and make efforts to draw in members of the host organization community to participate in the implementation. At the same time, practitioners will need to be culturally sensitive to differences in assumptions, world views, and expectations that are likely to occur in diverse communities.

A dilemma facing all practitioners in implementing a model prevention program concerns the potential conflict between *fidelity* and *adaptation* (Rappaport & Seidman, 1979). Stolz (1984) noted that a major controversy in the field of knowledge diffusion and utilization has to do with whether a model program should be used in a form as close to the original tested form as possible (fidelity) or whether to encourage organizations to modify the innovation and therefore enhance the likelihood of local acceptance (adaptation). Future research must distinguish between core program features, which are its effective ingredients and should not be altered, and adaptive features, which can be changed to suit local circumstances.

Sensitivity to the Needs of Ethnic Minority Groups

A principal issue of the 1960s was the lack of adequate services to underserved populations, particularly minority groups (Gurin, Veroff, & Feld, 1960; Robinson, DeMarche, & Wagle, 1960). Throughout the years, treatment programs have been improved to address such issues as folk practices (Comas-Diaz, 1981) and the effects of racism (Thomas & Sillen, 1972).

Unfortunately, an area that has not kept pace is that of prevention program development for minorities. Although most community mental health centers were mandated to provide prevention programs, such programs quite often only involved community education and, at best, secondary prevention efforts. Primary prevention programs geared primarily toward underserved populations, therefore, are still very much needed. In reviewing model prevention programs, Task Force members attended to this need by ascertaining whether a program addressed issues of relevance to minority groups. Although some of the identified programs met this criterion, more primary prevention programs are needed for underserved populations.

Policies for Prevention Research and Funding

Policymakers who plan for the nation's future health and mental health care needs would do well to consider this Task Force report. The findings reported in this volume argue strongly for the efficacy of preventive efforts. Clearly, carefully designed programs whose procedures are implemented systematically can prevent the occurrence of significant emotional and behavioral problems.

The health, mental health, and social problems addressed by the interventions described in this volume include mental retardation, substance abuse, school failure, adolescent pregnancy, marital instability, cardiovascular disorder, reactive depression, and child abuse. These are important, prevalent, and difficult problems in modern society, each of which results in significant health care costs and gives rise to significant "ripple" effects for families and friends who must also cope with these problems. The overall costs associated with these health and mental health problems are sizeable; they will grow unless some efforts are undertaken to bring them under control.

It may be of special interest to policymakers that many of the findings reported in this volume were obtained with limited funding, and, frequently, unlimited skepticism. How many more proven programs would we have identified if predictable funding for prevention research and development had been available? The message of this volume is not that unlimited funds should be made available for the immediate, national dissemination of all of its component programs. Rather, we hope to highlight potential benefits to the nation's health through the selective funding of systematic adoptions of proven interventions. Such a step would add to the knowledge necessary to justify later widespread program dissemination that can help to meaningfully address significant national problems.

The programs described in this volume also refute the argument that emotional and behavioral disorders cannot be prevented. Both the diversity and reliability of findings reported provides evidence to support the efficacy of prevention programs. We can only hope that such encouraging findings will influence subsequent research funding decisions.

Preventive intervention research is characterized both by its complexity and longitudinal nature. To grow in healthy ways, such work needs adequate support in terms of funds and time. Solid evidence of preventive effects requires longitudinal field research with a corresponding commitment of long-term reliable commitment and support. In turn, the fact that we have been able to identify these model programs suggests that with further research the number of viable models will continue to expand. With that expansion, the nation's control over its health and mental health problems will also increase.

These programs should be especially enlightening for people with interest in the efficacy and cost-effectiveness of early intervention programs. Across different settings, populations, and procedures, investigators who developed model programs provide strong evidence of the value of such interventions. Even so, considerable additional efforts are needed for these programs to become available to all who stand to benefit from them. Successfully disseminated, however, they can have far-reaching effects on the nation's overall educational strength and emotional health.

Benefit-cost issues. A critical issue for policymakers and for the general public as well is the benefit-cost analysis in evaluating preventive program models. Both technical and value issues must be addressed before benefit-cost evaluation methodology can be applied thoughtfully to preventive programs.

First, it is worth noting that some preventive programs may never be truly cost beneficial in the narrow sense. Nonetheless, a society may choose to develop and implement them because they reduce human suffering, increase human dignity, or otherwise reflect the society's deepest human values. Preventive programs should not be rejected simply because the program does not save money in the short term. It is inevitable that as sophistication in conducting research and evaluation on preventive programs grows, benefit-cost questions will be raised and researchers will attempt to do benefit-cost analyses on preventive programs.

An outstanding example of such a pioneering benefit-cost evaluation effort is the Perry Preschool Program described by Schweinhart and Weikart in chapter 5. In *Changed Lives,* Berrueta-Clement, Schweinhart, Barnett, Epstein, and Weikart (1984) documented the costs of early education and the benefits resulting from the positive program outcomes. As the authors observed, "changes in economic success, self-sufficiency, and social responsibility can be predicted quantitatively from observed effects at age 19" (p. 89).

In commenting on these findings, Gramlich (1984) made several important points that policymakers and prevention researchers should consider. First, benefits from prevention programs may increase over time. Short term evaluations of benefits may show that they are either small or nonexistent, but benefits may accrue as children are engaged in less crime, depend on welfare less, or begin to reap the benefits of higher levels of educational achievement.

Another critical issue is that sensitive benefit-cost analyses should identify gainers and losers in society. In Gramlich's (1984) analysis, he identified net social benefits received by participants in the program, taxpayers, and potential victims of crime. As Gramlich observed, elected officials are concerned about who gains and who loses as well as how big the overall gain or loss actually is. Benefit-cost analyses of the Perry Preschool Program suggest that the total net benefit to preschool participants themselves is approximately $5,000. On the other hand, total net benefit to taxpayers and potential crime victims is estimated at around $23,000 for one year of preschool experience by the time the program recipients are 19 years of age.

However, sensitive policy decisions about the benefits and costs of preventive programs must recognize that some preventive programs may help realize ideals that we value as a society (i.e., dignity and reduction in human suffering) even if they do not save money. Nevertheless, we expect that many preventive programs will indeed reduce costs to society, and sensitive benefit-cost analyses will need to tell us which societal actors tend to gain or lose. Although preventive programs are time consuming to develop and evaluate, their cost is trivial compared to the social costs of drug abuse, school dropout, depression, or delinquency. As the latter type of health care costs continue to soar, we are becoming more aware that for every problem of this kind, someone is paying the bill in tax dollars, insurance premiums, or health costs paid by employers.

Conclusion

The inventiveness and tenacity of researchers, committed practitioners, and community members is needed to promote widespread application of programs such as those reported in this volume as the preventive services offered in many communities. So far, the overwhelming majority of health dollars are spent for chronic care of health and mental health problems, many of which are preventable. It is unlikely that we can continue permanently on this path. Although the drama of "curing" mental and physical health problems has been compelling in the past, the task of prevention is the most critical one for our future.

References

Berrueta-Clement, J. R., Schweinhart, L. J., Barnett, W. S., Epstein, A. S., & Weikart, D. P. (1984). *Changed lives: The effects of the Perry Preschool Program on youths through age 19.* Ypsilanti, MI: Monographs of the High/Scope Educational Research Foundation, No. 8.

Bloom, B. L. (1979). Prevention of mental disorders: Recent advances in theory and practice, *Community Mental Health Journal, 15,* 179–191.

Comas-Diaz, L. (1981). Puerto Rican espiritismo and psychotherapy. *American Journal of Orthopsychiatry, 5*(4), 636–645.

Gramlich, E. M. (1984). Commentary on *Changed lives.* Chapter in J. R. Berrueta-Clement, L. J. Schweinhart, W. S. Barnett, A. S. Epstein, and D. P. Weikart (Eds.), *Changed lives: The effects of the Perry Preschool Program on youths through age 19.* Ypsilanti, MI: Monographs of the High/Scope Educational Research Foundation, No. 8, pp. 200–203.

Gurin, G., Veroff, J., & Feld, S. (1960). *Americans view their mental health: A nationwide interview survey.* New York: Basic Books.

Price, R. H., & Lorion, R. P. (1987, October). Prevention programming as organizational reinvention: From research to implementation. Paper presented at the meeting of the American Academy of Child and Adolescent Psychiatry, Washington, DC.

Price, R, H., & Smith, S. S. (1985). *A guide to evaluating prevention programs in mental health.* (DHHS Publication No. ADM 95–1365). Washington, DC: U.S. Government Printing Office.

Rappaport, J., Seidman, E., & Davidson, W. S. (1979). Demonstration research and manifest true adaption: The natural history of a research project to divert adolescents from the legal system. In R. F. Manoz, L. R. Snowden, & J. G. Kelly, and Associates (Eds.), *Social and psychological research in community settings* (pp. 104–144). San Francisco: Jossey-Bass.

Rice, R. E., & Rogers, E. M. (1980). Reinvention in the innovation process. *Knowledge: Creation, diffusion, utilization, 1,* 499–514.

Robinson, R., DeMarche, D. F., & Wagle, M. (1960). *Community resources in mental health.* New York: Basic Books.

Stolz, S. B. (1984). Dissemination of standardized human service models. In S. C. Paine, C. T. Bellamy, and B. Wilcox (Eds.), *Human services that work: From innovation to standard practice* (pp. 235–245). Baltimore: Paul H. Brooks Publishing.

Thomas, A., & Sillen, S. (1972). *Racism and psychiatry.* New Jersey: Citadel Press.